THE SUPER GOSPEL

By Robert C. Ferrell

Robert C. Ferrell

The Super Gospel

Copyright © 2011
by Robert C. Ferrell

All rights reserved.

Printed in the United States of America. No part of this book may be used or reproduced in any manner whatsoever without written permission except in the case of brief quotations embodied in critical articles and reviews.

Fifth Estate, Post Office Box 116,
Blountsville, AL 35031

First Edition

Cover Designed by An Quigley

Printed on acid-free paper

Library of Congress Control No: 2011921491

ISBN: 9781936533053

Fifth Estate, 2011

THE
SUPER GOSPEL

A HARMONY
OF ANCIENT GOSPELS

By

Robert C Ferrell

Robert C. Ferrell

To Nancy

FOREWORD

The Super Gospel is many different Christian sources compiled into a single, readable text. Although many acknowledge and accept the canonical gospels of Matthew, Mark, Luke, and John, people are becoming increasingly aware of other gospels that once circulated throughout the greater Christian world. Many different forms of Christianity arose within it, and thus there grew to be divisions. Each group held its own version of Christianity as apostolic and genuine, and other groups as heretical and inauthentic. As time progressed, power struggles within and among these various groups began to obscure the fact that the writings themselves all spoke of the same Jesus--a loving Jesus, a forgiving Jesus, an accepting Jesus.

Differences within and among these groups were emphasized--and sometimes manufactured--in order to generate hatred, mistrust, and divisions between them. These feelings thus began to dominate our Christian thinking, even to the point where Christians were branding other Christians as heretics and killing them. The New Testament speaks of this in many places; "The love of the many shall wax cold," and "Friend shall turn against friend." Did the Church quench the Holy Spirit by these actions? Theology at best is a contrivance of man, and as such is inherently flawed, and is therefore not able to act as the true light. "The true light was he which lights up every man that comes into the world."

What could possibly act as an antidote to these traditions? What could possibly lift this curse of intellectualism and speculation and doubt from our shoulders? What could possibly unite us after all of these years? What if the unthinkable were to happen? What if there was more than what we were told? What if we were to discover that the same God had authored all these works?

If we would only take the time to align the documents themselves and set aside all preconceived notions of what they are supposed to mean in terms of theology and scholarship, carefully arranging the words as to subject matter, chronology, and affinity, and placing them where they most logically belong, we could arrive at a higher understanding of the Logos. We could then put these words to the test, comparing "Scriptural things to Scriptural things" to "try the spirits to see if they are from God." The best way to do this would be to simply let them speak for themselves. Put them all where they fit best and see if they form a sensible document.

The story begins with Mary's parents, Anna and Joachim, two very kind and generous people who despite living righteously in the eyes of God and men, remain childless into their old age. One day, when Joachim is offering his animals to the Lord in the Temple of God, the high priest, who sees his lack of children as a sign of God's disapproval, publicly chastises him. Humiliated, Joachim takes his herdsmen with him into a distant land to hide away from everyone he knows, including his wife Anna, who mourns for her barrenness and the loss of her husband. Angels then appear to both Anna and Joachim letting them know that they will indeed have a child, Mary, whose name will someday be the "talk of the earth." Mary is then born to Anna in her old age.

After three years in her parents' house, Mary is dedicated to the Temple in Jerusalem, where she remains until she is twelve. The priests then order her to take a husband. When, however, she refuses, the priests assemble and draw lots to determine who should foster her until she is ready to wed. Joseph, an elderly man, is chosen, and Mary goes to live with him for two years, "lest she should pollute the temple."

After the two years have passed, the priests again assemble to select a husband for Mary. After Joseph holds his own rod back and no sign appears, an angel reveals to the high priest that Mary should be given to the man who had "held back his rod." Joseph is then loudly summoned before the gathering; the sign of a dove coming "out of his rod and onto his head" confirms that Joseph is to be her husband. Mary then goes to live as his betrothed. There the archangel Gabriel announces to her that she will give birth without a "man's seed." After this, Mary runs away to live with her cousin Elizabeth, where she remains for three months, and returns to Nazareth

Joseph soon returns from a building project and discovers that she is pregnant. He questions her story and accuses her of adultery until her virginity is revealed to him in a dream. An officer of the priest then catches sight of Mary and reports to the high priest that "the 'virgin' is pregnant." Mary and Joseph are immediately summoned before the High Priest, interrogated, and given the "water of the Lord's testing." After Joseph shows "no sign of guilt," Mary is given the same test, and the sign of guilt does not appear. Since no guilt is found on either of them, the Priest declares that they are innocent, and so they go home rejoicing and praising God.

After this, during the reign of Quirinius in Syria, Augustus Caesar orders that a census be taken. Joseph and Mary are therefore compelled to travel to Jerusalem. On the way to Bethlehem, however, her time comes to bring forth. Joseph quickly finds Mary a cave to conceal her, and then goes out to seek for midwives. But as he is on his way, he is met by a midwife's apprentice, who tells him that a "young man," probably an angel of God, had come running up and crying out that a "virgin was about to give birth." They therefore make their way to the cave.

After Joseph goes out to find even more midwives for Mary, we are treated to the spectacular events that accompany the birth of Jesus. We see him descend through each of the seven heavens. And as he enters into this world, everything in creation literally comes to a halt. The people, the animals, and the earth all stop moving as the dazzling light is brought forth in the cave. Jesus is at this point a nearly weightless being of light, and he speaks to his mother from the cradle.

When Joseph returns, he cannot even see the child for the brilliance of the light. The first of these other midwives then goes in and believes, but when she tries to convince the other one, Salome, who is waiting outside, she insists on "proving her status." After Salome has inspected Mary, her hand begins to wither and burn. An angel of the Lord then tells her to touch the infant and

The Super Gospel

worship him. Her hand is then restored and she runs around telling everyone about it. An angel then appears to her and orders her to keep these things to herself. The shepherds then visit, and after a few days, Joseph and Mary take Jesus up to the temple, where they present him to Simeon, and Anna prophesies about him. Then we have the visit of the Magi, the Slaughtering of the Innocents, and the Journey into Egypt.

At first we see that nearly anything that touches Jesus has the power to heal, from his swaddling cloth, to even his bathwater. His childhood abounds with stories of miracles, like his ability to form clay animals and bring them to life, to heal the ill, and to reveal to his teachers things that they had never heard of before. He does, however, cause many problems for his parents. The people they live and work around object to his working of miracles on the Sabbath, his brash and defiant attitude towards his elders, and his ability to kill or injure people with his word alone.

And though he would often undo the damage he had done, people would get angry and call him a sorcerer, forbid their children to play with him, and snub the entire family. So Joseph and Mary found themselves shunned wherever they would go, which ranged from Egypt to Judea to Galilee. It is even pointed out that, "It is truly mysterious that the Lord of every nation should be moved around all over like this--back and forth across so many lands." The story of his childhood culminates in his return to the temple at the age of twelve, where we are given more details as to just what Jesus said to the learned men that so impressed them. After this, we have the death of Joseph the Carpenter.

The Ministry section of the Gospel contains many interesting details about Jesus, such as his physical description, a second transfiguration, his refusal to flee to King Abgar in Edessa and avoid crucifixion, and the hymn he sang with his disciples before his agony in the garden. It is, however, the astonishing sayings from sources like the Gospel of Thomas and the Agrapha--or the various sayings of Jesus that are scattered all over the writings of the Early Church Fathers--that dominate this section. These sayings give this part of the gospel a character all its own. After all, in this section lie his greatest teachings, such as the Sermon on the Mount and the so-called Apocalypse of Jesus, both of which are far more detailed and nuanced with the addition of these lesser known sayings and sections. Here we are confronted with teachings that we were perhaps not ready to accept in the early Church age, teachings that give us more insight into our own angelic nature and the governance of the heavens.

Most of the time, these sayings correspond to an already existing verse, and thus there can be no better fit. One such example is Jesus at the Feast of Tabernacles. John, in chapter 7-verse 11, reads, "On the final and most important day of the Feast, Jesus stood and cried aloud, 'If anyone is thirsty, let him come to me and drink.'" Here the Gospel of Thomas has a similar passage. Since the verse fits here better than anywhere else in gospel literature, at this point a would-be gospel compiler would or should insert saying 108: "Anyone who drinks from my mouth will become like me! I will, in fact, become that man, and the hidden things will open up to him." At this point, yet another verse seems in order, a quote from the Heavenly Dialogue by Origen in his

Robert C. Ferrell

work, Against Celsus 8:15: "Many are those who circle the well, yet no one ever draws from it. Why fear now when you've come so far? Isn't it clear to you that I lack neither courage, nor a weapon." At this point, I continue with John through chapter 8-verse 1. "Whosoever trusts in me, as it says in the Scripture, 'Rivers of living waters will flow forth from him.'" And in so saying, he spoke of the Spirit, which they who believed in him would soon receive." Seeing the verses together where they best fit reveals to us an impressive teaching about ourselves and our relationship to Christ. We come to Jesus to drink. Drink from where? His own mouth! The water is therefore his inspired word. If we make his words our words, then we will also speak these inspired words. Jesus will then come to live in us and open the hidden things up to us. It is important to recognize where we are in the teaching now, as people who get their words directly from him, and not through others. The next verse speaks to those who don't accept the "water" from the well--which really means the inspired words, they will not "drink," meaning they will not accept them. Where it says, "Many are those who circle the well, yet no one ever draws from it. Why fear now when you've come so far? Isn't it clear to you that I lack neither courage, nor a weapon." The weapon is, of course, the depth of his inspired word. Here Jesus is the well, but how do the rivers of living waters flow from the one who comes to him? Because Jesus becomes that man and the spirit flows through him!

Such insights, however, sometimes require the proper grouping and ordering of sayings to form a single coherent teaching. If these books were meant to be pieced together some day, then one such "self-assembly of verses" would clearly take place while Jesus and his disciples are on the road to Galilee. Combining sayings 7, 11, 60, 87, 106, 111, and 112-from the Gospel of Thomas yields the following exchange: "A Samaritan was carrying a lamb on his way into Judea. "<How come> that man <has to> carry that lamb?" Jesus asked his students. "So that he might kill it and eat," they responded. "He will not eat it while life is still in it," Jesus observed, "but only after he has butchered it, so that what he eats is nothing but a carcass." "He cannot do so otherwise!" they reasoned. "Such indeed is your circumstance," Jesus continued, "Find a place for yourselves to live, or you might also become a carcass--and like a carcass be devoured! Blessed is the lion that the man consumes so that the lion becomes human; and cursed is the man that is eaten by the lion so that the lion takes on humanity! How miserable the body that depends upon a body, and how miserable the soul that depends upon these two. Accursed is the flesh that is governed by the soul, and accursed is the soul that is governed by the flesh. This heaven will pass away, as will the next. Indeed the dead do not have life, nor will the living ever die. Back when you would eat what was dead, you used it to feed what was alive. And now that the light is shining on you, what will you do? On the day that you were one, you split in two, so when you are two what ever will you do? When you join the two into one, you will be transformed. Then, as the Sons of Humanity you will say to the mountain, 'Move away!' and it will be moved. The skies will roll up before you, and the earth will too, and whoever receives his life from the One Who lives forever

The Super Gospel

will never see death." (Does not Jesus himself affirm, "Of one who has come to see the truth of his nature, the world is not worthy?")

Now even though it could be said that this hypothetical exchange never really took place, an interesting question is why it can be done at all. It should not be possible to arrange these verses such that they answer their own questions unless the author had somehow intended the reader to discover this. Given the chance, these works actually harmonize with both the canonical traditions and with each other. Combining them reveals the unity of thought that lies behind them, showing there to be a greater Source behind them.

The Passion Narrative is far more detailed in this gospel than in the canonicals alone, with Pilate going to even greater lengths to save Jesus from crucifixion. Many people vouch for him before the crowds, retelling the stories of his miracles and his healings, attesting to the betrothal of his father and mother, and pleading for his life. Here we also learn that when Pilate does pass sentence against Jesus, it is at the request of Herod. As Jesus hangs upon the cross, the Apostle John flees to a cave on the Mount of Olives for fear, where Jesus visits him and gives him a vision of a cross of light. In this vision, Jesus explains that though the lower, human aspect of himself, truly hung upon the cross, the Logos remained unnoticed upon it; that the Word was what suffered, the Word was judged, and the Word was what died. From the point of view of the Scriptures, then, the religious authorities' crucifixion of Jesus was to represent an as yet unknown mystery--that the Scriptures would be put on trial, suffer death at the hands of the religious authorities, and be raised again on the "third day," or in the third millennium, "for with the Lord, a day is as a thousand years and a thousand years are as a day." After it is revealed to John "...that the Lord put every single detail into symbolic language, as a gift to be given to mankind, that their hearts might be transformed thereby and thus receive deliverance," he returns to the cross with this understanding, where Jesus entrusts Mary to his care and places his spirit into the Father's hands.

After this, "...the Lord himself look[s] down on earth from out of heaven to hear the groaning of the fettered and to liberate the sons of the slain." He descends into Hades, frees the captives, reconciles Adam and Eve and the other prisoners to himself, throws Satan and Hades down into Tartarus, and leads the saints up into heaven. And "...the bodies of many of the righteous who had died already were seen raised back up to life. They came out of their graves and, following the resurrection of Jesus, entered into the Holy City and appeared to many of its citizens...." After this, his spirit returns to the tomb, where he is resurrected and with the help of two angels emerges from it having "...spoken to the 'spirits in prison.'" His stature now ascending into the heavens, he transforms himself into a man and appears to Mary Magdalene, he then shows himself to the other women, and later hides his true appearance to the two men on the road to Emmaus.

Despite the number of reports attesting to the fact that Jesus had arisen bodily and appeared to the women, and even to Peter, the disciples still do not believe. Later, Jesus materializes before the disciples in the locked room, chastises them for their lack of faith, and reveals to them that the reign of Satan has passed, but that other, terrible things still lie ahead. Here is where I place the Dialogue of the Savior, a document that I went to great pains to restore, followed closely by the Gospel of Mary Magdalene, two post-resurrection, but pre-ascension gospels that delve into the deceptive nature of the material realm, the judgment of the Archons, or Governing Angels that keep us from ascending to the presence of God and the heavenly light. After this, we have the reappearance of Jesus to the disciples and to Thomas, where he shows him his hands, his feet, and his side.

Then he appears to them by the Sea of Galilee, where they cast their nets and bring their haul ashore. Then we have the Great Commission. From this point forward, three documents, the Epistle of the Apostles, the Apocalypse of Peter, and the Sibylline Oracles intertwine to describe the spiritual state of the coming age, complete with images of spiritual consequences for the various crimes of mankind. The punishments are extremely graphic in nature, but are not to be taken on a literal level. There are numerous cues as to their meaning in terms of mankind's spirit, soul, and body. It is a picture of the spiritual condition of mankind all the way up to the Day of Judgment.

The Disciples then weep and mourn for the 'sinners' and their fate, whereupon Jesus informs them that, "To all of these, His righteous ones, the eternal God Who governs all, will grant them something further still: When they ask Him to rescue mankind from the unquenchable fire and perpetual grinding of teeth, He will give them what they long for. And I say definitively, that at that time, I will deliver out of torment whomsoever my righteous and elect ones should ask of me." After this, Jesus reveals the angelic nature of the exalted man to Peter, James, and John, "...these two men appeared to us, standing there before the Lord, but we were not able to look their way and see their faces, for they beamed forth even more light than the sun. Their garments were luminous beyond words, and beyond compare, such as has never been seen by any man in this world. The gentleness thereof no mouth can express, nor can any heart conceive of the glory of their adornment or the beauty of their faces. Astonishing and wonderful was their appearance. The greater one, I would venture to say, shone more in his brilliance than a crystal. And we were all amazed at the sight of them. Their bodies were even whiter than snow, and had a redness surpassing any rose. That redness, moreover, was mingled with the whiteness thereof. It is simply not possible for me to put their beauty into words. They had curly hair that framed their faces and shoulders in a delightful manner. And around their foreheads there was a crown of nard--like a garland woven out of nard blossoms--and beautiful blooms of different hues, like a rainbow on the water, (or) in the air was [their] hair; so finely fashioned was their form, and [they] were decked out in all manner of ornamentation. And when we looked on them in all of their splendor we marveled in their presence, and we were startled by their sudden appearance." The future glory of the saints is then described, "And [we] stood there trembling with fright, but we all looked upward and saw the sky spreading apart. We could see flesh-bearing men approaching and welcoming our Lord, along with Moses and Elijah. And we heard the voices of many angels as they rejoiced and proclaimed, "Oh priest, gather us in your glorious light." And as they were approaching the heavenly firmament, we heard him say, "Go in peace!"

The Lord sent forth his twelve apostles as he rose into the sky, but he was not changed into the form of the angels there. Satan himself, and the angels of that firmament saw him there and worshiped him. And great was the anguish in that place, as they cried out, "How did our Lord come down here to our sphere and we not notice his greatness, seeing in him that he was the King of Glory? Only now do we recognize that this was the majesty that was on him even from the sixth heaven." The Lord then ascends through the six other heavens and takes his seat to the right hand of the Most High. Then the disciples go joyfully back into Jerusalem, remaining in the temple, and praising God ceaselessly.

And after receiving their instructions, they report to Peter and his companions. Afterward, Jesus himself puts them to work as ambassadors in charge of spreading the holy and imperishable word of eternal salvation from one end of the earth to the other. So they go and preach it everywhere, the Lord working with them, confirming the word with the signs that follow.

ABBREVIATIONS

1Cor	First Corinthians
1Pet	First Peter
1Thess	First Thessalonians
2Bar	Second Baruch
2Clem	Second Clement
2Esd	Second Esdras (Fourth Ezra)
2Pet	Second Peter
AcA&M	Acts of Andrew & Matthias
AcAn	Acts of Andrew
AcJn	Acts of John
AcPt	Acts of Peter
AcThad	Acts of Thaddeus
Acts	Acts of the Apostles
AnaPlt	Anaphora Pilatae
ApPt	Apocalypse of Peter
ArIn	Arabic Infancy Gospel
Arundel404	Latin Infancy Gospel (Arundel MS 404)
AsIs	Ascension of Isaiah
BMary	Birth (Nativity) of Mary
ClemAlex	Clement of Alexandria
ClHm	Clementine Homilies
Dec	The Decensus
DecLtA	The Decensus, Latin A
DecLtB	The Decensus, Latin B
DSav	Dialogue of The Savior
DTry	Dialogue of Justin with Trypho
Egtn	Egerton Gospel
EpAb	Epistle of Abgar
EpAp	Epistle of the Apostles
GEb	Gospel of the Ebionites
GEgp	Gospel of the Egyptians
GHeb	Gospel of the Hebrews
GMary	Gospel of Mary Magdalene
GNaz	Gospel of the Nazoreans
GNc	Gospel of Nicodemus
GPh	Gospel of Philip
GPt	Gospel of Peter
GTh	Gospel of Thomas
GThGr	Gospel of Thomas (Greek Fragments)
HJC	History of Joseph the Carpenter
IgEph	Ignatius of Antioch to the Ephesians

InTh	Infancy Gospel of Thomas
InThL	Infancy Gospel of Thomas (Latin)
John	Gospel of John
LJB	Life of John the Baptist, by Serapion
Luke	Gospel of Luke
Mark	Gospel of Mark
Matt	Gospel of Matthew
OSol	The Odes of Solomon
PEv	Protevangelion of James
POxy	Papyrus Oxyrynchus
PsMt	Gospel of Pseudo-Matthew
QBar	Questions of Bartholomew
Qur	Gospel Material Preserved in the Quran
Rev	Book of Revelation (Apocalypse of John)
Rm	Epistle of Paul to the Romans
SbOr	Sibylline Oracles
SMk	The Secret Book of Mark
TrdMth	The Traditions of Matthias

TEXTUAL NOTES

< > Pointed brackets indicate words that have been supplied.

[ ] Denote changes made necessary by the combining of texts.

[...] Denotes that words that cannot be supplied or conjectured.

( ) Indicate parenthetical remarks and supplied conjunctions.

{ } Braces denote various introductions and conclusions.

Robert C. Ferrell

TABLE OF CONTENTS

INFANCY 1

INTRODUCTION	31
MARY'S PARENTS	32
JOACHIM'S CENSURE	33
ANNA'S LAMENT	33
AN ANGEL APPEARS TO ANNA	34
AN ANGEL APPEARS TO JOACHIM	36
AN ANGEL AGAIN APPEARS TO ANNA	38
BIRTH & INFANCY OF MARY; JESUS' FAMILY LIFE	39
MARY IN THE TEMPLE	41
ABIATHAR ASKS MARY TO WED HIS SON	43
MARY GOES TO LIVE AS JOSEPH'S WARD	44
MARY ORDERED TO WED	44
JOSEPH CHOSEN TO TAKE MARY	46
MARY SPINS THE SCARLET AND THE PURPLE	48
THE FORETELLING OF JOHN'S BIRTH	48
ELIZABETH'S SECLUSION	50
THE ANNUNCIATION	50
MARY VISITS ELIZABETH	53
THE BIRTH; NAMING OF JOHN	54
JOSEPH DISCOVERS THAT MARY IS PREGNANT	55

THE TRIAL OF JOSEPH AND MARY	57

INFANCY 2

INTODUCTION TO THE ARABIC INFANCY GOSPEL; JOSEPH AND MARY TRAVEL TO BETHLEHEM	60
THE BIRTH OF JESUS	61
THE SHEPHERDS VISIT	67
JESUS' CIRCUMCISION	68
MARY TAKES JESUS TO HER FAMILY; THE PRESENTATION	69
JESUS' GENEALOGY	71
THE MAJI VISIT	71
JOSEPH'S WARNING	73
SLAUGHTER OF INNOCENTS; MURDER OF ZECHARIAH	73
JOURNEY INTO EGYPT	76
ARRIVAL IN EGYPT; 365-IDOLS TOPPLE	78
JESUS REVIVES A DRIED FISH	79
JESUS INFURIATES A TEACHER	79
THE FALLEN IDOL; AND THE POSSESSED BOY	80
THE ROBBERS FLEE	81
POSSESSION CURED	81
MUTENESS HEALED	82
SATANIC OPPRESSION AND SKIN DISEASES CURED	82
WITCHCRAFTS OVERCOME	83
TITUS AND DUMACHUS	85

Robert C. Ferrell

THE IDOLS TURN INTO SAND	86
THE SPRING AT MATAREA	86
THE HOLY FAMILY MEETS WITH PHAROAH	86

INFANCY 3

RETURN TO JUDEA; TO GALILEE	87
JESUS' BATHWATER CURES VARIOUS ILLNESSES	87
THE TWO WIVES AND THEIR SONS' ILLNESSES	88
THE HEALING OF BARTHOLOMEW	89
BATHWATER CURES	89
ANOTHER CURED BY BATHWATER	90
GIRL AFFLICTED BY SATAN	91
FIRE FROM THE SWADDLING CLOTH	91
JUDAS STRIKES JESUS	92
A BOY WRECKS JESUS' POOLS AND DIES	92
INFANCY GOSPEL OF THOMAS INTRODUCTION	93
JESUS CLARIFIES WATER, QUICKENS CLAY ANIMALS	93
BOY SCATTERS JESUS' FISH POOL	94
BOY ATTACKS JESUS AND DIES	95
JOSEPH ADMONISHES JESUS; HIS REPLY	95
ZACCHAEUS TAKES JESUS AS HIS PUPIL	96
JESUS ASTONISHES ZACCHAEUS	97
ZACCHAEUS TAKES JESUS TO LEVI	98
BOYS ROUGHHOUSING ON THE ROOF	100

JESUS HEALS A MAN'S FOOT	101
JESUS DRAWS WATER WITH HIS GARMENT	101
THE THREE MEASURES OF GRAIN	102
JESUS, MARY, & SALOME HELP JOHN THE BAPTIST	102
JESUS COMMANDS CLAY ANIMALS	104
MIRACLE AT THE DYER'S	104
ANOTHER MIRACLE AT THE DYER'S	104
JESUS STRETCHES THE THRONE	105
THE BOYS WHO TURNED INTO GOATS	106
THE KING KILLS THE SERPENT	106
ONE GRAIN YIELDS A HUNDRED MEASURES	107
THE LIONS WORSHIP JESUS	107
THE LIONS CROSS THE JORDAN WITH JESUS	108
JOSEPH AND JESUS STRETCH THE BEAM	108
JESUS' SECOND VISIT TO A TEACHER	109
FINAL ATTEMPT TO EDUCATE JESUS; JESUS TEACHES AS A TORRENT OF LIVING WATER	110
JOSEPH HEALS ANOTHER JOSEPH	111
JESUS BLOWS ON JAMES' SNAKE BITE	111
JESUS REVIVES A DEAD CHILD	112
JESUS RAISES A CONSTRUCTION WORKER	112
JESUS BLESSES HIS FAMILY; THE GLORY OF GOD SHINES UPON HIM	112
JESUS STAYS BEHIND IN THE TEMPLE	113

JESUS ASTONISHES AN ASTRONOMER AND A PHILOSOPHER	113
JOSEPH AND MARY DISCOVER THAT JESUS IS MISSING	114
JESUS BEGINS TO HIDE HIS ACTIVITIES; DILIGENTLY STUDIES THE LAW	115
INTRODUCTION TO THE LIFE OF JOSEPH THE CARPENTER; INSTRUCTIONS TO SPREAD THE GOSPEL	115
THE DEATH OF JOSEPH	116

MINISTRY 1

INTRODUCTION TO JESUS' MINISTRY; HIS PHYSICAL DESCRIPTION	124
MINISTRY OF JOHN THE BAPTIST	124
JOHN BAPTIZES JESUS	126
JESUS' GENEALOGY	127
THE TEMPTATION	128
JOHN'S TESTIMONIAL; THE FIRST FOLLOWERS	128
JESUS TURNS WATER INTO WINE	129
THE FIRST PURGING OF THE TEMPLE	130
NICODEMUS VISITS JESUS	131
JOHN'S FINAL ATTESTATION	132
ON THE ROAD TO GALILEE	132
THE SAMARITAN WOMAN	133
JESUS HEARS OF JOHN'S IMPRISONMENT; RETURNS TO GALILEE	134
PETER, ANDREW, JAMES, & JOHN FOLLOW JESUS	135

JESUS CURES A FEVER	136
DENIAL IN NAZARETH	136
CASTING OUT DEMONS	137
JESUS HEALS THE SICK	138
JESUS EXPANDS HIS HEALING MINISTRY	138
THE BIG CATCH	139
JESUS HEALS A SKIN DISEASE	139
JESUS HEALS A PARALYTIC	140
JESUS CALLS MATTHEW (AND LEVI)	141

MINISTRY 2

THE PARALYTIC AT BETHESDA	142
THE LORD OF THE SABBATH	144
THE MAN WITH THE SHRIVELED HAND	145
JESUS HEALS THE SICK	145
JESUS COMMISSIONS TWELVE APOSTLES	146
SERMON ON THE MOUNT	146
THE FAITHFUL CENTURION	154
JESUS EXPLAINS WHY HE CHOSE THE TWELVE	154
JESUS RAISES A DEAD MAN	155
JOHN THE BAPTIST'S INQUIRY	155
JESUS CONDEMNS THE CITIES	156
WOMAN WASHES JESUS' FEET	157
THE WOMEN'S CONTRIBUTION TO JESUS' MINISTRY	157

CAN SATAN CAST OUT SATAN?	158
THE LEADERS ASK FOR A SIGN	159
FUTILE REPENTANCE & THE LIGHT OF THE SPIRIT	160
JESUS' TRUE FAMILY	160
PHARISAISM DENOUNCED; THE SIX CURSES	161
THE TEACHING OF THE HOLY SPIRIT	162
THE DANGERS OF WORLDLINESS	162
BE WATCHFUL	163
JESUS BRINGS ABOUT A DIVISION	164
JESUS DEMANDS REPENTANCE	165
PARABLE OF THE SOWER	165
WHY JESUS USES PARABLES	166
THE WHEAT AND THE TARES	167
THE SEED GROWS BY ITSELF	168
THE MUSTARD SEED	168
THE WOMAN AND THE LEAVEN	168
THE WOMAN AND HER JAR OF MEAL	169
JESUS SPEAKS TO THE PEOPLE ONLY IN PARABLES	169
JESUS EXPLAINS THE WHEAT AND THE TARES TO HIS DISCIPLES	169
TREASURE HIDDEN IN THE FIELD	169
THE PEARL OF GREAT PRICE	170
THE LARGE FISH	170
THE TWO KINDS OF FISH	170

CLOSING PARABLES	170
THE WINDS AND THE WAVES OBEY JESUS	171
HEALING THE DEMONIAC	171
THE FEAST AT LEVI'S	173
JOHN'S FOLLOWERS QUESTION JESUS	173
RAISING OF JAIRUS' DAUGHTER; HEALING OF THE BLEEDING WOMAN	174
JESUS HEALS THE TWO BLIND MEN	175
JESUS "DISHONORED IN HIS OWN HOUSE"	175
JESUS IN THE GENTILE TEMPLE	176
BOUNTIFUL HARVEST; FEW LABORERS	178
THE TWELVE SENT OUT AS A WITNESS	178

MINISTRY 3

THE DEATH OF JOHN THE BAPTIST	181
JESUS FEEDS FIVE THOUSAND	182
JESUS REJECTS AN EARTHLY KINGDOM	183
JESUS WALKS ON THE SEA	183
IN GENNESARET	184
THE LIFE-GIVING BREAD	185
CLEAN HANDS--CORRUPT HEARTS	186
IN TYRE AND SIDON	188
JESUS HEALS THE BLIND, MUTE, LAME & CRIPPLED	188
JESUS FEEDS THE FOUR THOUSAND	189
THE SIGNS OF THE TIMES	189

THE LEAVEN OF THE PHARISEES, SADDUCEES, AND HEROD	189
HEALING THE BLIND MAN IN BETHSAIDA	190
THOMAS' INSIGHT & JESUS' WORDS TO HIM: PETER'S INSIGHT	190
JESUS BEGINS TO TEACH OF HIS PASSION & RESURRECTION	191
JESUS TEACHES ABOUT DISCIPLESHIP	192
THE TRANSFIGURATION	192
A SECOND TRANSFIGURATION	193
JESUS REVEALS THAT JOHN THE BAPTIST IS ELIJAH	193
THE DEMON THE DISCIPLES COULD NOT CAST OUT	194
JESUS AGAIN EXPLAINS TO HIS DISCIPLES ABOUT HIS DEATH	195
JESUS, PETER, AND THE SHEKEL	195
WHOEVER IS LEAST IS GREATEST	195
JESUS INSTRUCTS PETER TO FORGIVE	197
THE SOLEMNITY AND PRICE OF DISCIPLESHIP	198
JESUS' BROTHERS URGE HIM TO REVEAL HIMSELF	198
JESUS SECRETLY HEADS FOR JERUSALEM	199
JESUS AT THE FEAST OF TABERNACLES	199
THE WOMAN CAUGHT IN ADULTERY	201
DISPUTATIONS	201
HEALING OF THE MAN BORN BLIND	204
THE GOOD SHEPHERD	205
THE SEVENTY TWO SENT OUT	206

THE GOOD SAMARITAN	208
MARTHA AND MARY	208
PRAYER & THE PARABLE OF THE PERSISTENT NEIGHBOR	209
JESUS HEALS THE BENT WOMAN	209
THE MUSTARD SEED AND THE THREE MEASURES	210
THE DEDICATION FEAST	210
JESUS WITHDRAWS TO THE JORDAN; ASKS A STRANGE QUESTION, & WORKS A MIRACLE	211
ENTER THROUGH THE STRAIGHT GATE	211
JESUS IS WARNED ABOUT HEROD	212
HOW TO ATTEND, AND HOW TO GIVE A FEAST	212
THE REJECTED INVITATION	213
THE COST OF DISCIPLESHIP	213
THE LOST SHEEP AND THE LOST COIN	214
THE PRODIGAL SON	214
THE CLEVER MANAGER	215
THE RICH MAN AND LAZARUS	216
FORGIVENESS AND FAITH	217

MINISTRY 4

JESUS RAISES LAZARUS	218
THE PHARISEES CONSPIRE TO EXECUTE JESUS	219
THE GRATEFUL LEPER	220
THE COMING OF THE KINGDOM	220

THE UNJUST JUDGE; THE PHARISEE & THE TAX-COLLECTOR	221
JESUS TEACHES ABOUT DIVORCE	222
JESUS AND THE CHILDREN	223
THE PITFALL OF WEALTH	223
THE WORKERS IN THE FIELD	225
JOURNEY TO JERUSALEM	225
ZACCHAEUS THE PUBLICAN	227
THE TEN MINAS	227
BARTIMAEUS AND HIS COMPANION	228
ARRIVAL IN BETHANY; MARY ANOINTS JESUS	229
THE TRIUMPHAL ENTRY	229
THE WITHERED FIG TREE	231
THE SECOND CLEANSING OF THE TEMPLE	232
THE SECOND ENCOUNTER WITH THE FIG TREE	232
CHRIST'S AUTHORITY CHALLENGED	233
WHO IS THE TRUE WORKER?	233
PARABLE OF THE WICKED HARVESTERS	233
THE INVITATION TO THE WEDDING FEAST	235
GIVE CAESAR WHAT BELONGS TO CAESAR	235
THE WIFE OF THE SEVEN BROTHERS	236
WHICH COMMANDMENT IS THE GREATEST?	237
"DAVID CALLS HIM 'LORD'"	237
EXPOSING THE SCRIBES AND THE PHARISEES	238

THE WIDOW'S MITE	240
THE HOUR HAS COME	240
THE APOCALYPSE OF JESUS	241
THE TEN VIRGINS	246
THE PARABLE OF THE TALENTS	247
THE COMING OF THE MESSIAH	248
THE CONSPIRACY AGAINST JESUS	249
MARY ANOINTS JESUS	250
JUDAS STRIKES A BARGAIN	250
KING ABGAR OFFERS JESUS ASYLUM	250
THE PASSOVER PREPARATIONS	252
JESUS WASHES THE FEET OF THE DISCIPLES	252
JESUS IDENTIFIES JUDAS AS HIS BETRAYER	253
LOVE ONE ANOTHER	254
JESUS PREDICTS PETER'S DENIALS	254
THE BREAD AND THE CUP	255
THE FAREWELL DISCOURSE: THE WAY, THE TRUTH, & THE LIFE	255
THE TRUE VINE	257
OPPOSITION	257
"I AM GOING TO THE ONE WHO SENT ME"	258
THE FAREWELL PRAYER	258
THE PARTING HYMN AND DANCE	260
AGONY IN THE GARDEN	262

THE ARREST   263

PASSION 1

PROLOGUE TO THE ACTS OF PONTIUS PILATE   265

JESUS BEFORE THE SANHEDRIN   265

PETER'S DENIALS   266

JESUS CONDEMNED BY THE SANHEDRIN   268

JUDAS COMMITS SUICIDE   268

THE JEWS ACCUSE JESUS BEFORE PILATE   269

JESUS BEFORE PILATE   272

HEROD TRIES JESUS   276

JESUS' TRIAL BEFORE THE PEOPLE   276

THE CRUCIFIXION OF JESUS   279

JOHN'S VISION OF THE CROSS OF LIGHT   282

THE OVERTHROW OF HADES   284

JOHN THE BAPTIST   287

ADAM AND SETH   288

DAVID   289

JEREMIAH   289

ISAIAH   289

THE SAINTS   290

JESUS SURRENDERS HIS SPIRIT   290

SIGNS ACCOMPANYING JESUS' DEATH   291

CHRIST'S BURIAL   292

THE END OF DARKNESS	293
THE THIEF	293
DAVID'S OUTCRY	293
JOSEPH DETAINED	294
THE JEWISH RULERS BEGIN TO SENSE THEIR GUILT	294
THE SEALING OF THE TOMB	295
THE HARROWING OF HELL	295
CHRIST DESCENDS INTO HADES	296
JESUS SEIZES SATAN	296
JESUS DRAWS ALL THE SAINTS TO HIMSELF	297
THE TESTIMONY OF ADAM AND EVE	297
THE TESTIMONY OF THE SAINTS	297
EVENTS OF THE SABBATH: MANY VISIT THE TOMB: THE SYNAGOGUE RULERS SCHEDULE AN ASSEMBLY: THE WOMEN BUY SPICES FOR JESUS	298
THE SIGN OF VICTORY	298
LEAVING HADES	298
THE RESURRECTION	300
THE ASCENT INTO PARADISE	300
HABAKKUK	301
MICAH	301
INTO PARADISE	301
THE PENITENT THIEF	302
THE EARTHQUAKE AND THE REPORT TO PILATE	302

JOSEPH NOT FOUND	303
THE WOMEN FIND THE TOMB OPEN; JESUS APPEARS TO MARY MAGDALENE & THE OTHER WOMEN	303
THE REPORT OF THE SOLDIERS TO THE JEWS	305
REPORT TO THE DISCIPLES; THE VISIT OF THE THREE WOMEN	306
APPEARANCE TO JAMES	307
THE WALK TO EMMAUS	307
THE REPORT FROM EMMAUS	308

PASSION 2

JESUS REVEALS HIMSELF TO THE ELEVEN	309
THE DIALOGUE OF THE SAVIOR	309
JESUS' SECOND APPEARANCE TO THE TWELVE	318
THE MISSION OF THE APOSTLES	319
MARY ASKS JESUS ABOUT THE NATURE OF HIS FOLLOWERS	325
PETER'S OBJECTION TO MARY	326
THE GOSPEL OF MARY	326
APPEARANCE AT THE LAKE OF TIBERIAS	329
THE GREAT COMMISSION	330
THE FORTY-DAY INTERIM	330
JESUS TEACHES ABOUT PAUL	331
INTRODUCTION TO THE APOCALYPSE OF PETER	332
HIS DISCIPLES ASK IF THE TIME OF HIS COMING IS AT HAND	332

AN EXHORTATION	333
THOSE WHO ARE SEALED	334
THE GREAT MULTITUDE	334
THE FIG TREE	335
COMING OF ENOCH AND ELIJAH	336
SIGNS OF THE END	336
MORE PLAGUES, THE COMING OF THE ELECT	337
THE SPIRITS AT THE JUDGMENT	339
JUDGMENT DAY	339
THE GRAINS OF WHEAT	340
A FIGURE OF THE RAISING OF MANKIND AND OF JUDGMENT	340
THE CALAMITIES, DESTRUCTION BY FIRE	341
THE PUNISHMENT OF THE WICKED	342
THE BLASPHEMERS	343
THOSE WHO FORSOOK RIGHTEOUSNESS	343
WANTON WOMEN AND MEN	343
THE MURDERERS AND THEIR ACCOMPLICES	344
THE SLAIN BEHOLD THEIR KILLERS	344
THOSE WHO ABORT THEIR CHILDREN	344
THE ABORTED	344
THE PERSECUTORS AND BETRAYERS OF THE RIGHTEOUS	345
THOSE WHO DOUBT & BLASPHEME GOD'S WAY OF RIGHTEOUSNESS	345

THE LIARS WHO KILLED THE MARTYRS	346
THOSE WHO TRUSTED IN THEIR RICHES	346
USERERS	346
CULTISTS	346
THE IDOL WORSHIPPERS	347
THOSE WHO FORSOOK THE WAY OF GOD	347
THOSE WHO DISHONOR THEIR FATHER AND MOTHER	347
THOSE WHO DISOBEY THEIR PARENTS & THEIR ELDERS	347
THOSE WHO DID NOT PRESERVE THEIR VIRGINITY	348
DISOBEDIENT SERVANTS	348
SELF-RIGHTEOUS HYPOCRITES	348
THE FIERY STREAM OF JUDGMENT	348
THE RIGHTEOUS BEHOLD THE PUNISHMENT OF THE WICKED	349
THE APOSTLES' CONCERN FOR THE SINNERS	350
THE WISE & THE FOOLISH VIRGINS	351
THE SINNERS RELEASED FROM HADES	352
EXHORTATION TO PREACH	353
EXHORTATION TO PETER	354
A VISION OF THE RIGHTEOUS	355
THE ASCENSION	357

INFANCY 1

INTRODUCTION
(Luke 1:1-4; John 1:1-18)

Since it is clear that many have painstakingly tried to stitch together a narrative regarding matters which have been proven to our own satisfaction, even as did those who from the very beginning were eyewitnesses and humble administrators of the word; it seemed right that I should follow suit; accurately ordering and writing to you from a loftier view, most noble lover of God, that you also might come to see the certainty in the things that you were taught.

In the first place, there was the Word, and this Word had to do with God, and this Word was God. This was the very basis for drawing near to God. Everything was brought into being because of it, and apart from it not so much as one thing ever came to pass. For within it there was life, and that light was enlightenment for all of mankind, and that light continues to shine through all of the darkness, without that darkness ever perceiving it.

God sent out a man whose name was John. He came to attest to that light, that all might come to believe in it through him. Not that he was that light, but he did come as a witness to that light. The true light was he who illumines all men by his coming into the world.

He was in the world, and the world came into being because of him, yet the world never recognized him. He joined in among his own, but they refused to accept him. To as many as trusted in his good name, however, and did come to accept him, he gave the chance to become God's own children; brought forth through neither bloodline, nor the will of the flesh, nor the slightest effort on the part of men, but the agency of God instead. The Word put on flesh and lived among us, and we recognized his preeminence as God's only Son, brimming with spiritual life, being the embodiment of truth. John has aptly testified of him, and resoundingly proclaimed, "This was the same one who appeared before me bringing word that through me he would rise to prominence." And from this man, or rather him in the fullest sense, each of us also receives this gift: true spiritual experience as opposed to mere spiritual intercession, because through Moses came the law, whereas through Jesus, the Christ, came the gift of spiritual fulfillment, along with the embodiment of truth. No one ever saw God clearly before; the only begotten son is revealing him now from the heart of the Father.

MARY'S PARENTS
(BMary 1:1-6; PsMt 1, 2; PEv 1:1, 2)
Jerusalem

{Here begins The Book of the Birth of the Blessed Mary and the Childhood of our Savior; which was written in Hebrew by the Most Reverend Apostle Matthew.}

The holy and majestic Virgin Mary was born in the city of Nazareth, descended from David's royal bloodline, and received her instruction in the Lord's temple in Jerusalem. Her father's name was Joachim and his family was from Galilee and the city of Nazareth. Her mother's name was Anna, and her family was from Bethlehem. They lived plainly and honestly before God; piously and blamelessly in the sight of men.

According to The Chronicles of the Twelve Tribes of Israel, Joachim, a wealthy man of Judah's line, was in Jerusalem at this time. He shepherded his own sheep, and loved the Lord wholeheartedly and with all integrity. His entire concern was for the well-being of his herds; and from the food that they produced, he fed every God-fearing person, honoring God by offering a twofold charity to everyone who served Him, and who worked at teaching. He brought all of his offerings before the Lord, saying, "What I bring as a sacrifice for my own sins will be dedicated to the Lord, that He might be appeased with me. What is over and above that will be for the people to use." So his entire income--his lambs, his sheep, his wool, and everything else that he owned--was split three ways: one part was devoted to orphans, widows, foreigners and the needy; another to the temple, its officials, and those who worship God; and the third part he reserved for his own needs and those of his entire family. He practiced this level of generosity from the age of fifteen years, and all the while God compounded his flocks and his wealth, such that there was no one else like him in all of Israel. When he was twenty, he married Anna, the daughter of Issachar, who shared his lineage from David. They practiced this decent way of living for about twenty years; being approved by God and respected by men, yet she bore him neither sons nor daughters.

The Great Day of the Lord was approaching, and the people of Israel were bringing their oblations. Now during the festal days, Joachim was gathering his gifts before the Lord in the company of some other people who were offering their incense up. And this priest named Reuben rose to his feet, walked over to Joachim and said, "It is unlawful for you to stand here alongside these others and present your offerings ahead of those who are sacrificing to God, seeing that you have fathered no children in Israel." (But they had solemnly pledged that if God should bless them with a child, they would consecrate it to the service of the Lord; which was why they went to the Lord's temple during every feast of the year.)

JOACHIM'S CENSURE
(BMary 1:7-12; PEv 1:3-7)
Jerusalem; The Hill Country

Now when the Dedication Feast was approaching during the high priesthood of Issachar, Joachim and some others of his tribe traveled up to Jerusalem. When he saw Joachim and his companions bringing their offerings, he snubbed both him and his gifts, demanding, "Why would a childless person like you be so presumptuous as to come and stand here alongside those who are not? God will never accept any offerings from you," he added. "He hasn't even deemed you worthy to have children! Remember that the Scripture reads, 'Accursed are all who fail to father a son in Israel.'" He said, moreover, "You ought first to free yourself from that curse by fathering a child, and only then should you bring your offerings into the presence of the Lord."

Taken aback by such a shameful and public censure, Joachim ran away from the Lord's temple in tears. He felt discouraged and said to himself, "I will check the register to see if I am indeed the only one in Israel who has not brought up any children." So he consulted the archives of the twelve tribes and learned that all of the upright in Israel had indeed raised up children. Then he recalled that even as his days were drawing to a close, God blessed the patriarch Abraham with his son Isaac. Now since Joachim was so depressed, he did not wish to go back home and face his wife and neighbors who, after all, had been there and had heard all that the high priest had spoken, and feared that they might publicly humiliate him as well. He therefore did not go back home, but withdrew instead into the mountains of a faraway land with his herdsmen, so that his wife Anna might hear nothing about him. There he set up his tent, and after some time he started fasting. "For forty days and forty nights I will not eat or drink anything," he said to himself. "My prayer will be my only food and drink until the Lord my God visits me."

ANNA'S LAMENT
(PEv 2:1; 2:8-3:7; PsMt 2, 3)
Jerusalem

His wife Anna sang two elegies, and uttered a double lament: "I will weep for my widowhood and wail for my barrenness." For because she had heard nothing of what had become of Joachim, she complained to God, and in tears did she plead, "Oh Lord, Great and Powerful God of Israel, You have given me no children; why have You taken my husband as well? Behold, it has been five months since I have seen him, and I have no idea where he might be. If I knew that he were dead, I could at least bury him." Then she entered into the courtyard of his house in the depth of her sorrow, fell to her face and prayed, pouring forth her requests to the Lord.

And afterward, even though she felt dejected, Anna got up from her prayers, took off her mourning clothes, washed her hair, and put on her wedding garments. At about the ninth hour, she went for a walk in her garden and saw a laurel tree there. And sitting down beneath it, she begged the Lord, "Oh God of Our Fathers, hearken to my prayer and bless me even as You blessed the womb of Sarah and graced her with her son Isaac."

Then Anna looked into the sky and sighed. And noticing a nest of sparrows in that laurel tree, she sang the following elegy:

> "Poor little me! Who gave me life?
> What womb brought me forth?
> For I was born only to be cursed before the people--
> Even the sons of Israel.
> And I was censured; they ridiculed me
> And threw me out of the Lord's temple.
> Poor little me! With what am I to be compared?
> I am not to be compared with the birds of the sky,
> Because, oh my Lord, even the birds of the sky
> Produce for You.
> Poor little me! With what am I to be compared?
> I am not to be compared with the speechless beasts,
> Because, oh my Lord, even the speechless beasts
> Produce for You.
> Poor little me! With what am I to be compared?
> I am not to be compared with the earth's wild animals,
> Because, oh my Lord,
> Even the wild animals of the earth produce for You.
> Poor little me! With what am I to be compared?
> I am not to be compared with these waters,
> Because, oh my Lord, even these waters produce for You.
> Poor little me! With what am I to be compared?
> I am not to be compared with this earth,
> Because even this earth is productive in its season
> And praises You, oh my Lord."

And she spoke sorrowfully saying, "Lord God Almighty, the One Who has given posterity to all living things; every creature, be they either tame or wild; to serpents, birds, and fish as well, that they might all take pleasure in their young. Only I am deprived of Your generous gift. But You, dear God, know that from my wedding day, I promised in my heart that if ever You gave me a son or a daughter, I would give them back to You, to serve You in Your sacred temple."

AN ANGEL APPEARS TO ANNA
(BMary 3:1-5; PEv 4:1, 2; 2:2-7; PsMt 2, 3)
Jerusalem

And behold, even as she was saying all this, one of God's angels suddenly appeared to her and said, "Anna, Anna, do not be afraid! Do not think that what you see is some delusion, for I am the angel who has presented your petitions and charitable donations in the presence of God. The Lord God has heard your plea and ordained seed for you. You will conceive and give birth, and your child's name will be the talk of the whole earth. All generations will marvel at what you are to bear; even until the end of the age." "As my Lord is the Living God," Anna replied, "if a child is given to me, be it either a boy or a girl, I will give it to the Lord my God, and it will serve Him all the days of its life." Then the angel said to her, "I have been sent to you to let you know that you are to bear a daughter. You are to name her Mary, and she will be favored above all other women. And as soon as she is born, she will exhibit qualities like those of the Lord. She will be brought up in her father's house until the three years of her weaning run out, then she will be given to the service of the Lord. She will never set foot off the temple grounds until she reaches the age of discretion. In short, in that place she will serve the Lord, fasting and praying day and night, keeping away from every unclean thing, and never lying with a man. This will be unparalleled--a virgin will give birth to a son in a pure and undefiled manner; without sleeping with a man, a young woman will bring forth the Lord, who will rescue the world through his divine nature, power, and labors." And after he had spoken this, the angel vanished from her sight. But because she had seen all this and heard such words, she withdrew to her bedroom in fear and dread, threw herself over her bed as dead, and stayed there all day and night in prayer and trembling.

When all of this had taken place, she called her servant to herself and said, "Do you not see how my widowhood has deluded me and caused me no end of confusion? Even so, you have been unwilling to come in and visit me!" Now the Great Day of the Lord was approaching, so her servant Judith asked Anna, "How long are you going to wallow in your self-pity, because the Lord's Great Day is nearly upon us and you will be unable to do any mourning then. Behold, here is a head-covering. A seamstress had given it to me, but because I am just a servant I cannot wear it. Why not take it to yourself instead, since it so greatly befits your regal appearance!"

"Go away!" Anna replied, "I will not accept this thing from you. The Lord has humiliated me and who knows but that some evildoer has not given it to you. Your passing it on to me might only get me caught up in your sin!" Somewhat sullenly, Judith replied, "And how am I supposed to bring a curse down on you seeing that you never even listen to me? The Lord God has sealed your womb that you might not bring forth any children in Israel. If God Himself has closed your womb and taken your husband away from you, what could I possibly do to you?" And when Anna heard that, she raised her voice and wept aloud.

AN ANGEL APPEARS TO JOACHIM
(BMary 2:1-14; PsMt 3)
The Hill Country

Joachim, meanwhile, was alone on the mountains feeding his flocks. One day a young boy appeared to him and asked, "Why not go back home to your wife?" "I have been with her for twenty years now," explained Joachim, "and it has not been God's will to give me any children through her. With shame and reproach have I been cast away from the temple of the Lord. Why should I return to her seeing that I have already been completely scorned and driven out? So as long as God gives me light in this life, I will simply stay here with my sheep. With a little help from my servants, I will give the poor, the orphans, and the God-fearing their portions." And after he had spoken this, the young man, an angel of the Lord, stood there bathed in a dazzling light! Now because Joachim had been rattled by the visitation, the angel who had shown himself to Joachim tried to console him, saying, "Do not be shaken by my manifestation to you, for I am the Angel of the Lord, sent to you by Him in order to let you know that He has heard your prayers and seen your alms. He has also seen your humiliation and heard the unjust accusations leveled against you with regard to your childlessness. But it is on account of their own sins that God punishes people, and not their physical condition. Whenever He closes a woman's womb, He has its miraculous opening in mind; so that what it brings forth might be seen as the gift of God, and not as the result of mere passion. For was not Sarah, the mother of your people, childless until her eightieth year? And did she not bring to pass the blessing promised to every nation, bringing forth Isaac at such an old age?

"And Rachel, who was so favored by God and beloved of Jacob, went on for a long time before she ever bore a child, yet she later went on to bear Joseph, who not only governed Egypt, but also spared many nations a famine's death. And even though both of their mothers were barren, who among the Judges was braver than Samson, or holier than Samuel? But if reason should fail to convince you of the soundness of my speech, that many who were barren have conceived in their old age and brought forth to their surprise, this very day I have appeared to your wife as she sat weeping and praying, and comforted her. Know, therefore, that your wife Anna will bring forth a daughter from your very own seed, and you have abandoned her without even knowing this. You are to name her Mary, and she is to be set apart to the Lord's service from the time of her birth, even as you have promised. She will be filled with the Holy Spirit from her mother's womb, and will remain within the temple of God, where the Holy Spirit will live in her. She will never eat or drink any unclean thing, and will speak only with those inside the Lord's temple, and never outside with the rest of the world, that she might avoid slanderous and evil suspicions. She will, moreover, be venerated above all other holy women, such that no one will be able to say that any woman before her was ever like her, nor indeed will anyone in this world come along hereafter who ever will be. And even as she will be born in a miraculous fashion, so also in due course will she bear in a way unparalleled--while yet a virgin she will bring forth the Most High God, Who will rescue all nations, as His name, Jesus, signifies.

"Get down from these mountains, therefore, and return to your wife, whom you will find is pregnant. God has raised up a seed inside her, and you will thank Him for it. Her child will be blessed, and so will she. Indeed, she is to be made the mother of everlasting blessing. And as a sign of what I have told you, as soon as you arrive at the Golden Gate in Jerusalem, you will meet up with your wife Anna, who, though downcast over your not returning sooner, will be joyful at the sight of you."

Then Joachim worshiped the angel and said, "If I have found favor in your eyes, then come, sit in my tent awhile and bless your servant." But the angel corrected him, saying, "Do not say 'servant,' but 'fellow servant,' for we both serve a single Master. But my food cannot be seen and my drink is invisible to men. You should therefore not invite me into your tent. If, however, you were ready to offer me something, sacrifice it instead as a burnt offering to the Lord." And taking a spotless lamb Joachim said to the angel, "I would never have taken it upon myself to present a burnt offering to the Lord had you not first commanded me and given me the priestly authority to do so." "I would never have said that you could," the angel replied, "unless I had first known the will of the Lord." And as Joachim was offering up his sacrifice to God, the angel ascended with the fragrance of the smoke right up into the sky.

Then Joachim fell to his face and prayed from the sixth hour until dusk. And the young men and hired hands who were with him there, unaware of why he was lying there face down, supposed that he had passed away. They hurried over to him and, with great difficulty, they lifted him up off of the ground. And when Joachim related the vision of the angel to them, they were stricken with alarm and amazement, and advised him to do according to the angelic vision and hurry back home to his wife just as soon as possible. And even as Joachim was considering whether or not he ought to go back, a deep sleep overwhelmed him. And behold, the angel who had shown himself to him before when he was awake now appeared to him in his sleep and said, "God has appointed me to be your guardian angel. Go down therefore, and return to Anna in complete assurance, because the merciful deeds that you and your wife have performed have been spoken in the presence of the Highest. God is giving you fruit such as has never been given to either prophet or saint; nor will ever be given hereafter."

Now when Joachim stirred from his slumber, he went down, summoned his herdsmen and related his dream to them. "Bring me ten spotless ewe-lambs," he instructed them, "that I might give them to the Lord my God. Bring me also twelve unblemished calves, which will be for the elders and the priests, as well as a hundred young he-goats, which will be for the entire nation." Then they worshiped the Lord. "See to it that you never again disregard an angel's words!" they cautioned Joachim. "Let us rise up and move on! We will return at a leisurely pace, feeding our flocks along the way."

AN ANGEL AGAIN APPEARS TO ANNA

(BMary 3:6-10; PEv 4:3-5:5; PsMt 3)
Jerusalem

Now after they had traveled for thirty days and drawn near, behold, two angels of the Lord came and appeared to Anna, who was standing in the midst of prayer, and (one of them) proclaimed to her, "Look, your husband Joachim is coming with his driver and his droves of sheep, cattle, and goats. An angel, you see, has come down to him from the Lord saying, 'Joachim! Joachim! The Lord Himself has heard your prayer. You must leave this place at once, for your wife Anna is to bear you a child.' Get up therefore, and as proof of what I have told you, set out for Jerusalem, and when you reach that entrance which, because it is overlaid with gold, is referred to as 'The Golden Gate,' you will meet up with your husband, whose safety has so concerned you, for he is coming back to you. When you see these things happen as I have described them, believe that everything else I have spoken to you will certainly come to pass." So with all speed, she and her maidens went out to greet him. They each therefore left their places as they had been told by the angels, and they each arrived at the specified place, where they met up. Anna, nearly exhausted from standing and waiting at the gate so long and praying for him to show, lifted up her eyes; and behold, she saw Joachim approaching in the distance with his droves! Now when Anna saw Joachim coming, she ran up to him, threw her arms around his neck, offered up her thanks to God and said, "Now I am certain that the Lord God has regarded me highly; for I was a widow, but now I am a widow no more; barren, but now I have conceived a child." Then they, exulting in their respective visions and fully convinced that they would bring forth a child, paid their debt of gratitude to the Lord, who honors those who exercise humility. Then, after they had praised the Lord, they both went home, and Joachim spent his first day home at rest.

The following day he went to offer up his beasts, saying in his heart, "The frontlet of the priest will clearly reveal whether the Lord is favorable toward me." And as Joachim was offering them up, he ascended to the Lord's altar, looked into the plate on the forehead of the priest, and saw no sin within himself. "Now I am certain," said Joachim, "that the Lord God has favored me and forgiven me of all my sins." And fully vindicated, he left the Lord's temple and went down to his house, where they lived in joy and complete assurance that God would do what He had promised. And when word of this had gotten around, there was much joy among all of their friends and neighbors, inasmuch as the entire nation of Israel offered them congratulations.

THE BIRTH AND INFANCY OF MARY
DETAILS ABOUT JESUS' FAMILY LIFE
(PEv 5:6-8:1; BMary 3:11-4:11;
PsMt 4, 5, 42; Qur 3:35-36)
Jerusalem

So Anna conceived and then proclaimed, "Lord, please accept what's in my womb, for I am consecrating it to Your service, for You surely know and hear all things." And during her ninth month, after coming to full term, Anna gave birth. "What have I borne?" she asked the midwife. "A little girl," the midwife said. And Anna cried out, "Today my soul is magnified! Lord, I have brought forth a daughter and named her 'Mary.' Protect her and all of her children from that Accursed One, Satan!" then she lay down. And when the time of her purification had passed, Anna began to nurse the child. Then, on the eighth day, they named her Mary, as the angel had instructed them, for her name will never fade.

And the girl grew more robust with each day that passed. Now when she was six months old, her mother set her on the ground to see if she could but stand on her feet. And after taking seven steps, she returned to her mother's lap. Then Anna lifted her up and exclaimed, "As my Lord is the Living God, you will no more walk upon this ground until such time as I take you into the Lord's temple." She then converted Mary's nursery into a sanctuary and allowed nothing defiled or polluted to pass through. Then Anna sought assistance from the Jewish virgins, and they took Mary to themselves, serving her, caring for her, and keeping her amused.

And on Mary's first birthday, Joachim readied a great banquet and invited all of the priests, teachers of the law, and the elders--even the entire nation of Israel. And he presented the girl to the priests, who blessed her, saying, "God of our Fathers, bless this child and give her an illustrious reputation that shines eternally throughout the generations." And all who were there replied, "Amen! Amen! Amen!" From there they took her over to the chief priests, who blessed her, saying, "God of the Highest heaven, look upon this little girl and grace her with a perfect and unsurpassable blessing."

Then her mother took her into her nursery and suckled her there, singing this song to the Lord:

"I will praise the Lord with a song,
For He has come and cleared me
Of the dishonor heaped upon me by my enemies.
And the Lord has given me virtue in its full fruitage,
Unparalleled--yet everywhere before Him!
Who will proclaim to the sons of Reuben
That Anna is nursing?
Listen closely, you twelve tribes of Israel,
Anna is nursing!"

She then placed Mary to sleep on her bed in her recently enshrined nursery and then returned to serve at the feast. After the banquet, they left rejoicing and praising the God of Israel.

The child grew apace as the months went by, and when she was two years old, Joachim said, "Let's take her up to the Lord's temple, for we made a promise which we must fulfill. Otherwise the Lord might curse us and refuse our offering." But Anna said, "We should wait until the three years have passed, so the girl will no longer yearn for her father and mother." "Very well," said Joachim, "we can wait." And when the child turned three, the time allotted for her weaning ran out, so Joachim said, "Summon the Jewish virgins and light a torch for each of them, so that the girl might not return heart and mind distracted from the temple of the Lord." Joachim and his wife Anna gave all diligence to this right up to the time that they reached the Lord's temple with the sacrifices they had brought to offer God. There they entered the young Mary into the Society of Virgins, where the other virgins stayed, praising God both night and day.

Now around the temple and before its doors were fifteen steps to climb, which correspond to the fifteen Psalms of Ascent, and the temple was built into the mountain in such a way that the altar for burnt offerings, being outside, could not be approached except by these. The holy and virgin Mary's parents placed her on the first step before the temple doors and, according to the practice, went to change out of their traveling clothes and into some that were nice and clean. Meanwhile, the Lord's Virgin, not needing anyone to help or lead her, ascended all of the steps one by one so quickly that she did not even look behind, nor did she seek out her parents as other children typically do. Anyone would have thought her to be of a proper age.

The priest then hugged and blessed Mary. "The Lord has magnified your name throughout the generations," he said, "for at the close of this age the Lord will unveil His plan to deliver all of the tribes of Israel through you." Then the priest placed her on the third step of the altar, and the Lord filled her with such joy that her feet started dancing, and all of the families of Israel adored her. Her parents, who had each been running around looking anxiously for the child until they found her in the temple, were equally amazed. The priests were also taken aback. This was how the Lord chose to bring to pass this wonderful work--to show forth the greatness that the Virgin would one day come to embody by means of this marvel done in her childhood.

> Then Anna, filled with the Holy Spirit, said before them all:
> "The All-Powerful Lord, the God of Hosts,
> Has come to visit His people in holiness and benevolence,
> Being ever mindful of His Word;
> To cut to size the hearts of the Gentiles
> Who had been rising up against us,
> And convert them to Himself.
> He has unstopped His ears to hearken to our prayers,
> And silenced the gloating of our enemies.
> The barren one has become a mother,
> Bringing forth joy and celebration to Israel,
> For behold the gifts that I have brought
> To offer to my Lord!
> And powerless were my adversaries to stop me,

For you see, God has opened their hearts to me,
And given me eternal gladness."

And after her parents had offered up their sacrifices and completed their pledge, even as the law directs, they left the Virgin in the temple housing with the other virgins who were to be brought up there, and they returned to their own home, exulting in the Lord, amazed that the girl did not turn back.

Now it was during that same year that Anna was widowed. Anna and Emerina were sisters, you see, and Emerina was the mother of Elizabeth, who brought forth John the Baptist. And because Anna, the mother of the blessed Mary, was so beautiful, she married Cleophas by order of the Lord after Joachim had passed away. Now within a year she bore a second daughter through Cleophas, whom she likewise named 'Mary.' Anna then gave this Mary over to Alphaeus to wed. She later bore him James, the son of Alphaeus, and also Philip, his brother. Her second husband, Cleophas also died before the child could be born, so an angel commanded her to take a third husband by whom she bore her third daughter, Salome, whom she would also refer to as 'Mary.' Anna then gave her in marriage to Zebedee, through whom she bore the sons of Zebedee, James and John the evangelist.

MARY IN THE TEMPLE
(Luke 1:5-7; BMary 5:1, 2; PEv 8:2;
PsMt 6; Qur 3:37; QBar 2:15-21; LJB pt.1)
Jerusalem

{With the aid of God and His divine guidance, we begin to write about the life of that holy man, John the Baptist, the son of Zechariah. May he intercede on our behalf. Amen.}

In the days of Herod, the King of Judea, there was this Levite priest of Abijah's course whose name was Zechariah, of the tribe of Judah. He was a prophet who arose at that time from among the children of Israel. And he had a God-loving wife, whose name was Elizabeth, and she was of the daughters of the line of Aaron, of the tribe of Levi. Both were righteous in God's sight, and blamelessly lived according to all of the Lord's commandments and ordinances. And because they had both grown old and Elizabeth was barren, they remained without children.

Mary's Lord graciously accepted her and placed her under the care of Zechariah, and everyone in Israel held her in the highest of regard. By the time that she was three, she walked so gracefully, spoke so fittingly, and praised God so passionately, that everyone was impressed by her. So amazed were they, in fact, that she was not thought of as a child at all, but even as a thirty-year-old adult. And as the Lord's Virgin matured, He modeled her into an exemplary child. She grew more holy every day, and was the fulfillment of the Scripture written in the Psalms that reads, "Her parents delivered her over, but the Lord nurtured her," and she remained continuously in prayer. So truly beautiful and splendid was her appearance, that one could hardly look her in the face. She always kept herself busy with her woolworking. So much so, as a matter of fact, that from her youth she could do everything that even the elderly women could not. And this was her daily schedule: from dawn until the third hour, she would pray; from the third hour until the ninth, she would weave; and from the ninth hour on, she would return to her prayers. She would not stop until an angel of the Lord would visit her, at which point she would eat food right out of his hand. Every day she spoke with them, and every day she received visitors from God, which kept her from every form of evil and caused her to overflow with the richest of blessings. It was in this way that she became ever more perfect in the work of God.

And she never rested a bit from praising God, even when the older virgins would leave off, so that when it came to exaltations and vigils to God, no one was found to surpass her, nor indeed were any more knowledgeable in the wisdom of God's law. No one was more meek or modest, none could sing more beautifully, nor was any more complete in virtue. Truly she was steady, unmoving, and constant; and each day she grew closer to perfection. No one ever saw her get angry, or heard her speak wickedly. Her speech was marked by such eloquence, that it was quite clear that God was in her tongue. She prayed without ceasing, and diligently searched the law, ever mindful lest with so much as a single word she should sin against any of her companions. She was concerned that through her laughter, or the sound of her melodious voice, she should cause offense; or that her elation should, perchance, betray any misconduct or arrogance on her part to one of her companions. She glorified God ceaselessly, and if anyone ever greeted her, she would simply respond, "Give thanks to God," that she might never have to leave off, and this is where the custom among men of saying, "Give thanks to God," when greeting one another came from. She nourished herself exclusively on the food that the angel would hand-feed her daily, and would distribute every morsel that the priests would give her to the poor. The angels of God were frequently seen talking with her, and would obey her without question. If anyone who was sick ever touched her, he would return home healed that very hour.

"One day," Mary related, "while I was living in God's temple and receiving my food from an angel's hand, someone who had the appearance of an angel revealed himself to me, but I could not make out His face, and He did not have a cup or any bread in his hand like the angel did that came before. Right away the temple's veil was ripped in two and the earth shook with tremendous force, and because I could not look at Him, I fell to the ground. But He reached beneath me and lifted me up. And I looked into the heavens and behold, a dewy cloud came down and drenched me from my head to my feet; and with His robe, he dried me off. And the 'angel' greeted me, saying to me, 'Hello there, you favored one and chosen vessel, everlasting mercy to you.' Then He struck the right hand side of his robe and out came a giant loaf, and He placed it on the altar of the temple, ate therefrom and gave some to me. Once again He struck his robe on the left hand side, and out came a giant cup that was brimming with wine. He placed it on the temple's altar, drank therefrom and gave some to me.

Then I looked at them again and I saw that the bread and wine had been restored to the way they were before.

And He said to me, 'Three years from now I will send you My Word, and you will bear Me My Son. He will renew everything in all of creation. My beloved, go in peace, and My peace will be with you.' And after telling me all of these things, He disappeared before my eyes, and the temple was restored to the way it was before."

ABIATHAR ASKS MARY
TO WED HIS SON
(PsMt 7; PEv 8:3)
The Temple, Jerusalem

Now when Mary turned twelve, the priests all got together and said, "Behold, Mary is now twelve years old. What are we to do with her, for we do not wish to see the pollution of the holy place of the Lord our God." Abiathar the priest offered numerous gifts to the other high priests in exchange for Mary's hand in marriage to his son. But Mary utterly refused, saying, "It can never be that I should ever know a man, or that a man should ever know me." All of the priests, and her family as well, kept saying to her, "God is shown love through children, and is worshiped in progeny, even as it has ever been among the children of Israel." "God is worshiped through chastity," answered Mary. "This was first demonstrated through Abel, before whom there was none among mankind who was righteous. God was pleased with his offerings, but Abel was mercilessly slain by the one who did not please Him. He received two crowns as his reward; one for his offering, and one for his virginity, since his body remained unsullied. And since Elijah also kept his body undefiled the whole time that he was in the flesh, he was taken up therein. And now, since I have been in God's temple from the time of my youth, I have come to learn that virginity can be pleasing to God. So because I am able to offer to God the thing that He holds dear, in my heart of hearts I have firmly decided that I ought never to know any man."

MARY GOES TO LIVE AS JOSEPH'S WARD
(HJC 2-4; BMary 6:1)
Bethlehem

Now there was this elderly man named Joseph who was from the family and city of King David, the Judean town of Bethlehem. This man was trained in all knowledge and wisdom, and had been made a priest in the Lord's temple. He was skilled in his carpenter's trade, and he took a wife as other men do-- fathering four sons, whose names were Judas, Justus, James, and Simon; and also two daughters, whose names were Assia and Lydia. In due course, the wife of the righteous Joseph, a woman who was bent on holiness in all that she did, passed away. But that venerable man Joseph, my father according to the flesh, and husband to my mother Mary, went off to his business and practiced carpentry with his sons.

Now my blessed, holy, and unblemished mother Mary was already twelve years old by the time the honorable Joseph had become a widower. Her parents had dedicated her to the temple when she was three, you see, and for nine years she lived in the temple of the Lord. Then, when the priests recognized that the saintly and God-loving Virgin was coming of age, they talked it over with one another. "Let us try and find a just and pious man," they agreed, "to whom we may entrust Mary until such time as she should wed, just in case what normally happens among women should take place within her while housed in it--for should we fail to do this thing, we might bring God's wrath down on ourselves."

So they promptly sent word, and assembled twelve elderly men from the line of Judah. They wrote out the names of the twelve tribes of Israel, and the lot fell upon the elderly, devout, and upright Joseph. Now when at last the priests were resolved, they said to my blessed mother: "Go with Joseph, and remain with him until it's time for you to wed." So the righteous Joseph accepted my mother and took her away to his own home. And Mary found the Lesser James heartbroken and downcast over the recent loss of his mother, so she looked after him in his father's house; and this is why Mary is spoken of as the mother of James. From that time forward Joseph left her at home and went away to his carpenter's shop and practiced his trade. And after living in his home for two years from the time that he took her in, Mary was fourteen years of age.

MARY ORDERED TO WED
(BMary 5:3-17; PEv 8:3-6; PsMt 8)
The Temple, Jerusalem

And it happened that by the time Mary had reached the age of fourteen, every upright person who had ever met her respected her lifestyle and manner of speaking, and no malicious person could accuse her of any wrongdoing. Then the Pharisees affirmed that because she had turned fourteen, and because it had been such a longstanding practice, no woman who had reached that particular age should remain within the temple of God. So the high priest issued this decree: "All fourteen-year-old virgins who have reached physical maturity, and who reside in the temple's public housing, should return to their own homes and seek to be wed in accordance with the custom of their nation." Mary, the Lord's Virgin, was the only one to refuse, even though the other virgins were eager to comply, saying that she could not for the following reasons: that both she and her parents had given her to the Lord's service and that, moreover, she had pledged her virginity to the Lord, which was a vow that she was determined never to break by sleeping with a man.

This put the high priest in a difficult spot because he realized that he could not annul the vow, disobeying the Scripture that reads, "vow and pay," nor did he wish to set a precedent that would seem foreign to the people. So he ordered all of the prominent people of Jerusalem and its surrounding areas to convene during the approaching feast, and to offer up their recommendations as to the most prudent option for such a difficult situation. And after they had gathered together, he said to them, "Look, Mary has turned fourteen in the temple of the Lord. What should we do to keep her from polluting the Lord's temple?" They all agreed that it would be best to consult the Lord and to seek His advice. They therefore said to the high priest: "You serve at the Lord's altar. Enter into the sanctuary and pray with regard to her situation, and we will comply with whatever the Lord should reveal to you." Then they joined together in prayer, and the high priest took the breastplate of judgment, entered into the holy of holies and prayed her circumstances over. Then an angel of the Lord appeared to him and said, "Zechariah, Zechariah, go and gather all of the widowers from among the people." And all who were there heard a voice coming from the ark and the mercy seat, which said that the virgin ought to be betrothed to the one determined according to the prophecy out of the book of Isaiah, for Isaiah says,

"A staff will proceed from the stem of Jesse,
And a flower will bud from its root,
And the Spirit of the Lord will rest upon him;
The Spirit that enkindles wisdom and understanding,
The Spirit that delivers power and instruction,
The Spirit that conveys knowledge and virtue,
And the Spirit that inspires an awe of the Lord will direct him."

And so it happened that they came across the idea of sending a herald out to the Israelite tribes and gathering them together in the Lord's temple on the third day.

JOSEPH CHOSEN TO TAKE MARY
(BMary 6:1-7; PEv 8:7-16; PsMt 8)
The Temple, Jerusalem

So in accordance with this prophecy, he ordered every available and eligible man of David's line to bring his own rod up to the altar. The man from whose staff a flower would bud, and upon which the Lord's Spirit would alight in the form of a dove would be the one to whom the Virgin should be betrothed. And the criers went throughout the Judean countryside. The Lord's trumpet then blared and everyone came running up. Among them was Joseph, who tossed aside his carpenter's ax and joined in the gathering. And when they had all assembled in one place, the high priest Abiathar got up and ascended to a higher step, that all of the people might see him and hear. And when he had gotten them to quiet down, Abiathar declared, "Sons of Israel, listen! Open your ears and hearken to my words. From the time that Solomon built this temple, it has housed virgins--the daughters of kings and of prophets, of priests and of high priests--and great and venerable were they. But when the time was right they followed in the footsteps of their mothers, and were married off, and so were deemed to be pleasing to God. But Mary has found a new way of life for herself; promising to continue in her vow of virginity to God. For this reason, I think it is right to determine into whose care she should be given by asking God and receiving His response." These words were accepted by the synagogue, so the priests cast the lot on the twelve tribes, and it fell upon the tribe of Judah. "Tomorrow," the priest announced, "let all who are without a wife come together, staff in hand." So Joseph brought his rod along, as did all the younger men, each of whom took his staff up to the high priest. But when everyone else handed their rods in, Joseph held his own rod back. After he had taken the staffs, the high priest entered into the temple and prayed. And after he had finished his prayer, he gathered them, returned with them, and distributed them among the men; but no sign appeared on any of them. So when nothing that the heavenly voice had spoken of seemed to happen, the high priest decided that it would be best to once again consult the Lord, Whose answer was that the virgin should be engaged to the one man in the whole crowd who had not turned in his staff.

Joseph handed in his rod, and when the high priest had received them all, he sacrificed to the Lord God and sought an answer from Him. "Put their staffs into God's holy of holies," the Lord instructed him, "and leave them all there. Tell them to return tomorrow and receive their rods back. Let Mary be delivered into the keeping of the man who shows this sign: 'when his staff is returned into his hand, a dove will issue from its tip, and fly away into the sky.'"

So they all assembled early the next morning, and incense was offered up. The high priest then entered into the holy of holies and brought out the rods. He handed them back out again, but no dove came from any of them. The high priest then donned the twelve bells and the priestly robe, entered into the holy of holies, burnt an offering and said a prayer. An angel of the Lord then appeared to him and said, "Here is the shortest staff. You did not count it up or take it out with the others, though you brought it in with all the rest. Now after you have taken it out and given it to its owner, the sign that I spoke to you about will appear." Joseph was therefore exposed, because the staff belonged to him. He had been passed up, so to speak, that on account of his old age he might not get her--and neither did he wish to ask for it back. And as he stood there meekly, last of all, the high priest thundered, "Joseph! We are all waiting for you to come and get your staff." Now because the high priest had called him with such vehemence, Joseph went up trembling. So he received his staff after everyone else had received theirs. Now as soon as he had reached out his hand and taken hold thereof, from out of the sky flew a beautiful dove, which was even whiter than snow, and perched upon it. Then the dove flew off of it and onto Joseph's head. And after flying around the rooftops of the temple for quite awhile, it flew away into the heavens.

Now everyone saw clearly that the virgin was to be betrothed to him, so they congratulated the old man and said, "Father Joseph, you have been blessed in your old age, for God has deemed you to be worthy of Mary." Then the priests all counseled Joseph: "You must accept her, for out of the entire line of Judah, God has chosen you alone to take the Lord's virgin into your care." But Joseph answered them sheepishly, "I am an old man, with sons of my own; she is but a little girl. I have children already, so why are you giving me this young maiden, who is even younger than my grandsons? I protest for fear of becoming an object of ridicule in Israel." "Joseph," the high priest Abiathar cautioned, "you ought to fear the Lord your God and call to mind what he did to Dathan, Abiram, and Korah; how the earth was ripped apart and all of them were swallowed up. It was for their disobedience (and) contempt for God's will that they perished. Watch out Joseph, and realize that all of this could come to pass in your house too. It most certainly will happen if you scorn what God demands." "Truly I do not despise God's will," Joseph replied, "but I will foster her until I know to which of my sons it is His will to give her. Let some of her virgin friends be given her for companionship and consolation." "Five virgins will indeed be conceded," the high priest Abiathar responded, "but only until the day comes for you to take her to yourself, for she cannot marry anyone but you." So Joseph, growing fearful, accepted Mary into his charge, along with Rebecca, Sephora, Susanna, Abigea, and Zael, the five (other) maidens who were to live with her in Joseph's house, and to whom the high priest would give the silk, the blue, the choice linen, the scarlet, the purple, and the fine flax. "Mary," said Joseph, "I have accepted you from the Lord's temple, but for now I must leave you in my house to go away and do some building. I will come again for you, and may the Lord watch over you."

MARY SPINS THE SCARLET AND THE PURPLE
(PEv 9:1-5a; PsMt 8)
Jerusalem; Bethlehem

A council of priests assembled and said, "Let us fashion a veil for the temple of the Lord." And the high priest declared, "Summon the undefiled virgins of the line of David," and the officers went looking and found seven. The high priest then called to mind that Mary, too, was of David's line, so the officers went and got her as well. Then they gathered them into the Lord's temple where the high priest declared, "Cast lots before me to see who will weave the golden thread, the white, the linen, the silk, the blue, the crimson and the royal purple." The royal purple and the crimson fell to Mary's lot, so she accepted them and took them home. Then, so as to provoke Mary, the other virgins taunted, "Since you are after us all, and younger than us all, and ever so modest, you truly deserve to be awarded, and to accept the purple." Then they started calling her 'The Virgin Queen.' And even as they were saying these things, the angel of the Lord appeared in their midst and said, "These words will not have been spoken as a mere insult, but uttered as a most prophetic truth." They naturally trembled at the sight of the angel and the words he had spoken; so they asked Mary to forgive them and to pray on their behalf. Mary then took the scarlet thread and began to spin. This marks the time when Zechariah became unable to speak.

THE FORETELLING OF JOHN'S BIRTH
(Luke 1:8-25; PEv 9:5b;
Qur 3:38-41; 19:2-10; 21:89-90; LJB pt.2)
Jerusalem

Now Zechariah was ever presiding in the temple of the Lord. And it happened that, even as he was executing his priestly duties in the sight of God, according to his custom (and) the order of his course, and the manner of his priestly office, it was his lot to enter into the Lord's temple and burn incense at the time of the lighting thereof. Now every time Zechariah would look in on Mary in the temple, he found that she had all of this food with her, so he asked her, "Mary, where does all this food come from?" "All of this food comes from God," she replied. "He gives generously to whomever He pleases." After hearing this, Zechariah secretly called upon his Lord and prayed, "Lord, You hearken to my every prayer. My bones all creak, and my head has aged to a lustrous gray, yet never have I prayed to You in vain. Lord, do not let me leave this world without an heir, but give me righteous children. Now, because my wife is barren, I fear that my cousins are in line to replace me. Even so, You are over all who inherit. Give me a son who is favored in your eyes--one who will be not only heir to me, but also to the house of Jacob." And even as he stood praying in the temple, his answer came: an angel of the Lord suddenly appeared to him, standing to the right of the altar of incense. Now Zechariah grew anxious when he saw the angel, and he froze with fear. The angel therefore said to him,

> "Zechariah, have no fear, but rejoice instead;
> For your humble prayer has been heard.
> Your wife Elizabeth will bear you a son,
> And you are to name him John;
> A name that none before him has been called.
> God is inviting you to celebrate in the birth of John.

You are to be joyful and glad,
And his appearance will bring rejoicing to many.
He will be great in the eyes of God,
For he will give his strength to the Word of God.
He is destined to be honorable and virtuous;
A prophet and an honest man
Who will never partake
Of wine or strong drink.
And he will be filled with the Holy Spirit
While yet in his mother's womb.
And he will transform many hearts
Among the children of Israel,
That they might turn again to the Lord their God.
And the Lord's face will be toward him
As he goes forth in the spirit and power of Elijah,
That he might turn the hearts of the fathers
Toward their sons,
And the hearts of the disobedient,
That they might live according to the wisdom of the just;
To train a people to readiness,
That they might be prepared for the Lord."

Now Zechariah was taken aback by what had been said, and doubt overtook him, for he had as yet not fathered any children. He did not recall the case of Abraham, who was foremost among the Patriarchs, to whom God had given Isaac after having reached the age of one hundred years, nor did he call to mind his wife Sarah who was just as barren as his own wife was. "Lord," Zechariah inquired, "how can I be sure of this? How am I to father a son seeing that old age has crept up on me and also my wife, who is barren?" "This is all the will of God," the angel replied, "He always does as He sees fit. This was how your Lord put it, 'For [Me] this is nothing, [I] brought you into being, and you were nothing before that!'" "Show me Lord," Zechariah said. "Give me a sign!" "I am Gabriel," the angel replied, "who stands in the presence of God Himself. I was sent to speak to you and to give you this wonderful news. Now behold, since you did not believe the words I spoke, though your body will otherwise remain intact, you will be unable to speak with any man except through signs, until the passage of three days and nights, the time allotted for these things to happen. Keep your Lord forever in your thoughts, praising Him both dusk and dawn." Then the angel vanished from his sight.

Meanwhile the people who had been waiting for Zechariah, were wondering why he had been in the temple so long. When he finally came out of it, he was unable to speak, and they could tell that he had seen a vision while in it, and he continued to speak to them in signs. And when his time of service had ended, he returned to his home. And Elizabeth came to learn of this (from God.) "[I] hearkened to the prayer of Zechariah and gave him John, removing the barrenness of his wife. Together they vied in good works and called on [Me] in all honesty, fear, and submission."

ELIZABETH'S SECLUSION
(LJB pt.3)
Judea

Now in those days Elizabeth conceived and remained in seclusion until her fifth month, for she felt rather ill at ease, fearing to appear in public, seeing that she was aged and pregnant, and milk was leaking from her breasts. So she kept to herself, closed off in isolation in a room of her house, as did Zechariah. The door that stood between them remained shut tight, and they spoke to no one at that time.

THE ANNUNCIATION
(Luke 1:26-38; BMary 7:1-21; PEv 11:1-3;
HJC 5; SbOr 8:459-471; PsMt 9;
Qur 3:45-49; 19:16-22a; LJB pt.4)
Nazareth

Now during the sixth month of their engagement, when Elizabeth was in her sixth month of pregnancy, God sent Gabriel, the angel of His Spirit, to the Virgin Mary, who was betrothed to Joseph, of the line of David, in the Galilean city of Nazareth. This took place when she first arrived in Galilee, in order to announce to her the conception of our Savior, and the way that it would come to pass.

First of all, Gabriel was revealed in his holiness and might. Mary took a pitcher and went out to draw some water, and while she was at the well, he approached her. And behold, there came a voice: "Hello there, exalted one, rejoice! You are more blessed than all women, for the Lord is with you." And she looked left and right to see where it could be coming from, because the saying troubled her greatly, and she wondered what such a statement might mean. And she went back into her house and put down the jug. And still shaken, she took the purple thread, sat down and started working with it.

The next day, the archangel addressed the young woman a second time in words. Mary was at the fountain filling her pitcher when the angel of the Lord appeared to her and said, "Mary, how blessed are you, for you have readied a place in your womb for the Lord to live. Just look, the heavenly light will come and dwell in you, and through you will illumine the world."

And on the third day, he approached her again in a similar way, entering in the form of an unspeakably beautiful young man, filling the room she was in with a blinding light, even as she was working with her fingers on the purple. And behold, the Lord's angel stood before her; and when Mary saw him, she trembled with fright, (and) said, "May the Merciful One shield me from you." And he addressed her in the most genial way imaginable, saying,

"Hello, Mary, most acceptable of the Lord's virgins!
Oh Virgin who is full of splendor, the Lord is with you!
You are blessed among women,
And blessed also is the fruit of your womb Jesus.
Blessed are you above all women!
Blessed (indeed) are you beyond all men who have ever been born!
For God has chosen you alone.
He has created you unblemished
And exalted you above all other women."

And when Mary heard these words, she began to shake with fear. The Lord's angel then declared, "Mary, do not be afraid, for you have received God's favor. I am your Lord's messenger, here to bring you a holy son. Behold, you are to conceive in your womb, and bring forth a king who fills not only the entire earth, but the heavens as well; and whose rule spans from generation to generation. Mary, show your obedience to the Lord by bowing down and worshipping with the worshippers. God is inviting you to rejoice in a Word from Him. His name is Jesus, the Christ, the Son of Mary. He will show his greatness in this world and the one that is to come, and God will greatly honor him. He will preach to all men from the cradle to his final day, living virtuously all the while."

But to the Virgin, such celestial light was nothing new; for she, being no stranger to the faces of heavenly angels, was not alarmed by the sight of the messenger, nor was she awed by the brilliance of the light, but the angel's words did trouble her greatly. "What could such a fantastic greeting possibly mean?" she wondered. "What might it foreshadow, or what might come of it?" And through divine inspiration the angel responded to her thoughts, saying, "Mary, do not be alarmed and imagine that by my greeting I meant anything that is inconsistent with your chastity--for it is because of your purity that the Lord has favored you.

Behold, while preserving your virginity,
And apart from any kind of sin,
You are to conceive in your womb,
And by His Word bring forth a son,
Whom you are to call Jesus.
He will be great, for he will rule from sea to sea,
And from the heads of the rivers to the ends of the earth.
And he will be called the Son of the Most High God;
For the one born into a lowly state upon the earth
In reality rules from one which is exalted in heaven.
The Lord will give him the throne of his forefather David,
And he will reign over the house of Jacob for endless ages,
And there will be no end to his kingdom.
He is King of Kings, and Lord of Lords,
Infinite and eternal is his heavenly reign."

"Lord," said Mary, "tell me how these things can be? How is it possible for me to bear a child without a man's seed, seeing that in line with my vow I have never slept with, (or) touched any man, nor ever have I been unchaste?" (The Virgin did not reply to the words of the angel as though she disbelieved them, but merely to find out how these things would come about.) To this the angel responded, "Mary, do not think that you will conceive by sleeping with a man as others do, but as a virgin, you will conceive, as a virgin you will bring forth, and as a virgin you will give suck." And when she heard that, she thought it over and asked, "Then will I conceive by the Lord, the Living God, and give birth even as other women do?" "Not at all, Mary," said the angel of the Lord, "for the Holy Spirit will draw near to you, and the Lord's power, free from the slightest taint of lustful passions, will overshadow you, so that what you bear will be completely holy, because it will be conceived without sin, and be called the 'Son of God' upon his birth. And you are to name him Jesus for he will save his people from their sins. This is the way that your Lord put it, 'This is simple enough for [Me]. He will be a sign to all mankind, and a blessing that comes straight from [Me]. [My] decree will surely come to pass.' This is how the will of God is: whenever He ordains anything whatsoever, He need only say 'appear' and it appears. To him will He reveal the wisdom of the Writings, the Torah and the Gospel--and He will send him out to preach among the Israelites. He will say, 'I am giving you a sign from your Lord--I will form the shape of a bird from mud, and breathe into it. Through God's power it will be changed into a living bird. And through the power of God, I will heal the leprous and the blind, and raise the dead back up to life. I will give you orders as to what to eat and what to lay up in your homes. If your faith is pure, surely this will be a sign for you. I have come in order to confirm the Torah that has been revealed to you already, as well as to make lawful certain things you've been denied. This is the sign that I bring to you straight from the Lord; now honor God by obeying me! God is both my Master and yours: therefore do all things for Him, for that path indeed is straight.'

"Now behold, Elizabeth, your kinswoman has also conceived a son in her old age; and she that was thought to be barren is now in her sixth month, for no word of God will be robbed of its strength. With God, you see, nothing is impossible." Then Mary, harboring no doubts in her heart, stretched out her hands and lifted up her eyes to heaven and said to the archangel: "Behold the servant of the Lord! May these things all be to me as you have said." "Virgin," the archangel replied, "accept God into your unblemished heart." And as he spoke, he breathed God's perfection into her who had ever been a virgin. She was stricken with alarm and amazement as she listened. And even as she stood and trembled, her mind raced and her heart throbbed on account of the mysterious words that she had heard. But soon she rejoiced, and her heart received its healing from the selfsame voice. The young woman laughed so hard that her face turned red, and her heart filled with awe as she reeled in joy. Courage, then, was given her, and a Word flew into her womb; quickly putting on the flesh, coming to life and taking the form of a child within her--(and) even so did Mary conceive. The angel then saluted her and left her presence. "I, (Jesus,) chose her myself, according to my Father's will, and the counsel of the Holy Spirit, and was formed out of her flesh by a means so mysterious that it defies the created reason."

MARY VISITS ELIZABETH
(Luke 1:39-56; PEv 12:1-3; Qur 19:22b; LJB pt.5)
Jerusalem, The Highlands of Judea

So Mary finished up the purple and the scarlet and gave them to the priest, who blessed her, saying, "The Lord God has exalted your name, Mary, and your praises will span the generations of the earth." Then Mary rose up quickly in joy, and left in haste to a faraway place--to the home of Zechariah and Elizabeth, her kinswoman, who lived in a Judean town nestled in the hills. Now Mary was amazed that Elizabeth could be expecting a child, and so kept saying in her heart: "How great and wonderful are Your deeds, oh Almighty God, for You have given children to an aged woman who had been barren. I will not leave off walking until I have visited her and seen for myself the marvelous thing that God has brought to pass in our days: a virgin who will bear a child, and a barren woman who will give suck." She knocked at the door and called to her. And when Elizabeth heard Mary's cry, the baby leapt within her womb. Then Elizabeth, filled with the Holy Spirit, cried aloud, "Blessed are you above all women, and most holy is the fruit of your womb." And she put down her scarlet, and with great joy and gladness, raced to the door and flung it open. Now as soon as she saw Mary there, she worshiped her and said, "How can it be that the mother of my Lord should visit me? For behold, no sooner did the sound of your call enter into my ears, than did the child in my womb jump for joy and give you praise! And blessed indeed is she who believed, for the things spoken to her by the Lord will certainly be fulfilled." Then the devout and holy virgin embraced the true turtledove, and the Word baptized John while yet in his mother's womb. Then David appeared in their midst and proclaimed: "Mercy and truth have joined together, and virtue and peace have kissed one another." Just then, John stirred within the womb as if striving to come out and meet his Lord. And as they went into the house, Mary (and) Elizabeth (together) said:

> "My soul truly magnifies the Lord,
> And my spirit has delighted in God my Savior,
> For He has looked upon the lowliness of His servant:
> Behold, from this time forward all generations
> Will honor me,
> Because He that is all-powerful
> Has done marvelous things to me;
> And His name is 'Holy.'
> His mercy is from generations to generations
> And is on those that fear Him.

With His arm, He has shown His might;
To disperse those whose hearts imagine proud things.
He has pulled the rulers out of their thrones,
And replaced them with the oppressed.
He has heaped good things upon the hungry,
Plundered the rich and banished them.
He has brought deliverance to His servant Israel,
That He might call to mind His forbearance,
Even as He swore to our ancestors;
Toward Abraham and his children for all of eternity."

But after they had greeted each other, Mary lost sight of the mysterious things that the Archangel Gabriel had revealed to her. And looking toward heaven, she groaned, "Lord, who am I that all the people of the earth should venerate me?" Now for three months, until Mary's time was near, she remained with Elizabeth, and her womb grew with each day that passed. Mary was sixteen years old by the time that all of these astonishing things came about, and she returned to her home for fear of the Israelites and hid.

THE BIRTH AND NAMING OF JOHN
(Luke 1:57-80; Qur 19:11; LJB pt.6)
The Highlands of Judea

Now Elizabeth came to full term and brought forth a son, and there was great joy and gladness in her house. Her family and her neighbors, hearing how the Lord had shown her compassion, rejoiced along with her. So on the eighth day they came to circumcise him, intending to name him after his father Zechariah. "Not so," his mother insisted, "his name is supposed to be John." "There is no one in your family with this name," they protested. Elizabeth therefore said to them: "Ask his father what his name should be." Now when Zechariah came out of the temple, they gestured to him, "Tell us what you'd have us name him?" And he motioned for a tablet to write on and wrote out, "His name is John," and none of them could believe these words. All of a sudden, he could open his mouth, and his tongue was free to speak. Zechariah therefore praised the Lord, (and) urged them all to glorify him morning and evening. Everyone grew fearful, and news of these things spread throughout the hills of Judea. Now because the hand of the Lord was upon him, all who heard it took these things to heart, and they asked, "What is this child destined to become?" And filled with the Holy Spirit, his father Zechariah, mindful of the gift he had received from God, prophesied concerning his son John the Baptist:

"Praise the Lord, the God of Israel,
For He has come and freed His people
And lifted up a horn of salvation
For those of us of the house of His servant David,
Even as He had foretold in ancient times

By the mouth of His holy prophets,
Deliverance from our enemies,
And from the grasp of those who hate us.
To show forbearance to our predecessors,
And call to mind the holiness of the promise;
The solemn pledge that He made to our father Abraham,
To grant that we be saved
From the clutches of our enemies
And to serve Him without fear,
In purity and virtue in His sight every day of our lives.
Yes, child, and you will be known
As the prophet of the Most High
Since you will go ahead of Him to clear His way;
To give knowledge for the deliverance of His people
In His pardoning of their sins,
For tender is the mercy of our God,
Which is why He will look upon us from above
As the dawn breaks forth,
(And even now that day is dawning.)
To shine on those who live in darkness;
Underneath the shadow of death;
To guide our steps on the road to peace."

At that time John was living in prosperity, and for two years he nursed at the breast of his mother. The joy of God was on his face, and he grew up strengthened in the Spirit.

JOSEPH DISCOVERS THAT MARY IS PREGNANT
(BMary 6:6, 7/8:1-11; PEv 13:1-14:2;
Matt 1:19-24; PsMt 10, 11; HJC 5; AsIs 11:4)
Capernaum; Bethlehem; Nazareth

Even as all of this was going on, Joseph, because he was a carpenter, was busily at work on a house-building project near the seaside district in Capernaum, where he remained for nine months. Now after the nine months had passed, as the customary engagement ceremonies were drawing to a close, three months after Mary's conception, that venerable man Joseph left the building site and returned to his hometown of Bethlehem to get his house in order and to supply the provisions necessary for the wedding. But Mary, the Lord's Virgin had returned to her parents' home in Galilee, along with the seven other virgins who were of the same age and period of weaning, and who had been appointed by the priest to care for her. And Joseph left Judea and traveled on to Galilee, planning to visit the Virgin there, for it was by then nearly three months from their time of engagement.

Behold, by the time Joseph entered into his home, Mary was in her sixth month of pregnancy. Now she was his betrothed, so it soon became clear to him that she was expecting, for she could not hide it from him--after all he did have free access to her and did speak familiarly with her, so he naturally came to know.

When he realized that my virgin mother was pregnant, he was stunned, and so entirely taken with distress, that he started to shake. He slapped himself upon the face, dropped to the ground upon sackcloth and wailed, "With what semblance am I to face the Lord my God? What intercession am I able to offer on behalf of this young woman? She was a virgin when I accepted her from the Lord's temple, but I have not protected her. Who has betrayed me? Who has carried out such wickedness; violating this virgin in my very own home? Could it be that my life has become like Adam's? For Adam was by himself in his time of prayer, when the serpent crept up and found Eve alone and beguiled her; and a similar fate has befallen me. My Lord, my God, take my spirit, for I would rather die than live!" And the virgins who had been with Mary asked him, "What are you saying, Master Joseph? We are quite convinced that no man has laid his hand on her. We know for sure that she has not sullied her innocence and that she has, in fact, preserved her virginity, for God Himself has protected her. We have kept our eyes on her; and she continues ever with us in our prayers. Every day an angel of the Lord speaks with her; and every day she is fed by an angel's hand. How any evil could enter into her, or how there could be any sin within her we do not know, but if you want us to tell you what we think it is, it is that nothing less than God's angel has impregnated her." "Are you trying to tell me that an angel of God has gotten her pregnant?" Joseph replied. "Why are you trying to deceive me? Truly, it is more likely that someone disguised as an angel from God has seduced her." And he sobbed as he spoke these things and asked, "How am I going to look when I enter into the Lord's temple? How am I to hide my circumstances from the priests of God? What am I supposed to do?" And after he had spoken this, it occurred to him that he should run away, and secretly put her away as well.

Then Joseph got up from the sackcloth, summoned Mary to himself and asked, "Why have you who were cared for by God, forgotten your God and done this thing? Why have you who were hand-fed by an angel and raised in the holy of holies gone and debased your very soul?" And through her tears, she sobbed, "I am chaste and have never slept with any man." "As my Lord is the Living God," Joseph replied, "I don't know why this has happened to me." And he could not even bring himself to eat or drink anything that day on account of his sorrow and dread.

And Joseph left her there, unsure as to which course it would be best to take. He grew all the more anxious and confused the more he tried to figure out what he should do with her, for he was a righteous man and was not eager to expose her, nor as a pious man was he willing to stigmatize her with the reputation of a whore. "If I should cover up her sin," he said, "I will be opposing the law of the Lord, and if I should expose her to the children of Israel, I fear that I might be handing over innocent blood to the sentence of death, for what is in her may indeed be from the angels."

He therefore determined firmly to terminate their engagement quietly, and to divorce her secretly. And when he had decided this, he started to devise a scheme to hide Mary and put her away: he planned to get up in the middle of the night, leave her there and live in seclusion, but night fell upon him as he was working out the details. Now behold, later on that evening that holy prince of angels, the angel of the Lord's Spirit, Gabriel, came to this earth with an order from my Father, and spoke to Joseph in his dreams, saying, "Joseph, son of David, do not be afraid! Do not fear to take this child, nor hesitate to take Mary as your wife. Do not think unseemly thoughts about the Virgin, and do not imagine for a moment that she is guilty of fornication, for it is by means of the Holy Spirit that she has conceived, and among all women is the only virgin who will ever give birth. And she will bring forth a son--even the very Son of God--whom you are to name 'Jesus,' which means 'The Savior,' for he will save his people from their sins." Now all of these things came to pass in order to fulfill what the Lord had spoken through the prophet: "Behold, the virgin will conceive and bring forth a son, whom they will call Immanuel;" which means 'God in our midst,' when interpreted. "He will rule all nations with a rod of iron." And after saying all of this to him, the angel left his presence.

And at midday, Joseph rose up from his slumber, gave praise to the God of Israel, and thanked Him Who had shown him such mercy. He then shared his dream with Mary and the other virgins who were there. And after receiving assurances from the angels and from Mary, he confessed, "I have sinned in my mistrust of you." And he did not divorce her, but kept her instead as the angel had instructed him; and she remained there with him. Even so, he did not speak these things to anyone.

THE TRIAL OF JOSEPH AND MARY
(PsMt 12; PEv 15:1-16:2-BMary 8:12; AsIs 11:5, 6)
Jerusalem, The Hills of the Countryside

A rumor started to get around that Mary was pregnant, so Annas, the teacher of the law, came to Joseph and demanded, "Why have you not seen fit to join in our assembly?" Joseph replied, "Because my travels tired me out and I took it easy on my first day back." Then Annas caught sight of Mary and saw for himself that she was with child. He hurried to the priest and said: "Joseph, for whom you have borne witness, has done a terrible thing!" "What is it?" the high priest asked him. "He has deflowered the virgin whom he received from the Lord's temple," Annas replied, "consummating his marriage to her without telling it to the children of Israel." "Has Joseph really done this thing?" the priest inquired. "Send officers and you will find that the 'Virgin' is pregnant." Some officers then went and verified that it was true, bringing Joseph and Mary back with them to the court. The temple officers seized Joseph and led him before the high priest. He (and the other) priests began to accuse him, saying, "How could you have been cheated out of a wedding like this; a virgin whom God's own angels nurtured as a dove in the temple, who never sought the company of any man, and whose understanding of God's law was unexcelled?

Why have you done this kind of thing? Had you not defiled this maiden, she would be a virgin today." But Joseph swore on oath that he had never even touched her, saying, "As my Lord is the Living God, I am not to blame for the state she is in." "Do not perjure yourself," the priest rejoined. "Own up to the facts; you have failed to bow your head beneath the hand of power, and have consummated your marriage without telling it to the children of Israel, and have thereby denied a blessing on your children." Joseph did not speak a word, so the priest demanded, "Restore the 'virgin' that you took from the Lord's temple." As Joseph wept in bitterness, the priest announced, "I will give you both to drink of the water of the Lord's testing, and it will witness to you of your sins." He then brought it over to Joseph to drink and sent him out into the hills, and he returned to them unchanged.

"As God lives," the high priest Abiathar said to Joseph, "I will therefore give you to drink of the water of the Lord's testing, and He will immediately show the sign of your sin." So Joseph was also called before the altar and given the water of the Lord's testing, out of which should anyone drink and walk around it seven times, will expose his guilt, for if he has spoken a falsehood, God will show it in his face. Joseph drank it gladly and went around the altar, and not a trace of guilt appeared on him. So the priests, the officers, and the people there exalted him, saying "Blessed are you, for evil was not found in you."

Then a great crowd of Israelites gathered around, and Mary was ushered into the Lord's temple. The priests, her neighbors, and even her parents clamored to Mary: "Confess to the priests that you, who were hand-fed as a dove by angels in God's temple, have committed sin." And calling Mary to themselves, they asked, "What excuse can you possibly give? What sign will He give over and above the pregnancy that is clearly revealed in your own womb?" And the priest demanded, "Why have you who were raised in the holy of holies, hand-fed by an angel, heard hymns and danced in His presence, done this, humbling your very soul and forgetting the Lord your God? Since Joseph has been cleared with regard to you, we will only accept one answer from you: Tell us who it was that seduced you. It would truly be better for you to confess than to have the wrath of God revealed as a sign on your face, exposing you before us all." But Mary burst into tears and replied, "As my Lord is the Living God, I am untainted before Him and have never slept with any man." But he had Mary drink as well, and venture out into the hills, whereupon she also returned unchanged.

Mary then stood firmly, and boldly proclaimed, "If there is any evil or defilement in me, or if there has ever been in me any lust or lasciviousness, may the Lord expose me before everyone here, that they might learn a lesson from my case." And she approached the altar of God in complete assurance, drank the water of testing, and went around it seven times, and not a trace of guilt was found in her.

Seeing that she was pregnant, yet still displayed no sign of guilt, all of the people stammered, and were bewildered. But, as is common in crowds, some of them became disorderly and complained to one another. Some of them blessed her, saying that she was holy and pure; but others, motivated by doubts, denounced her, saying that she was wicked and defiled. Then Mary, seeing how her integrity had not rid the people of their doubts, confidently said to them: "As God, Adonai of the multitudes, in whose sight I stand lives, I have never slept with any man, nor has it ever crossed my mind, seeing that from the time of my youth until this day I have been ever mindful of this vow. And I made this pledge my offering to God from early in my childhood, that I might dwell uprightly with Him Who made me; live solely in Him with Whom I share my convictions; and remain spotlessly and exclusively with Him."

Then the priest declared to them, "If the Lord God has not revealed any sins in you, then neither will I judge you," and he let them both go. Then everyone started kissing her and asking her to forgive them for their vicious mistrust. Joseph and Mary then left for his house, joyfully praising the God of Israel. Everyone, including the priests and the virgins led her home, rejoicing, celebrating, and loudly proclaiming, "Blessed be the name of the Lord, who has revealed your holiness to Israel." And after this, Joseph married the virgin and guarded her, living separately alongside her for two months; never approaching her or lying with her, but keeping her as a perfect virgin as the angel had instructed him.

INFANCY 2

INTODUCTION TO THE ARABIC INFANCY GOSPEL; JOSEPH AND MARY TRAVEL TO BETHLEHEM
(Luke 2:1-6; BMary 8:13, 14; PEv 17:1-18:1;
PsMt 13; ArIn 1:1, 4-6; AsIs 11:7; HJC 7; Qur 19:23-26)
Nazareth; Jerusalem; The Road to Bethlehem

{We found the following reports written in the Book of Joseph the High Priest, who some say is Caiaphas:}

Now it happened shortly after the two months, in the three hundred and ninth year of the reign of Alexander, when Joseph the Carpenter was living apart from his wife Mary in her house, that a registration was imposed according to the edict of Augustus Caesar the king: that everyone in the inhabited world should register in his own town. (This registration was the first to take place during the governorship of Quirinius in Syria.) So everyone returned to enroll in their own home towns. It was needful, therefore, for Joseph to sign on with Mary (in Bethlehem), because they, being of the tribe of Judah, and the stock and lineage of David, were both from there. By then it was approaching nine months from her time of conception, and by then Mary was great with child.

"I will enter my sons," (said Joseph,) "but what am I to do with this girl? How am I to register her? As my wife? I am too embarrassed to admit that! Perhaps as my daughter! I cannot, for the children of Israel are all aware that she is not my daughter. No, on this, the Lord's Day, the Lord will do as He sees fit." So the aged and righteous Joseph got up, packed some essentials, saddled his donkey, and seated her on it. Joseph then left the city of Nazareth, his son leading and himself trailing behind. They passed through Galilee and entered into Judea, then traveled on to Jerusalem and Bethlehem.

And as they were approaching the third milestone, Joseph turned around and noticed Mary looking sad, so he thought within himself, "Perhaps the child within her is causing her anguish." Later on, Joseph turned around and saw her laughing out loud, so he asked her, "Mary, why do I see laughter on your face one minute and sorrow on it the next?" And Mary replied to Joseph, "I can see two peoples with these eyes of mine: one of them weeping in bitterness and one triumphing in utter joy."

When they reached the halfway point along the road to Bethlehem, Mary called out to Joseph, "I see two nations before me, one weeping and the other rejoicing." "Sit quietly upon your beast," answered Joseph, "and speak only when necessary!" A handsome young man, all dressed in white, appeared before them there and asked, "Joseph, why did you say that the words that were spoken by Mary concerning the two peoples were superfluous? For she saw the Jewish people weeping because they have abandoned their God; and the Gentile people rejoicing because they have drawn near to the Lord, even as He promised to our forefathers Abraham, Isaac, and Jacob: for the time has now come for a blessing to be extended toward all the nations of the children of Abraham!"

And after he had spoken this, they drew near to the cave. And the angel commanded the donkey to stop, for it happened at that point that the time for her to give birth had come. Mary then let Joseph know that it was her time, and that she would be unable to make it into town. The angel then told Mary to come down from her beast. "Joseph," said Mary, "take me off of this donkey, for the child within me is struggling to come out." And Joseph helped her down from it. And the throes of childbirth drove her to the base of a palm, where she lamented, "Oh that I had only died before and passed into oblivion!" And from within a voice cried out, "Do not be sad, for below at your feet, your Lord has provided you with a brook. Now if you should shake the palm a bit, it will drop fresh, ripe dates into your lap. Eat, drink, and rejoice therefore; and if you should meet with anyone, merely say, 'I have sworn a fast to the Lord this day, and will not speak with any man.'"

And (Joseph) asked her, "Where am I to take you in this forsaken place that I might conceal your disgrace?" "Enter into an underground cavern which has never seen the light of day," the angel replied, "but which has forever been choked with darkness." Joseph found a cave nearby, and Mary said, "Let us enter into it," and he took her inside. Now as soon as Mary entered the cave, it began to shine as bright as the sixth hour of the day. And the light, which came from God, was such that so long as Mary was there, be it either night or day, there was never any lack thereof.

THE BIRTH OF JESUS
(Luke 2:7a; Matt 1:25; PEv 18:1-20:3; PsMt 13; IgEph 19;
SbOr 8:471-476; BMary 8:15; LtIn 73, 74-in Arundel Ms 404;
ArIn 1:2, 3, 7; AsIs 10:7-31, 11:8b-14; OSol 19:6-11)
In a Cave Between Jerusalem and Bethlehem;
The Seven Heavens

And Joseph, leaving his sons to care for her, went out to seek for a Jewish midwife in the region of Bethlehem. Now behold, a girl drew near with a birthing chair and came to a stop. Both of them were startled, and Joseph asked her, "Girl, where are you going with that chair?" "My mistress has sent me here," she answered, "because a young man came running up and crying out, 'Hurry now! Come and assist in a remarkable birth, because for the first time ever a virgin will bring forth.' Now as soon as my mistress heard this, she sent me out ahead of her. Look, here she comes now!" And behold, there was this woman coming down from the hills. Joseph turned around and saw her approaching, so he went up to her and they introduced themselves to one another. "Mister," the midwife asked Joseph, "where are you headed?" And he answered her, "I am in search of a Jewish midwife." And the woman asked him, "Are you an Israelite?" "Indeed I am," Joseph replied. The woman then asked him, "Who is this 'virgin' who is ready to bring forth in this cave?" "It is Mary," answered Joseph, "my betrothed, who was educated in the Lord's temple." "Is she therefore not your wife?" the midwife asked him. "Well, she was betrothed to me," Joseph replied, "but it was the Holy Spirit that brought about her conception." "Is what you say indeed the truth?" the midwife asked him. "Come and see it for yourself!" responded Joseph. And she followed him to the mouth of the cave, where they came to a stop. "Come and have a look at Mary," he directed her, so both of them went inside. And even as she was about to enter into the innermost chamber, behold, a luminous cloud shone brilliantly within it, and the midwife froze with fear.

"Behold," Joseph cried aloud to Mary, "I have brought you a midwife, Zachel, who is standing outside at the opening. Not only does she not dare to enter, but indeed finds it impossible to do so." When Mary heard this, she grinned. "Do not smile," Joseph complained, "but be prudent, for she has come to examine you and see if you need medicine." He asked the midwife to go inside and have a look, and she stood before Mary.

"Now as I was going in," (the midwife later reported,) "I saw the virgin looking up and facing heaven. And although she seemed to be talking to herself, I truly believe that she was praying to and praising the Most High God. And when I came up to her, I said, 'Tell me, my daughter, do you not feel any pain? Is there no part of your body in anguish?' Yet she remained motionless; fixed like a solid rock toward heaven." And for several hours, Mary allowed herself to be observed. And when the Lord was about to be born, Joseph went away to seek midwives.

And (in my vision) I, (Isaiah,) heard the voice of the Most High, the Eternal One, my Lord's Father saying to my Lord, the Son, the Christ, the one who is to be called Jesus, "Withdraw from here and pass through the heavens. You must descend below the skies of that world to dwell within that sphere, and further descend as far as the angel in Sheol, but you will by no means travel as far down as destruction and perdition. And you are to take on the appearance of those of the five heavens, and must take care to transform yourself into the image of both the angels of the sky, and those in Sheol. Not a single angel of that realm will perceive that you are Lord with me over their angels of governance and those of the seven heavens. And they will fail to grasp that you are with Me when with the utterance of the skies I summon you unto Myself-- along with their angels and stars--until My voice ascends to the sixth heaven, that you might pass judgment upon and utterly destroy the rulers, angels, and 'gods' of that realm, along with the domain that they control. For they have all denied Me and said, 'We are all alone, and there is no one here but us.' After this, you will rise again from the dead, rising from the 'gods' of death and entering into your true stature. And you are to wear no disguise in any of the heavens, but in the fullness of your splendor will you rise up and sit to My right, and the princes and powers will worship you, as will each and every angelic being and authority, be they in heaven, on earth, or in hell." These are the instructions that I heard the Great and Glorious One giving to my Lord.

And I could see the Lord departing from the seventh heaven and entering into the sixth. The angel who had accompanied me from that world was with me, and he said, "Isaiah, look and see, that you may understand the disguising and descent of the Lord." Then I looked, and when the angels of the sixth heaven saw him, they exalted and venerated him, for he had not been changed into the form of the angels there. And as they were praising him, I sang praises to him right along with them. And when I saw him descend into the fifth heaven, he transformed himself to resemble the angels there; and they did not exalt or venerate him when they saw him, for his appearance was like their own. He then went down into the fourth heaven and changed his appearance into that of the angels who were there, and when they saw him, they neither exalted nor venerated him, for his form was just like theirs. Again, I saw him descend into the third heaven, that he changed himself into the form of the angels there. Now the gatekeepers of that realm demanded the password, so to keep from being known, the Lord spoke it to them. And when they saw him, they did not exalt or venerate him because his appearance was like their own. Again, I saw him descend into the second heaven, where the gatekeepers likewise demanded the password, and the Lord provided it. Then I saw him disguise himself to look like the angels of the second heaven, but because he looked like them, they did not exalt him when they saw him. And when I saw him descend into the first heaven, he spoke the password to the gatekeepers there. Then he disguised himself to appear as the angels to the left of that throne, and they neither praised nor worshiped him because his appearance was like their own. (As for myself, no one even questioned me on account of the angel who was guiding me.) And once again, he descended into the sky where the Prince of this World resides and spoke the password to those on the left hand side, and because his form was just like theirs, they did not exalt or venerate him there. Quite to the contrary, they were jealously contending with one another, for there is an evil power and a competition over trivial matters in that place. And I saw him descend and disguise himself to resemble the angels of the air, and they did not exalt him there, because he looked like one of them. He did not speak the password to them, nor did they even question him, for they were busy pillaging and beating one another.

Now as for the virginity of Mary, and the way that she brought forth, and the passion of the Lord, they were all concealed from the Prince of This World. Even though these mysteries were shouted out loud, God brought them about in complete silence. So how was all this shown to the world? Up in the heavens a star far more luminous than any other blazed forth. No words could express its brilliance; its incomparability left men utterly perplexed. The sun, moon, and stars surrounded it in harmony, but this star outshone them all. Then extreme bewilderment ensued; where could this star, which was so different from its companions, have come from? Everywhere, magic disappeared before it--all the spells of sorcery were broken, and superstition was removed. The ancient kingdom of darkness was about to be undone; for God, by coming down in human form, was ushering in a new order of eternal life. Now what God had devised was being brought to pass; and everything from that day forth was thrown into disarray on account of this design to destroy death.

"As I was walking along," (Joseph recalled,) "I came to a stop and then looked up. There I saw the clouds astonished. And gazing upward further still, I saw birds motionless against the unmoving sky. Then I looked around me and saw work hands who were sitting at a table. A bowl had been placed before them, and their hands were in it, but they were not moving them to feed themselves. And those in the process of eating were no longer chewing. Those who were lifting their food were putting none of it down, while those whose food was near to their lips were putting none of it into their mouths. Everyone was looking up. And behold, sheep that were being driven along stood still and did not advance, while the hand of the shepherd whose rod was set to strike them remained frozen in its place. Then I glanced over to see what the river looked like. I could see a number of young goats, some with their muzzles over and others with theirs in the water, but none of them were drinking. And just as suddenly, everything returned to normal." By then the sun was going down.

"At that moment," (the midwife related,) "everything came to a complete stop. There was an utter and fearful silence--even the winds stopped blowing! The leaves did not rustle on the trees, nor did the waters babble, for the rivers all stopped flowing, and the oceans ceased their undulations. All that the waters bring forth grew still. There was no human voice to be heard, and the silence was complete--for the very pole stopped spinning at that moment and time nearly ground to a halt. All of them were taken with fear and everyone stopped talking. We were all anticipating the Most High God and the end of the world."

When the moment was ripe, God showed His power visibly. Fixated on heaven, the Virgin stood and became as white as snow, for the fulfillment of all good things was near. "My soul indeed is magnified," the midwife exclaimed, "and these eyes of mine have seen great things, for this very day has brought about the deliverance of Israel!" And immediately the cloud withdrew from the cave, and was replaced by a light so bright that our eyes could not endure the sight. The light brought forth even as the dew from heaven condenses upon the earth. And even as it blazed, she bore a son by virgin birth. And as he was coming forth, the luminous beams intensified to a level far brighter than the sun, filling the entire cave with their brilliance. And with it came the most fragrant odor imaginable; more redolent than any aromatic ointment. (Now even though among mankind this is thought to be an incredible miracle, for God the Father and God the Son, nothing at all is considered miraculous.) The merry earth shuddered as the child came forth; the heavenly throne burst out in laughter as creation celebrated in joy, (and) a dazzlingly brilliant star was worshiped among the Magi. The angels encompassed him at his coming, and the voices of many invisible beings joined together in chorus and shouted, "Amen!"

Immediately upon his birth, he stood to his feet, and worshipping him the angels proclaimed, "Glory to God in the heights and peace to men of goodwill on earth." "Mary looked in astonishment with her own eyes and saw the infant, and exalted the one to whom she could see she had borne. As for the child, he radiated a bright and beautiful light, which was like the rays of the sun. He was indeed a sight to behold, for his mere arrival pacified and brought to rest the entire world." After her astonishment had faded, her womb became even as it had been prior to conception, and she bound him up in swaddling cloths.

"I, however, was amazed," (the midwife continued,) "and I stood there stunned, staring in utter astonishment at the spectacularly bright light that had just been brought forth. But in time the light withdrew and began to take on the form of a newborn child. Soon its appearance changed to that of a normal infant born after the usual fashion. And as he came with all of these visible signs, Jesus spoke to his mother from the cradle, saying, 'Mary, I am Jesus, that Son of God and servant; that Word which you have brought forth, even as the angel Gabriel announced to you, and my Father has sent me here to save the world.'

"And growing ever the more daring," (the midwife related,) "I bent down to pick him up and touch him with my hands. What was startling to me was that unlike other babies who are born on this earth, he weighed nearly nothing at all! I looked him over closely and could find no flaw upon him anywhere, but found him instead to be as luminous in body as the dew from the Most High God. And since he weighed nearly nothing at all, he was effortless to carry. He was magnificent to behold, (and) for some time he astounded me by not crying as other babies do. And as I held him in my arms and gazed into his face, he let out the most joyful laugh--and when he opened up his eyes, they pierced me through with just a glance. All of a sudden, a bright light beamed forth from his eyes like a lightning flash. 'This has been a great day for me,' [I] exclaimed, 'for I have seen something completely new!'" Then Jesus went and nursed at the breast of his mother Mary.

Now Joseph (had) ventured off to see if he could find [any midwives] for Mary, and after he had found her some, he came back. He spotted an elderly Jewish woman coming from Jerusalem. By the time Joseph arrived at the cave with the old woman, it was already past sunset. "Kind woman," said Joseph, "please come this way and enter this cave. There you will see a young woman who is about ready to give birth." Both of them then went inside, and behold, everything there shimmered with a light that was brighter than lamplight and candlelight--it was, indeed, even brighter than the sun! By that time, the child was already wrapped up in swaddling clothes and nursing at the breast of his mother, Saint Mary. And the two of them were taken aback by the spectacle of light. And when her husband Joseph saw her there, he said to her, "Tell me what has startled you?" Immediately, his eyes were opened and he could see the newborn child. And he praised the Lord, because the child had arrived as foretold by the lot. They then heard a voice proclaim, "Relate this vision to no one!"

"I have brought you two midwives," Joseph said to Mary, "Zelomi and Salome. They are standing out by the mouth of the cave, but the light is so intense that they dare not come inside." When she heard all this, Mary smiled. "Stop smiling!" said Joseph. "Be sensible and allow them to inspect you. What if you should need their medicine?" Mary then gave them her permission to enter. And when Zelomi came inside, she said to Mary, "Please let me have a look at you." And after Mary had agreed to the examination, the midwife exclaimed, "Lord, oh Almighty Lord, have mercy on us! Never before has it been heard, nor ever even imagined that a mother should show every sign of virginity after milk has come into the breasts and a son has been brought forth! But she has suffered neither loss of blood, nor the slightest pain in giving birth. As a virgin she has conceived, as a virgin she has borne a child, and a virgin she remains."

"Are you the mother of this boy?" the elderly woman asked Saint Mary. "Indeed I am," Saint Mary affirmed. "You are completely unlike other women," the elderly lady replied. "Even as there is no child who can compare with my son," explained Saint Mary, "neither is there any woman who can compare with his mother." "My Lady," the aged woman replied, "I have come here to receive an eternal blessing."

Now the midwife came out of the cave and Salome greeted her. "Salome! Salome!" the midwife shouted, "I must tell you of this novel sight; a virgin has given birth, something that her condition forbids!" And when Salome, the other midwife, heard that, she scoffed, "As my Lord is the Living God, I will not believe what I have heard--that a virgin has given birth--unless I first examine her (and) prove it with my own finger!"

And Zelomi entered in and said, "Mary, prepare yourself, for there is no small controversy brewing over you." And when Mary heard these words, she lied back down and readied herself. Then Salome came in and demanded, "Mary, allow me to inspect you and see whether what Zelomi has told me is true." And Mary gave her permission to examine her. So Salome went inside, made her ready, and proved her status. And when she had inspected her as she had said and withdrawn her hand, it began to wither up. And overcome with anguish and horrible pain, she started weeping bitterly. "What misery for my sin and doubt," Salome shouted, "for I have tempted the Living God. Just look, my hand feels like it is burning with fire and falling right off!" And dropping to her knees, she wept and pleaded before the Lord, "Oh God of my fathers, consider my case; for I am a child of Abraham, Isaac, and Jacob! Do not humiliate me before the children of Israel, but restore me to the destitute; for as You are well aware, oh Lord, I offer my services in Your name, and my payment comes from You alone. Oh Lord God, You know that I have always worshiped You and cared for those who live in want. Never have I taken pay from widows and orphans, nor have I ever turned the poor away empty-handed. Now behold, I am made to suffer for my lack of faith, for I sought to put Your virgin to the test for no reason whatsoever."

And even as Salome was recounting these deeds, a young man dressed in glistening clothes, an angel of the Lord, (appeared and) stood beside her. "Salome! Salome!" he cried aloud, "The Lord your God has heard your prayer. Go right now, and worship the babe. Touch him with your hand and he will heal you, and joy and deliverance will be to you, for he is the Savior of all the world, and of all who trust in him." "Place your hands upon the child!" our Lady Saint Mary bid her. So she quickly approached the infant and adored him, saying, "I will truly worship this child, for an illustrious king has been born to

The Super Gospel

Israel!" Then Salome touched the hem of his swaddling clothes and immediately her hand was healed, and she was restored as she had implored.

And upon her restoration, she got up to leave, testifying along the way, "From this day forward, I will serve this child and care for him!" And as she was leaving the cave, she started crying out and proclaiming the marvelous things that she had seen--the way that she had suffered and the healing that she had received--and great numbers were persuaded by her testimony. Now behold, an angel of the Lord cried out to her, "Salome! Salome! Let no one hear of the wonders you've seen until this child enters Jerusalem!" But stories about him circulated widely throughout Bethlehem. Some of them claimed, "The Virgin Mary has brought forth before even two months of marriage." Many others contended, "Mary did not really give birth; the midwife never went up, and we heard no cries or anguish of birth." All of them were blind to him; everybody knew of him, but they did not know where he came from.

Joseph then (went and) entered his name into the register; for Mary's husband was a son of David, from the tribe of Judah. So it happened that my mother, the Virgin Mary, brought me forth in Bethlehem; in a cave near to the tomb of Rachel, the wife of Jacob the patriarch, and the mother of Joseph and Benjamin. She became a gracious mother, and it was not without reason that her labor and her childbirth were free from anguish; for she did not seek after a midwife because the Father used her as a conduit of life itself. She, driven by her intense determination, gave birth manfully, and her childbirth came about precisely as it had been foretold, and was effected by an extreme power. And in her love was deliverance, in her guardianship was benevolence, and in her declaration was grandeur.

THE SHEPHERDS VISIT
(Luke 2:8-20; ArIn 1:2, 3, 19-21; PsMt 13; SbOr 8:477-479)
The Cave, Between Jerusalem and Bethlehem

The newly born infant was revealed to those who are obedient to God: drivers of cattle, herders of goats, and shepherds of sheep. There were shepherds staying overnight in a nearby place keeping watch over their flocks in the field. An angel of the Lord (came and) stood near to them, and the glory of the Lord shone all around them, and all of them were taken with fear. "Do not be afraid," the angel reassured them, "for behold, I am bringing you great news of unbounded joy that everyone will come to know: for this very day, in the city of David, a Savior has indeed been born, the Anointed Lord. And this will be a sign for you: you will find a baby lying in a manger, all bound up in swaddling clothes." And suddenly, a vast array of the heavenly host appeared to them and joined the angel who was praising God, saying, "Glory to God in the highest, and peace on earth to men who please Him." Then the angels rose up from their midst and into the sky, and the shepherds said to one another, "Let us all make our way to Bethlehem this very instant and see what the Lord has revealed to us." They hurried there and found Mary with Joseph, and the baby lying in the manger. And after the shepherds had seen it, they went inside, lit a fire (and) made known the words that were spoken to them about this child, and also about the angels they had seen at midnight, praising and worshipping the God of heaven and proclaiming, "The Anointed Lord and Savior to all, has been born to us. Through him will deliverance be restored to Israel."

All were celebrating in delight. Just then, the entire array of the heavenly host appeared to them, praising and worshipping the God of Perfection. And since the shepherds were doing the same by then, the cave came to resemble a glorious temple, for the tongues of men and angels joined to worship and give praise to God for the birth of Christ the Lord. When the elderly Jewish woman saw all of these evident miracles, she also gave God praise and said, "Oh God of Israel, I thank you for granting that my eyes should see the birth of the Savior of the World!"

And all who heard the shepherds speak marveled at the things they said. But Mary committed their words to memory and pondered them within her heart. And as the shepherds were returning, they exalted God and gave Him praise, for all that they had seen and heard came to pass as they were told. And a powerful star, larger than any other seen since the world began, beamed over the cave from dusk until dawn. The Jerusalem prophets, moreover, affirmed that this star was the sign of the birth of the Christ; the one destined to restore the covenant not only to Israel, but also to the other nations. And Bethlehem was proclaimed to be the providential birthplace of the Word.

JESUS' CIRCUMCISION
(PsMt 14, 15; ArIn 2:1-4; Luke 2:7, 21)
A Stable; Bethlehem; The Cave

Three days after the birth of our Lord Jesus Christ, Mary ventured out of the cave. Now because there was no room for them at the inn, she entered into a stable (and) laid the child in a manger, where an ox and a donkey worshiped him. It was then that the words of the prophet Isaiah, "The ox knows his owner, and the donkey his master's feeding trough," had their fulfillment. So without ceasing did the animals, the ox and the donkey, worship him who was in their midst. Then the words that were spoken by the prophet Habakkuk, "You are revealed between the two creatures," were fulfilled. For three days Joseph stayed in the same place with Mary, and on the sixth, they traveled on to Bethlehem and kept the Sabbath there.

And when the time came for him to be circumcised, that is, the eighth day-- upon which the law dictates that a child must be circumcised, they performed it in the cave. They named him Jesus, which was what the angel had called him prior to his conception in the womb. And after the child had undergone parhithomus, or circumcision, the elderly Jewish woman took the foreskin and umbilical cord and preserved them in an alabaster jar filled with aged spikenard. Her son happened to be a pharmacist, so she cautioned him, "Be careful not to sell this alabaster jar of nard-oil, even if someone should offer you three hundred denarii for it." This same alabaster jar was later procured by Mary the sinner, who poured it over the head and feet of our Lord Jesus Christ, and wiped it off with the hair of her head.

MARY TAKES JESUS TO HER FAMILY; THE PRESENTATION
(Luke 2:22-39; ArIn 2:4-10; AsIs 11:15, 16b, 17b; PsMt 15; Qur 19:27-33, 43:63)
Jerusalem

When Mary's period of purification as required by the Mosaic Law had passed, Joseph (and Mary) took him to Jerusalem to present him to the Lord. Mary came bearing him to her family. "Mary," they said, "this is an astonishing thing. Sister of Aaron, your father was never a whoremonger, nor ever was your mother a harlot." She gestured to them and pointed to the babe. "How are we to speak with an infant in a cradle?" they questioned her. Then Jesus spoke right up and said,

"I am God's servant.
He has placed the book into my hands
And decreed my prophethood.
I have come to give you wisdom,
And to make plain many of the issues
That currently divide you.
His goodness follows me wherever I go.
He has instructed me to pray continuously
And to give alms to the poor my whole life long.
He has encouraged me to honor my mother,
And has driven evil and foolishness far from me.
I was blessed on the day of my birth,
And will be blessed on the day of my death,
And may peace rest on me
On the day of my resurrection.
Honor God by obeying me.
God is both my Master and yours,
So do all things for His sake,
For this path is truly straight."

And ten days later, forty days after his birth, they presented him before the Lord in His temple, in accordance with what's written in the Law of the Lord, "Every male that passes through the womb must be given to the Lord." They also offered up a sacrifice in keeping with the law of the Lord: "A pair of turtledoves, or two young pigeons." Now behold, in the Jerusalem temple there was this righteous and religious man named Simeon who was one hundred and twelve years old. He was anticipating the consolation of Israel, and the Divine Inspiration was upon him. And the Holy Spirit revealed to him the Lord's response--that he would not die before having seen the Lord's Messiah, the Son of God, alive and in the flesh. Simeon entered into the temple completely inspired, and the parents of the infant Jesus brought him in with them, so that they could do to him as the law directs. And at that moment--when his mother, Saint Mary the Virgin, cradled him in her arms--the elderly Simeon overflowed with boundless joy, for he saw the boy as a glorious beam of light. And the angels worshiped him, surrounding him as guardians around their king. And as soon as Simeon saw the child, he cried aloud, "God has come to visit His people, and the Lord has brought His word to pass." Then Simeon hurried over to Saint Mary, stretched out his hands to her and took Jesus into his arms. After taking Jesus into his robe, Simeon kissed his feet, worshiped him, and paid his respects to God, saying,

"Lord, let Your servant go in peace,
In accordance with Your word;
For these eyes of mine have seen Your deliverance
Which You have readied in the sight of all:
To uncover a light for the Gentiles
And the glorification of Your people Israel."

His father and mother were amazed by the things that were said of him. And Simeon blessed them and prophesied to his mother Mary,

"Behold, this child is set for the falling and rising
Of many in Israel,
And as a sign that's spoken against.
And your soul will also be pierced by the sword,
So as to expose the thoughts of many hearts."

And there was also in the temple a certain prophetess by the name of Anna, the daughter of Phanuel, who was of the tribe of Asher. She married as a virgin and lived with her husband for seven years before being widowed, then lived eighty-four years more in the temple of the Lord, fasting and worshipping day and night without ever leaving. And at that moment, she came up to them and offered her thanks and praises to God. Anna also worshiped the boy and came to share in Mary's joy, saying to those who were there and awaiting the deliverance of Israel all about him, "In him lies the redemption of the world."

And after completing all that was required by the law of the Lord, they set out for Nazareth in Galilee. While in Nazareth he nursed at the breast of his mother as any other infant would, so that he might remain concealed. And this was hidden from the heavenly realms, and the 'gods' and rulers of this earth.

JESUS' GENEALOGY
(Matt 1:1-17)

Matthew's Version

The account of the genealogy of Jesus, the Christ--the son of David, the son of Abraham:
Abraham fathered Isaac, Isaac fathered Jacob, and Jacob fathered Judah and his siblings. Judah fathered Perez and Zerah through Tamar, Perez fathered Hezron, Hezron fathered Ram, Ram fathered Amminadab, Amminadab fathered Nahshon, Nahshon fathered Salmon, Salmon fathered Boaz through Rahab, Boaz fathered Obed through Ruth, Obed fathered Jesse, and Jesse fathered King David. David fathered Solomon through her who had been Uriah's wife, Solomon fathered Rehoboam, Rehoboam fathered Abijah, Abijah fathered Asa, Asa fathered Jehoshaphat, Jehoshaphat fathered Jehoram, Jehoram fathered Uzziah, Uzziah fathered Jotham, Jotham fathered Ahaz, Ahaz fathered Hezekiah, Hezekiah fathered Manasseh, Manasseh fathered Amon, Amon fathered Josiah, and Josiah fathered Jeconiah and his brothers at the time of the Babylonian exile. After the exile into Babylon, Jeconiah fathered Shealtiel, Shealtiel fathered Zerubbabel, Zerubbabel fathered Abiud, Abiud fathered Eliakim, Eliakim fathered Azor, Azor fathered Zadok, Zadok fathered Akim, Akim fathered Eliud, Eliud fathered Eleazar, Eleazar fathered Matthan, Matthan fathered Jacob, and Jacob fathered Joseph, who was husband to Mary, who brought forth Jesus, the one who is called the Christ.
So it came about that fourteen generations passed between Abraham and David, fourteen generations passed between David and the Babylonian exile, and fourteen generations passed between the exile into Babylon and the Christ.

THE MAJI VISIT
(Matt 2:1-12; ArIn 3:1-10; PEv 21:1-4;
PsMt 16, 17; HJC 8; LJB pt.8)
Jerusalem; Bethlehem

Now more than two years after Jesus had been born in Bethlehem, during the reign of Herod the king, Joseph was ready to travel on to Judea. At that time, there was a great disturbance taking place in Bethlehem of Judah over some Magi who had come from the east bringing marvelous gifts to Jerusalem, in keeping with the prophecy of Zoroaster. "Where," they were asking, "is the king of the Jews who has been born to you? We have seen his star in the east and have come to worship him." But Satan went and informed Herod the Great, father of Archelaus, about these things. Now when King Herod caught wind of it, he was disturbed by all that he had learned of the Magi, and all of Jerusalem likewise, seeing that the boy was the King of the Jews. And he wanted to kill him that very instant. So shaken was he, as a matter of fact, that he assembled all of the scribes, Pharisees, chief priests, and teachers of the law from among the people and asked them where the prophets had foretold the birthplace of the Messiah would be. "What is written about this Messiah?" he inquired. "Where is he supposed to be born?" "In Bethlehem of Judah," they answered him, "for this is how the prophet worded it:

'And you, Bethlehem, of Judah's land,
Are in no way least among the princes of Judah;
For a leader will arise from you
Who will shepherd my people Israel.'"

Then King Herod dismissed them all. And secretly summoning the Magi to himself, he asked, "What was this sign that you saw that showed that a king had just been born?" "We saw how a star outshone all of these others," the Magi answered, "dimming them inexpressibly, such that these stars no longer gave light. This is how we came to know that a king had been born unto Israel. We have come to worship him." Herod then asked them the time of the star's appearance to them, and learned from them the precise time that the star had appeared. Then he sent them off to Bethlehem with these words: "Go right now and investigate! Uncover every detail having to do with this child, and after you have tracked him down, bring me a report, that I might come and worship him too." And hearing the king, they went their way. Now behold, the star that they had seen back east, guided them, going before them until they arrived at the cave where the child was. And when the Magi saw the star, they rejoiced in inexpressible delight. It came to rest over the head of the cave, so they went inside and saw the child seated on the lap of his mother Mary, and they prostrated themselves in worship. Then they opened the treasures they had brought to them and presented the holy Mary and Joseph with generous offerings. Each of them offered the child gifts (and) gold; one gave him gold, another frankincense, and a third one gave him myrrh.

And rather than pronouncing a blessing upon them, our Lady Mary took one of the swaddling cloths that the young child was wrapped-up in and offered it to them, which they accepted from her as a glorious gift. And when they would have gone back to King Herod, even as they slept, God (sent) an angel to warn them in a dream not to return, so they set out for their native land by another route. Soon an angel appeared to them in the semblance of the star which had guided them on their way before; and they followed the light thereof until they came into their own land.

And upon their arrival, kings and princes came up to them and posed all manner of questions to them, such as, "What did you do?" and, "What did you see?" and, "What was your trip like?" and, "Who did you meet along the way?" But they handed them the swaddling cloth that Saint Mary had given them and held a banquet in its honor. Then they lit a fire, which they worshiped according to the custom of their nation. Then they cast the swaddling cloth into the flames, which received and preserved it. After the fire had been put out, they pulled it from the ashes unharmed, just as though the flames had never touched it. Then they started kissing the cloth, placing it over their heads and eyes. "Without question," they affirmed, "the truth of this is impossible to doubt, and it is truly astonishing that the fire was powerless to char it, much less to devour it." Then, with the utmost of regard, they took the cloth and treasured it alongside their other hallowed possessions.

JOSEPH'S WARNING
(Matt 2:13-15; ArIn 4:1-4; PEv 22:2; InThL 1a; LJB pt.8)
Jerusalem; The Cave; The Road to Egypt

Herod began to recognize that the Magi had been away too long, and were not going to return to him, so he called for all the priests and sages. "Tell me," he (again) prodded, "where is the Christ supposed to be born?" "In the Judean town of Bethlehem," they answered him; whereupon he began to plot in his mind the death of the Lord Jesus Christ. Now this was the same Herod who called for the beheading of my friend and kinsman John. And he likewise sought me out, imagining that mine would be an earthly kingdom.

Now behold, after the departure of the Magi, the day before these things took place, the Lord's angel appeared in that pious old man Joseph's dream (and) warned him as he slept, saying, "Get up! Take the young boy and his mother, Mary, and as soon as the rooster crows escape from those who seek to slay him through the desert and into Egypt. Wait there until I say otherwise, for Herod is going to try to hunt down and murder the young child." Now when Mary heard that the babies were about to be killed, she grew terrified, took the boy, wrapped him up in the swaddling cloth, and placed him into an ox's feeding trough. And that night Joseph rose up, and as he was planning his trip, dawn started to break. He then took me, the young boy and my mother Mary by night and set off for Egypt as the angel had commanded him, and I rested in her bosom. He stayed in Egypt until after the death of Herod that what the Lord had spoken through the prophet, "Out of Egypt I have called my son," might be fulfilled.

THE SLAUGHTER OF THE INNOCENTS
AND THE MURDER OF ZECHARIAH
(Matt 2:16-18; PEv 22:1, 3-24:1; PsMt 17; LJB pt.9)
Bethlehem

Now when it was clear to Herod that the Magi had mocked him, he was enraged. And wishing to take and murder them, Herod ordered his executioners to travel down every road, but he could not track them down. Then Herod sought after the Master in order to put an end to him, but he could not find him. He therefore sent his executioners to Bethlehem and its surroundings, and started putting the children to death. (And as) Herod (had) commanded, (they) slaughtered every male child age two and under, according to the precise time given to him by the Magi. It was then that the word spoken through the prophet Jeremiah was fulfilled,

"In Ramah a voice was heard
Wailing in horrible anguish.
Rachel was weeping for her children;
And nothing could console her,

For they no more."

Now Elizabeth heard that the executioners were out searching for John, and fearing that her son would be killed with the other children, she immediately took him to Zechariah in the temple. "Oh my lord," Elizabeth implored, "let us take our son John to another land, that we might save him from that unbeliever Herod, who is slaughtering children on account of Jesus the Christ. Mary and Joseph have already escaped into the land of Egypt. Let us go this very moment, so that they don't kill our son, and turn our joy into sorrow." "I must not abandon my service in the temple of the Lord," Zechariah said, "only to enter into a foreign nation that is teeming with idol worshippers." "What am I to do therefore," she asked him, "that I might save my infant son?" "Rise up," the old man said to her, "and venture forth into the wilderness of 'Ain Karim. There, by the will of God, you will find refuge for your son. If they should come here seeking him, they will shed my blood instead of his." And how great was their sadness at their parting! The faithful Zechariah took the child into his arms, blessed him, kissed him and lamented: "Oh John, my son, how deep is my pain! Oh glory of my later life! They have taken from me the glory of your face, which is so very full of grace." Then Zechariah took him into the temple and blessed him, saying, "May God guard you along your path." Just then, Gabriel, the head of all angels, came down from heaven and into their midst carrying a garment and a leather belt, and said to him: "Zechariah, take these clothes and put them on your son. God is sending them down from heaven. This clothing belongs to Elijah, and this belt is of Elisha." So the blessed Zechariah accepted them from the angel, prayed over them and presented them to his son, binding on him with the leather belt the garment of camel's hair. Then he took him back to his mother and instructed her: "Take him out into the desert, for the hand of the Lord is upon him. I have come to learn from God that he is to remain in the wilderness until the day that he's revealed to Israel." Then, with weeping, the blessed Elizabeth took the child; and Zechariah, also weeping, said to him, "I know that I will never again look on you with these eyes of flesh. Go in peace and be led by God." Then Elizabeth walked away with her little boy.

After this, she took John and fled into the hills with him. She looked left and right for a place to conceal him, but there was nowhere for him to be hid. "Mountain of God," Elizabeth wailed, "accept a mother and her child." Now because Elizabeth was unable to climb, the mountain suddenly split down the middle and received her. A light was there to show the way, for an angel of the Lord traveled with them and looked after them, and they entered into the wilderness of 'Ain Karim, where she remained with him.

And so it happened that when King Herod sent troops to Jerusalem to slaughter the children, the executioners came and started putting them to death until sunset. This all happened on September seventh. Herod sent officers to Zechariah in an effort to track down John. "Zechariah," they demanded, "tell us where you've hidden your son!" "I am the servant of God," he replied, "here at work in the temple of the Lord. I have no idea where my child could be." The servants then left and passed these things on to Herod, whereupon he seethed and raged, "His son is to reign as king over Israel!" Again, he sent inquiry to him, "Where is your son? You had better own up, because as you well know, your very life is in my hands!" And the agents went and apprised him of this. "I am indeed a martyr of God," Zechariah said. "Spill my blood, but the Lord himself will take my spirit, for you are shedding the blood of an innocent man at the very threshold of the Lord's temple." And as they were on their way back to their king, behold, Satan approached them and asked: "How can it be that you have left the son of Zechariah without killing him? He is hidden away in the temple with his father. Do not spare him, but kill him instead, that the king may not be enraged with you. Return for him, and should you fail to find the son, kill the father in his stead." The officers did as Satan had said, and returned to the temple early in the morning, where they came across Zechariah, who was standing in his service to the Lord. "Where," they demanded, "is your son? You are hiding him in here somewhere!" And Zechariah replied: "There is no child in this temple." "You most certainly are hiding him here," they insisted. "You are shielding him from the king." "Oh, you most merciless fiends!" Zechariah said. "Your king laps up blood like a lioness! How long will you shed the blood of the innocent?" "Bring out your son," they answered him, "that we might slay him. For if you should refuse to do it, then we will kill you in his stead." Then the prophet answered them: "As for my son, he has fled into the wilderness with his mother, and I have no idea where he might be."

Now after Zechariah had bidden farewell to Elizabeth and his son John, he blessed the boy and made him a priest. Then he handed him over to his mother, and she bid him, "Pray for me, my blessed father, that God might make my way bearable in the wilderness." And he responded, "May the One Who caused us to bring forth our child in our old age, guide you both along your way." Then she accepted the child and entered into the wilderness where not a single soul resided. (How truly great and commendable is your case, oh blessed Elizabeth. You did not ask for anyone to travel along with you, though you knew neither of the way nor of any place to hide. You did not seek to take any food or water for the child to [eat or] drink. You did not demand of his father Zechariah: "To whom are you sending me in this desert region?" The wilderness at that time had neither a monastery nor an assembly of monks that you might say: "I will go and live among them with my son." Likewise, when Herod's executioners came to [you,] Zechariah, demanding, "Where is your newborn son, the child of your old age?" you did not deny the truth and claim: "I do not know of any such child," but in truth did you respond: "His mother fled with him into the wilderness.") Now after Zechariah had spoken these words to the officers with regard to his son, they slew him there inside the temple. And Zechariah was murdered as the day was dawning, and the children of Israel did not know that he'd been killed.

But as the priests were leaving at the salutation hour, Zechariah was not there to offer the customary benediction. And the priests stood around waiting for Zechariah; to welcome him with a prayer and offer praise to the Most High

God. But when he did not come out, they feared the worst. Even so, one was bold enough to go inside. He looked around, and beside the altar he saw congealed blood. Then he heard a voice that said, "Zechariah has been slain, and his blood will not be wiped clean until his Avenger comes." These words terrified him, and he left to inform the other priests about what he had seen. And they steeled themselves to enter therein, and saw firsthand just what had been done. The fretwork of the ceiling wailed, and the priests tore their robes from top to bottom. And they found his dried-up blood, but they could not find his corpse. And with deep regret they went out and let the people know about the murder of Zechariah. And all the tribes of the people heard about it and mourned for him. The priests therefore placed his remains in a shroud, and then for fear of the wicked one, laid it to rest in a hidden burial ground near the body of his father Berechiah. Now his blood seethed upon the earth for fifty years, until Titus, the son of the Roman Emperor Vespasian, came and demolished Jerusalem--destroying the Jewish priests for spilling the blood of Zechariah, as the Lord had himself decreed. They mourned him for three days and nights. After that, the priests all got together to determine who was fit to replace him, and by lot they installed Simeon. This was the same one to whom the Holy Spirit had revealed that he would not see death before having seen the Christ in the flesh.
{Conclusion to the Protevangelion of James}
 {I, James, penned this narrative while yet in Jerusalem. And at the time that the uproar began, I got away into the wilderness until after the death of Herod, when the disturbance in Jerusalem had died down. And I praise the Lord God, Who graced me with wisdom enough to record an account such as this to you spiritual ones who love God, to Him belong glory and dominion forever. Mercy to all who worship our Lord Jesus Christ. May he be worshiped forevermore. Amen.}

THE JOURNEY INTO EGYPT
(PsMt 18-22; cf. HJC 8; InThL 1b)
Between Bethlehem and Egypt

 As soon as Joseph and Mary came to a cave, they decided that they should rest in it, so Mary climbed down from her mount, seated herself, and placed the boy Jesus upon her lap.
 There were three young men who traveled with Joseph, and also a girl named Salome, who traveled with Mary. Now behold, many dragons suddenly came thundering out of the cave! And when the boys caught sight of them, they shrieked in horror. Jesus then came down from his mother's knees and stood to his feet before the beasts, which worshiped him and went their way. It was then that the words spoken through the prophet David were fulfilled, "Dragons, praise the Lord--from upon the Earth, and the depths of the seas." And the boy Jesus ordered them not to injure anyone, and he traveled on ahead of them. But Joseph and Mary were very concerned that the dragons would do harm to the lad. "Do not be afraid," Jesus consoled them, "nor think of me as just a child,

for I am now and have always been the embodiment of perfection. No woodland creature can help but be gentle in my presence."

Lions and leopards worshiped him also, walking with them across the desert, traveling ahead of Joseph and Mary, bowing their heads and showing the way wherever they would go. They worshiped Jesus with sincere veneration, and wagged their tails in submission to him. When Mary first saw all of the lions and the leopards and the many other wild animals that were thronging them, she began to grow concerned. But the little boy Jesus gazed into his mother's eyes with the most pleasing expression and said, "Mother, do not be afraid, for they have not come to harm you in any way. Much to the contrary, they are eager to attend to you and me both." With this assurance he dispelled all of the fear that she had in her heart. The lions continued to walk with them, injuring neither them, nor the oxen, nor the donkeys, nor any of the pack animals that were carrying their provisions in the least. They were even docile toward the sheep and the rams that they had brought from Judea. They walked among wolves and none of them had any fear, nor did a single one do harm to another. Then what was spoken by the prophet, "Wolves will eat alongside lambs, and lion and ox will eat hay with one another," was fulfilled. Two oxen hauled [the] wagon that was filled with their provisions, and the lions guided them along the way.

And on the third day of their journey, as they were traveling along, it happened that the extreme heat of the desert sun started to overwhelm Mary. So when she caught sight of a palm tree, she said, "Joseph, I would like to rest awhile under the shade of this palm." Joseph promptly took her over and helped her get down from her beast. And as Mary rested there, she looked into its canopy and saw a profusion of date clusters. "Joseph," she said, "how I long to eat of the fruit of this palm; if only there were some way for us to pick some!" "I'm truly surprised that you're speaking this way," Joseph replied, "even considering how you would like to eat the fruit of this tree when you can plainly see how high it is! I am far more concerned with our lack of water, for our skins have been depleted, and we don't have enough for ourselves, much less our livestock." Then the boy Jesus, lying in his mother's lap with an amused look on his face, commanded the palm, "Lower your branches, oh palm, and refresh my mother with your fruit." Now as soon as the palm tree heard these words, it immediately bowed its top all the way down to Mary's feet; and they ate their fill of the fruit they had plucked. And after they had picked it clean it remained there lowered, awaiting the command to stand from the one who had ordered it to bend. "Palm tree," cried Jesus, "rise up now and strengthen yourself! Become like the trees in my Father's paradise and cause your roots to open up a hidden spring, so that we might have enough to drink." Just then it stood tall, and cold, crystal clear water began to gush from between its roots. And when the people who were there saw the fountain of water they all rejoiced and gave thanks to God. All of them then drank their fill, as did their livestock and the other beasts.

The following day as they were on their way, at the very hour that their journey had begun, Jesus turned to the palm and said, "Palm tree, here is the blessing that I will give to you: my angels will take off one of your branches and plant it in my Father's paradise. I will, moreover, present you with this mark of distinction: to anyone who prevails in any challenge, it will be said, 'You have received the palm of victory.'" And even as he was saying these things, behold, an angel of the Lord appeared to them, stood atop the palm, plucked one of its branches off, and flew away, branch in hand, into the sky. Now after they had taken it in, they prostrated themselves as dead. "Why are you so full of fear?" he questioned them. "Are you not aware that this palm, which I have arranged to be transplanted into paradise, is to be readied for the holy ones in the place of bliss, even as it has been readied for us today in this desert?" And they rose up strengthened in their joy.

After this, as they journeyed on, their saddle straps broke, (and) Joseph said to Jesus, "Lord, we are all about to broil in this heat. If it should seem good to you, please allow us to travel alongside the sea, that we might lodge in the coastal towns." "Joseph," said Jesus, "do not fret; I will shorten the distance that you must go, so that what would have required thirty days to pass, you will complete this very day." And right as he was saying this, behold, the mountains and townships of Egypt came into view just ahead. And after Joseph had left his home and withdrawn into Egypt, he remained there for an entire year, until the anger of Herod had diminished. And Jesus was two when he came into Egypt.

ARRIVAL IN EGYPT; THE 365-IDOLS TOPPLE
(PsMt 22-24; InThL 1:1c)
Sotinen, Greater Hermopolis, Egypt

They entered joyfully and exultantly into the region of Hermopolis. And as Jesus was walking through a field of grain, he reached out his hand and grabbed hold of some ears. After roasting them upon a fire, he crushed them and ate. They then entered the Egyptian city of Sotinen. Now since there was no one there from whom they knew to seek hospitality, they went into a certain temple known as the Egyptian Capitol Building. Three hundred and sixty-five idols had been set up in that place, each receiving religious devotion and hallowed rituals on its particular day. The Egyptians who lived in that town would enter into the capitol, where the priests would tell them how many sacrifices to offer up that day, corresponding to the regard in which the 'god' was held.

And it happened that as soon as Mary took the young boy into the temple, every idol in that place fell flat on its face, and each of them was lying there face down on the floor, smashed and demolished in a show of their powerlessness. Then was fulfilled the word of the prophet Isaiah: "Behold, the Lord will enter Egypt on a swift cloud, and all that the Egyptians have crafted will be cleared away at his coming."

And when that city's ruler Affrodosius was notified, he and his entire army marched toward the temple. And when the temple priests caught sight of Affrodosius entering into that place, in the full strength of his military might, they felt certain that he would retaliate against those who had overthrown the idols. But when he entered into the temple and saw all of the gods lying there face down, Affrodosius went up to Mary, who was holding Jesus in her arms, and worshiped him.

Then he confessed to his army and his supporters, "Our gods would never have fallen in his presence, nor would they have remained here prostrated before him unless he were God over our gods; so even though they cannot speak, they silently acknowledge his lordship. If we should fail to do as we see our own gods doing, then we are all in danger of infuriating him and being devastated like Pharaoh, King of the Egyptians, who drowned with his whole army in the sea for not acknowledging such a masterful authority." Then everyone in that place put their faith in the Lord God through Jesus Christ.

JESUS REVIVES A DRIED FISH
(InThL 1)
Sotinen?

And on entering into Egypt, they lived for a year as boarders in a widow's house. When Jesus was three, he joined in with some boys that he saw playing. He placed a dried-up fish into a tub and said, "Breathe," and it started to respire. "Release the salt within yourself," he commanded the fish, "and jump into the water." And it did as he had said. Seeing, then, what he had done, the neighbors went and informed the widow who was housing his mother Mary; and as soon as she found out about it, she evicted them.

JESUS INFURIATES A TEACHER
(InThL 2)
Sotinen?

And as Jesus was walking through town with his mother, he looked up and saw an instructor who was teaching his students. Behold, twelve sparrows were fighting there, and they fell from the wall and into the teacher's lap as he was lecturing them. When Jesus saw it, he came to a stop and burst into laughter. The instructor, marking his amusement, became enraged. "Go get that boy," he told his students, "and bring him right back here to me!" And as soon as they took hold of him, the teacher pinched his ear and asked, "What have you seen that you think is so funny?" "Look into my hand," he answered, "is it not full of grain? I revealed the grain to these birds, and distributed it among them. It was at their own peril that they made off with it; for they were all fighting over the division of this grain!" And Jesus did not leave that spot until they had divided it. The instructor therefore threw both Jesus and his mother out of town.

THE FALLEN IDOL
AND THE POSSESSED BOY
(ArIn 4:5-23)

A Large Egyptian City

And they approached a large city that housed an idol which received the sacrifices and pledges from all the other Egyptian gods and idols. Now there was a priest nearby who would attend to it and, as often as Satan spoke through it, pass along to the Egyptians and the others every word that it would speak. This priest had a three-year-old son who was possessed by a legion of demons, and would utter many senseless things. Now whenever the demons would exercise their power over him, the boy would tear his clothing and walk around naked, throwing rocks at everyone in sight. The city's inn was near to the idol, and when Joseph and Saint Mary entered that city and checked into the inn, the residents were all amazed. All of that idol's judges and priests gathered before it and asked, "What does all this fear and terror that has gripped our region forebode?" "Truly the unknown and unrivaled God is visiting us," the idol replied. "He is no doubt the Son of God, and no one but he is worthy of adoration. The entire nation trembled at his fame, and his arrival has brought this present fear and dread upon us; and we do ourselves shrink before his tremendous might." And even as he said this the idol fell, and its collapse prompted everyone from the land of Egypt and parts beyond to run away.

The next time the disorder overcame the son of the priest, however, he went into the inn where Joseph and Saint Mary were staying and approached those from whom everyone else had fled. And when our Lady, Saint Mary, had finished washing the swaddling cloths of the Lord Jesus Christ, she hung them over a post to dry. The demon-possessed boy pulled one off and wrapped it around his head, whereupon the demons spewed out of his mouth as crows and snakes, and flew away from him in haste. The boy was healed once and for all by the power of the Lord Jesus Christ, and he began to offer thanks, and to sing songs of praise to the Lord, who had made him well. When his father saw that his boy was again in health, he prodded him, "Son, tell me what has become of you. Explain to me how you were restored!" "As soon as those devils got hold of me," his son replied, "I went into the inn, where I met a very beautiful woman--and her young boy was there with her. She had just washed his swaddling cloths and hung them over a post to dry. Then I took one and placed it over my head, at which point the demons came out and fled." When his father heard all of these things from him, he jumped for joy and cried aloud, "My child, this might just be that boy--that Son of the Living God--who brought all of creation into existence; for the very moment that he came to us the idol was destroyed, and every single god, overwhelmed by a higher power, fell flat on its face." In this was fulfilled that prophecy that reads, "Out of Egypt I have called my Son."

THE ROBBERS FLEE
(ArIn 5:1-6)
Egypt, on a Road Frequented by Robbers

The Super Gospel

    When Joseph and Mary heard that this Idol had fallen down and been destroyed, they grew fearful. And trembling they said, "Back when we were still in Israel, Herod put all of the infants that were in and around Bethlehem to death because he sought to murder Jesus. If the Egyptians should hear that this idol has fallen down and shattered to bits, they will set us all ablaze!" They therefore sought refuge where bandits lie in wait for passersby, to steal their clothing and their wagons, to bind them up and carry them off. And even as Joseph and Mary drew near to it, these robbers perceived their approach as a king with a mighty army, attended by legions of horses, complete with drums and trumpet blasts announcing the departure from his city. The sound of it so frightened them, that they left everything they had stolen behind and ran. When this happened, those who had been captured got up and untied one another--each one took what was their own and they all went on their way. When they saw Joseph and Mary approaching, these people asked them, "Where is that king that we all heard--who so alarmed the bandits that they ran away, leaving us all here free and unharmed?" "He is following after us," said Joseph.

POSSESSION CURED
(ArIn 6:1-4)
An Egyptian City

    They entered into another town where there lived a demon-possessed woman in whom Satan, the one condemned for rebellion, had made himself at home. One night, as she was going out to draw some water, she found that she could not keep her clothing on or stay inside of any house. Still, no matter how many times anyone had tried to chain her up, she had broken free and made her way into desert places, where she would on occasion lie in wait at crossroads and places of worship to cast stones at people, and she brought great hardships on her friends.

    Saint Mary felt for this woman the moment she laid eyes on her; and Satan fled away from her in the shape of a young man, screaming, "Mary, I am utterly tormented by you and your Son!" So she was freed of her affliction, but when she recognized her nakedness, the woman blushed and hid from the eyes of men, put on some clothes and went back home. She then related the story to her father and her family--who, by the way, happened to be the most prominent people in that town--and they showed themselves greatly hospitable to Joseph and Saint Mary.

MUTENESS HEALED
(ArIn 6:5-9)
Another Egyptian City

    The following morning they were given the necessary provisions for their journey, and they headed out. They came into another town around sunset, where a marriage was about to be performed. But the bride had become unable to speak to such an extent that she could not even open her mouth on account of some magical spells that some sorcerers steeped in the Satanic arts had cast on her. But when this speechless woman saw Mary on her way into town bearing the Lord Jesus Christ in her arms, she reached out to him and held him in her embrace, hugging and kissing him all over; moving him back and forth and squeezing him against herself. Immediately the string of her tongue was loosed, and her ears were cleared, and she started singing praises to God, the One Who had healed her. So the people of that town were overjoyed that night, and they truly believed that God and His angels had come down to them. They stayed there for three whole days, being shown true veneration and great hospitality.

SATANIC OPPRESSION AND SKIN DISEASES CURED
(ArIn 6:10-37)
Another Egyptian City

Then, after receiving provisions for their journey, they traveled on. They entered into another town, where they truly wished to lodge, for it was a popular place. There was a woman in this town who had gone to the river to bathe one day, and behold, Satan, the Accursed One, sprang on her in the form of a snake and wrapped himself around her body; and he wrenched her every night thereafter. When this woman saw our Lady, Saint Mary, with the child, the Lord Jesus Christ, in her arms, she asked the Lady Saint Mary to hand the little one over to her, so that she might kiss and hold him in her arms. Now when Mary handed him over--even as she was taking hold of the child--Satan suddenly took off and abandoned her, and that woman never saw him again. Everyone in that place immediately broke into praises to the Most High God, and the woman gave them generous gifts.

The next day, that same woman bought perfumed water with which to bathe the Anointed Lord, and set it aside. Another girl was there whose skin was white with leprosy, and as soon as she was sprinkled with it, and had scrubbed herself off, her skin disease was washed away. So the people all proclaimed, "There can be no doubt that Joseph, Mary, and this boy are gods, since they do not seem like mortal men." And as they were getting set to travel on, the girl who had been afflicted by her skin disease approached them and asked if she could come along. And they answered that she could, so the girl traveled on with them until they came to a town in which stood the palace of a great king, and that place was near to the inn where they were staying. One day, when the girl went to visit the prince's wife, she found her grieving and suffering terribly, so she asked her, "Why are you weeping?" "Please don't ask me why I weep," she pleaded, "for I am under such a trial that I dare not tell a soul about it!" "But if you'll confide in me," the girl replied, "and disclose to me the nature of your personal suffering, then I might just be able to find you a remedy." "Then you must keep it to yourself," the princess insisted, "and not tell anyone about it! I have been married to this prince who reigns over many regions as a king, and had lived with him for quite a while before I bore him any children. At long last he managed to get me pregnant, but wouldn't you know, I gave birth to a leprous son! Now as soon as my husband saw him, he immediately denied his paternity and said, 'You either take and destroy him, or else send him off to a nurse in a place so far away that he will never be heard from! As for you, look to yourself, because I never want to see you again!' So here I am, languishing and grieving over my horrible situation. Oh, for my son! Oh, for my husband! Do you get the idea?" "I have found a remedy for your plight that I know you can trust," the girl replied, "even the one who is called Jesus, the son of the Lady Saint Mary. You see, I also had a skin disease, but then God washed me clean of it." "Where," asked the woman, "is this God of whom you speak?" The girl answered, "He is staying right here in your very own home!" "But how is this possible?" the princess said. "Tell me where this child could be!" "Behold," the girl replied, "you know Joseph and Mary? The child who is with them is called Jesus; and he was the one who freed me from my own illness and suffering." "Well then," the princess asked, "just how were you cleansed of it? Will you at least explain that much to me?" "Why, of course I will," the girl replied. "After I had bathed the boy, I took the water used to wash his body, and poured it over myself, and my skin disease disappeared." The princess then got up and showed herself hospitable to them, throwing a banquet in Joseph's honor before a great many men. The following day, she took perfumed water in which to bathe the Lord Jesus, and later poured some over her own son, whom she had brought along, and immediately he was freed of his leprosy. She then sang praises of thanks to God, saying, "Oh, Jesus! How blessed is the mother who bore you! Is this how you restore mankind: making them even as you are yourself with the very water that was used to clean you off?" Then she offered lavish gifts to our Lady, Saint Mary, and bid her farewell with every conceivable honor.

WITCHCRAFTS OVERCOME
(ArIn 7:1-35)
Several Egyptian Cities

After this, they came to another town and decided to lodge there. So they went to the house of a man who had just completed his nuptials, but due to the influence of some sorcerers, could not consummate his marriage. But they spent the night at this man's house, and he was relieved of his affliction. Early the next morning, as they were gathering their things to go their way, the newly wedded man did not let them go, but instead showed them great hospitality. Even so, they traveled on the following day.

And they entered into another town, where they saw three women who were weeping and wailing as they were leaving a certain graveyard. As soon as Saint Mary saw them, she asked the girl who had sought to travel with them, "Would you please go over to those women and find out what is troubling them, and what circumstances they are under." They did not answer her question though, but questioned her instead, "Who are you, then, and where are you headed? For the day has nearly passed, and the night is on its heels." "We are travelers searching for an inn in which to stay," the girl replied. "Follow us," they answered them, "You can come and stay with us." So they followed after those women, and were ushered into a brand new house--all decorated with every kind of furniture imaginable. By now it was winter, and the girl entered into the parlor and found the women there, crying and lamenting over their plight, even as they had before. A mule was standing next to them all draped in silk. A black feedbag was hanging from his neck--and they were kissing him and feeding him. But when the girl remarked, "Ladies, that's a fine looking mule you've got there!" they all burst into tears and said, "What you see as a mule was once our brother, born from the very same mother as we. For when our father passed away, he left us with a large estate, and this was our only brother. We tried to find him a suitable companion, thinking that he should wed as others do, but some woman got jealous and cast a spell on him without our knowing. Then one night, right before dawn, when the doors to the house were still shut tight, we saw that our brother here had been changed into a mule, as you can plainly see. And we, being in the sorry state that you see us in now, having no father to console us, have sought the services of all the sages, wizards, and sorcerers in the world, but they have not helped us in the least! So now when we find ourselves feeling down, we get up and travel with our mother to our father's grave. And after we have cried it off, we all simply come back here."

And as soon as the girl had heard all this, she said, "Now take heart, and have no fear, for truly a cure for what ails you is near. It is, in fact, right here with you--even in your very home! I was a victim of a skin disease, you see, but when I saw this woman with her child Jesus, I sprinkled my body with the bathwater that his mother had used to wash him off, and in that instant I was healed. Now I am certain that he can bring your troubles to an end. Get up, therefore, and go over to my lady Mary, and after you have brought her into this room, share your secret with her. And while you are at it, ask her to show you compassion for the circumstances you are under." The moment the women heard what the girl had said, they went quickly to our Lady, Saint Mary, introduced themselves to her, seated themselves before her and wept. "Oh, our Lady, Saint Mary," they pleaded, "show us some compassion, for our house is without a head, and we have no one who is older--neither father or brother--to lead us either in or out! What you see as a mule over here was once our brother. Some woman using witchcraft has brought him to his present state. And for this reason do we beg of you, please have pity on us all!" When she heard this, Mary felt sorry for them, so she took the Lord Jesus, placed him on the back of the mule and said, "Oh, Christ Jesus, through your absolute power, restore this mule into a man, having the same sense as he had before." The Lady, Saint Mary, had scarcely finished speaking these words when the mule returned to the form of a young man without any deformity whatsoever. Then he, his sisters and his mother all worshiped our Lady, Saint Mary. Then they lifted up the child and held him out above their heads, kissing him, and proclaiming, "Oh Jesus, Savior of the World, how blessed is your mother! How blessed and joyful are the eyes that see you!" The two sisters then confessed to their mother, "Truly, it was the Lord Jesus Christ who helped our brother, restoring him to his prior state; but it was also through the kindness of that girl who told us about Mary and her son. So seeing that our brother here is not yet wed, it seems good that we should marry him to this servant girl of theirs. So they consulted Mary about it, and when she had given them her consent, they threw a stylish wedding for her."

So their sorrow turned to gladness, and their grieving into joy. And they dressed up in their finest clothing and bracelets, and began to celebrate and to be festive. Then they all broke out in song, and soon they were all exalting and praising God, saying, "Jesus, oh son of David, who changes sorrow into joy, and misery into elation!" And after these things, Joseph and Mary remained there with them ten days more, receiving tremendous appreciation from them. And after Joseph and Mary had gone away, they all went home weeping, but none of them wept more than the girl.

TITUS AND DUMACHUS
(DYSMAS AND GESTAS)
(ArIn 8:1-7)
The Desert, Where Bandits Lie In Wait

And as they moved on from that district, they came into a desert, where they were warned about all of the robbers that lurked therein. Joseph and Saint Mary therefore waited until nightfall to pass through. And even as they journeyed forth, they caught sight of two bandits who were sleeping on the road--and many of their companions were sleeping nearby. These two robbers were named Titus and Dumachus. "Dumachus," Titus implored him, "I beg you, please allow these people to pass us quietly by, so that no one in our band might notice them." Now Dumachus refused to do it, so once again he said to him, "I will give you forty goats; and look, here is my belt, take it also as a pledge." And he handed it over to Dumachus even as he was bargaining with him, so that he might not sound the alarm. When our Lady Saint Mary saw the kindness that this robber had done them, she informed him, "The Lord God will forgive you of your sins and place you at His own right hand." "Mother," the Lord Jesus said to her, "in thirty years' time, the Jews will crucify me in Jerusalem. These two thieves will be crucified alongside me; Titus will be to my right, and Dumachus to my left--and Titus will pass into paradise even before I do." "My son!" said Mary, "God forbid this should happen to you!"

THE IDOLS TURN INTO SAND
(ArIn 8:8)
Another Egyptian Town

Then they traveled to another town, where several idols turned into mere sand dunes at their approach.

THE SPRING AT MATAREA
(ArIn 8:9-11)
Matarea, Egypt

After this, they traveled on to that sycamore tree, a place that is now called Matarea. And there in that region the Lord Jesus caused a fountain to spring forth, and Saint Mary washed his coat in it. And the sweat that dripped from the Lord Jesus in that land produces a medicinal oil.

THE HOLY FAMILY MEETS WITH PHAROAH
(ArIn 8:12-13)
Memphis, Egypt

From Matarea they moved on to Memphis, where they met together with Pharaoh. For three years they remained in Egypt, and the Lord Jesus performed all kinds of miracles which are neither to be found in the Gospel of the Infancy, nor the Gospel of Perfection.

INFANCY 3

RETURN TO JUDEA; TO GALILEE
(Matt 2:1-23; Luke 2:40; ArIn 8:14-17;
PsMt 25; InThL 3; HJC 9)
Egypt, Judea, Nazareth

But after three years had come and gone, Herod passed away. (Now he died from the worst death that you can imagine, paying the price for those innocent children, whose blood he so wickedly shed.) After the death of that evil despot and the passing of Joseph from Egypt, (an angel of the Lord) led him out into the desert until those who sought after the boy's life were no longer a threat and Jerusalem was once again at rest. Behold, an angel of the Lord appeared to Joseph in a dream, saying, "Get up! Take your young child and his mother into Israel, for those who sought to kill him are dead." And behold, one of the Lord's angels came (also) to Mary, saying, "Take the child and return to the land of the Jews, because the ones who were trying to kill him have themselves passed on." Joseph therefore got up, took the young child and his mother and entered into Israel. The closer he drew to Judea, however, the more reluctant he became to enter into it. (Joseph, you see, had heard that Herod had passed on and that his son Archelaus was reigning in his stead, so he was afraid to go there.) And on his arrival in Judea, an angel of God appeared to him in a dream, warning him: "Joseph, travel on to the city of Nazareth and settle in that place." So Joseph and Mary got up and left with Jesus for the region of Galilee, and they entered into Nazareth, where she had an inheritance from her father; that what was spoken through the prophets, "He will be called a Nazarene," might be fulfilled. And Joseph returned to his carpenter's trade, earning a living with his own two hands; for he would never have tried to live off of another man's labor; (even) as the Mosaic Law forbids. And he thanked the Lord God for His kindness, and for giving him such an understanding. It is truly mysterious that the Lord of every nation should be moved around all over like this--back and forth across so many lands. And the boy grew, and became strong, and extremely wise. And God endowed him with His nature.

JESUS' BATHWATER CURES VARIOUS ILLNESSES
(ArIn 9:1-11)
Bethlehem

Later, after they had entered into Bethlehem, they came across several victims of a grave disorder that had become so serious that most children who suffered from it would die. A woman there had a son who was afflicted thereby, and was standing at the door of death. And she brought him to our Lady, calling on her as she was bathing Jesus Christ. "Oh my Lady Mary," the woman implored her, "consider the misfortune of my son, who is wracked by such extreme pain." And hearing her, Mary said, "Take and sprinkle him with a little bit of that water with which I have just now finished bathing my son." Then she took some of that water, even as she had been told, and mottled her boy who, worn out by tumultuous sufferings, had drifted off. After sleeping but a little while, he was restored to health and he awoke. Thrilled by this turn of events, the mother returned to Saint Mary, who replied, "Offer up your praise to God. It is He Who has healed your son."

A neighbor of the woman whose son had been made well was nearby, and this woman's boy was also suffering from the very same illness. His eyes had nearly closed forever, and day and night she mourned for him. The restored boy's mother then suggested, "How about taking your son to Mary as I have done? I took my boy to her as he was in the throes of death, and the water with which she had washed the body of her son Jesus healed him." As soon as the other woman heard what she said, she went there also. And after getting hold of some of the same water, she used it to wash her son as well. After she had done this, his eyes and his body were immediately restored to the way that they had been before. And when she returned to Saint Mary with her boy, our Lady told her to offer thanks to God for the recovery of her son, but to avoid telling anyone about what had been done.

THE TWO WIVES AND THEIR SONS'
ILLNESSES
(ArIn 10:1-14)
Bethlehem

In that very town, there were these two wives of one husband, each of whom had a boy who was ill. One of them, whose name was Mary, had a son named Cleophas. She got up, took her son with her, and went to visit Jesus' mother, our Lady Saint Mary. She offered her a fine, luxurious rug, and pleaded, "Oh my Lady Mary, please accept this rug from me in exchange for a tiny piece of swaddling cloth." Mary then agreed to it, so when the mother of Cleophas left, she fashioned a garment from it, placed it upon her boy, and he was relieved; but the son of the other wife died.

Out of this disparity there arose a conflict in the running of the house. Each mother had been taking a turn every other week. When Cleophas' mother Mary's turn came around, she fired up the furnace to bake some bread and left her son nearby as she stepped away to get some flour. The competitor wife, seeing the boy unattended, grabbed him, threw him into the sweltering oven and ran off quickly. When Mary came back and saw her son Cleophas lying in the midst thereof, which was just as cool as it had been before being heated, she recognized that the rival wife had tossed him into the flames. After she had pulled him out, she took him over to the Lady Saint Mary, and explained to her what had happened. "Keep this to yourself," she said. "I need to know that you will not tell these things to others."

Afterward, the enemy wife was drawing water at the well, and seeing Cleophas playing nearby, and no one around to witness it, she snatched him up and threw him in. Some men came to the well to draw some water and saw the boy sitting there on the surface, and were taken aback at the sight. Then they gave praises to God and pulled him out with ropes. His mother came and took him straight to our Lady Saint Mary, saying solemnly, "Oh my Lady, see what my rival has done to my son! See how she has thrown him down a well, and I have no doubt but that sooner or later she will be the death of him." "God Himself will avenge your cause," replied Saint Mary. A few days later, the other wife came to the well to draw some water, and her foot got caught by the rope in such a way that she fell headlong into the well, even as befit her case. And those who rushed to help her out found her head bashed in and her bones in splinters. So she came to a sorry end, and the saying of the prophet who wrote, "They made a deep well, but ended up falling into the pit that they had dug," was fulfilled in her.

THE HEALING OF BARTHOLOMEW
(ArIn 11:1-8)
Bethlehem

In that city there was yet another woman who had twin sons who had fallen prey to a disease. And after one had died, she took the other, who was himself on the verge of death, cradled in her arms to our Lady Saint Mary. And she pleaded through her tears, "Oh, my Lady, please help me in my distress. Not long ago I had two sons, but I have just now buried one and can see that the other one is on the brink. Behold, I am desperately seeking mercy from God, and am offering up my prayers to Him." "Oh my Lord," the woman said, "You are kind and gracious and giving. You have given me two sons and taken one again to Yourself, please leave me this other one." And sensing the depth of her despair, Saint Mary felt sorry for her and said, "Rest your boy on the bed of my son, and lay the clothes of my child on him." The very moment she had laid him who had just closed his eyes in death onto the bed where the Anointed was lying, and the scent of the clothes of the Lord Jesus Christ hit the lad, his eyes popped open, and he cried to his mother for bread, which when he had taken some, he promptly ate. "Oh my Lady Mary," confessed His mother, "now I am convinced that God's powers work through you, such that your son is able to heal children, who are by nature like him, as soon as they come into contact with his clothing." The boy who was cured like this is the same one who is called Bartholomew in the Gospel.

BATHWATER CURES
(ArIn 12:1-6)
The Cave Outside Bethlehem

Now there was a leprous woman who came to the mother of Jesus, our lady Saint Mary, and pleaded, "Help me, my Lady." "What kind of assistance are you seeking?" Saint Mary inquired. "Will you ask for silver or gold, or would you have your leprosy cured?" "Who can do this thing for me?" the woman asked.

"Just wait until I have bathed my son Jesus and put him down to rest" she said,. The woman waited as advised, and after Mary had laid Jesus down to sleep, she gave her some of the water she had used to wash his body and said, "Take some of the water and pour it over yourself." And when the woman had complied, she received her cleansing and so praised God, thanking Him with all her heart.

ANOTHER CURED BY BATHWATER
(ArIn 12:7-22)
Jerusalem?

After staying there with her for three days, the woman went away and into town. And as she was going in, she met up with a certain prince who was married to the daughter of this other prince. But when this prince went in to examine her he saw evidence of leprosy--a star-like sign between her eyes--and he immediately nullified their marriage vows. When the woman saw the two in such a state, pouring forth a flood of tears, she asked them why they all were weeping so. "Do not pry into our affairs," they said, "for we are not even able to breathe our circumstances to anyone." Even so she prodded them to share their case with her more fully, suggesting to them that she might be able to help them. So after showing her the maiden with the mark of her disease between her eyes, she said, "I, the very one who stands before you now, also suffered from the same disease, but when my dealings brought me to Bethlehem, I entered into this cavern and saw a woman there whose name was Mary, and her son Jesus was there with her. And seeing me in my leprous state, she felt for me and offered me some of the water with which she had washed the body of her son. And when I had sprinkled myself with it, I became clean." At that point the woman asked, "Young lady, would you be so kind as to take us to the Lady Saint Mary and let us meet her?" And after she had agreed to it, they got up and traveled over to our Lady, taking some very costly gifts along with them. And when they had gone in to her, they presented their offerings to her, and revealed to her the skin disease of the young lady that they had brought with them. At that point Saint Mary said, "May the mercy of the Lord Jesus Christ be with you." Then she offered them some of the water that she had used to wash the body of Jesus Christ, and instructed them to cleanse the diseased woman with it. And when they did as they were told, the woman was immediately healed, so these and some others who were there exalted God and returned in joy to their own town, praising God for what had been done. And on hearing that his wife had been cured, the prince again took her into his house and took her hand in marriage, giving praise to God for restoring his wife.

GIRL AFFLICTED BY SATAN
(ArIn 13:1-13)
Jerusalem?

In that place there also lived this girl who was tormented by Satan. That filthy spirit, you see, would often appear to her in the form of a dragon and swallow her whole. He sucked so much blood from her, in fact, that she looked just like a corpse. Every time she would come to her senses she would hold her head in her hands and scream, "How wretched I am, seeing how there is none to save me from this wicked dragon!" Her father and mother cried for her and lamented, as did all the others there; and all who were there would feel particularly bad for her whenever they would hear her weeping, wailing, and crying out, "Oh my friends! Oh my family! Is there no one who can save me from this murderer?"

The prince's daughter, whose leprosy had completely vanished, upon hearing the wailing of that girl, went all the way up to the roof of her palace and saw the girl's hands wrapped around her head, surrounded by her sorrowful companions, and pouring forth a stream of tears. She then asked the possessed girl's husband if his mother-in-law were living, and he let her know that both her mother and her father were indeed alive. Then she had the girl's mother sent to her. And as she caught sight of her approach, she asked her mother, "Is this possessed girl here your daughter?" "Yes, young lady," she woefully and sorrowfully confessed, "I was the one who gave birth to her." The prince's daughter then replied, "Tell me all about her state, because I am here to tell you that I once had a skin disease, but the Lady Mary, the mother of Jesus Christ, healed me of it. If you'd like to see your daughter cured, then take her to Bethlehem and ask to see Mary, the mother of Jesus, and have no doubts as to whether your daughter will recover, for I believe with all my heart that you will go back home rejoicing over your daughter's restoration." And when she had finished speaking, she got up and took her daughter there. Then she went up to Mary and shared her girl's circumstances with her. And when she had listened to her story, Mary gave the woman some of the water that she had used to wash off the body of her boy Jesus, and asked her to pour it over that of her daughter. She also gave her one of the swaddling cloths of the Lord Jesus, saying, "Take this cloth and show it to your adversary every time that you see him." And she bade them peace and sent them off.

FIRE FROM THE SWADDLING CLOTH
(ArIn 13:14-20)
Judea

After leaving that town and returning home, the hour that Satan would typically show up and take control of her came around. The accursed spirit suddenly showed himself to her in the likeness of an enormous dragon. On seeing this, the girl was terrified, but her mother said, "Daughter, have no fear, but allow him to draw near to you. Then reveal to him the swaddling cloth that was given to us by our Lady Mary, and let us see what comes of it." Then Satan approached her in the form of a terrifying dragon and the girl became so afraid that she began to tremble with violence. But even as she held the swaddling cloth to her head and about her eyes, where the dragon could see it, flames shot out and the dragon was pummeled with fiery cinders. What a wonder was brought about through all that had happened, for just as soon as the dragon caught sight of the swaddling cloths of the Lord Jesus, fire shot out of it and bespattered his eyes and face. "Why should you and I meet like this, Jesus, son of Mary?" he shrieked loudly. "Where am I to run and free myself from you?" So he fled away from her in fear. She, being freed from her torment, sang songs of praise and thanks to God along with everyone else who was there at the time that this miracle took place.

JUDAS STRIKES JESUS
(ArIn 14:1-10)
Judea

Satan had taken possession of the son of another woman in that region. As often as Satan would take control of this boy, whose name was Judas, he would go around biting everyone in sight; and if there was no one around, he would bite his own hands and limbs. The mother of this wretched boy, hearing about Saint Mary and her son Jesus, rose up quickly and carried her child in her arms to our Lady Mary. Meanwhile James and Joses had taken the young Jesus to play with some other children. And while they were out, they all sat down alongside him. Then Judas, the possessed boy, came and sat down to his right. And when Satan was working through him in his usual manner, the boy attempted to bite the Lord Jesus. But because he was not able, he struck him so hard against his right hand side that he cried aloud. Now just as soon as he did this, Satan left the lad and ran away like a mad dog. This very child, the one who struck Jesus, and out of whom Satan fled in the form of a dog was he who betrayed him to the Jews--Judas Iscariot. And the Jews pierced him with a spear on the very spot where Judas had stricken him.

A BOY WRECKS JESUS' POOLS AND DIES
(PsMt 26)
Galilee, by the Jordan River

And when he had returned from Egypt, by the time that he was four years old, it so happened that he was playing in Galilee by the banks of the Jordan with some other youngsters on a Sabbath Day. Now as he was sitting there, Jesus fashioned seven puddles out of mud, each complete with its own viaducts. And at his command the waters rushed into them and out again. Then one of those boys--a child of Satan who was jealous of Jesus--stopped up the channels that were feeding these pools and demolished all that Jesus had made. "Curse you, you son of the devil!" Jesus reproached him. "Will you tear down my hard work?" And right away the one who had done this dropped dead. The dead boy's parents then loudly denounced Joseph and Mary, complaining, "Your boy has killed our son, and now he is dead." And when Joseph and Mary heard the clamoring of the parents and the convergence of the Jews, they went out to where Jesus was. Privately, however, Joseph confided to Mary, "I do not dare to lecture him. You must therefore chasten him, and be sure to ask him why it is that he stirs the people's anger against us and forces such animosity upon us." And when Mary went and questioned him, "Oh my Lord, what did he do that he should die?" Jesus replied, "He deserved to die for scattering all that I worked so hard to build." Then his mother pleaded with him, "My Lord, do not conduct yourself like this, for everyone is up in arms against us." And Jesus, not wishing to cause his mother grief, kicked the boy who had died in the rump with his right foot and ordered him, "Get up, you child of darkness! Because you have destroyed all that I had worked so hard to make, you are unfit to enter my Father's rest." Then the one who had died got back up and ran away. And at Jesus' command, the water gushed back through the channels and into the puddles.

THOMAS' INTRODUCTION
(InTh Greek 1)

{Here begins the book of the holy Apostle Thomas the Israelite philosopher regarding the discourse on the childhood of the Lord. I, Thomas the Israelite, have felt the need to inform you brothers from among the Gentiles, filling you in on the mighty childhood deeds that our Lord Jesus Christ brought to pass in our land from the age of five forward, even as he spoke bodily in the city of Nazareth.}

JESUS CLARIFIES WATER AND QUICKENS CLAY ANIMALS
(InTh 2(3); QBar 2:11; PsMt 27)
Galilee

When Jesus was five years old, he was playing near the shallow crossing of a stream. He diverted some of the flowing water into puddles and with a word he gave command and they instantly clarified.

Afterward, Jesus took some clay out of the puddles he had formed and, before them all fashioned twelve sparrows from it, representing the twelve apostles. There were many other children who were playing with him there. A certain Jew, when he saw what Jesus was doing as he played there on the Sabbath Day, hurried over right away to his father Joseph. "Look, the boy informed him, your son is playing down by the river. He has taken mud and made twelve sparrows with it, which is unlawful for him to do, thereby desecrating the Sabbath Day." And when he heard this, Joseph hurried to the spot. And as soon as he got there, the boy said to him: "See? Your son, by doing work, is violating the Sabbath! He has fashioned twelve sparrows out of clay." And Joseph chastened Jesus, saying, "Why do you break the Sabbath with such unlawful acts?" But when Jesus heard Joseph, he offered no reply, but instead turned toward the sparrows, clapped his hands and cried aloud before them all, "Fly now, and go your way! Sail throughout the world and live, calling me to mind your whole life long." And at the sound of his word they all flew into the air, flapping and chirping loudly even unto the ends of the earth. And when Joseph saw this miracle, he was astounded. And when the Jews saw it, they too were astounded. Everyone, in fact, upon seeing such wonders, was astounded. Many who were there praised Jesus and offered him thanks, but a few others denounced him--still others went and notified the high-ranking priests and the leaders of the Pharisees that Joseph's boy Jesus had performed great signs and wonders in the sight of Israel. And word got around to the Israelite tribes.

BOY SCATTERS JESUS' FISH POOL
(InTh 3(2); ArIn 19:16-21; PsMt 28, 29)
Galilee

Jesus left his mother in the house one day after a rain, and went to play on a riverbank with some boys. After making some ponds they dug little channels, drawing some of the river water into the small fish ponds. Then Jesus said to the waters: "Clarify and become fresh," and they all became so right away. The Lord Jesus had also formed twelve sparrows around his puddle, placing three on each of the sides. But this all happened on the Sabbath, and the son of a Jew named Annas, a temple priest, happened along and saw them making all of these things and protested, "Are you making images of clay on the Sabbath Day?" Then he hurried over to them and ruined all of their ponds. But when the Lord Jesus clapped his hands over the sparrows he had fashioned, they took off chirping.

Soon the son of Annas the scribe again stood nearby, branch in hand before them all, this time with Joseph. And with bitter anger, he took the willow branch and approached Jesus' fish pond to break down its dams that he had fashioned with his own two hands. And upon destroying the ponds with the branch, the waters that had flowed into it streamed out again. He sealed off the inlet, moreover, and broke down the channel supplying it. And when Jesus saw what he had done, he was angry, and he reproached the boy who had destroyed his levees, "You disrespectful fool! What an evil, godless, and lawless one you are! In what way were these ponds harming you that you have felt the need to drain them?" Then the water disappeared and the Lord Jesus reproved him, "Oh evil seed most foul! Oh, son of death! Oh, devil's workshop! The fruit of your seed will be powerless indeed! Your roots will parch, and your fruitless branches wither. Behold, you will travel no further; but you also will waste away like a tree and sprout neither leaves, nor roots, nor any fruit; and your very life will evaporate even as this water has, and you will become as dried-up as the stick which you now hold." Moments later, as he headed off along his way, the boy fell down before them all; withering up suddenly and completely, thus surrendering his spirit and passing on. Then Jesus left that place and entered into Joseph's house.

Now when the youngsters he was playing with saw what had happened, they were astonished and went to the dead boy's father and let him know. He then ran over to the scene and saw that the youth was dead. The withered boy's parents then carried him away, grieving over the loss of this child. And they took Jesus straight to Joseph, chastening him, "What kind of boy do you have that does such things?" Then Joseph, trembling, took hold of Jesus and went with him and his mother (back) into his house.

BOY ATTACKS JESUS AND DIES
(ArIn 19:22-24; InTh 4; PsMt 29)
Nazareth?

One evening, after a few days had passed, Jesus was again walking home through the midst of town with a very frightened Joseph. And behold, a certain boy, another evildoer, threw a stone at Jesus and ran quickly up to him from the front wishing to make a laughingstock of him or even injure him if at all possible, pounding him so soundly against his shoulder that he slammed against the ground. Jesus became furious and condemned the boy, "May you go no further on your way (so as to) return from it unharmed! And even as you have knocked me down, so also will you fall to the ground, but you will never recover." And in that instant the boy fell dead.

Some who had witnessed the event, however, including the dead boy's parents shouted, "Where could this boy have come from, seeing how every word he speaks is true, and is carried out in fact, sometimes before he even utters it?" They all came up to Joseph, bringing with them the parents of the dead boys. And they started to reprove him saying, "Because your son does things like this, you may no longer live with him alongside us in this town. Take Jesus away from here--or else kindly teach him to bless and not to curse, for he is killing our children, since every word of his has an immediate effect."

JOSEPH ADMONISHES JESUS; HIS REPLY
(InTh 5; PsMt 29)
Jerusalem

Joseph then went up to Jesus, calling the boy privately to himself. Now after Joseph had seated himself upon his chair, the boy came and stood before him there. Joseph then reproved him saying, "Why do you do these kinds of things? Many of these people are heartbroken already because of you, and therefore they despise and harass us. Many of them are now talking bad about you and deride us both on your account, and we have no choice but to endure it." Jesus answered them, "According to the knowledge of this age, unless a father has taught his son, he is not considered wise. Even so, the Father's curse cannot hinder any man unless he is an evildoer. I recognize that these words are not coming from you, so for your sake I will speak no more. In either case, these people will be punished." And those who had accused him were at that moment all made blind, and all who saw it were terrified and taken aback, and they proclaimed, "Good or bad, everything that this boy speaks becomes an action--and indeed, a miracle!" And when they had established that Jesus had done this, Joseph got up and pulled him hard by the ear. Then Jesus stared him down in all severity, crying out, "That is quite enough! For you to seek and not to find is one thing," the boy angrily rebuked, "but for you to act in so reckless a manner is quite another. Are you not yet convinced that I'm not truly your own? Do not provoke me!" Then they banded together against Jesus, and denounced him to Joseph. Now when Joseph saw what was going on, he grew fearful over the furious outcry of the Israelites. Jesus then grabbed the dead boy by the ear and lifted him up before them all, and they could see that he was scolding him as a father would scold his own son. The spirit of the boy was then returned and he was raised again to life, and all were amazed at his restoration.

ZACCHAEUS TAKES JESUS AS HIS PUPIL
(InTh 6:1-12,(6); ArIn 20:1-4; PsMt 30)
Jerusalem

There was also a certain teacher in Jerusalem named Zacchaeus who was standing nearby and had heard what Jesus had said to his father. He was stunned that a mere child such as he would speak such things. And seeing that Jesus could not be vanquished, and recognizing the power that was within him, he was incensed, and started fearlessly, foolishly, and rudely denouncing Joseph, "Don't you think that you should turn your son over to me, so that he might learn worldly wisdom and respect for other people? It is clear to me that you and Mary care more about your own son than you do the elders of Israel and what they have to say of him. You ought to have shown us all--the entire congregation of Israel--a little more respect, so that he might like other children and be better liked by them, and that he might receive a proper Jewish education." Joseph, however, questioned them, "Who, I ask, is capable of taking him on and teaching him anything? If you think that you can do it, then we are more than willing to let you try and provide him with a common education."

And a few days later he went up to Joseph, saying, "You know, your boy really is quite clever, and he has tremendous insight. Why not turn him over to me so that he might learn his letters? I will teach him all there is to know of them. I will also teach him the proper way to address his elders, giving them all their due respect as fathers and forefathers, as well as how to get along with those who are his age." Joseph agreed and told Saint Mary.

The next day Joseph took Jesus by the hand and led him over to Zacchaeus saying, "Very well, Rabbi, take this boy and teach him letters." "Brother," he responded, "if you will turn him over to me, I will cast light on the Scriptures for him, convincing him that he ought to bless everything and curse nothing." And Jesus, hearing what Zacchaeus had said, burst into laughter and answered them, "The lessons to which you refer, and the principles that underlie them are sufficient for an ordinary person's education, and as such ought to be kept by them; but your law courts are alien to me. You speak as you can understand, but I understand much more than you can, for before the ages came about I AM. I even know when your fathers' fathers were born; yet I have no fleshly father. You who read from the law and know about it do indeed hold to it; but I existed before the law was given. Since, however, you imagine that no one else's learning is a match for your own, I will teach you a thing or two about the things to which you refer that no one could possibly expound, unless he were worthy. For when I am exalted in this world at last, I will bring to an end all reference to your lineage. You see, you do not yourselves recall the occasion of your birth. I not only know when all of you were born, but also how much longer you will live on this earth." "Oh, oh, oh!" they all responded in amazement. "What a great and incredible mystery this is. We have never heard any such claims before. No one else has ever said such things, not even the prophets themselves, or the scribes, or the Pharisees. We know where this boy came from. He is scarcely even five years old. Where does he get off saying things like this?" The Pharisees declared, "We have never heard such claims from any other child of his years." But Jesus replied, "Does it surprise you that a child would say such things? How is it that you do not believe me when I speak these words to you? All of you were astonished when I revealed to you that I knew when you were born. I will go even further than this, so that you might marvel all the more. I have both seen Abraham and spoken with him-- the one who you call 'father'--and Abraham has seen me too!" Everyone there was taken aback, and no one even dared to speak. And Jesus added, "I have been in your midst as a child among your children, and you have not even come to know me. I have spoken to you as with the wise, and you have failed to comprehend my speech. Indeed, you are more childish than I am, and your faith is stunted."

Once again he said to them, "You find it hard to believe that I know how many years have been given you to live? Believe me; I know when the world was formed. Behold, though you don't believe me now, when the day comes that you see my cross, you will know that I am telling the truth." And when they heard these words they were all appalled.

JESUS ASTONISHES ZACCHAEUS
(ArIn 22:1-6; InTh 6:3-7:4(7))
Jerusalem

Zacchaeus wrote out the Hebrew alphabet and one by one pronounced for him all of the letters from [Aleph] to [Taw], asking him question after question. He said "[Aleph]" to him, and the boy said "[Aleph.]" The teacher repeated, "[Aleph,]" and so the boy repeated it also. Then, the third time that the master said "[Aleph,]" Jesus looked right at him and demanded, "You who do not know the [Aleph] according to its proper sense, how ever will you teach anyone about the [Beth]? You hypocrite, if you know the [Aleph], then explain it to us; only then will we believe you when you teach about the [Beth]." Then Jesus started to examine the teacher on the topic of the first letter, and the teacher could not answer. And the boy taught Zacchaeus loud enough for all to hear,

"Listen, teacher, and pay close attention to the composition of the first letter; how it has lines and a stroke intersecting the two down the center, as you can see, intersecting, rising up, dancing there and turning together; three signs, each alike, subordinate to, yet supportive of one another, all of them the same dimensions. There you have it--the lines of the [Aleph]!"

Now when Zacchaeus the instructor heard so many allegorical interpretations of the first letter being elucidated by the boy, he was bewildered by his answer, and his exposition, and was utterly amazed and could give him no reply. And beginning at [Aleph], Jesus expounded all twenty-two letters without any prompting whatsoever. Then Zacchaeus confessed to the people there, "How miserable and wretched and troubled I am. By taking this boy to myself, I have gotten only shame. I beg you, Joseph, take this boy away from me, for I cannot bear the way he looks at me so demandingly. I cannot understand in the least the things about which he speaks. This child cannot be of this world. Perhaps he was born before the world was formed. What belly could carry him? Whose womb could nourish him? My friend, I am undone; he utterly perplexes me--I cannot even begin to scale the heights of his understanding. I have fooled myself, and been disgraced thrice over. I had sought after a student, but have instead gotten a teacher. I am, my friends, completely ashamed that a mere child such as he has gotten the better of an old man like me. Depression and death overwhelm me on account of this lad. I cannot look him in the face--and when everyone goes around saying that I have been bested by a little boy, how am I supposed to reply? What am I to say about the first letter and its lines as he explained it to me? My friends, I have no idea, for I understand neither beginning nor end."

And turning to Joseph he remarked, "Without a doubt, brother, this child was not born of this earth, so I implore you, brother Joseph, take him back home with you. Be he a god or an angel or some other magnificent being I do not know, and cannot say."

ZACCHAEUS TAKES JESUS TO LEVI
(ArIn 20:7-12; PsMt 31; InTh 8)
Jerusalem

Then the doctor of the law, master Zacchaeus urged Joseph and Mary a second time, "Turn the boy over to me and I will take him to Master Levi--he will teach him letters and give him an education!" Then Joseph and Mary pacified Jesus and took him over to the school so that the elderly Levi might teach him letters. And from the moment he entered that place, Jesus remained silent. And starting with the first letter, Aleph, Master Levi kept saying just that one letter to Jesus, and ordering him to explain it, but he held his peace and gave no answer. Then Master Levi, his instructor, grabbed his storax rod and cracked him over the head with it. Then Jesus, standing up to his teacher Levi, demanded, "Why did you hit me? You can be quite sure of this: the one who has been stricken can teach the one who struck him much more than he could ever learn from him. You see, I can teach you all about what you claim to know.

The Super Gospel

Everyone who speaks, and everyone who hears is as blind as the noise of brass or the clang of a cymbal; which cannot hear the sounds they make." To Zacchaeus he added, "Every letter from Aleph to [Taw] is understood by the way that it's composed. Explain what the [Taw] is first, and then I will make clear to you what the Aleph is." And once again he said to him, "How can those who know not the Aleph, ever come to know the [Taw], seeing how hypocritical they are? Say what Aleph is first and then I will believe you when you expound to me the Beth." Then, one by one, Jesus started asking about the names of each, and said, "Let the law teacher explain to us what the first letter is, or why it has so many triangles, which gradually flow from pointed to broad, bringing together, drawing across, and reaching over; being perpendicular, prostrate, and curving." And when the teacher threatened him with a whipping, the Lord Jesus expounded the meaning of the letters Aleph and Beth to him. He also pointed out which parts of the letters were straight, which were diagonal; which of them had double strokes; those with and without points; the reason that one preceded another; and he began to make plain to him one thing after another, explaining things that his instructor had never so much as heard of before, nor read out of any book.

And when Levi heard this, he was surprised at such an arrangement of letters and names, and started loudly denouncing Jesus before them all, "Does he even deserve to live on this earth? No, he ought to be hung instead upon a giant cross! He can put out any fire and talk his way out of any punishment." The Lord Jesus went on to explain to the teacher, "Listen carefully to the way that I speak them." Then he started plainly and intelligibly to pronounce, "Aleph, Beth, Gimel, Daleth..." and all of the others to the end of the alphabet. Upon hearing this, the teacher was so beside himself that he cried out, "I honestly believe that this child lived before the deluge and was born before Noah. What womb gave rise to him? What mother brought him into this world? What breasts nursed him? I flee from his presence. I cannot endure the words from his mouth, and my heart is amazed at the sound of such speech. I do not believe that any man could comprehend his expositions unless God were with him. Now I--pitiful fool that I am--have allowed myself to become a joke in his eyes, for the whole time that I was thinking of him as a student, ignorant of who he was, I have come to see that he is my better. Now what can I say? Because I cannot endure the words that this boy speaks, nor do I find myself able to plumb their depths, I must surely leave this town. For seeing as how I am able to grasp neither beginning nor end of his exposition, an old man like me stands vanquished by a little child. It is no small matter to ascertain even the first thing about him. I tell you most assuredly, and do not lie when I say that from where I stand, the actions of this boy, the source of his speaking, and the thought that underlies his objective, seem to have nothing to do with those of mortal men. Hence I cannot tell whether he is a sorcerer, or a god, or if, perhaps, there is some angel of God speaking through him. From where he derives his essence, or from where he came, or what ever will become of him I cannot say." Turning to Joseph, he confessed, "You brought me a boy who is more knowledgeable than any master, as though he were in need of learning."

And turning to Mary the teacher affirmed, "This son of yours has not the slightest need of any teaching."

And even as the Jews were attempting to console Zacchaeus, the boy Jesus started to smile and to laugh out loud. Then he said to the sons of Israel who were standing there listening, "Let those among you who have borne no fruit now bring it forth, and let those whose hearts are blind now see, those who are lame now walk straight, the poor enjoy good things, the dead come back to life, and everyone be restored to their original stature to live in Him Who is the fountainhead of life and of eternal sweetness. I have come down here from on high that I might bring a curse on these for their own good, so that I might summon them again to what is above, even as it has been decreed by the One Who sent me."

And when the boy Jesus had spoken these things, those who had fallen victim to grave disorders were immediately healed. After that, no one dared to say a thing to him, or to hear anything from him, or to anger him for fear that they might be cursed by him and thereby suffer harm.

BOYS ROUGHHOUSING ON THE ROOF
(ArIn 19:4-11; InTh 9(8); PsMt 32)
Nazareth

Joseph and Mary then went away and took Jesus into the city of Nazareth, and he lived with his parents there. A few days later, on the first day of the week, Jesus was playing on a housetop in Nazareth with some other youngsters. One of them shoved another headlong to the ground from the upper floor, whereupon the child died. And when they saw it, all of the other children who had been playing with him ran away, leaving Jesus standing there by himself on the housetop where the boy had been pushed off. Now when the dead boy's parents heard of it, they ran over to that place in tears. And when they found the dead boy lying on the ground and Jesus standing up above, they supposed that he had pushed him down. And the dead boy's parents, who had not witnessed the event, confronted Joseph and Mary, saying, "Your son has thrown our boy to the ground, and now he is dead." But Jesus held his peace and did not answer. Then they looked up at Jesus and denounced him, accusing him of having thrown him off: "Surely it was you who threw our boy from the top of that house!" Joseph and Mary quickly ran over to where Jesus was; and his mother questioned him, "My Lord, tell me, was it you who pushed him down?" But Jesus denied it, answering, "I did not throw him off--he jumped down from it himself. He was simply being careless and hurled himself from the roof to his death." But they shouted and threatened him, saying, "Our son has been killed, and this is the one who murdered him!" And sizing up the situation, the Lord Jesus answered them, "Do not accuse me of a crime that you have no way of proving. Let us go and ask him ourselves. He will tell us what really happened." And immediately Jesus jumped down from the roof and yelled out as loud as he could, "Zeno! Zeno!" For that was the young boy's name. And Zeno answered Jesus, "Yes, Lord?" "Was I the one who pushed you from the roof to the ground?" Jesus asked him. "Get up and say who threw you down!" And at his word, the boy got up and worshiped Jesus saying, "Lord, you were not the one who threw me down. That indeed was someone else. Rather, it was you who raised me from death to life!"

And when they saw what had happened, everyone was astounded, including the parents of the previously dead boy. And when the Lord Jesus advised those who had gathered around to consider the boy's words carefully, they praised God for the miracle. And the parents praised God for the sign that Jesus had shown and worshiped him. Joseph, Mary, and Jesus then moved on to Jericho.

JESUS HEALS A MAN'S FOOT
(InTh 10(9))
Jericho

A few days later, in a nearby corner of that neighborhood, there was this man chopping wood who lost control of his ax, splitting open and severing the sole from his foot. He was bleeding so freely that he was near to death. Such a disturbance then arose in that place that many people ran up to him and gathered all around him. The boy Jesus ran there also, shoving his way through the midst of the crowd. He then took him by the foot, and healed the young man with just a touch. Then Jesus ordered him, "Get up! Split your wood, and think of me." The man got up and worshiped him, thanked him, and then began to split his wood.

And seeing what had happened, everyone there also gave thanks and marveled, worshipping the lad and confessing, "Without a doubt the Spirit of God is alive in this child."

JESUS DRAWS WATER
WITH HIS GARMENT
(ArIn 19:12-15; InTh 11(10); PsMt 33)
Jericho

Now when Jesus was six years old, his mother handed him a pitcher and sent him out with some children to draw water from the well and return with it. He pulled it out completely full, and after he had drawn it out, as he was walking in a crowd, one of the children bumped against him and hit the jug, whereupon he stumbled and it broke! And going over to the well, he laid out the garment he was wearing, drew up as much well water with it as had been in the pitcher, and carried it to his mother in his robe. And when his mother saw this astonishing miracle, she pondered it within herself, and she was completely amazed; she then hugged and kissed him all over. Mary etched this and all of the other wonders that she had seen in her heart, keeping the mysteries she had seen him perform to herself.

THE THREE MEASURES OF GRAIN
(PsMt 34)

Jericho

On another day, Jesus took a tiny measure of grain from his mother's storehouse and went out to the field and seeded it himself. Then it sprang forth and grew, bearing increase with astonishing speed. In time he harvested it alone; and it yielded him three measures, which he freely gave to his many friends.

JESUS, MARY, AND SALOME
HELP OUT JOHN THE BAPTIST
(LJB pt.10)
The Wilderness of Judea

Now as for the blessed John, he wandered with his mother out in the desert, and God supplied locusts and wild honey for him to eat, even as it had been spoken to his mother about him, that he might not let any unclean food pass through his mouth. After five years had come and gone, the devout, exalted, and aged mother Elizabeth passed away and the holy John sat weeping over her body. He had no idea how to enshroud or bury her, for he was but seven-and-a-half at the time of her passing. (Now the blessed Elizabeth died on the same day as had Herod, which was February the fifteenth.)

Jesus, who could see both the heavens and the earth, saw his cousin John sitting and wailing over his mother. And Jesus also started weeping at length, but no one knew the cause of his tears. When Mary saw the grieving of Jesus, she asked him, "Why are you weeping? Did Joseph or someone else scold you?" "No, mother," answered the Mouth Abounding with Life. "The truth is that Elizabeth, your aged kinswoman, has left my dearly beloved John an orphan. Even now he is weeping over her body, which is lying on the mountain."

When Mary heard this, she began to mourn over the loss of her kinswoman. "Weep not, dearest mother," Jesus consoled her. "We will go and visit her this very hour." And even as he was saying this to his mother, a bright cloud came down and settled in between them. Then Jesus said, "Call upon Salome, and have her come along with us." Then they all climbed onto the cloud, which flew them out to the wilderness of 'Ain Karim where John was sitting, and Elizabeth's body was laying. The Savior then commanded the cloud, "Drop us off on this side of it." Then the cloud, without delay, traveled there and went away. But the sound carried over to John. And when John heard the noise of their approach, he was afraid and abandoned the body of his mother. He then heard a voice that said, "John, do not be afraid. I am your kinsman Jesus. I have come with my mother to see to the proper burial of your own hallowed mother Elizabeth, for she is near of kin to my mother and me." When John heard this, he turned around and headed back in the direction of Christ and his mother Mary and embraced them. Then the Savior said to his mother, "Mother, Salome, rise up and wash her body off." They bathed it in the spring from which she used to wash herself and her boy. Mary then held John close and wept with him, cursing Herod for his many crimes.

Then the Angels Michael and Gabriel came down from the heavens and dug a grave. "Go now," said the Savior, "and return with the souls of Zechariah and Simeon the priest, that they might sing as you bury her body." Immediately Michael returned with the souls of Simeon and Zechariah, who placed the shroud over Elizabeth's body and sang for rather a while. Now the mother of Jesus wept, as did Salome, and the two priests traced the sign of the cross upon her corpse and prayed over it three times before laying it to rest in the grave. Then they buried her body there, sealing the plot with the sign of the cross, and they each returned in peace to their places. For seven days Jesus and his mother remained with John--consoling him on the loss of his mother, and teaching him how to survive in the desert. Then Jesus said to his mother, "Let us move on to where I can resume my work." And Mary burst into tears over the isolation of the young boy John, so she suggested, "Since he has been left an orphan and there's no one here to care for him, we will take him home with us." But Jesus replied, "This is not the will of my heavenly Father. He is to remain in the wilderness until the day that he's revealed to Israel. He will not remain in a wasteland full of wild beasts, but will instead walk in a desert full of prophets and angels, as though there were great multitudes of people there. Archangel Gabriel is also with us, and I have charged him with protecting John and granting him power from on high. What is more, I will make the water from this spring as sweet and pleasing to him as his own mother's milk. Who was it that watched over him in his youth? Oh, mother, do I not love him more than the world itself? Zechariah loved him too, and I have decreed that he should also come and care for John, for though his body lies buried in the ground, his soul indeed lives on."

Jesus spoke these words to his mother in the wilderness, even as John remained behind. They then climbed back onto the cloud, and John watched and grieved as they left him there. Mary agonized and mourned for John saying, "How wretched I feel, seeing you alone out here in the desert. Where is your father Zechariah? Where is your mother Elizabeth? Let them come today and weep alongside me." "Mother," Jesus reassured her, "do not weep over this child, for I will never forget him." And even as he was saying these things, behold, the cloud picked them up and carried them off to Nazareth. And while in Nazareth, Jesus fulfilled all things human except for sinning. And John lived in the desert with great simplicity and devotion. God and His angels were with him there, and his only nourishment came from grasses and wild honey. He prayed without ceasing, fasted often, and remained in expectation of the salvation of Israel.

JESUS COMMANDS CLAY ANIMALS
(ArIn 15:1-7)
Jericho?

One day, when the Lord Jesus was seven years old, he was playing with some friends of his who were about his age. As the boys were playing, they molded clay into various shapes--donkeys, cattle, birds, and other creatures. Each of them was boasting to the others about how much better their own was, and each of them was attempting to outdo the others. Finally the Lord Jesus said to the young men, "I will order the forms that I have fashioned to walk." And right away they started walking, and when he ordered them to return, all of them came back to him. He had, moreover, modeled images of sparrows and other birds, which flew around when he ordered them to fly, stayed in place when he said "hover," and ate and drank when he gave them food and drink. After a while, the boys went off and reported to their parents all that had happened, and their fathers all admonished them, "From now on, children, beware of his companionship, for he is an enchanter. Steer clear of him and have nothing at all to do with him, for from this time forward you are forbidden ever to play with him."

MIRACLE AT THE DYER'S
(ArIn 15:8-15; InTh: Paris Manuscript #239)
Jericho?

On another day, when the Lord Jesus was playing and running around with the boys, he passed by the shop of a dyer named Salem. There were many clothes in that shop belonging to the people of that town; each with orders to be dyed in various ways. He saw a young man dipping some clothing and leggings into a rather gloomy color, dying them according to the instructions given by each of his customers, and placing them into the vat. The boy Jesus, entering into the dyer's shop, approached the young man who was doing this, took all of the garments and threw them into the dryer. When Salem returned and saw that the clothes had all been ruined, he started to rant and to rave, and to take Jesus to task, saying, "Oh Son of Mary, what have you done to me? You have not wronged me alone, but my neighbors as well. They all wanted their clothing to be dyed properly, but you came along and ruined them entirely!"

Then the Lord Jesus answered him, "I will restore each and every piece to whatever color you wish." And he immediately started pulling the cloths from out of the dryer, and they all were colored as the dyer had intended. And when the Jews saw this amazing miracle, they all started praising God.

ANOTHER MIRACLE AT THE DYER'S
(GPh 37, 47; Qur 2:138)

The Lord entered into the shop of a dyer named Levi, took seventy-two different pigments and poured them all into the vat. Now as Jesus took them out, they all turned white. Then he said, "The Son has come as one who dyes in the selfsame manner."

God is a dyer, and even as the excellent dyes are called "true," and fuse with everything that is colored within them, so it also happens to whomever God dyes. Even as His are dyes of immortality, so also do they achieve eternal life by means of His tinctures. These days what God dips, He dips in water. We soak in the dye of God. Who can boast of a dye that is better than God's? Truly we will worship Him!

JESUS STRETCHES THE THRONE
(ArIn 16:1-16)
Jerusalem

Now whenever Joseph would go into town, he would take the Lord Jesus along. Whether his work involved making gates, milking buckets, sieves, or crates, anywhere that he would go, the Lord Jesus would go there with him. Now any time Joseph was working on something that needed lengthening or shortening; widening or narrowing, the Lord Jesus would reach his hand out toward it, and it would immediately become as he needed it to be. He therefore had no need to complete any job with his own two hands, for Joseph was not an expert in this line of work.

The king of Jerusalem once summoned Joseph and instructed him, "I want you to fashion a throne for me of precisely the same dimensions as the place where I usually sit." Joseph agreed and started working on the project. He labored for two whole years in the palace of the king before he was able to finish it off, and when he brought it to the spot to fit it in, he found that it was two spans short of the commissioned size on either side. And when the king saw it, he seethed with rage at Joseph. Joseph was so distraught over the king's anger, that he did not even eat his supper, but went straight to bed, taking nothing with him to eat.

The Lord Jesus then inquired, "What are you upset about?" "Because," Joseph replied, "I have wasted two whole years of labor in this effort!" "Do not fear," Jesus reassured him, "neither should you be distraught. You take hold of one side of the throne, and I will take hold of the other, and we will stretch it to its proper length." And when Joseph did what Jesus had said, and each had pulled as hard as they could, the throne obediently stretched itself to fit the space exactly.

When those who were standing there saw it, they were all astounded and gave praise to God, for this throne was made from the same kind of wood as was used in Solomon's day, decorated as it was with many intricate figures and designs.

THE BOYS WHO TURNED INTO GOATS
(ArIn 17:1-10)
Jerusalem?

On another occasion the Lord Jesus went out into the street, saw some young boys playing together, and went over to them to join in. But as soon as they caught sight of him, they all hid themselves from him, leaving him to look for them. The Lord Jesus came up to the gate of a certain house and asked the women standing there, "Where did all of those boys go?" And when they said that there were none around, the Lord Jesus asked them, "Who then are those that you can plainly see in that archway over there?" "Those are three-year-old goats," the women replied. Then Jesus shouted, "Hey you goats, come on over to your shepherd!" And the boys came out and frolicked all around him like goats. And when the women saw that, they were utterly astounded, and trembled. And right away they worshiped the Lord Jesus, begging him, "Oh Jesus, our Lord, and son of Mary, you are without question the Good Shepherd of Israel! Have mercy on your maidservants, who stand in your presence, Lord, and have no doubt that you have come to save and not destroy."

Then the Lord declared to them, "The children of Israel appear even as Ethiopes compared to the rest of mankind." "Lord," the women replied, "you know all things, and nothing can hide itself from you; but now we are asking you--even appealing to every mercy that is within you--to restore these boys to their prior state." Then he said, "Come on you guys, let's go and play!" And right in front of those women, the goats all changed back into boys.

THE KING KILLS THE SERPENT
(ArIn 18:1-19)
Jerusalem?

In the month of Adar, Jesus gathered the boys together, arranging them as would a king. They spread their clothes out on the ground so that he could have a seat. Then they fashioned a garland of flowers and placed it on his head. They then arrayed themselves to his left and right as guardians of the king. Now if anyone happened to pass him by, the boys would take hold of them and drive them along saying, "Come on over here and pay the king his due respect, that all may go well with you along your way."

And even as they carried on like this, some men came along bearing a boy upon a mat. This child, you see, had gone to gather wood up on the mountainside with some friends of his, where he came across a partridge's nest. He reached out his hand to collect the eggs, and without warning a venomous viper shot out of it and struck him on his hand. Then he shouted for his friends to come and help him out. But by the time they got to where the young boy was, he was already lying like a corpse upon the ground. His neighbors showed up a little while later and carried him back into town. Now when they arrived at the place where the Lord Jesus sat enthroned as a king-- and the other boys standing as his guardians--the youngsters raced to head off the snake-bitten child and said, "Come with us and pay the king the respect he is due."

When, however, out of their unbearable grief they declined, the boys compelled them, forcing them to against their wills. And when they got to the

Lord Jesus, he said, "Tell me why you are carrying that child?" And when they said that he had been bitten by a snake, the Lord Jesus said, "Let us go and slay that serpent." But when that boy's parents begged to be excused, seeing that their son was all but dead already, the young men said to them again, "Did you not hear the king's pronouncement, 'Let us go and slay that serpent'? Will you disobey him?" So they brought the stretcher back, though it really was against their wills. And when they arrived at the nest, the Lord Jesus asked the boys, "Is this where that serpent likes to hide?" "Yes it is," they all replied. Then the Lord Jesus called to the viper, and it slithered out submissively to him. And Jesus commanded the serpent, "Go right now and suck out all of the venom that you've injected into that boy!" So it skidded over to him and sucked all of it back out of him. Then the Lord Jesus cursed it, and the snake burst open and died.

And he placed his hand upon the lad, restoring him to his former state. And when the boy began to cry, the Lord Jesus said to him, "Wipe away your tears, for the day is coming when I will take you on as one of my disciples." This is he who is referred to as Simon the Canaanite in the gospel.

ONE KERNEL OF GRAIN YIELDS
A HUNDRED MEASURES
(InTh 12)
Jericho?

Once again, during the sowing season, the boy went out with his father to sow grain in their field. Now even as his father sowed, the boy Jesus planted but a single grain. And after harvesting and tossing it, he garnered fully one hundred measures from it. Then he called the needy of that town to the threshing floor and distributed the grain among them, and Joseph gathered what remained. He was eight when he worked this wonder.

THE LIONS WORSHIP JESUS
(PsMt 35)
Jericho, The Jordan River

There is this road which passes from Jericho over to the place on the Jordan River where the children of Israel had crossed over; and it is said that the Ark of the Covenant once rested there. Now Jesus, who by then was eight years old, left Jericho and headed out for the Jordan. This path was not safe for men to walk because over by the side of the road, not far from the riverbank, there was this cave where a lioness lay nursing her cubs. Jesus came from Jericho knowing full well that a lioness had recently brought forth a litter in that place, and he went right in before them all. Now as soon as the lions caught sight of Jesus, they all ran up and adored him. And the whole time that Jesus sat within the cave, the little cubs rubbed up against him and played with him, even as the older lions kept their distance and lowered their heads, worshipping him and patting their tails affectionately upon him. Now those who were standing off in the distance, unable to see Jesus said, "He would never have offered himself to the lions unless he or his parents had committed some serious offence." And as these people were speculating to one another, overwhelmed by their grief, behold, Jesus suddenly came out of the cave in plain sight of them all; the pride of lions going before him, and the cubs playing with each other all around his feet. And Jesus' mother and father stood, heads bowed, in the distance as they looked on. The others also kept their distance on account of the lions, not daring to approach them. Then he said to the people there, "How far superior are the untamed animals to the likes of you, seeing how they both recognize and venerate their Lord, whereas you men, even though you have been made in the image and likeness of God, have no idea who He is! Wild animals sense me and become docile; whereas men look right at me and do not even acknowledge me."

THE LIONS CROSS THE JORDAN
WITH JESUS
(PsMt 36)
The Jordan River

After this, the waters of the Jordan spread to the right and to the left, and Jesus went across before them all, attended by the lions. Then loud enough for all to hear, Jesus called out to the lions, "Now go in peace along your way, injuring no one, and may no man do you any harm until you return to the place from which you came." And they bid him farewell through their cries and their gestures. They then moved on to their proper domain.

JOSEPH AND JESUS STRETCH THE BEAM
(InTh 13(11); PsMt 37)

And when Jesus was eight years old, Joseph was commissioned by a wealthy young man to build for him a bed of six cubits, because at that time he was working as a carpenter specializing in wooden plows, yokes for oxen, farm equipment, and beds. Now Joseph went out to the field to collect some wood, and Jesus went along with him. He ordered his servant to cut a beam with an iron saw to the given length. But he did not keep to the specified measure, cutting one of the timbers a bit too short. And after sawing two wooden planks, he produced one and placed it up against the other. Then Joseph, noticing that one board was shorter than the other, grew troubled. He then measured it and confirmed that it was wanting, so he became frustrated and was not sure what to do about it. As he started thinking about what he should do, he headed off to find another. Now when Jesus saw what had happened, he understood that Joseph was perplexed; that from his point of view the situation seemed hopeless. He therefore comforted him, saying, "Come now, let us take hold of both ends of these beams and position them together, lining up the ends; for by fitting them together precisely and pulling them to ourselves, we will make the one the same as the other." And Joseph, unsure of what Jesus had in mind by saying this, did as he was told, since he knew full well that Jesus could do whatever he willed. So Joseph grabbed the ends of the two wooden beams and pressed them flush against the wall beside him, and Jesus took the opposite ends. Once again Jesus said, "Hold tight to this shorter piece." And Joseph, still bewildered, took hold of it. Jesus then grabbed the other end and stretched it to himself until it was the same as the other beam. "From now on," Jesus assured him, "be anxious for nothing, but go back now and finish your work, even as you have agreed to do, with nothing whatever to stand in your way." His father Joseph took it all in and was dumfounded. Then he hugged and kissed the boy, saying in his heart, "How blessed I am that God has given me a son like this!" Then Joseph went ahead and finished the job, even as he had promised.

And as soon as they returned to town, Joseph explained all that had happened to Mary. Now when Mary heard about and had seen the glorious miracles that were done by her Son, she exulted, worshipping him along with the Father and the Holy Spirit, now and forevermore; throughout an eternity of ages. Amen.

JESUS' SECOND VISIT TO A TEACHER
(InTh 14; PsMt 38; ArIn 20:13-16)
Jerusalem?

When all of the people started urging Joseph and Mary to enroll Jesus in a school so that he might learn his letters, Joseph came to accept just how much the boy truly understood for a child of his years, and that he was becoming much more mature. So he, not refusing, decided that Jesus should not go on any longer without learning them, and complied with the order of the elders. They took him to school a second time around, to an even more learned teacher, who would instruct him in human knowledge. "First I will teach him Greek," the teacher said to Joseph, "then I will move on to Hebrew." That teacher, you see, knew all about the knowledge that this boy possessed and it frightened him. Even so he wrote out the alphabet for him and went over it with him for several hours; but Jesus did not answer him. Then the instructor started teaching him in a forceful way, saying, "Say Alpha!" Then Jesus challenged him, "If you are such a clever teacher, and know the letters so well, then tell me the strength of the Alpha, and I will show you that of the Beta--or, if you prefer, you may tell me first what is the Beta, and then I will explain the Alpha." Now the teacher was enraged at this, but when he lifted his hand to flog the child, and beat him over the head, the boy winced in pain and cursed him, and his hand immediately withered. Then he fell face down to the ground and died. Then the boy returned to the house of Joseph and Mary.

Joseph, however, grew anxious and fearful. He called Jesus' mother Mary over to himself and issued her the following command: "Never again will we let him out of this house. Do not let him set so much as a single foot outside the door, because everyone who angers him ends up dead. Know that my soul suffers almost to death because of him! Who knows but that one day someone might strike and kill him out of rage!" "Oh man of God," Mary replied, "do not even think this way, but have faith instead that the One Who sent him as one born among mankind will keep him from all spite and in His name guard him against all evil."

FINAL ATTEMPT TO EDUCATE JESUS; JESUS TEACHES LIKE A TORRENT OF LIVING WATER
(InTh 15; PsMt 39)
Jerusalem?

Now a little while later the Jews asked Joseph a third time to coax Jesus into being schooled by yet another teacher. This teacher--someone who was close to Joseph--advised him, "Bring the boy to me at my school; and if I can win him over, perhaps I'll be able to teach him letters." And Joseph, knowing that it was impossible for any man to teach him anything, since his knowledge came from God alone, answered him, "Brother, if you think that you can teach him, then go ahead and take him to yourself." Joseph and Mary, fearful of the people, intimidated by the rulers, and broken by the priests, went ahead and delivered him up to the school despite the misgivings of Joseph. The boy, however, went along cheerfully. And Jesus walked boldly into the classroom, saw the book on the podium and, moved by the Holy Spirit, pulled it from the instructor's hands even as he was teaching from the law. Then in the sight and hearing of all, Jesus started reading and teaching them from out of the law, though he did not read from the words inscribed. It was instead through the power of the Living God that he opened his mouth and, by means of the Holy Spirit that he taught them all--as a never-ending flood of water gushing from a fountain of life! And it was with this kind of power that he taught the people the sublime things of the Living God. And the hearts of the people seated there changed to absolute astonishment upon hearing such words from him. And a great crowd gathered around, and they stood there, listening in amazement over the excellence of his teaching and the fluency of his speech. Everyone there, including the teacher, who dropped to the ground in adoration, was utterly astounded that a mere child like him could bring such things as these to light.

But as soon as Joseph heard of it, he grew anxious and raced over to Jesus at the school, wondering to himself if this teacher might, for his lack of experience with him, be dead already. But when the schoolmaster caught sight of Joseph, he confessed, "Brother, I realize that I took this boy on as a pupil, but he is brimming with all grace and wisdom. This is no mere student that you have brought to me, but a great teacher! Who can hear the words he speaks? Brother, I beg you, take him home with you." This fulfilled the Scripture that reads, "The river of God overflows with water. Their food You have readied, for even thus is the preparation thereof." And when the boy heard all these things, he quickly smiled at the teacher and said, "Because you have spoken so aptly and testified so truthfully, the one who was stricken will now be made whole." And just then his former instructor was healed. Then Joseph took the young man and returned to his home.

JOSEPH HEALS ANOTHER JOSEPH
(PsMt 40)
Capernaum

After this, because their enemies had been acting so spitefully toward them, Joseph took Jesus and Mary and went away to Capernaum by the sea. Now during the time that Jesus was there, there lived this other, rather wealthy man whose name also happened to be Joseph. But this man had withered up and died from an illness, and was laying lifeless on his bed. Now when Jesus heard the townspeople sorrowing and wailing and grieving over the departed, he asked Joseph, "Why not do this man a kindness that's in line with your benevolence, seeing that you and he both share the same name?" Joseph then inquired of Jesus, "How is it within my authority or capacity to do anything for this man?" And Jesus answered him, "Take the cloth off of your head and lay it over the face of the man who is dead, and say to him, 'The Anointed One is saving you.' The lifeless man will then be restored and rise again from his bed." Joseph, when he heard what Jesus had said, quickly rose up and ran into the house of the deceased, placed the cloth he had been wearing around his head over the face of the man on the bed and said, "Jesus is saving you." And the man who had died immediately got up from his bed and asked, "Who is this Jesus?"

JESUS BLOWS ON JAMES' SNAKE BITE
(ArIn 19:1-3; InTh 16; PsMt 41)
Bethlehem

They moved on from Capernaum to Bethlehem, where Joseph could stay with Mary and Jesus in his own house. One day Joseph summoned his eldest boy James and sent him out into the garden to collect herbs and firewood for the stew and return home with them. The young Jesus, however, tagged along behind him into the garden without either Joseph or Mary knowing about it. When they got to the spot where the firewood was, James started gathering vegetables, and behold, a poisonous snake shot out of its hole and bit James on the hand, whereupon he started yelling and screaming in great pain. Then he grew faint and cried out in anguish, "Oh, no! No! An accursed snake has bitten my hand!" The Lord Jesus, who was standing there across from him, hearing his cries of agony and seeing him in this state--all sprawled out and nearly dead--ran up to him, took him by the hand, and with nothing but a puff to the wound, he cooled it off, and James was immediately healed. His pain disappeared, and the serpent split apart.
    Joseph and Mary, when they heard the cry of James and the call of Jesus, ran to the garden unaware of what had happened, and found the snake dead and James healed.

JESUS REVIVES A DEAD CHILD

(InTh 17)
Bethlehem?

Now after this had come to pass, there happened to be a little child who lived near Joseph who had died from an illness, and his mother was crying out in bitter anguish. Hearing that horrible wailing and the ensuing commotion, Jesus hurried over there, found the child dead, laid his hand upon his chest and said, "I say to you, do not die, but go and live at your mother's side." And looking up, the child laughed. "Take this boy and suckle him," he instructed the woman, "and remember me." Now when the bystanders saw it, they were all amazed and they confessed, "Without a doubt, this lad is either himself a god or else he is an angel of God, for every single word he speaks brings about a reality." And Jesus left them there and went to play with some other children.

JESUS REVIVES A DEAD CONSTRUCTION WORKER
(InTh 18)
Bethlehem?

Some time later a rather large disturbance broke out where a house was being built, so Jesus got up and headed there. When he saw a man lying there dead, Jesus took him by the hand and said, "Get up sir, and do your work!" And the man rose right up and worshiped him. And when the people saw this thing, they were all astounded, and cried aloud, "This boy assuredly comes from heaven, since he has delivered so many from death, and as long as he remains alive, he has the power to save them all."

JESUS BLESSES HIS FAMILY; THE GLORY OF GOD SHINES UPON HIM
(PsMt 42)
Bethlehem?

Joseph took his sons, James, Joseph, Judah, Simeon, and his two daughters to a banquet. Jesus and his mother Mary met them there, along with her sister Mary, daughter of Cleophas. And when they had all arrived, he sanctified and blessed them all.

(The Lord God had given this Mary over to Cleophas and Anna, her father and mother, since they had presented Jesus' mother to the Lord. She was known by the same name, Mary, that her parents might feel somewhat consoled. Now Jesus would always be the first to eat, for not one of them would ever venture to dine, drink, recline at table, or break bread unless he had blessed them first. And if for some reason he was not present, they would wait around for him. And whenever he did not wish to come for food and drink, then neither did Joseph, Mary, or any of his brothers, the sons of Joseph. These brothers of his would obey him with all severity, seeing his life as the light of a lamp. And whenever Jesus would sleep, be it either night or day, the glory of God would shine on him. May all praise and honor be to him forevermore. Amen and amen!)

JESUS STAYS BEHIND IN THE TEMPLE
(Luke 2:41-43a; ArIn 21:1-8; InTh 19:1a)
Caravan to Nazareth, The Temple in Jerusalem

Every year, Jesus' parents would go to the Passover feast in Jerusalem. And when he was twelve years old they traveled up, as their custom was. And after the feast was over and they had satisfied the number of days required, they all started out for home. And even as they were all returning, the Lord Jesus headed back for Jerusalem. His parents knew nothing about him staying behind in the temple among the teachers, elders, and learned men of Jerusalem. He posed many questions to them and answered them concerning many issues having to do with their expertise.

For example, Jesus asked them: "Whose son is this 'Messiah'?" "David's," they replied. Jesus therefore questioned them, "Then why in the Spirit does David call him 'Lord' when it states, 'The Lord said to my Lord "Sit here to my right until I have made all who oppose you a stool for your feet?"'" Then this particularly eminent Rabbi prodded him, "Have you read books?" "Not only have I read books," Jesus replied, "but also what is in those books." Then he gave them a detailed explanation of the books of the Law--the rules, the legislations, and all of the riddles that were interwoven into the prophetic Scriptures--matters that were too profound for the mind of any ever to unravel. At that point the Rabbi said, "I have never seen, or even heard of such things before! What do all of you suppose will become of this boy?"

JESUS ASTONISHES AN ASTRONOMER
AND A PHILOSOPHER
(ArIn 20:9-21)
The Temple in Jerusalem

And when this astronomer who was there asked the Lord Jesus, "Have you ever studied astronomy?" he answered him by revealing to him the number of spheres and celestial objects, together with their triangular, square, and sextile facets; which ones moved prograde and which ones moved retrograde, their various proportions and their various forecasts, along with many other depths, never yet plumbed by the minds of men.

There was also this Philosopher among them who was very skilled in medicine and the physical sciences, who asked the Lord Jesus, "Have you ever studied medicine?" He answered him with an explanation of both medicine and its theoretical underpinnings. Moreover, he defined precisely what lies above the powers of nature, along with all that is subject thereto; the physical potential, and the interactions between the body and its fluids, and how they respond to one another. He also revealed the number of its constituent parts, such as bones, arteries, veins, and nerves; the various physical aspects of the body, namely warmth and dryness, coolness and moisture, as well as their various functions; how the soul controls the body, and the various senses and modalities that are open to them; the capacity for language; desire and anger; and last of all, the composition and decomposition of the body; and a whole host of other subjects that have eluded the grasp of all mankind. Then that philosopher got up and worshiped Jesus, saying, "Oh Jesus, my Lord! From now on, I will follow you and work for you."

JOSEPH AND MARY DISCOVER THAT JESUS IS MISSING
(Luke 2:43b; InTh 19:1b-5; ArIn 21:22-29)
Caravan to Nazareth, The Temple in Jerusalem

But his parents imagined that Jesus must have been in the crowd with them somewhere. And after they had done a full day's walking, they went looking for him among their kin, and when he was nowhere to be found, they grew troubled and headed back to the city to search for him. They found him at last on the third day, sitting in the temple amid the Teachers, hearing the law and posing questions to them. And all of those who heard him there were astounded by his understanding and his exposition. And everyone there paid careful attention to him and wondered how in the world a mere child like this could throw so much light on passages from out of the law and parables within the prophets, leaving the elders and the Teachers of the People utterly unable to speak.

It was even as they were all addressing these and other issues that the Lady Saint Mary came walking in after having wandered around all over with Joseph for three days seeking after him. And when she saw that he was seated in the presence of doctors, asking them questions and giving them answers, Joseph and Mary were both astonished. Then his mother Mary approached him and asked, "Why have you put us through all this, my child? I'll have you know that your father and I have gone through a great deal of trouble in searching for you, and we worried about you all that time!" Jesus then replied to them, "Why did you go looking all over? Were you not aware that it was needful for me to be employed in the house of my Father, taking care of His affairs?" But they failed to grasp the sense in which he meant for them to hear his words.

But the scribes and Pharisees then spoke up, "Are you the mother of this lad?" "Yes I am," she replied. "Oh Mary," they all confessed, "how joyful are you among women! You are truly blessed to have brought forth a boy like him, for such a blessing has God lavished on the fruit of your womb! Never before have we seen or heard such glorious and excellent wisdom." Jesus then rose up and followed his mother, going down with them, and traveling with them on to Nazareth, where he lived in obedience to them. His mother treasured up all that had been said in her heart. And Jesus waxed ever wiser and wiser, growing continually in grace and stature; and in the esteem of God and men. To him be boundless glory forevermore. Amen.

JESUS BEGINS TO HIDE HIS ACTIVITIES;

DILIGENTLY STUDIES THE LAW
(ArIn 22)
Nazareth

This marks the time when Jesus began hiding his miracles and secret works. He dedicated himself to a careful study of the law until the end of his thirtieth year, the age at which the Father acknowledged him openly at the Jordan with the sound of His voice, and the Holy Spirit in the form of a dove, addressing him with this declaration from the sky above: "This is My Son, whom I love and in whom I take delight!" He is the one we worship with all honor, because he brought us from the womb of our mother; calling us into being and bringing us to life. He who for our sakes has taken on a human form and rescued us, that he might embrace us with eternal kindness, and freely show us the greatness and abundance of his mercy and goodness. May all glory, praise, power and dominion be to him from now on and forevermore. Amen.

INTRODUCTION TO THE LIFE OF JOSEPH THE CARPENTER; INSTRUCTIONS TO SPREAD THE GOSPEL
(HJC Intro, 1)

{In the name of God; three Who are comprised of one. The narrative of the death of our father, the aged and venerable Joseph the carpenter. Brothers, may his blessings and his prayers sustain us all. Amen.

His entire lifetime amounted to one hundred and eleven years, and his passing from this world took place on the twenty-sixth of Abib, which is also known as Ab. May we be upheld by his prayer! Amen. And it was truly none other than our Lord Jesus Christ who disclosed this narrative to his most reverend disciples on the Mount of Olives; all about the labors of Joseph, and also of his final days. And the holy apostles preserved this address, and left it in written form in the Jerusalem library. May their prayers sustain us all! Amen.}

One day it happened that our Lord, God, and Savior Jesus Christ, was sitting on the Mount of Olives with his followers who had gathered there. And he addressed them as follows: "Brothers, friends, and sons whom the Father has chosen out of all mankind; you know how I have frequently spoken to you about the crucifixion I must undergo, and of the death that I must endure in order to redeem Adam and his children, and how I will arise from death. I will now entrust you with the teaching of the sacred gospel which has been preached to you already, so that you might make it known around the world. I will, moreover, give you power from on high, filling you with the Holy Spirit. And you are to preach repentance and the remission of sin throughout each and every nation. For if a man could find so much as a single cup of water that is from the world to come, it would seem far greater and more vast to him than the collective riches of this earth. Moreover, the ground covered by even a single foot in my Father's house is beyond the wealth of the entire world. Truly a single, joyful hour in the home of the godly is more gracious and dear than a thousand years among evildoers: since their wailing and mourning will never cease, nor ever will their tears stop flowing, nor will they even once enjoy any comfort or rest.

"And now, oh my distinguished members, go and proclaim this in every nation, saying to them, 'Truly the Savior, the Administrator of Justice, is looking diligently into the inheritance that is due. And the angels will throw down their opponents and fight on their behalf on the Day of Battle. And he will closely scrutinize every senseless and baseless word that mankind has spoken, and they will all be forced to give account. For even as death is inescapable, so also will every single one of man's works, whether they are good or bad, be spread out on the Day of Judgment.' Also, be sure to relate to them this message I am giving you today, 'Let not the strong man glory in his might, nor the rich man in his wealth; but if any man must glory, let him glorify the Lord.'"

THE DEATH OF JOSEPH
(HJC 10-32; ArIn 22:7b)

After many years had come and gone, the elderly Joseph arrived at a ripe old age. Despite working continuously, his body never grew frail, nor did his vision ever fail, nor ever did his teeth fall out, nor was he ever senile his whole life long; but he, like a young lad, went about his business spryly and energetically, with his arms and legs intact and free from aches and pains. His lifetime amounted to one hundred and eleven years in all, stretching his days to their furthest extent.

Now two of Joseph's oldest boys, Justus and Simeon, were married and had their own families. Both of his daughters were also married and living in their own homes. That left Joses and the Lesser James living in Joseph's house with my virgin mother. I lived with them blamelessly as one of his sons, calling Mary my mother and Joseph my father, doing whatever they would tell me to. I never defied them, but always obeyed them no matter what they would say, even as other men who are brought forth on this earth are inclined to do. I never did provoke them to anger, nor did I talk back to them, or contradict them, either. On the contrary, as the apple of my eye did I lavish them both with love and affection.

And after all this, it happened that the death and passing from this world of the pious and elderly Joseph was drawing near, as is the case for every man that is born of this earth. And even as he was at the point of death, an angel of the Lord informed him that his passing was near. He therefore grew fearful and perplexed. He then rose up and traveled on to Jerusalem. And when he went into the Lord's temple, he poured forth his prayers before the sanctuary, pleading, "Oh, God, author of every solace; God of all pity, and Lord over the whole human race; God of my soul; God of my body; and God of my spirit; I worship You and plead with You. Oh, my Lord, my God, if my days are at an end, and the hour of my passing from this world is at hand, I beg of You, send Michael, the great prince of Your holy angels, to accompany me, that my miserable soul might leave this tortured frame of mine without incident; free from any threat or fear. For unspeakable fear and dread seize all bodies on their dying day; be they either male or female, wild or domestic animal, or whatever crawls along the ground, or flies through the air. Every creature under heaven that breathes in the breath of life becomes panic-stricken as their souls fearfully and woefully pass away from their bodies. Oh, my Lord and my God, let Your holy angel be there to help ease the separation between my body and soul, and do not let the face of the guardian angel appointed to me from the time of my birth turn away from me now; but may he accompany me on my journey even until he brings me to You. Let his expression be pleasing to me and comfort my heart, and let him go with me in peace. Let not the demons approach me with their frightful faces on the way that I must go, until I arrive in Your delightful presence. Let not the gatekeepers keep my soul from paradise. Show not forth my sins so as to condemn me before the terror of Your judgment seat. Do not permit the lions to lunge on me, nor allow the swells of the fiery sea to overwhelm my soul before I have gazed upon Your face, so glorious and divine; for every soul must face these things. Oh, God, most upright Judge, Who with justice and fairness will pass judgment on all mankind, and will pay them back for what they have done. Oh, my Lord, my God, I beg of You, draw near to me with Your compassion, and shine Your light upon my path, that I might draw near to You; for You are a fountain overflowing with every glorious thing, and are possessed of everlasting glory. Amen."

And it happened afterward that when he had returned to his own home in Nazareth of Galilee, Joseph was stricken by an illness that confined him to his bed. And it was at that time that he passed on, as is the lot of all mankind. This disease, you see, completely overwhelmed him. From the day that he was born, he had never yet suffered such an affliction, and truly it pleased Christ to arrange this end for the righteous Joseph. And for forty years he remained unwed; afterward he cared for his wife another forty-nine until she died. And one year after she had died, the priests entrusted my mother, the blessed Mary to him, to look after her until such time as she should wed. She lived in his house for two whole years; and during her third year in the house of Joseph, when she was fifteen, she brought me into this world by a means so mysterious that no created being can recount it, nor yet understand it, but only myself, my Father, and the Holy Spirit, who are of one substance with me.

The age of my father therefore, that venerable old man, was one hundred and eleven years, as it had been decreed by my Father in heaven. And it was on the twenty-sixth of Abib that his soul left his body. For it was then that the choice gold started to lose its luster, and the silver to wear out through use. (By this I mean his wisdom and his intellect.) He also refused all food and drink. And having lost his carpentry skills, he began to let his business go. And so it happened that, in the early morning hours of the twenty-sixth day of Abib, that that honorable man, the aged Joseph, lay upon his bed, surrendering his troubled soul. He therefore opened his mouth and cried:

"Cursed was the day I was brought into this world!
Cursed was the womb that carried me!
Cursed were the bowels that moved for me!
Cursed were the feet that I sat and rested on!
Cursed were the breasts that nursed me!
Cursed were the hands that carried me
And cared for me until I was grown!
For in sin was I conceived,
And in sin did my mother long for me.
Cursed are my lips and my tongue,
Which have brought up and spoken foolishness, scandal,
Lies, ignorance, ridicule, gossip, dishonesty, and hypocrisy!
Cursed are my eyes,
Which have gazed upon scandal!
Cursed are my ears,
Which have rejoiced in the slanderous words of others!
Cursed are my hands,
Which have taken things that were not theirs!
Cursed are my stomach and my guts,
Which have longed for forbidden foods!
Cursed is my throat, which as a blazing fire
Has consumed all that it has come across!
Cursed are my feet, which have taken paths offensive to God!
Cursed is my body, as is also my pathetic soul,
Which has already deserted God, Who fashioned it!

What will I do when I am made to stand before the Righteous Judge; when He will demand an account for all the deeds that have been accumulating from my youth? Cursed is every man who dies in his sins! Behold, that same event that overtook my father Jacob as his soul sailed away from his body has truly overtaken me! Oh, how miserable I am today, and fit to be mourned! God, however, and no one else, will concern Himself with my body and soul; and deal with them as He sees fit."

Then I went over to Joseph and found his soul in its distress, for he was suffering terribly. And I said to him, "Bless you, father Joseph! How are you feeling, oh man of honor?" And he responded, "Bless you too, my beloved son. Truly do I say to you that pain and fear encompass me, but my soul grew still when I heard your voice. Oh Jesus of Nazareth! Jesus who rescues me! Jesus who sets my soul free! Jesus who defends me! Oh, Jesus! How sweet is your name in my mouth--and in the mouths of all who cherish it! Oh All-Seeing Eye, and All-Hearing Ear, hearken to the words I speak! I worship you and serve you today in all humility, and my tears rain down before your face. You are my God, and my Lord, even as the angel has reminded me so many times, particularly on that day when wayward thoughts tossed my soul to and fro concerning the holy and virgin Mary, of whom I was secretly plotting to rid myself, though she was bearing you within her womb. At the time that I was weighing my options, behold, these angels of the Lord appeared in my sleep, and related this incredible mystery to me: 'Joseph, son of David, do not fear to take on Mary as your wife. Do not be sad or speak such unbecoming words with regard to her conception, for she is carrying the child of the Divine Inspiration, and will bring a son into the world, who will be called Jesus, since he will free his people from their sins.' Oh my Lord, please do not permit me to suffer because of my lack of knowledge concerning your birth, neither of the mystery involved. Oh my Lord, I also recall the occasion when that boy died of a snakebite--how his family wished to turn you over to Herod, accusing you of killing him--but even so, you brought him back from death and restored him to his mother and father. How I then came up to you, grabbed your hand and admonished you, 'Watch yourself, my son!' At that time you answered me, 'Are you not seen as my fleshly father? I will show you who I truly am!' For all of these reasons, my Lord and my God, please do not be mad at me, nor call me to account for that instance. I am your servant, your servant girl's son; but you are my Lord, my God and my Deliverer, and assuredly the Son of God."

Now when my father Joseph had spoken this, he was worn from all his weeping. And I could see that death clearly held him in its sway. Then my unblemished virgin mother stood to her feet, walked over to me and said, "Oh, my beloved son, this honorable old man Joseph is even now at the point of death." "Oh, dearest mother," I replied, "truly the burden of death is shared by all things that are brought forth on earth; for death has its way with all of mankind. Even you, oh virgin mother, must experience the same fate as other mortals. Nevertheless, neither your departure, nor that of this righteous man, qualifies as the true death, but rather as eternal life. Furthermore, even I must die with regard to the body that I got from you. Even so, rise up dearest mother of mine, and go over to the blessed old man Joseph, that you might bear witness to all that takes place as his soul rises up from his body."

My spotless mother Mary walked over to where Joseph was and went inside. There at his feet I sat and watched over him, for by then the signs of death could be seen in his face. And that honorable old man lifted up his head and fixed his eyes upon me, but had no strength to speak to me on account of the pains of death that had taken him. But he kept on gasping for air, and I held his hands for an entire hour, at which time he turned and looked at me, motioning to me not to leave his side. At that moment, I held my hand up to his chest, and sensed his soul around his throat, ready to depart its chamber.

And when my virgin mother saw me touching his body, she felt his feet. And when she found that they were lifeless and cold, she said to me, "Oh, my beloved son, truly his feet are stiffening, and are even now as cold as snow." She then called Joseph's sons and daughters, saying, "Come now, all of you, and gather all around your father; for he is surely at the gates of death." Then his daughter Assia remarked, "Oh my brothers, this is certainly the same affliction that claimed the life of my own dear mother!" And she mourned and wept in bitterness; whereupon all of Joseph's other children likewise cried alongside her, my mother and myself weeping along with them.

And glancing southward, I saw Death already drawing near, and all of Gehenna with him, closely guarded by his army and his helpers; flames shooting out of their clothing, faces, and mouths. And when my father Joseph saw them coming, his eyes welled up with tears, and at that moment he groaned in a very strange way. When I saw him gasping furiously, I pushed Death back, and all his minions. And I called upon my Holy Father and said, "Oh Father of Every Mercy--the All-Seeing Eye and the All-Hearing Ear--hearken to my prayers and petitions on behalf of the elderly Joseph. Send in the brightness of all Your angels, Michael, the Prince of Angels, together with Gabriel, the Proclaimer of Light. Allow the entire host of them to walk alongside the soul of my father Joseph until they bring it near to You. This is the moment when my father needs Your compassion the most." (And I say to you also that each and every saint--indeed each and every man that is born to this world, be they either just or corrupt--must necessarily pass away.)

Then Michael and Gabriel approached the soul of my father Joseph. Then they took and wrapped it in a glistening cloth. This was the means by which his spirit was given into the hands of my good Father, Who granted him peace. None of his children yet knew that Joseph had died. And the angels defended his soul from the demons of darkness who were blocking the way, glorifying God until they had conveyed it into the abode of the devout.

Now his corpse was lying flat on its back and devoid of blood. I therefore reached out and straightened his eyes, shut his mouth with my own hand, and said to the Virgin Mary, "Oh, mother of mine, where is that ability which he so aptly showed throughout his lifetime in this world? Sadly, it has gone away, and is as though it never was." And when his children overheard my conversation with my spotless and virgin mother, they knew that he had breathed his last, and they burst into tears and mourned for him. "Your father's death," I explained to them, "is in truth not really death, but rather it is endless life: for he has been freed from this world and its concerns, and has moved on to endless and eternal rest." And hearing these words, they tore their clothes and wept aloud.

And the people of Nazareth and Galilee converged on the scene when they heard their weeping,. And they wept from the third hour all the way until the ninth. At the ninth hour they all went to the bed of Joseph, where they rubbed his body with precious ointments and raised it up. But I prayed that same prayer to my Father in the heavenly language which I had made with my own hand before I was carried in the womb of my mother Mary. And when I had completed it, I said "Amen," and the entire host of angels appeared. And I ordered two of them to extend their glistening robes and to enshroud the body of the blessed old man Joseph in them.

At that point I spoke to Joseph, saying, "The stench of death and corruption will have no power over you, nor will so much as a single worm ever come from out of your body. None of its limbs will ever be broken, nor will a hair on your head be moved from its place. Oh Joseph, my father, no part of your body will ever be lost, but it will remain intact and never decompose, even until the thousand-year feast. I will bless and repay in the assembly of virgins anyone who should make an offering on your special day. And on the day of your memorial, whosoever should feed the wretched, the poor, the widows, and the orphans in your name from the work of his hands will never lack anything good as long as he lives. And to anyone who has so much as offered a cup of water or wine to drink to either widow or orphan in your name, I will place him in your care, that you may travel along with him as he enters into the millennial feast. And to every man who should offer a gift on the day of your commemoration, I will bless and repay in the assembly of virgins: to one I will give thirty times over, to another, sixty, and to yet another, a hundred. And as for anyone who should write down the story of your life, and of your labors, and of your passing from this earth--and even this narrative that is from my mouth--him I will commit to your keeping as long as he lives. And when his soul leaves his body and he has parted from this realm, I will burn the book of his sins and not afflict him with any penalty on Judgment Day; but he will travel through the sea of flames, passing across without trouble or pain. And to every poor man who can offer none of these things, this will be what he should do: if a son is born to him, he is to name him Joseph, so that neither poverty nor untimely death might ever come to pass in that house."

After this, the leading men of that town gathered together at the spot where Joseph's body had been placed, bringing with them burial shrouds with which they wished to wrap him up, according to the way the Jews prepare the bodies of their dead. But they found that his shroud held tight--clinging like iron to his body--for when they would have taken it off, they found it impossible to loosen or budge, nor could they find a linen edge, which astonished them to no end. Finally they carried him over to a place where there was a cave and opened the gate so they could lay his body to rest alongside those of his forebears. Just then I called to mind the day that he traveled with me into Egypt, and of the tremendous hardships that for my sake he was compelled to endure. And I mourned his passing for quite some time; saying as I was sprawled out over his corpse: "Oh Death, which causes all knowledge to disappear and brings about tears and sorrows in abundance, surely it is my Father, God Himself, who has given you this power. Because men perish for the transgression of Adam and his wife Eve, and Death does not spare anyone. Even so, nothing ever happens to anyone, or is brought upon him without my Father commanding it first. Surely there have been men whose lives reached nine hundred years; but even these have passed away. And though there were others who lived even longer, all of them have come to this end, and not one of them can say, 'I have never tasted death.' For the Lord does not send the same affliction twice; hence it has satisfied my Father to inflict it upon mankind but once.

"Death goes out the very instant that it sees the order coming down from heaven, and says, 'I will go forth against that man, and afflict him most grievously.' Then, in a flash it sets upon the soul and overpowers it, doing with it as it pleases. Because Adam violated my Father's decree, you see, and failed to act in line with His will, the anger of my Father seethed over him, and He then condemned him to death; and this was how Death came into the world. If, however, Adam had kept my Father's laws, Death would never have gotten the better of him. Don't you know that I could ask my Father to send me down a chariot of fire to take my father Joseph's body up to the peaceful place that it might live among the spirits there? But because of Adam's disobedience, the trouble and violence that come with Death has befallen all of mankind. And it is for this reason that I myself must die in the flesh; that I might secure grace for those who are my handiwork."

Having said this, I embraced the body of my father Joseph, and wept over it. Then they opened the mouth of the tomb and placed his body into it, near to that of his father Jacob. And at the time of his passing, he had lived one hundred and eleven years. Never had a tooth in his mouth pained him, nor had his eyesight ever grown dim, nor ever did his body bend, or his strength ever fail him, but he worked at his carpenter's trade even until his dying day, which was on the twenty-sixth of Abib. And after Joseph, who was worn out by old age, had died and received a burial alongside his forebears, the blessed Mary went to live with her sisters' children.

And when we apostles heard these words from our Savior, we rose up in joy and prostrated ourselves in his honor. "Oh Savior of us all," we implored him, "show us your grace. Now we all have heard the life-giving word! Even so, we still have questions about the fates of Enoch and Elijah, oh Savior of ours, for they were both reprieved from death. For truly they dwell in the place of the just even unto this very day, nor have their bodies known decay. Even so, that aged carpenter, Joseph was, after all, your father according to the flesh. And you have ordered us to go throughout the world and preach to them your holy Gospel; and you have said, 'Relate to them the account of the passing of my father Joseph, and honor him every year with a solemn holiday and festival, and let them know that anyone who takes anything away from this narrative, or adds anything to it, sins by so doing.' Yet we are especially eager to understand why it is that you did not cause Joseph to be immortal like these, though he called you his son from the day that you were born in Bethlehem, and you say yourself that he was both chosen and righteous?"

And our Savior answered us, "Truly my Father's prophecy regarding the disobedience of Adam has now been fulfilled. Everything is ordered by my Father according to His will and pleasure. For if any man should despise the commands of God, and in imitation of the devil continue to sin, his life is prolonged, that he might have a change of heart, and think about how he must be given over to death. If, however, anyone is quick to do good works, his life is also prolonged, that the more his life is lengthened and discussed, the more that upright men might imitate him. But when you see a man whose mind tends toward anger, his days are indeed cut short; for these are the ones who are taken in the prime of their lives. Therefore every prophecy that has been spoken by my Father concerning mankind must be fulfilled in every one of its aspects. Yet with regard to Enoch and Elijah, and how they are alive to this day in the very flesh in which they were born, and with regard to my father Joseph, whose body has not been spared as were theirs; indeed, even if a man were to live many thousands of years upon this earth, he would nevertheless at some point be compelled to exchange his life for death. And my brothers I say to you that Enoch and Elijah must return to this world toward the close of time and be slain as well. To be more specific, this will happen on the day of upset, terror, confusion, and evil. For because of the reproach with which he will be revealed, the Antichrist will mutilate the bodies of the four who are to disgrace him utterly when they expose him for his ungodliness during the time that they are alive, and he will pour their blood out like water."

"Oh, our Lord, God, and Savior," we asked, "who are these four about whom you have spoken, those whom the Antichrist will cut off on account of the reproach that they will lay to his charge?" "They are Enoch, Elijah, Schila, and Tabitha," the Lord replied. When we heard our Savior say this to us, we all exulted and rejoiced, giving glory and thanks to the Lord God, and our Savior, Jesus Christ. To him be glory, honor, dignity, power, authority, and praise, the good Father along with him, together with the life-giving Holy Spirit, from now on and forevermore. Amen.

{Here ends the complete Infancy Gospel, which through the aid of the Most High God has been completed in accordance with what we found written in the original.}

MINISTRY 1

INTRODUCTION TO JESUS' MINISTRY; HIS PHYSICAL DESCRIPTION
(Mark 1:1; Luke 3:1; Lentulus to Tiberius)
Judea

Here begins the gospel of Jesus Christ, the Son of God.

In the fifteenth year of the reign of Tiberius Caesar, Pontius Pilate was the governor of Judea, and Herod was the tetrarch of Galilee. Philip, his brother, was the tetrarch of Ituraea and Trachontis, and Lysanias was the tetrarch of Abiline. In those days there emerged, and to this day exists, a man of tremendous might named Jesus Christ, who is referred to as the Prophet of Truth by the Gentiles, and the Son of God by his own disciples, since he raises the dead and heals the ill. He is a man of average height, handsome and dignified in his appearance, giving those who look on him a feeling of love and at the same time fear. His hair is the same shade as an unripe hazelnut, and is straight nearly to his ears, but from that point down, it becomes darker, curlier, and shinier; flowing over his shoulders and parting down the middle of his head as is typical of Nazarenes. His brow is gentle and serene, and his face has neither wrinkles nor flaws, and its comeliness is enhanced by a slight ruddiness thereto. There is no defect to be found on either his nose or his mouth. His beard is full, and about the same shade as his hair; not too long, but parting a bit below the chin. His expression is one of mature simplicity, with sparklingly clear gray eyes. His rebuke is fearful, but his warnings are humane and motivated by love, that is to say he strikes a balance between lightheartedness and solemnity. On occasion he has wept, but he has never indulged in laughter. He stands tall and straight, with particularly arresting hands and arms. His manner of speaking is serious, measured, and down to earth; more captivating than the children of men.

THE MINISTRY OF JOHN THE BAPTIST
(Matt 3:1-12; Mark 1:2-8; Luke 3:2-18; John 1:19-28;
GEb 1, Quote by Epiphanius, Heresies 30.3;
GEb 3, Quote by Epiphanius, Heresies 30.13)
Judean Countryside Near the Jordan River

Now in the days when Annas and Caiaphas were high priests, the Word of God came to visit this man in the Judean countryside by the name of John, who was a descendant of Aaron the priest; the son of Zechariah and Elizabeth.

John turned up at the Jordan River and traveled throughout the regions of Judea to either side thereof, preaching a baptism that changed peoples' hearts; of rededication and forgiveness of sins, saying, "You must turn your lives around, for the kingdom of heaven is drawing near." This was he who was prophesied of in accordance with what is written in the Book of the Oracles of Isaiah the Prophet:

"Behold, I will send a messenger ahead of you
Who will make arrangements for your arrival.
The voice of someone crying in a wilderness,
'Everyone, make all things ready for
The coming of the Lord!
Make every one of his ways plain.
Every valley will be filled in,
And every mountain and hill will be made flat.
The crooked roads will be made straight,
And the bumpy roads will be made smooth.
Then all men will be convinced of God's salvation.'"

John's clothes were woven from camel's hair, and he wore a leather belt around his waist. For nourishment he ate locusts and natural, raw honey that tasted like manna, like a cake pan-cooked in oil. Everyone in the Judean countryside, the regions along the Jordan, and Jerusalem, went out to him. They confessed their sins and were baptized by him in the Jordan River.

But when John saw that many of the Pharisees and Sadducees were coming to him to be baptized, he cried out to them, "You brood of vipers, who counseled you to flee from the judgment to come? Produce results consistent with true penitence. Now do not say to one another, (or) think to yourselves that you can say, 'Our father is Abraham,' because I am telling you now that God can transform even these very rocks into children of Abraham. The ax is already laid at the roots of the trees, and every tree that fails to bring forth fit fruit will be chopped up and relegated to the flames."

And those who were assembled said, "Well then, explain to us what we must do?" And John replied, "Any man who has two garments should give to someone who has none, and whoever has food should do likewise." Tax-collectors were also coming to him to be baptized, so they asked him, "Teacher, what are we supposed to do?" And he replied, "Only collect the amount that's due." Then some soldiers who were there inquired, "What are we supposed to do?" And he responded, "Be content with what you earn, accuse no one falsely, neither extort any money from anyone."

All of these people were waiting in expectation, wondering to themselves if John were indeed the Messiah. Now this was John's answer to the priests and the Levites when the Jews of Jerusalem sent them out to ask him who he was. He did not fail to acknowledge, but freely admitted, "I am not the Messiah." They asked him, "Who are you then? You must be Elijah." "I am not!" He replied. "How about the Prophet?" He answered them, "No!" Finally they asked him, "Who are you, then. Give us a statement to take back to those who sent us. What is it that you say of yourself?" John answered them with the words of the prophet Isaiah,

"Mine is the voice of one crying in a wilderness,
'Make every one of his ways straight!'"

Now some from among the Pharisees who had been sent prodded him, "If you are not the Messiah, nor Elijah, nor the Prophet, then why do you baptize?" John responded to the people there and removed all doubt. This was what he had to say:

"I baptize you in the water of repentance,
But there is one who stands among you--
Someone who you do not know,
Someone who is greater than I.
He is following on my heels.
It is he who comes after me,
Whose sandals I am not fit to carry.
Nor am I so worthy as to bend down
And untie the laces thereof.
He will baptize you with Holy Spirit
And with fire.
His sifting fork is in his hand
To empty out his threshing floor
And gather his wheat into his barn.
But the chaff he will burn
In unquenchable flames."

All of these things took place at Bethany, on the other side of the Jordan, where John was baptizing. And John spurred them on with many such words, preaching the gospel to the people.

JOHN BAPTIZES JESUS
(Matt 3:3-17; Mark 1:9-11; Luke 3:21-3; John 1:29-32;
GHb 2, Quote by Jerome, Against Pelagians 3; GHb 3,
Quote by Jerome, Commentary on Isaiah 4, concerning
Isa 11:2; GEb 4, Quote by Epiphanius, Heresies 30.13;
Severus, Syriac Baptismal Liturgy; DTry 88:3)
The Jordan River

One day, when the people were being baptized, the Lord's mother and brothers said to him, "John the Baptist is washing for the forgiveness of sins. Let's all go and be baptized by him." "In what way have I erred?" Jesus replied. "Why should I go and be baptized by him? That would only be fitting if I did not understand my own teaching."
At that time Jesus came from Nazareth in Galilee over to the Jordan to be baptized by John. The next day John saw Jesus heading his way and said, "Behold, it's God's Lamb of Atonement for the sins of the world! This is the one I was talking about when I said to you, 'A man who comes after me surpasses

me, since he went before me.' I never did know him myself, but the reason I came washing with water in the first place was so that I might reveal him to Israel." Even so, Jesus also was baptized, though John tried to discourage him, saying, "I ought to be baptized by you, and here you are coming to me?" "Let it be this way for now," Jesus replied. "It is proper insofar as it allows for the forgiveness of all." Only then did John consent. Now John was standing up above the waters as Christ went down into them to receive baptism in the Jordan. And just then a great light blazed forth all around; and fire was visible upon the water, such that all who were there were afraid. And even as Jesus was praying there and being baptized, he rose up from the water and the sky started spreading apart. On his way up and out of the water, Jesus saw the sky splitting open and the entire wellspring of the Holy Spirit plunging down-- perching upon him in physical form like a dove (and) filling him. (For truly the Lord is the Spirit, and wherever the Spirit manifests, liberation ensues.) And a voice came from the sky: "You are My Son and I love you. You bring Me great joy! This very day I have become your Father. I awaited you in all the prophets, Son, biding My time until your arrival, that I might settle all things in you. For you are My rest, My firstborn Son, who rules forever." And right away a bright light illumined that place. And when John saw all of this, he asked him, "Who are you?" And once again a voice from the heavens confirmed, "This is My precious Son. He pleases Me immensely, (and) I accept him completely!" Then John knelt down before him and pleaded, "Lord, I beg you to baptize me!" But Jesus refused, saying, "That will not be necessary. This is the means by which all things are to be fulfilled." And Jesus was about thirty years old when his ministry began.

JESUS' GENEALOGY
(Luke 3:23-38; Rm 1:3, 4a; 9:5)
Luke's Version

And the human genealogy of the Christ is traceable through the forefathers. God's own Son, who was of the sons of David according to natural human lineage, (and) who by means of the sanctifying Spirit was confirmed with authority to be the Son of God. He was also considered to be the son of Joseph, who was the son of Heli, the son of Matthat, the son of Levi, the son of Melki, the son of Jannai, the son of Joseph, the son of Mattathias, the son of Amos, the son of Nahum, the son of Esli, the son of Naggai, the son of Maath, the son of Mattathias, the son of Semein, the son of Josech, the son of Joda, the son of Joanan, the son of Rhesa, the son of Zerubbabel, the son of Shealtiel, the son of Neri, the son of Melki, the son of Addi, the son of Cosam, the son of Elmadam, the son of Er, the son of Joshua, the son of Eliezer, the son of Jorim, the son of Matthat, the son of Levi, the son of Simeon, the son of Judah, the son of Joseph, the son of Jonam, the son of Eliakim, the son of Melea, the son of Menna, the son of Mattatha, the son of Nathan, the son of David, the son of Jesse, the son of Obed, the son of Boaz, the son of Salmon, the son of Nahshon, the son of Amminadab, the son of Ram, the son of Hezron, the son of Perez, the son of

Judah, the son of Jacob, the son of Isaac, the son of Abraham, the son of Terah, the son of Nahor, the son of Serug, the son of Reu, the son of Peleg, the son of Eber, the son of Shelah, the son of Cainan, the son of Arphaxad, the son of Shem, the son of Noah, the son of Lamech, the son of Methuselah, the son of Enoch, the son of Jared, the son of Mahalaleel, the son of Cainan, the son of Enos, the son of Seth, the son of Adam, the son of God

THE TEMPTATION
(Matt 4:1-11; Mark 1:12, 13; Luke 4:1-13;
GHb 4, Quote by Origen, Commentary on John 2)
Jordan River; The Wilderness (Mount Tabor)

Jesus, filled with the Divine Inspiration, returned from the Jordan and was guided by the Spirit, which sent him out to a solitary place in the wilderness to be tempted by the devil. "At that moment, my mother, the Holy Spirit took me, whisked me away by one of my hairs, and brought me to the great Mount Tabor." He spent forty days in the wilderness being tempted by Satan. He lived among the creatures of the wild, where angels looked after him. He ate nothing that whole time, so after fasting for forty days and forty nights, he was very hungry. Then the tempter showed up and enticed him, "If you really are the Son of God, then say the word and this stone, (indeed all of) these stones will be turned into bread." Jesus replied, "It is written: 'Man does not live on bread alone, but on every word that comes from the mouth of God.'"

Then the devil took him and led him to Jerusalem, the holy city and placed him on the pinnacle of the temple. He said, "If you really are the Son of God, then jump down from here. You see, it is written: 'He will order his angels to watch over you, to guard you carefully, and pick you up with their own hands, lest you should kick your foot against a stone.'" "It is written," Jesus answered, "'Do not tempt the Lord your God.'"

Again, the devil took him and led him up to a high place, to a lofty mountain and showed him all the nations of the world, with all of their trappings, in a moment of time. "All of this will I give to you," he baited him, "if you will bow and worship me. All of its power, and every bit of its glory will I give to you, for it has been placed into my hand, and I am free to offer it to whomever I choose. So it will all be yours if you worship me." And Jesus answered saying, "You get behind me, Satan! For it is written, 'You must worship only God, serving Him and no one else.'" Then, after the devil had run through every temptation, he left Jesus for a better occasion. Angels then came and ministered to him.

JOHN'S TESTIMONIAL; THE FIRST FOLLOWERS
(John 1:32-51; Papyrus Berolinensis 11710)
Bethany; Far Side of the Jordan

Then John gave this testimony: "I saw the Spirit coming down as a dove out of the sky, and lingering upon him. Had that One Who sent me to baptize in water not disclosed to me, 'The man upon whom you see the Spirit come down and remain is the one who will baptize with the Holy Spirit,' I would never have recognized him. I have seen, and do confirm that this one is the Son of God."

The next day, John was standing there with two of his followers. And as Jesus was walking along, John looked his way and cried aloud, "Behold--the Lamb of God!" And when the two of them heard what John had said, they started following after him. Jesus, turning around, saw them in pursuit and asked, "What are you seeking?" And they asked him, "Rabbi, (which means 'Teacher,') where are you staying?" And Jesus answered, "If you'd like to know, then come along!" They went with him and saw the place, and that day they all remained together until about the tenth hour. Andrew, Simon Peter's brother, was one of the two that heard John testify, and who afterward followed Jesus. The first thing he did was to go and find his own brother Simon. And he said to him, "We have found the Messiah, which means the Christ." Andrew then took Simon over to introduce him to Jesus. Jesus looked at him and said, "You are Simon, the son of John. You are to be known as Cephas, which means 'the stone.'"

The following day, he was of a mind to move on to Galilee, so Jesus found Philip, and bid him, "Follow me." Philip, you see, was from Bethsaida, the same city that Andrew and Peter were from. Philip went to get Nathanael and said, "You know the one about whom Moses wrote in the Law and the prophets? Well, we have found him! He is Joseph's son; Jesus of Nazareth." And Nathanael asked him, "Nazareth? Can a blessing come from there?" "You will see," Philip said. "Come on!" Jesus saw Nathanael approaching and said, "Look, an Israelite in whom there truly is no guile!" "How can it be that you know me so well?" Nathanael asked him. Jesus replied, "I saw you even before Philip summoned you. You were underneath the fig tree." "Rabbi," Nathanael confessed, "my Master--you are God's Lamb of atonement for the sins of the world! You are assuredly the Son of God!--the King of Israel!" "Nathanael, take a walk in the sun!" Rabbi Jesus answered him, "Do you believe that simply because I said to you that I could see you underneath the fig tree? You are going to see things that are far more impressive than this! Of a truth, and without a doubt," he said, "I am here to tell you that you are going to see the sky open up, and God's angels rising and falling on the Son of Man."

JESUS TURNS WATER INTO WINE
(John 2:1-12)
Cana, in Galilee; Capernaum

On the third day, there was a marriage in Cana of Galilee, and the mother of Jesus was there. Jesus and his disciples had also been invited. After the wine had run out, Jesus' mother said to him, "They are out of wine." "Woman," Jesus answered, "why are you bringing me into this? It is not my time just yet." And at this his mother instructed the servants, "Do whatever he tells you to!" Six stone water jugs were standing nearby, the type that the Jews use for ablutions. They were each from about two to three "measures" in capacity. "Fill those jugs up with water," Jesus commanded the attendants; so they filled them to the brim. Then he instructed them: "Now measure some out and take it to the banquet host." Then they did as they were told, and the one in charge of the feast tasted the water that had turned to wine. The host had no idea from where it had come, but the ones who had drawn the water out knew. Then he called the groom to himself and said, "Everyone else serves the better wine first, and after the guests are already drunk, the cheaper wine is then brought out. You, on the other hand, have saved the better wine until the end." This was the first of his supernatural signs, and Jesus performed it in Cana of Galilee. It was in this way that he showed his glory, and his students put their faith in him.

After this, he traveled down to Capernaum with his mother, his brothers, and all of his disciples and spent a few days there.

THE FIRST PURGING OF THE TEMPLE
(John 2:13-25; GTh 71)
Jerusalem

The Jewish Passover was approaching at the time that Jesus traveled up to Jerusalem. He came across men who were selling cattle, sheep and doves in the temple; and still others who were sitting at tables exchanging money. He then made a whip of cords and chased them from the temple grounds, together with their sheep and cattle. Then he poured out the changers' money and he flipped their tables over. Furthermore, he raged at those who were selling doves, "Take all of these things far from here! Do not turn my Father's home into a market!" Then his disciples called to mind how it was written, "I will be utterly consumed by those who covet the house of my Father." Then the Jews insisted, "What heavenly sign can you show us to prove your authority to do this?" "Level this temple," Jesus retorted, "and in three days I will restore it." The Jews then said, "Raise it up in three days will you? This temple took forty-six years to construct!" (But when Jesus said "temple," what he meant was his body.) "I will myself tear down this house," said Jesus, "and none will be able to rebuild it <but me.>" And after he arose from death, his disciples called to mind what he had said, then they believed the Scripture in light of the words that Jesus had spoken.

As he was attending the Passover feast in Jerusalem, many people saw the wonders that he was working, and put their faith in his good name. Jesus, however, would not give himself to them, for he knew all things. And having a complete understanding of human nature, he had no need for anyone to explain to him the kinds of things that people could do.

NICODEMUS VISITS JESUS

(John 3:1-21)
Jerusalem

There was this Jewish leader of the Pharisees, a man whose name was Nicodemus. He came to Jesus by night and confessed, "Rabbi, we are all aware that you are a teacher sent here from God, seeing how no one could possibly show forth the signs that you do unless God were working through him." "Truly, and most assuredly I say to you," Jesus replied, "unless a man is born again from above, he is unable to see the dominion of God." Nicodemus asked, "How is it possible for an aged man to be born anew? Can he reenter his mother's womb and in this way be born again?" "I say to you most assuredly," answered Jesus, "that unless a man is born of water and Spirit, he cannot attain to the kingdom of God. What the flesh gives birth to remains fleshly; and what the Spirit brings forth becomes spiritual. Do not be put off by my telling you that it is essential that your birth be from above. The Spirit whispers wherever it may--you can hear the voice thereof, but where it's from you cannot know, nor can you see where then it goes--and everyone to whom the Spirit gives birth lives like this." Nicodemus answered him, "Tell me how these things can be?" "Do you, a teacher of Israel, not understand these things?" Jesus replied. "Truly and most assuredly I say to you, we are talking about things that we do understand, and are speaking of things that our eyes have seen, and yet you question what we say. If I were to show you the things of heaven, how ever would you come to accept them, seeing that you doubt the earthly things I have explained to you already? And no one has ever gone up into the heavens except for the one who came down from the heavens, namely the Son of Man, who even now is in the heavens. The Son of Man must be hung up as Moses prefigured when he lifted up the serpent in the desert, that whoever should place their faith in him might come to have eternal life. For God's love so abounded toward those in the world that he offered up the only Son that was born to Him, that whoever should place their trust in him might come to have eternal life, and never die. God did not send His Son into the world to convict the world, but that through the Son, the world might be spared. The one who puts his faith in him is not convicted; the one who does not believe has sentence passed against him already because he has refused to trust in the name of the only Son that was born to God. This is how the distinction is made: the light has shined throughout the world, and men have preferred the darkness to the light, since their way of life was completely wrong. For everyone who does evil is repulsed by the light for fear that his deeds will be shown for what they are. But everyone who puts the truth into action approaches the light, that it might be recognized that God has used his labors to do His works."

JOHN'S FINAL ATTESTATION

(John 3:22-4:3)
The Jordan River; Aenon, Near Salim

After these things, Jesus and his followers entered into the land of Judea and baptized there; and he remained there with them. And John was also baptizing at Aenon near Salim because there was an abundance of water there; and the people came to him and were baptized. John, you see, had not yet been cast into prison. A dispute therefore arose between a Jew, (indeed) several Jews, and John's disciples with regard to ablutions. And they took the matter up to John, saying, "Rabbi, you know that man you attested to, the one who was on the other side of the Jordan with you? Well, now he is baptizing those who come to him." "No man can receive it," replied John, "unless they have been graced by heaven. Each of you knows that I confessed, 'I am not the Messiah, but that I am sent ahead of him.' It is the bridegroom who receives the bride. The groom's best man merely stands nearby, receiving his testimony and rejoicing at the sound of the bridegroom's voice. Now my joy is fulfilled at last, for now I must be diminished, so that he might be increased.

"The one who came down from above is the one who is set over all. He that is of the earth is formed of an earthly substance, and speaks from an earthly perspective. He that comes from heaven is greater than all. He testifies about what he has seen and heard, and still nobody catches on. Anyone conforming to his testimony receives this assurance: that God is straightforward. The one who is sent from God speaks the very words of God, for God in no way rations the Spirit. The Father loves the Son and places all things into his hands. Whoever puts his trust in the Son of Man has eternal life, but whoever denies the Son will not ever see life, for God's anger seethes over him."

When the Lord learned that the Pharisees had become aware of his recruiting and baptizing more students than John had been--even though it was his own disciples who were doing all of the baptizing, and not, as it were, Jesus himself, he left Judea for Galilee.

ON THE ROAD TO GALILEE
(GTh 7, 11, 60, 87, 106, 111, 112)
On the Road to Galilee

A Samaritan was carrying a lamb on his way into Judea. "<How come> that man <has to> carry that lamb?" Jesus asked his students. "So that he might kill it and eat," they responded. "He will not eat it while life is still in it," Jesus observed, "but only after he has butchered it, so that what he eats is nothing but a carcass." "He cannot do so otherwise!" they reasoned. "Such indeed is your circumstance," Jesus continued, "Find a place for yourselves to live, or you might also become a carcass--and like a carcass be devoured! Blessed is the lion that the man consumes so that the lion becomes human; and cursed is the man that is eaten by the lion so that the lion takes on humanity!

"How miserable the body that depends upon a body, and how miserable the soul that depends upon these two. Accursed is the flesh that is governed by the soul, and accursed is the soul that is governed by the flesh. This heaven will pass away, as will the next. Indeed the dead do not have life, nor will the living ever die. Back when you would eat what was dead, you used it to feed what was alive. And now that the light is shining on you, what will you do? On the day that you were one, you split in two, so when you are two what ever will you do? When you join the two into one, you will be transformed. Then, as the Sons of Humanity you will say to the mountain, 'Move away!' and it will be moved. The skies will roll up before you, and the earth will too, and whoever receives his life from the One Who lives forever will never see death." (Does not Jesus himself affirm, "Of one who has come to see the truth of his nature, the world is not worthy?")

THE SAMARITAN WOMAN
(John 4:4-42)
Sychar, Samaria

It was necessary for Jesus to pass through Samaria. He came to Sychar, a Samaritan town near the tract of land that Jacob left to his son Joseph; and Jacob's well was in that place. It was about the sixth hour. Jesus, therefore, being worn out from so much traveling accordingly sat down on the well. A Samaritan woman came up to it to draw some water. Since his followers had gone into town to buy some food, Jesus bid her, "Give me something to drink." So the woman of Samaria asked him, "Seeing how you are a Jew, and I am a Samaritan woman, why are you asking me for a drink?" (Jews, you see, have no dealings with Samaritans.) Jesus responded, "If only you had understood just what the gift of God is, and just who it is that is saying to you, 'Give me something to drink,' you would have asked it of him first, and he would have given you the water of life." "You have no bucket," the woman replied, "and this well is very deep. From where will you draw this 'life-giving water'? Are you greater than our father Jacob, who gave us this well, having drunk from it himself, even as his sons and his cattle?" "Everyone who drinks of this water," Jesus replied, "will grow thirsty again, but anyone who drinks the water that I will give will not ever thirst again; but the water I will give to him will become a fountain of water springing up to limitless life." "Mister," the woman answered, "give me some of this water so that I might not get thirsty again, and have to come walking all this way to draw." Jesus said, "Go! Send for your husband and return." "I have no husband," the woman replied. "How aptly you have phrased that!" said Jesus, "For you have had five. The one you are currently with is not truly your husband, so well have you spoken." "Mister," the woman answered, "I sense that you are a prophet. Our fathers worshiped right here on this mountain, yet your people say to ours that Jerusalem is the proper place for men to worship." "Woman," Jesus assured her, "believe me when I tell you that the hour is coming when you will worship the father neither on this mountain, nor yet in Jerusalem. You worship in ignorance, but we worship with understanding, since deliverance is from the Jews. But the time is coming--and is upon us--when the true worshippers will worship the

Father with inspiration, and with truth. The Father goes looking for people like that to worship Him. God is a spirit, and anyone who worships Him must worship Him in spirit and truth." "I know," the woman answered, "that the Messiah, the one who is called 'the Christ,' is coming; when that one does come, he will expound all things in detail." "I, who am speaking to you," Jesus revealed, "am that one!"

And his disciples showed up as he was saying all this. They were surprised to see him speaking with a woman, but no one asked, "What do you want?" or, "Why are you speaking with her?" So the woman left for the city, leaving her water pot behind. And she said to the people there, "Come! See a man who described to me all that I ever did. Would not this one be the Christ?" Immediately they streamed out of the town and over to Jesus. And as they were walking along, the disciples urged him, "Teacher, eat!" But Jesus replied, "I've got food to eat you know nothing about." The disciples then started asking each other, "No one brought him any food, did they?" And Jesus informed them, "My 'food' is this: That I might do according to the decree handed down to me by the One Who sent me, that I might bring His striving to an end. Now do not go saying that there is no harvest for four more months. Behold, I am telling you now to lift up your eyes and look on the fields, because they are white already and waiting to be picked! Anyone who gathers will receive wages and be collecting fruit that leads to endless life! This is so that those who sow may rejoice with those who reap. For the saying, 'One man sows and another man reaps' is true in this sense. I sent you to gather where before you never labored; others have worked it, and you are here to garner the fruits of their labors."

And many Samaritans from that city believed the woman's testimony, "He related to me all that I ever did," and so came to place their trust in him. When, therefore, the Samaritans came to him, they asked him if they could stay with him awhile; and he stayed there with them for two days. And many more believed through his testimony. And to the woman they affirmed, "Now we believe, not only through your preaching, but we have heard it ourselves and are sure that this is the Savior of the World!"

JESUS HEARS OF JOHN'S IMPRISONMENT AND RETURNS TO GALILEE
(Matt 4:12; Mark 1:14-15; Luke 3:19-20, 4:14, 15; John 4:43-45)
Samaria; Galilee

But after John had reproved Herod the tetrarch with regard to his sister-in-law, Herodias, and all of his other immoral acts, Herod added this to his list: he had John put into prison. And after John had been locked up, Jesus came to hear of his confinement. So after two days, he left that place and returned to Galilee in the strength of the Spirit, proclaiming the good news of God, and his fame spread throughout the land.

Now Jesus had already revealed that every prophet is dishonored in his own nation. When he showed up in Galilee, the Galileans accepted him. They had all been to the feast and had seen the wonderful things that he had done at the Passover in Jerusalem. And he taught in their synagogues, "The time is now, the kingdom of God is breaking forth! Turn your lives around and accept the wonderful news!" and everyone there exalted him.

PETER, ANDREW, JAMES,
AND JOHN FOLLOW JESUS
(Matt 4:18-22; Mark 1:16-20; AcJn 88, 89)
Beside the Sea of Galilee

As Jesus walked along the Sea of Galilee, he caught sight of two brothers; Simon, whose nickname was Peter, along with his brother Andrew. They, being fishermen, were casting a net into the sea. "Follow me," he called to them, "and I will make you fishers of men!" And right away they followed him, leaving their nets behind them.

Moving on from there, he saw two other brothers, James, the son of Zebedee, along with his brother John. And he called to them as they were preparing their nets in a boat with their father. For after Jesus had selected the two brothers, Peter and Andrew, he came up to me, and my brother James, saying, "Come to me for I have need of you." And my brother asked me, "John, what does this youth who called out to us from the shore desire?" "What youth?" I asked. "The one who is summoning us," he answered. "Brother James," I said to him, "we've been out to sea for way too long--you are seeing things! Can you not tell that the one standing there is a grown man, strikingly handsome and joyful of face?" "My brother," he answered, "that is not the one I see. Let us go and see what this is about." And they both got out of the boat. Now as [they] were getting off, [they] realized that he was helping [them] to guide [their] boat ashore. And right away they followed him, leaving their father Zebedee in the boat with the workers.

And as we were leaving that place, again wishing to follow him, he showed himself to me again; this time with a bald head and a long, thick beard. To James, however, he revealed himself as an adolescent boy whose beard was just growing in. We were both confused by this, and marveled over what we had seen. Still, the longer we followed after him, and the more that we thought about it, the more confused we both became. And another, even more incredible sight was revealed to me. Every time that I would try to see him as he truly was, I never could see him with his eyes closed, but when I looked, they were always open. He would on occasion seem to me as somewhat small and rather homely, but at other times he would appear as one whose stature reached into the sky. There was yet another wonder in him: when I would sit with him at the table, he would hold me to his heart and I would hold him close to mine. Sometimes his chest seemed soft and gentle, and sometimes it seemed as hard as a rock. Naturally I was confused by this and asked, 'What is this supposed to mean?'

JESUS CURES A FEVER

(John 4:46-54)
Cana, Galilee

Then he returned to Cana in Galilee, where he'd turned the water into wine. And the son of a certain nobleman was sick in Capernaum. Hearing that he had come into Galilee from Judea, this man went all the way out to Jesus and asked if he would return with him to heal his son, for he was at the point of death. "Unless you witness signs and wonders," Jesus replied, "you don't believe anything at all!" "Lord," said the nobleman, "come down before my child dies!" "Go your way!" Jesus replied, "Your son is alive!" And the man believed what Jesus said, and at that he went his way. And even as he was going back down, his servants met him and gave him this word: "Your son is alive!" He then asked, "At what time did he recover?" "The fever broke yesterday at about the seventh hour," they answered. The father then realized that it had happened during that same hour that Jesus had said, "Your son is alive!" And he and his household believed firsthand. This was the second sign that Jesus had shown, having come again from Judea into Galilee.

DENIAL IN NAZARETH
(Luke 4:16-31a; Matt 4:13-17; Mark 1:21a; GTh 31)
Nazareth; Capernaum

And he came to Nazareth where he had been raised, and entered into the synagogue on the Sabbath Day, even as his custom was. And he stood up to read, and was handed the scroll of the prophet Isaiah. And after unrolling the scroll, he found the part where it was written,

> "The Spirit of the Lord is upon me.
> He has anointed me, that I might preach
> The gospel to the needy;
> He has sent me to bring healing
> To those whose hearts are shattered;
> To proclaim liberty
> To the captives;
> And new sight
> To those who are now blind;
> To set free the downtrodden
> And to preach the acceptable year of the Lord."

And he rolled the scroll back up, handed it to the attendant, and sat back down. And the eyes of those in the synagogue fastened upon him. Then he said, "Today this Scripture is fulfilled in your hearing." And everyone testified about him and was astounded by the elegance of the words that came from his mouth. But some of them objected, "Is this man not Joseph's son?" "You will certainly speak this parable against me," said Jesus, "'Physician, heal yourself! Do all of those amazing works that we heard you did in Capernaum right here in your own town.' Most assuredly I say to you," he added, "no prophet is accepted in his own home town, and a doctor does not heal those who know him. But I will tell you how it truly is, there were plenty of widows in Israel in Elijah's day, when the sky was closed for over three years and six months, and a major famine swept over the land. But Elijah was not sent to any of these, but rather to a widowed woman in Zarephath of Sidon. And there were many lepers in Israel during the days of the prophet Elisha, and not even one of them was cleansed except for Naaman, the Syrian." And as soon as those in the synagogue heard these words, they seethed with rage, rose to their feet, and drove him up to a cliff on the hill on which the city was built, in an effort to throw him down. But he slipped right through their grasp, passing through their very midst.

And departing (with them) from Nazareth, Jesus moved on to Capernaum by the sea, a city of Galilee in the regions of Zebulun and Naphthali, and stayed there to fulfill what was spoken through Isaiah the prophet:

"Land of Zebulun
And land of Naphthali,
Seaward, past the Jordan,
Galilee of the Gentiles--
The people once living in darkness
Have seen a great light,
And for those in the kingdom and
Shadow of death,
The light has arisen."

From that time forward, Jesus started preaching, "Turn your lives around, for the kingdom of heaven is drawing near!"

CASTING OUT DEMONS
(Mark 1:21b-28; Luke 4:31b-37)
Capernaum

And when the Sabbath Day came around, Jesus entered into the synagogue and started teaching the people there, and they were all astounded by his doctrine, for his teaching was convincing, and he taught them as someone with authority, and not as those who teach the law. There was a demon-possessed man in the synagogue, who at that moment, overcome by an evil spirit screamed out as loud as he could, "Leave us be! What have you to do with us, (and) we with you, Jesus of Nazareth? Have you come to do away with us? I can see you. I know who you are--the Holy One of God!" But Jesus stopped him, saying, "Do not say another word, but leave this man!" And the filthy spirit caused him to convulse, and he shrieked with a deafening voice and threw him down before them all and went away without doing him any harm. Everyone was so surprised that they asked one another, "What is this? Some new doctrine? With power and dominion he even commands the wicked spirits, and they depart!" And word about him quickly spread through the nearby parts of Galilee.

JESUS HEALS THE SICK
(Matt 8:14-17; Mark 1:29-34; Luke 4:38-41)
Capernaum

After they had left the synagogue, they went to the home of Simon and Andrew, accompanied by James and John. Simon's mother-in-law, you see, was stricken with a very high fever and was lying in bed, and they told Jesus about her state and asked him to help her out. Jesus, on entering into Peter's house, saw his mother-in-law fever-stricken and bedridden. At that point, he went up to her, stooped over, took hold of her hand, rebuked the fever, and it left her. At that point he helped her up, and she stood up right away and started serving them.

From dusk until after sunset that evening, the people brought all who were afflicted by this sickness or that up to Jesus, together with many who were demon-possessed. The whole town gathered at his doorstep, where he healed many of those who were variously afflicted by laying his hands on each of them. Furthermore, he drove out many demons, casting them forth with merely a word. The demons left many people, screaming, "You are indeed the Son of God!" But he reproved them, and would not permit the demons to utter so much as a single word since they could see that he was the Christ. All of this came to pass in order to fulfill what had been spoken through Isaiah the prophet: "He shouldered our weaknesses and bore our illnesses."

JESUS EXPANDS HIS HEALING MINISTRY
(Matt 4:23-25; Mark 1:35-39; Luke 4:42-44)
Galilee

As daylight was approaching one morning, Jesus rose up under cover of darkness, left the house, and ventured forth to pray in a secluded spot. Simon and his companions went searching for him, and when they found him they said, "Everyone is looking for you!" "Let's move on to the next town," he said, "that I might preach in that place too. This, you see, was why I came to begin with." The people who were searching for Jesus, when they got to where he was, took hold of him and tried to keep him from leaving them. But Jesus said, "It is only right that I should preach the great news of God's kingdom to the other townships also, for this is why I was sent." So Jesus went all around Galilee teaching and preaching in their synagogues, proclaiming the wonderful message of the kingdom, casting out demons and curing every illness and malady among the people. And news of him spread throughout Syria, and they brought all of the sick up to him, along with those who were suffering from various diseases and afflictions--the demon-possessed, the insane, and the paralyzed--and he cured them. Many groups from Galilee, the Ten Cities, Jerusalem, Judea, and the regions beyond the Jordan followed him all around, and he continued to preach in the synagogues of Galilee and the land of the Jews.

THE BIG CATCH
(Luke 5:1-11)
Lake of Gennesaret (Sea of Galilee)

One day Jesus was standing over by the Lake of Gennesaret and the people were pressing up against him to listen to the Word of God. And he spotted two boats that were near to the shore, whose fishermen had gotten out of them to wash their nets. Jesus then got into the one that belonged to Simon, and asked him to pull away from the shore a bit, and he taught the assembly while seated in the boat. And when he had finished speaking, he said to Simon, "Launch out into the deeper waters and drop your nets that you might draw." "Teacher," said Simon, "we have fished all night and not caught anything, but I will drop the net as you have said." And they signaled to their partners in the other boat that they should come and help them out. They came and filled them to the sinking point. At this, Simon Peter fell to his knees and confessed, "Go away and be done with me, Lord, for I am an evil man." Peter, you see, and all who were there, were thoroughly astounded by the number of fish that they had caught; as were the sons of Zebedee, James and John, who were partners with Simon. "Have no fear, Simon," Jesus reassured him, "for from this time forward, you will be a fisher of men." And they brought their boats back to the shore and followed him, leaving everything behind them there.

JESUS HEALS A SKIN DISEASE
(Matt 8:2-4; Mark 1:40-45; Luke 5:12-16; Egtn 2:1, 4)
Galilee

And behold, it happened that while he was in one of those towns, there was this man who was blanketed by leprosy. Now when he caught sight of Jesus, he came up to him and fell to his knees (and) his face in worship. "Lord Jesus," he said, "my teacher! As a result of keeping company with lepers, and eating alongside them in the poorhouse, I myself contracted leprosy. If you will, you can make me clean." And Jesus, moved with compassion, reached out his hand and touched him, saying to him, "That is truly my desire; therefore be cleansed." And even as he said this, the leprosy went away, and the man was cleansed. And immediately Jesus gave him a stern warning and ushered him out, saying to him: "See to it that you say nothing to anyone, but do go and allow the priest to examine you, and offer the sacrifice that is called for by Moses, both for your cleansing and as a sign to them--and no more sinning!" But he left that place and started preaching blatantly, and speaking the matter so extensively that Jesus could no longer enter into any town openly. And the stories about him grew even more widespread, and great multitudes were gathering both to hear him and to be healed by him of their illnesses. And he withdrew into solitude to pray. And though he was way out in isolated places, they nonetheless came out to him from every region.

JESUS HEALS A PARALYTIC
(Matt 9:1-8; Mark 2:1-12; Luke 5:17-26)
Capernaum

Now a few days after this, Jesus boarded a boat, crossed over the sea and entered again into his own town of Capernaum. And he was rumored to be in a certain house. So many rushed to fill the place that there was not the tiniest bit of room--even as far back as the door--and he preached the gospel to the people there. Pharisees and lawyers from Galilee, Judea, and Jerusalem were sitting there also. And the Lord's healing power was with him to restore the sick. Now behold, some men approached him, and four of them were carrying a paralytic on a stretcher, and they made quite an effort to get him into the house and lay him right across from Jesus, but the crowd kept them from doing so. Still, they were determined to get him in and set the man before him. Now they could find no way to get through on account of the crowd, so they climbed up to the roof of the house, undid the part above Jesus, opened it and let down the stretcher that the paralytic was lying on right through the tiles and into the crowd facing him, with the man still on it! And marking their determination, Jesus said, "My friend, my son, be of good cheer! Your sins have been forgiven you."

Some law teachers were seated there, and in their hearts they were wondering, "Why does this man put it that way? What he speaks is blasphemy! Who is this blasphemer, anyway? Who besides God has the power to pardon sins?" And picking up on their deliberations, he immediately knew in his spirit what their hearts were considering. Jesus therefore questioned them, "Why do your hearts think (or even) entertain such wicked thoughts? What is easier to say to this paralyzed man: 'Your sins have been forgiven you,' or to say, 'Arise! Pick up your bed and walk'? It is so that you might recognize that the Son of Man has power over the sins of the world, and has the authority to grant pardon." And to the paralytic he said, "Rise up, I say! Now take your bed and walk back home." Just then the man got up before them all, took hold of his mat--the thing he had been lying on--and traveled home praising God, and they all saw it. They were all spellbound and astonished, and they started glorifying God, Who had given such power to men, saying, "Today we have seen incredible things; we have never seen the likes of this!"

JESUS CALLS MATTHEW (AND LEVI)
(Matt 9:9-10; Mark 2:13-14; Luke 5:29-28;
GHb 5, Quote by Didymus,

Commentary on Psalm 184, regarding Psalm 33)
Capernaum

Now as he was moving on, Jesus saw a tax-collector named Matthew seated at the tax booth. "Follow me!" Jesus said, whereupon Matthew got right up and followed him. Now as he was walking along the lakeshore, he saw the son of Alphaeus, a tax-collector whose name was Levi sitting at his spot at the tax-collector's post. (Scripture, you see, seems to equate Matthew with Levi, but they are actually two different people. Matthias, the one who took the place of Judas, is in fact Levi. He is the one who has two names; something that the Gospel of the Hebrews makes clear.) "Follow me!" Jesus said. And Levi stood, leaving everything behind, and followed him.

MINISTRY 2

THE PARALYTIC AT BETHESDA
(John 5:1-47; GTh 52; Egtn 1:1-9:Quote By Pseudo-Cyprian,
On The Unbelief Of The Jews 4; Clementine Homilies 3.53)
Jerusalem

A short time later, there was a feast of the Jews and Jesus went up to Jerusalem to attend. Now in Jerusalem there is this pool over by the sheep gate, which in Aramaic is called "Bethesda." It has five colonnades surrounding it, and all manner of the ailing--the blind, the lame, and the paralyzed--were lying in wait for the rousing of the water. (Every once in a while, you see, an angel would come down to the pool and stir the water up. The first one in after this upset would be cured of whatever malady had afflicted them.) A man who had been disabled for thirty-eight years was in that place. Jesus saw him lying there, and knowing that he had been there a long time asked him, "Would you like to be made whole?" "Lord," the lame man answered him, "I've got no one to help me in at the stirring thereof; for even as I am inching toward it, someone always beats me there." "Get up!" said Jesus, "Pick up your bed and walk." Right away the man was healed, and he picked up his bed and walked away. Now it was the Sabbath Day, so the Jews said to the restored man, "Today is the Sabbath! The law prohibits you from carrying that bed." But the man replied, "The very one who healed me also said to me, 'Pick up your bed and walk.'" "Who is this 'man' who told you to pick up your bed and walk?" they demanded. The one who had been healed had no idea who it was that had healed him, for Jesus had slipped away into the crowd. A short while later, Jesus met him at the temple and said, "Behold, you are restored to your former state. See to it that you stop sinning, or something far worse might befall you." The man left that place and informed the Jews that it was Jesus who had healed him.

The Jews, therefore, were looking to deliver Jesus up to death, for he had dared to perform these acts on the Sabbath. "My Father ministers up to now," Jesus explained, "and now I minister just like Him." Then the Jews were even more determined to put him to death, for not only was he violating the Sabbath, but was also calling God his Father, making himself out to be equal to God. Jesus therefore answered them, "I say to you in all truth, the Son is unable to act on his own. He is only able to do as he sees his own Father doing, for the Son sees what the Father does and he does things just like Him. For the Father loves the Son, and fills him in on all He does. And He will, moreover, make known things that are even more astounding than this, that all of you might be amazed. For in the same way that the Father raises the dead and gives them life, so also does the Son give life to whomever he will. Moreover, the Father judges no one, but has relegated the judgment of all things to the Son. This is so that everyone might respect the Son every bit as much as they respect the Father. Whoever dishonors the Son also brings dishonor upon the Father Who sent him. I say to you most assuredly, anyone who hears my word and believes in Him Who sent me here, has transcendent life and will not be judged, but has passed right through death and into life. Assuredly I say to you, the time is approaching, and truly is upon us, when the dead will hear the voice of the Son of God, and in hearing they will come alive. Because in the same way that the Father has life within Himself, so also has He decreed that the Son should have life within himself. And He has given him complete authority, for he is the Son of Man.

"Do not be surprised at this, because a time is coming when all who are in the grave will hear His voice and resurrect; those who have acted righteously will arise to be enlivened, and those who have acted wickedly will arise only to be sentenced. I cannot do whatever I please. I judge according to the way I hear, and as such my judgment is fair, seeing that I do not act by my own whims, but only as the One Who sent me wishes me to. And if I should speak of myself alone, then my testimony will not stand. There is another who will testify on my behalf, and I am quite sure that His testimony regarding me is true. You sent envoys out to John, and he has testified to the truth. Not that I accept the testimony of men; but this I say for your salvation. John was a lamp that was burning bright, and for a time you were eager to bask in his light. But I am backed up by a testimony that is greater than John's. What I am working on now, you see, is the very task that was given to me by the Father, and it does of itself confirm that the Father has sent me. Moreover, the Father Who sent me has already borne me out. Never have you heard His voice, nor ever have you seen His form, and neither is His word alive in you. That much is certain, seeing that you do not trust in the one whom He has sent." <Jesus said> to the scribes, "<God will judge> all who behave unfairly, <so look to yourselves> and not me. <You imagine that you judge the same way that> He does, how does He?" And turning to the leaders of the people, he said: "Pore over the writings then. You study the Scriptures meticulously, supposing that through them, you will have eternal life. Yet you reject me out of hand, in spite of the fact that these very Scriptures point to me, that you might draw near to me and thereby receive endless life.

"I do not accept the praises of men. Indeed I know how it is with you. You do not have God's love in your hearts. For even though I come bearing the very stamp of my Father, you do not believe in me. If, however, someone else should come along acting in line with his own will, you will all be sure to embrace him. If you accept commendation from each other, while not attempting in the least to receive the glorification that comes from God alone, how ever will you come to believe?

"Now do not imagine that I will be the one to arraign you before my Father. Moses, upon whom you've pinned your every hope, stands as your accuser." "We know that God spoke to Moses," they said. "But as for you, we have no idea <where you came from.>" "You are now charged with not accepting those <whom Moses endorsed,"> Jesus answered. "Had you believed Moses, you would have believed me, for I am the one about whom he wrote to your forefathers, saying, 'The Lord our God will raise up a prophet for you from among your brothers, who will be to you even as I am. Hear him, therefore, in all things. And whosoever will not hear that prophet will die.' How will you ever believe what I say if you do not accept the things that he wrote?"

His followers said to him, "Twenty-four prophets have spoken in Israel, and all of them were pointing to you!" Then Jesus said, "You are speaking of the dead, and overlooking the Living One who is in your midst. I, the one who speaks in the prophets, am here with you, speaking to you." <Some people in the crowd started to gather> stones together <in order to pummel> him. <The leaders then> took hold of him and tried to arrest him and deliver him over to the people, but because the time for him to be handed up had not yet come, they failed to apprehend him. The Lord therefore of his own eluded their grasp and got away from them.

THE LORD OF THE SABBATH
(Matt 12:1-9a; Mark 2:23-28; Luke 6:1-5; Luke 6:5-in Codex Bezae Cantabrigiensis)
Galilee

One Sabbath Day at about that time Jesus was cutting through some wheat fields. As they walked along his hungry disciples started picking some of the heads, rubbing them between their hands and eating the grains. When some of the Pharisees saw what they were doing, they prodded Jesus, "Look, your followers are breaking the Sabbath! Why are you (and) your disciples doing what's unlawful on the Sabbath Day?"

"Have you never read what David did when he and his companions were hungry and lacking?" Jesus explained. "He entered into the house of God during the days of Abiathar the high priest, and they ate of the consecrated bread. He also shared some with his companions. He and his friends ate of that sacred bread, which was prohibited to them, but authorized for the priests alone.

"Have you not also read in the Law that on the Sabbath the priests who serve in the temple profane that day and remain undefiled? I say to you that someone greater than the temple is here. If only you had known what was meant by the words, 'I long for mercy and not sacrifice,' you would not have passed sentence against those who have committed no crime." "The Sabbath was designed for the sake of mankind," Jesus explained, "and not mankind for the sake of the Sabbath. So the Son of Man is indeed Lord even over the Sabbath," and at that he went away. That same day he saw someone doing work on the Sabbath, and said to him, "Sir, if you understand what you are doing, then you are to be commended, but if not, then curse you--you are nothing but a lawbreaker!"

THE MAN WITH THE SHRIVELED HAND
(Matt 12:9b-14; Mark 3:1-6; Luke 6:6-11; GNaz 4,
Quote by Jerome, On Matthew 2, Regarding Matthew 12:13)
Galilee

At another time, on another Sabbath, he entered into their synagogue and started to teach. Now a man was there whose right hand had withered. (Some Pharisees and scribes among them were looking for grounds upon which to bring charges against Jesus, so they watched him carefully to see if he would heal the man on the Sabbath Day.) This stonemason cried out for relief, "I was once a worker of stone, and earned my way with these two hands. Jesus, I implore you; please heal me, that I might not be reduced to begging for my food in shame." But Jesus was aware of their thoughts and said to the man with the withered hand, "Get up! Stand right here before the crowd." He therefore rose and stood nearby. "Is it lawful to heal on the Sabbath Day?" they asked him. "I will put the question to you like this," Jesus countered: "Which act done on the Sabbath Day is in line with the law: to perform an act of kindness, or to commit an act of wickedness; to save someone's life or destroy it?" But they did not answer him. "Should any of you have but a single sheep," Jesus asked, "and it should slip into a ditch on the Sabbath, would you not take hold and pull it out? How much more precious is a human being than a sheep! For this reason it is lawful to perform an act of mercy on the Sabbath Day." He looked out indignantly over them all, thoroughly pained at their unyielding hearts. "Reach out your hand," he said to the man. The man then did as he was told, and his hand was completely restored, and was every bit as good as the other. But the people seethed with rage and began discussing among themselves just what they ought to do to him. The Pharisees and the Herodians then went out and started devising a scheme to murder Jesus.

JESUS HEALS THE SICK
(Matt 12:15-21; Mark 3:7-12)
Beside the Sea of Galilee

Sensing this, Jesus left that place with his followers and went out to the lake, and a great crowd from Galilee followed after him. When they heard about all that he was doing, throngs of people came out to him--from Judea, Jerusalem, Idumea, the regions beyond the Jordan, and all around Tyre and Sidon. And he healed those who were sick among them, charging them not to reveal who he was. He asked his disciples to ready a little boat for him on account of the crowds, to keep the people from crushing him. He had healed so many, you see, that the diseased were shoving their way through to but touch him. Every time the wicked spirits caught sight of him, they would fall down before him and shout, "You are God's Son!" But he strictly ordered them not to tell anyone who he was. All of this came to pass in order to fulfill what had been spoken through Isaiah the prophet,

"This one is My chosen servant,
My beloved, the one in whom I take delight.
My Spirit will I rest on him,
And he will reveal justice to the nations.
He will not argue or cry aloud;
Nor will his voice be heard in the streets.
He will not so much as snap a damaged reed,
Or put out even a smoldering wick,
Until he guides justice to its conquest.
All the nations will trust in his name."

JESUS COMMISSIONS TWELVE APOSTLES
(Mark 3:13-19; Luke 6:12-16; GEb 2:1,
Quote by Epiphanius, Heresies 30.13)
Galilee, near Capernaum

In those days, Jesus went into the hills to pray, and to petition God the whole night through. And even as the morning dawned, he called his hand-picked disciples to himself and selected twelve from among them and appointed them, designating them as his apostles, that they might travel with him, possess the power to cast out demons, and be sent out to speak, "This man named Jesus, who is about thirty years old, has sent us." The twelve he appointed were Simon, the one he named Peter, and Andrew, his brother; James, the son of Zebedee, and his brother John--upon whom he bestowed the name Boanerges, which means the Sons of Thunder--also Philip, Bartholomew, Thomas, James, son of Alphaeus, Simon, also known as the Zealot, James' son Judas (also called) Thaddeus, and Judas Iscariot, who became a turncoat (and) betrayed him.

SERMON ON THE MOUNT
(Matt 5:1-8:1; Luke 6:17-7:1a; Acts 20.35b;
GPh 49; GNaz 3a, Quote by Jerome,
Commentary on Matthew 1, Regarding Matthew 6:11;
GNaz 3b, Quote by Jerome, Tractate on Psalm 135;
Quote from Origen, On Prayer, 2:2;
Cursive Ms 1424-(Quote following Matt 7:5);
2Clement 4:5; Traditions of Matthias,
Quote by Clement of Alexandria, Stromateis 2.9.45;
GTh 19, 24, 32, 36, 45, 47:1, 2;49,
58, 68, 69, 92, 93, 94/36-POxy 655;
Quote by Clement of Alexandria, Homilies 3.52;
GHb 6, Quote by Clement of Alexandria, Miscellanies 2.9.45;
Quote by Clement of Alexandria, Miscellanies 5.14.96)
On a Mountainside near Capernaum

He went down with them and arrived at a level place and stood, and many of his students were there. A sizable multitude from all parts of Judea, Jerusalem, and the coastal cities of Tyre and Sidon was there as well. All had come to hear him speak and to be healed of their diseases. Those who were afflicted by evil spirits were delivered from them, and they were trying to touch him, for power was flowing from him and healing each and every one of them. And seeing such enormous masses, he went up the mountainside, seated himself, and his disciples gathered around him. He looked out over his followers and began to speak to them, teaching them:

> "Blessed are the needy (and) the poor in spirit;
> For the kingdom of God is comprised of them.
> Blessed are you who are crying now
> For you are all about to laugh.
> Blessed are those who lament,
> For their consolation is drawing near.
> Blessed are you who are hungry now,
> For you are to be satisfied.
> Blessed are the humble,
> For they will inherit the earth.
> Blessed are those who hunger and thirst
> After righteousness,
> For they will be filled.
> Blessed are the compassionate,
> For they will be shown compassion.
> Blessed are the pure of heart,
> For they will see God.
> Blessed are those who aid in reconciliation,
> For they are to bear the name; 'Children of God.'
> Blessed are those who are hunted down
> On account of their virtue,
> For they comprise the kingdom of heaven.
> Blessed are they whose hearts have suffered greatly,
> For these have come to know the Father.
> Blessed are they who go without food,
> That the bellies of others might be filled.
> Blessed is the one who has toiled and found life.
> Blessed are the chosen ones who work alone,
> For you will discover the kingdom.
> Since it's from that place that you came forth,
> And to that place you will be restored!
> Blessed are those who came into being
> Prior to this existence.
> For though they came down to this realm,
> They will again exist eternally!
> For if you become a student of mine
> And examine my sayings closely,
> The very stones will become your servants,

> For there are five trees in Paradise
> That remain for you alone;
> They do not change from summer to winter,
> And their leaves are never shed.
> Anyone who knows of these will not ever taste of death.

Truly you are blessed when they detest you, exclude you, insult you, hunt you down and defame you; making yours an evil name; casting it aside and hurling every malicious and lying word against you--and all of it on my account--for the sake of the Son of Man! For whatever form your persecution takes, no basis will be found for it; and wherever persecution has befallen you, no standing is to be afforded. Celebrate and jump for joy, for beyond measure is the reward that awaits you in the heavens! This, you see, was the way their forefathers treated those who were prophets before you.

> But woe to the rich,
> For your comfortable days are behind you now!
> Woe to you who are well-fed now,
> For you are all about to starve!
> Woe to you who are laughing now,
> For you are about to howl and lament!
> Woe to you who are acclaimed by men,
> For that is exactly how their forefathers spoke of the false prophets.

You are the salt of the earth, but if the salt should lose its taste, what is there to season it? It is then no longer fit for anything but to be thrown into the dirt and trampled by men. You are illumination to this world; a well-defended city, sitting high upon a mountain cannot be hid, nor indeed can it be sacked. Also, no one lights a lamp and sets it under a grain bucket. Instead they place it high on a stand, and it enlightens all who are in that house. Let your light shine on all of mankind, that they might appreciate the goodness in the work that you are doing and likewise bring honor to your Father in the heavens.

"Now do not suppose that my coming nullifies the law or the prophets. My coming does not annul them, but rather completes them. I am telling you the simple truth when I say that not so much as a single jot, or the tiniest mark will be overlooked in the Law, but every detail is to be worked out until heaven and earth pass out of existence! So whoever voids the least of these commands, and teaches others to do the same will be despised in the kingdom of heaven; but whoever puts these teachings to work will be exalted in the kingdom of heaven. Believe me when I tell you that you will never get into the kingdom of the skies unless your virtue outshines that of the Pharisees and scribes.

"You have heard that it was said, 'Do not kill, and every murderer will be judged for it.' But I am telling you now that anyone who harbors anger against his brother without just cause will be judged for it. Moreover, anyone who says to his brother, 'You contemptible person!' will have to answer to the Sanhedrin. But anyone who calls you a 'fool' is right on the brink of the fires of Gehenna!

"For this reason, even if you are at the altar presenting your offering, and in the process recall that your brother has a grievance against you, put it down before the altar and go work things out first with your brother. Only then should you return and present your gift.

"You should try and settle things even as your enemy is dragging you to court. Otherwise he might place you into the hands of the judge, and the judge, into the custody of the bailiff, who may, in turn, throw you into prison! I say to you most assuredly, you will not be let out until you have paid back the last cent.

"You have heard that people have said, 'Do not cheat on your spouse.' I, however, am telling you now that anyone who looks a woman over and wishes to have his way with her is an adulterer already. If your right eye is a conduit of evil, then poke it out and throw it away. If your right hand is an instrument for wrongdoing, then cut it off and cast it aside. Better to lose a body part than to walk fully intact right into Gehenna!

"People have said, 'Anyone who puts away his wife has but to issue her a certificate of divorce.' I, however, am telling you now that anyone who divorces his wife for anything but unfaithfulness forces her into adultery, since anyone who marries this woman becomes guilty of adultery.

"Moreover, in ages past you have heard that it was said, 'Do not go back on your oaths, but follow through on your vows to the Lord.' But I am telling you to never swear. Do not swear by heaven, since it is the throne of God; nor by this world, since that is His footrest; nor by Jerusalem, since that place belongs to the Great King. Do not even swear by your head, since you can neither whiten nor darken so much as a single strand. Simply let your 'Yes' mean 'Yes,' and your 'No' mean 'No.' Anything more is of the evil one.

"You have heard it said, 'An eye in exchange for an eye, and a tooth for a tooth.' I am telling you otherwise. Do not oppose an evil man. If anyone should strike your cheek, turn the other one his way as well. Also, if someone wishes to sue you for the clothes on your back, let him have your underclothes. If anyone obliges you to go a mile, then go with him two. Should anyone ask you for something, then give it to them, and do not ignore the one who asks you for a loan.

"You have heard that it was said, 'Show love for a friend, but hatred for an enemy.' But I am saying to those of you who hear my words, show love to your enemies, blessing those who curse you, doing good to those who hate you, and extending your prayers toward those who wrong you. If someone should hit you on the cheek, turn the other one to him as well. If anyone should take your clothes, do not keep him from stealing your underclothes. Give to everyone who asks of you, and if anyone should take what's yours, do not insist on its return. This is so that you may be sons to your heavenly Father. He orders His sun to rise over the wicked and the righteous, and He sends rain upon both the virtuous and the sinful. How is it to your credit, (and) what reward can you hope to receive for loving those who love you back? Do not even the tax-collectors do that? Even 'sinners' show love toward those who love them. And if you only acknowledge your friends, what are you doing that these others are not? Do not even the pagans do this? And if you are only kind to those who show you benevolence, tell me how that makes you special? Even 'sinners' do as much as that. What credit can you hope to receive by lending to those from whom you fully expect to receive payment in kind? Even 'sinners' grant loans to 'sinners' in full expectation of repayment. Rather, show your enemies what love is, and perform acts of kindness even to them. It is more blessed to give than to receive. Should you have any money, do not lend it at interest. Present it instead to those from whom you will not receive it back. Grant loans to them without any terms of recompense, that way your return will indeed be great, and you will truly be the sons of the Most High, since He shows kindness toward the reprobate and the unappreciative alike. Embody mercy (and) perfection even as your Father in heaven embodies [them].

"Take pains to avoid doing kind works in public, for everyone to see. If you should, your Father in heaven will not reward you. So when you are helping out the impoverished do not proclaim it with trumpet blasts, receiving praises from men as do the hypocrites in the synagogues and in the streets. You can be sure that they have already received their wages. You, however, when giving to the poor, do not even inform your left hand of the doings of your right, that your giving might remain unseen. Your Father, Who examines all that is hidden, will pay you back.

"And do not pray on like the hypocrites do, for they all like to be seen by men; they stand in prayer before synagogues and at street corners. I am telling you the truth, they already have the payment they crave. When you pray, enter into your room, shut the door behind you, and pray to your Father, Who is hidden. Then your Father will pay you back, for He sees what is done in secret. And do not pray on like the pagans do, for they think that they will be heard for all of their blather. Your Father knows all about your needs way before you even ask, so do not seek to be like them. Here is a pattern for your prayers:

"Dearest Father in heaven,
Blessed be Your name!
May Your kingdom come,
And Your will be done on earth
As it is in heaven.
Give us this day
Our daily bread
(And that which is) for the next,
And forgive us our debts
As we forgive our debtors.
And lead us not into temptations,
But guard us against evil (and) the wicked one.
For the kingdom, the dominion and the praises
Are Yours for never-ending ages.
Amen.

You see, if you forgive what men do to you, then your Father in the heavens will forgive you, too. But if you don't forgive the sins of men, then your Father won't forgive your sins.

"Whenever you fast, do not go around looking dismal like the hypocrites do, because they make all kinds of faces so that men will be sure to see that they are fasting. I tell you most assuredly, they have the reward that they are after. But when you fast, rub anointing oil over your head, and scrub your face, so that people might not mark your observance. But your Father, Who cannot be seen, will indeed take note; and your Father, Who sees what is done in secret, will reward you.

"Do not hoard up wealth on earth, where moth and rust decay, and burglars break in and steal. Rather, stockpile riches in the sky, where moth and rust do not break down, and thieves do not purloin. For whatever the leaning of your heart, the things you value will be close at hand."

"Reveal to us your place of life," his disciples implored him, "since we all must seek for it!" He responded, "Those of you with two good ears, listen here! There is within a luminous being a light that shines throughout all things. If it should remain unlit, then everything will be obscured. The 'eye' is the 'lamp of the body;' if your eye is undivided, then your body will beam with light. But if your eyes should be divided, then your entire body will be eclipsed by darkness. If the light within should remain obscured, then that darkness is indeed profound!

"A person cannot ride two horses, nor yet can he draw two bows; neither can he serve two masters. He will either hate the one and love the other, or else be loyal to the one while disdaining the other. You cannot serve both God and Mammon.

"And for this reason do I say, do not fret about your life, what you are going to eat or drink; nor over your body, what you are going to wear. Is not life a weightier matter than food, and the body for more than mere clothing? Think about the birds of the sky; they neither plant, nor harvest, nor stockpile in barns, yet their heavenly Father nourishes them. Are you not more precious than these? Who among you can add an hour to his life, (or) a cubit to his height?

"And why trouble yourselves when it comes to your clothes? Think about the lilies in the field, which do not strive, nor do they weave. All the same, I can assure you that even Solomon decked in his finest apparel pales in comparison to even one of these. Fret not from daybreak until sunset, nor from sunset until daybreak <about> your <food>--the things that <you are going> to eat; <nor> <your clothes>--the things that you <are going> to wear. If God arrays field grass in such splendor, being here today and tossed into the flames tomorrow, will He not clothe you even better, oh you stunted of faith? <You are far> superior to the lilies, which neither strive nor <weave.> As for yourselves, when you have no clothes, what <ever will you put> on? Who is the One that can lengthen your life? The very Same will give you your clothes! So do not get all worked up, saying, 'What are we to eat?' or 'What are we to drink?' or 'What are we to wear?' The Pagans chase after all of these things, but your Father in heaven knows that you need them. Therefore seek His kingdom first, together with His righteousness, and every one of these things will be added on to you. Seek for things that are superior, and the inferior things will be given as well; seek after the things of heaven, and the things of the earth will be thrown into the bargain. For this reason, do not dwell on tomorrow, for tomorrow will dwell on itself. Each day, you see, has distresses sufficient for the duration thereof.

"Do not pass judgment, that judgment might not be passed on you. For to the extent that you judge, you will be judged, and to the degree that you calculate, it will be computed against you. Do not judge, and you will not face judgment. Do not criticize, and you will not be criticized. Pardon, and you will be pardoned. Give, and you'll receive it back--a heaping measure, all pressed down and densely shaken until it overflows generously into your lap. Whatever measure you use to mete it out, you see, will be used in measuring it back out to you."

And he spoke this parable to them: "Can one blind man be guide to another? Won't they both fall into a pit? An apprentice is not above his master, yet anyone who takes these principles fully to heart will equal his instructor.

"Why do you inspect your brother's eye for a tiny wooden splinter while ignoring the log that is in yours? How can you say to your fellow man, 'Brother, let me take that speck from your eye,' when you fail to see the plank in your own? You hypocrite! Remove the beam from your own eye first; only then will you see well enough to dislodge the bit from your brother's.

"Do not give hallowed things to dogs, for they might fling them onto a pile of dung. Neither cast your pearls before swine, for they might trample them into the mud, then turn on you and tear you to bits.

"Ask, and you will receive; seek, and you will find; knock and it will open for you. Everyone who asks receives; and the one who seeks is the one who finds; and to one who knocks, it is opened right up! Seek, and you will find, for before I would not tell you the things about which you were asking me then; I am anxious to explain them now, but you no longer seek for them. Recognize that the truth does not lie on the surface of things. Be in awe of the things that are before your eyes, and make this your starting point for further enlightenment! The ones who strive should not stop striving until they find. When they find, they will be shaken, and when they are shaken, they will be amazed, and will possess complete authority. And when they rule, then they will rest.

"Should any of your sons ask you for a loaf of bread, which of you would give him a rock instead? Were he to ask you for a fish, which of you would give him a snake? If, therefore, you know how to give good things to your children-- even though you are steeped in error--will not your heavenly Father bestow even greater favors upon those who ask of Him?

"Out of this principle flows the Law and the Prophets: What you would have others do for you, that's what you should do for them. Strive to enter through the narrow gate, for the large gate and the wide road through which so many enter leads to utter devastation. But how very few are those who come across that tiny gate and narrow path that leads to life!

"Be on the lookout for false prophets, for they come to you dressed-up like sheep, but beneath all that they are ravenous wolves. You can spot them by the fruit they bear. Do people pluck grapes from thorny bushes, or figs from prickly plants? Similarly, every tree that gives good fruit is useful, but a tree that delivers up no edible fruit is useless. No good tree puts forth bad fruit, (for) a good tree cannot yield bad fruit. Neither does a bad tree put forth good fruit, (for) a bad tree cannot yield good fruit. Every tree is recognized by what it bears. People do not pluck figs from thorns, nor do they garner grapes from brambles. Every tree that fails to yield fit fruit is chopped up and relegated to the flames. And so it will be that you will know them by their fruit. The virtuous man brings his goods up from his good heart's bounty, and the evil man brings up his own evil from his evil heart's inventory, and utters pure wickedness. Whatever fills his heart, you see, will flow forth from his mouth. For these people bring out abominations from what fills their hearts.

"And of those who say to me, 'Master! Master!' many will fail to enter into the kingdom of heaven--only the one who does the will of my Father in heaven. On that day, many people will say to me, 'Lord! Lord! Did we not use your name when we prophesied and cast out demons, and performed so many miracles?' I will therefore say to them clearly, 'Go away you evil men--I never even knew you!' If you rest upon my breast, yet ignore the will of my Father in heaven, I will shove you right off! Should each and every one of you be with me--even in my very bosom--and still not do as I say to you, I will shove you all aside and say, 'Get away from me! I have no idea where you evil workers came from!'

"Why do you cry out to me, 'Teacher! Teacher!' when you do not do as I instruct? For this reason, I will show you what he (and indeed) everyone who comes to me to hear my words, and acts on them is like. He is even as a wise house builder, who shoveled deep into the ground, fixed the foundation on bedrock, and on that rock he built his home. The rain beat down and the rivers rose up, and when a flood came, it beat against that house but was powerless to budge it on account of it's strength. The gales blasted and pounded away at that house, but it pulled through, for it was founded on the rock. But someone, (indeed) everyone, who hears my words and does not act on them is even as a senseless man who built his home upon the sand; upon ground without a foundation. The rain came down and the streams rose up; the winds blew hard and beat that house, and the instant that the flood hit it, it came down with a deafening sound, (and) it was completely destroyed!"

And after he had said these things, the crowds were taken aback by his teaching, for he taught them as an authority, and not at all like the scribes. And a host of people followed him down the mountainside.

THE FAITHFUL CENTURION
(Matt 8:5-13; Luke 7:1b-10)
Capernaum

Jesus then entered into Capernaum, where the servant of a centurion lay sick and on the brink of death. This servant was highly esteemed by his master. Now this centurion had heard about Jesus and had sent some Jewish elders up to him, asking him to come and heal his servant. When they got to Jesus, they begged him in all sincerity, "This man is worthy that you should do this for him, for he loves our people, and has even built us our synagogue." So Jesus went to that place with them.

After Jesus had entered into Capernaum, and had drawn near to the house, a centurion approached him, seeking assistance. (The centurion had sent some friends of his up to Jesus to say: "Lord, my servant boy is lying at home completely paralyzed in horrible pain.") "I will go and heal him," Jesus answered. "Lord," the centurion replied, "Do not go out of your way, for I am not worthy that you should come under my roof. I did not even come out to you, because I thought myself unworthy to. But if you would speak the word, my servant would improve. You see, I am myself a man who is subject to authority, and I have soldiers who answer to me. I say to one, 'Go!' and he goes; and to another, 'Come!' and he comes. I order my servant 'Do this!' and he does it."

When Jesus heard such things from him, he was surprised (and) impressed by him. And turning to the multitudes that were following him, he said, "I say to you in all honesty, never before have I met anyone in Israel with this kind of faith! I am telling you that from the east and from the west people are going to be seated at the same feast in the kingdom of the skies as Abraham, Isaac, and Jacob. But the people of the kingdom are going to be cast out, where it is dark, and where there will be weeping and grinding of teeth!" Then Jesus said to the centurion, "Go, and let it be as you believed." And his servant received his healing in that instant. And when the men who had been sent got back to the house, they found the servant there in perfect health.

JESUS EXPLAINS WHY HE CHOSE THE TWELVE
(GEb 2:2-5, Quote by Epiphanius, Heresies 30.13;
Quote by Clement Of Alexandria, Miscellanies 6.6.48)
Capernaum

After entering into Capernaum, Jesus went into the house of Simon, the one whom he nicknamed Peter. Then he said: "As I walked along the lake of Tiberias, I summoned John and James, the sons of Zebedee, then I called Simon and Andrew, then Thaddeus, Simon the Zealot, and Judas the Iscariot. After that I called you, Matthew, even as you sat at the tax-collector's booth, and you followed me. To represent Israel, therefore, I want you apostles to be twelve in number. Now I chose the twelve of you, deeming you to be worthy of me. I am sending you out into the world to make the gospel known to the world, that they might be sure that God exists. Make known the future things that will come about through faith in me, that those who hear and believe might indeed be saved."

JESUS RAISES A DEAD MAN
(Luke 7:11-17)
Nain

The next day Jesus moved on to a town called Nain, attended by his disciples and a very great multitude. And as he neared the gate of that town, there was this dead man being carried out--his widowed mother's only son--and many from that town were there with her. Now as soon as the Lord saw her, his heart went out to her. "Do not weep," he said to her. He then drew near to the casket and touched it, and the pallbearers stood motionless. "Young man," He said, "I order you to rise up now!" The one who had died sat up and started speaking. Jesus then restored him to his mother. They were all amazed and gave praises to God. "A great prophet has risen among us!" they all proclaimed. "God has come down to His people." This story about Jesus spread throughout the land of the Jews, and the regions beyond.

JOHN THE BAPTIST'S INQUIRY
(Matthew 11:2-9; Luke 7:18-35; GTh 46, 78, 85)
Galilee

John's disciples reported this to him, so when he heard in prison what the Anointed was doing, John called two of them up to himself, and sent them out to ask the Lord, "Are you the one for whom we were waiting, or ought we to seek another?" After the men had gotten to Jesus, they said, "John the Baptist has sent us here to ask of you, 'Are you the one who was to come, or should we wait for someone else?'" Right away Jesus healed many people who were afflicted by all manner of diseases, ailments, and evil spirits, and he gave sight to many of the blind. Then Jesus said to the messengers, "Go back to John and let him know all that you have seen and heard: the blind see, the lame walk, the lepers are cured, the deaf now hear, the dead are raised, and the gospel is preached to the poor. How blessed is he who does not take offense at me."

As the disciples of John were walking away, Jesus started speaking to the gathering about him: "What did you go into the wilderness to see anyhow; a mere wind-shaken reed? If this is not the case, then just what were you looking for; a man bedecked in silky-smooth finery? Leaders, then, and prominent men? Of course you didn't, for truth is lost on those who dress comfortably in magnificent, costly apparel and live luxuriously in royal palaces. What did you go all that way for then? To see a prophet? That's right, and much more than a prophet I can assure you, because this is the one about whom it is written in the place where it says: 'I am going to send my messenger ahead of you, who will ready the way that lies before you.' Adam arose out of an immense vitality and an incredible abundance, but he proved to be less worthy than you, for had he been of a comparable worth, he would never have tasted of death. I am telling you the truth when I say that from Adam down to John the Baptist no one who is born of women has come along who is so great that he should not feel compelled to lower his eyes to John the Baptist. Even so, whoever is least in God's heavenly kingdom and becomes a child will recognize the kingdom and become more illustrious than he. For from the time of John the Baptist, even to this very day, the kingdom of heaven has been suffering violence, and men of violence have seized it by force. For the Law and the Prophets prophesied all the way down to John; and he is that Elijah whose arrival was foretold--if you can but accept it. Someone who has ears will hear."

And everyone--even the tax-collectors--recognized the truth of God's way when they heard the words that Jesus spoke, for John had baptized them. But the Pharisees and the scribes, in refusing the baptism of John, rejected God's design completely on their own.

"What is a good thing for me to compare this generation with? They are like children sitting in the marketplaces, calling out to one another, 'We played a flute, but you did not dance,' and 'We sang a dirge, but you did not weep.' John, you see, did not come eating bread and drinking wine, and they say he's demon-possessed. But the Son of Man did come eating and drinking, and they say, 'Look, he's a glutton and a drunkard; a companion of tax-collectors and of "sinners!"' Wisdom, however, is defended by her children, (and) vindicated by her deeds."

JESUS CONDEMNS THE CITIES
(Matt 11:20-30; GTh 90)
Galilee

Then Jesus started denouncing the cities where he had done the greater portion of his works, for they were utterly without shame. "Curse you, Chorazin! Curse you, Bethsaida! Had the marvels that were worked in you been carried out in Tyre and Sidon, they would have long ago repented in sackcloth and ashes. But on Judgment Day Tyre and Sidon are going to fare better than you. As for you, Capernaum, will your praises reach the skies? Be assured that they will not! You will instead be thrown down into Hades! Had the kind of miracles that were worked in you been done in Sodom, it would still be here today. I am telling you that Sodom will be better off on Judgment Day than you will."

Then Jesus said, "Father, Lord of heaven and earth, I admire You for the way that You have concealed these things from intellectuals and scholarly types, and revealed them instead to mere children. Father, this was indeed a gratifying spectacle for You. My Father has placed all things into my hands; and no one knows the Son except for the Father; and neither does anyone know the Father except for the Son, and those to whom he chooses to disclose Him. All of you who work hard, yet are burdened all the more, come to me and I'll give you rest. Take my yoke upon yourselves and learn directly from me, because I am approachable and down-to-earth; and peace will overtake your hearts, for my yoke is gentle and my burden is light."

WOMAN WASHES JESUS' FEET

(Luke 7:36-50)
Galilee

A certain Pharisee invited Jesus to dine with him, so he set out for this man's house and sat at his table. And behold, there was this sinful woman of that town who, when she found out that Jesus was eating at the Pharisee's house, took an alabaster jar that was full of ointment, stood behind him and started washing his feet with her tears, and wiping them off with the hair of her head.
And she fervently kissed his feet and rubbed them with the ointment.
When he saw what was going on, the man who had bidden Jesus thought to himself, "If this man were really a prophet, not only would he know who was touching him, but also how sinful this woman is." "Simon," said Jesus, "there is something I must say to you." "Teacher," he answered, "do tell." "There were these two people who owed money to a creditor. One of them owed him five hundred denarii, and the other only owed him fifty. Now neither one could pay him back, so he canceled both their debts. Which do you think will love him the more?" "I imagine it would be the one he more generously forgave," Simon answered. "You have chosen rightly," answered Jesus. Then, turning to the woman he said, "Simon, do you really see this woman? I entered into your house and you gave me no water for my feet, but she has wet my feet with her tears and wiped them off with her hair. You did not so much as give me a kiss, but this woman has not stopped kissing my feet from the moment I came. You did not rub my head with oil, but she has poured perfume all over my feet. That is why I am telling you now that even though she owed a great debt of sin, because of her boundless love it has been forgiven her. But whoever has been forgiven but a little, also only loves a little. Jesus then revealed to her, 'Your sins have been forgiven you.'" Then those people grumbled to themselves, "Who is this man that pardons sins?" Jesus then bid the woman, "Go in peace, for your faith has made you whole."

ACKNOWLEDGMENT OF THE WOMEN'S CONTRIBUTION TO JESUS' MINISTRY
(Luke 8:1-3)
Galilee

After this Jesus went all around, through this town and that, preaching the wonderful news of God's kingdom. The twelve were in that place as well, together with some women that had been delivered from evil spirits and diseases: Mary, who is called 'Magdalene,' out of whom there came seven demons; Chuza's wife, Joanna, steward to Herod; and a host of others too, including Susanna. These all gave of their own substance to help keep them going.

CAN SATAN CAST OUT SATAN?
(Matt 12:22-37; Mark 3:20-30;
Luke 11:14-23; GTh 35, 43, 44, 70, 98)

Galilee

Then Jesus entered into a certain house, and once again so many people gathered within it that he and his followers could not even eat bread there. As soon as his family caught wind of it, they went over to get him, for they were all saying, "He has gone completely insane!" Then they brought this blind, deaf and demon-possessed man up to him, and Jesus healed him, driving out the demon of muteness, restoring both his speech and sight. And after the demon was gone, the hitherto speechless man began to speak, and the crowd was astonished, and they all began to wonder aloud, "Could this man be the Son of David?"

But when the Pharisees and lawyers come down from Jerusalem heard such talk, all of them began to say, "This man is possessed by Beelzebub! He is only driving out demons with the help of that Prince of Demons!" Others put him to the test by demanding some kind of heavenly sign.

Jesus, knowing their thoughts, called them over to himself and started speaking to them in parables. "How can Satan cast out Satan? Every nation divided against itself comes to ruin. No kingdom with an internal rift has any lasting dominion, and no house that is self-opposed can go on for very long, for every city or house that acts against itself has no prospects for survival. If Satan battles against (and) casts out Satan, he is torn apart (and) cannot abide. He is caught in a civil war, so how is his kingdom supposed to endure? His end has come! This I say because you claim that I cast out demons by Beelzebub. And if it is by Beelzebub that I am ousting demons, then by whom do your people cast them out? These will therefore be your judges. If, however, I cast out demons by God's own Spirit--the finger of God--then God's kingdom has risen upon you.

"The Father's kingdom is like someone who sought to kill a powerful man. Even before he left his home, he took his sword and thrust it into the wall to see if his hand would pass through. Then he slew the mighty one. When a stout man in full armor guards his own home, his possessions remain secure. But when someone stronger assaults and vanquishes him, he seizes the armor on which the man relied and distributes the plunder. To put it yet another way, how is it possible for anyone to enter into a strong man's home and make away with what he owns unless he first binds up the brute? Clearly, no one can go into his house and take of his things unless he ties him up ahead of time; only then will he be able to plunder the abode. Whoever is not for me is against me, and the one who does not gather with me only scatters. And truly this is why I say that every sin and blasphemy of mankind will be forgiven them; anyone who speaks a contemptuous word against the Father has forgiveness, and anyone who rails against the Son of Man has forgiveness, but no one who blasphemes the Holy Spirit has forgiveness; neither on the earth in this age, nor in heaven during the age to come, but is guilty of eternal sin." (This he said because they claimed that he had an unclean spirit.)

"How can you children of vipers speak anything reliably, seeing how thoroughly evil you are? For the mouth speaks what is from the heart. If you bring out what is in yourself, then what you have within you will deliver you. If you do not have it in yourself, then what you lack will do you in. The virtuous man brings choice things up from the good that he has stockpiled within, and the evil man brings vile things up from the sinfulness within himself. But I am here to tell you that on the Day of Judgment, men will be forced to answer for every word that they have spoken. For either by your words will you be acquitted, or else by your words you will be condemned." His followers asked him, "Who are you to speak this way to us?" "You do not recognize who I am through the words that I speak, but have instead become like the Jews, for they either love the tree and hate the fruit, or they love the fruit and hate the tree. Either make a good tree that gives only good fruit, or make a bad tree that gives only poor fruit, for a tree is known by the fruit it bears."

THE LEADERS ASK FOR A SIGN
(Matt 12:38-45; Luke 11:29-32)
Galilee

Then, as the gathering pushed forward, some Pharisees and lawyers bid him, "Teacher, we would like to see you perform some kind of miraculous sign." "Only an evil, unfaithful kind of people would need a sign," Jesus explained. "This is indeed a wicked nation! It always calls for signs and wonders, but the only sign that it will be given will be that of the prophet Jonah. For in the same way that Jonah was a sign to the Ninevites, so also will the Son of Man be a sign to this people. You see, for three days and three nights, Jonah was in the belly of a giant fish. And just like him, for three days and three nights, the Son of Man will be in the heart of the earth. The people of Nineveh will stand up at the judgment with this generation and pass sentence against it because they changed their ways at the preaching of Jonah, yet here and now stands someone who is greater than Jonah. The Queen of the South will rise up at the judgment alongside this generation of men and condemn them, because she came from the farthest reaches of the earth to hear the wisdom of Solomon, and here and now stands a greater than Solomon."

FUTILE REPENTANCE
AND THE LIGHT OF THE SPIRIT
(Matt 12:43-45; Luke 11:24-28, 33-36;
GTh 50, 74, 75, 79)
Galilee

"When an evil spirit leaves a man, it wanders about through arid places seeking repose, but finds it not, so it says, 'I will go back to my old home.' But when it gets there, it finds the house in good order and swept clean, but also vacant. It then goes and finds seven spirits even more disgusting than itself and they go in and make themselves at home, and that man winds up worse off than he started out. That is exactly how this generation of degenerates is going to end up!"

And as Jesus was saying these things, a woman shouted from the crowd, "How blessed is the womb that bore you and the breasts that nursed you!" But Jesus said, "No! How blessed are those who hear God's word and hold to it, for the days are coming when you will say, 'How blessed is the womb that never conceived and the breasts that never nursed.'

"No one lights a lamp and puts it in a hidden place, (or) underneath a basket. He puts it on a stand instead, so that those who go in might see by its light. The lamp of your body is your eye. When you've got good eyes, your entire body shines. But when they are bad, your whole body remains dim. You had better make sure that the light within you isn't really darkness instead. For this reason, if your whole body beams with light and there is no darkness in it, it will then be fully lit, just as though it were filled with lamplight. If they should ask you, 'Where are you from?' for their sake, explain to them, 'We came from the place of light, from where the light came into being all by itself and organized into images.' If they should ask you, 'Are you that light?' reveal to them, 'We are the ones whom the light brought forth, and we are the chosen of the Living Father.' If they ask you, 'What evidence is there that the Father is within you?' simply answer, 'It is movement and it is stillness.' Many are gathered around the drinking trough," he said, "but there is nothing in the well; many stand outside the door, but it is the solitary who enter into the bridal chamber."

JESUS' TRUE FAMILY
(Matt 12:46-50; Mark 3:31-35;
Luke 8:19-21, GTh 99)
Galilee

Jesus' mother and his brothers came to pay him a visit, but when they arrived at the place they could not get anywhere near him on account of the crowd. They wished to speak with him, so they sent someone in to call him out as they stood outside and waited for him. Even as Jesus was addressing the crowd seated around him, one of them informed him, "Your mother and your brothers are standing outside looking for you. They would like to see you and have a word with you." "Who is my mother," he asked them, "and who are my brothers?" Then he looked at those seated in a circle around him, and pointing to his disciples he said, "My mother and my brothers are here with me. You see, whoever hears the word of God and acts on it, carries out the will of God, Who is in heaven, who is my Father--they are my brother, sister, and mother; and these are the ones who will make it into my Father's kingdom."

PHARISAISM DENOUNCED;
THE SIX CURSES
(Luke 11:37-54)
Galilee

After Jesus had spoken, a Pharisee invited him over to eat with him, so he went inside and sat at the table. When the Pharisee observed that Jesus had not washed before the meal, however, he was taken aback. Then the Lord admonished him, "Now you Pharisees cleanse the outer surface of the dish and cup, but deep inside you are full of greed and vice. You fools! Did not the same One Who formed the outer also fashion the inner? You ought instead to offer to the poor what you have inside the dish--that way all things will come clean for you!

"Curse you Pharisees, because you offer God tithes of mint, rue, and every other kind of herb, yet you ignore justice and the love of God! You should have acted on the latter, and seen to it that the former did not remain undone.

"Curse you Pharisees, for you love the foremost seats in the synagogues and the salutations in the marketplaces!

"Curse you, because you are like unmarked graves, over which men pass without their knowing!"

"Teacher," one of the scribes retorted, "you are reproving us also with what you are saying." And Jesus answered him, "Curse you too, who teach the Law, because you weigh people down with loads that they can hardly manage, and you will not help them out with even one of your fingers!

"Curse you, because you set up tombs for the prophets when it was your own forefathers who murdered them! This is how you betray your approval of the deeds of your forebears: they killed the prophets, and you build them their tombs. And because of this, God in His wisdom has said, 'I will send them prophets and apostles, some they will kill, and some they will maim.' For this reason this generation will have to shoulder the blame for the blood of each and every prophet shed since the world began; from the blood of Abel to that of Zechariah, who was slain between the altar and the sanctuary. Most assuredly I say to you that the entire blame will fall upon this generation.

"Curse you scribes, for you have taken away the key to knowledge. You never did manage to find it yourselves and you have kept out those who would have gone in."

And as he was saying these things, the scribes and Pharisees all became thoroughly enraged, and started asking him a host of questions in an attempt to catch him in his words and thereby have something with which to charge him.

THE TEACHING OF THE HOLY SPIRIT
(Luke 12:1-12)
Galilee

At that time, when a gathering of so many thousands had assembled together in that place that they were stepping all over each other, he began to speak, cautioning his disciples, "You must guard against the leaven of the Pharisees, for it is all a pretense. Nothing has been obscured so completely as to fail in its revelation, nor is anything so secret that it will not be disclosed in full. For this reason, the things you uttered while it was dark will be heard when it is bright, and what you spoke secretly behind closed doors, will be heralded openly from the housetops. But I am telling you, my friends, stop being so fearful of those who, once they have put your body to death, can do nothing further to you. I will tell you, my friends, Who you ought rather to fear; fear the One Who after the killing has the power to cast you into Gehenna. Indeed I say, be fearful of this One! Do not five sparrows sell for two assaria? Yet not even one is forgotten by God. Indeed, every hair that is on your heads has its number, so stop being so spineless; you matter more than great numbers of sparrows. I am here to tell you that everyone who will acknowledge me openly before mankind, the Son of Man will acknowledge them openly before the angels of God. But anyone who denies me before mankind will be denied before the angels of God. And anyone who defames the Son of Man will be forgiven, but no one who maligns the Holy Spirit will be forgiven. And when they lead you before synagogues, rulers, and magistrates, do not think about how you ought to respond or what you should say, for on that day, the Holy Spirit will give you the words."

THE DANGERS OF WORLDLINESS
(Luke 12:13-34; GTh 63, 64, 72)
Galilee

And someone in the crowd yelled out to him, "Teacher, tell my brother to split his inheritance with me! Order that these brothers of mine divide with me the things of my father!" "Mister," Jesus answered, "who appointed me as judge or mediator between you? Who has made me out to be a divider?" And turning to his disciples he said, "I am not a divider, am I?" At that point he cautioned them, "Be on the lookout for covetousness, (and) steer clear of it, for one's life is not to be found in an abundance of possessions." And he spoke this parable to them, "There was this rich man with substantial means. Now he said, 'I will put my money into sowing, reaping, planting, and filling my storehouses with the goods, so as to lack nothing.' Now this rich man's field brought forth a great crop, and inwardly this rich man thought, 'What should I do? I do not even have enough space to store all of my harvest.' And he said, 'I know just what I will do, I will tear down the ones I have and build myself even larger ones, and there will I store all of my grain and my goods. Then I will say to my soul, "Soul, you have many good things on hand for many years to come, so sit back now--eat, drink, and enjoy."' 'You fool!' God rebuked him. 'This very night will they demand your soul from you--who then will inherit all that you have prepared?' Such did his heart imagine, yet he died that very night.

Anyone here with two good ears should understand. It is just like this with the one who hoards up for himself but is not rich when it comes to God."

And to his disciples he said, "For this reason do I say to you, do not be anxious about your life. Do not be concerned from dawn until dusk or dusk until dawn about what you will eat; nor about your body, what you will wear. Life is more important than food, and the body is better than its clothes. Consider the birds, which neither plant nor harvest, nor possess any barns or storehouses, yet God nourishes them. How far better are you to doves! Which of you can add an hour to his life or a cubit to his height? If you cannot do these minor things, then why trouble yourselves with these other details?

"Consider the lily; how does it grow? <You are far> superior to the lilies, which neither strive nor spin, but let me tell you that Solomon in all of his splendor was not decked-out like one of them. Now if God so dresses the grass of the field, which is here today, and tomorrow tossed into the oven, how much better will He clothe you, oh you limited of faith. Now concerning you; when you have no clothing, what ever will you put on? Who is the One that can lengthen your life? The very same will give you your clothes. Do not worry about what you will eat, or what you will drink--do not be concerned with this, for the nations of the world chase after these things, and your Father understands that you need them; but seek out first the kingdom of God, and all these things will be added on. Have no fear, oh little flock, because it was your Father's pleasure to give you the kingdom. Sell your things to give to the poor, and make bags for yourselves that do not wear out, a surefire treasure in the heavens, where no thief can approach, nor moth destroy; for wherever your treasure is, there will your heart be also.

BE WATCHFUL
(Luke 12:35-48; Justin Martyr--Dialogue with Trypho 47:6)
Galilee

"Keep yourselves clothed in readiness, and your lamps burning. Be like men who are awaiting their master when he comes back from the wedding feast, that they might open up the door for him the moment he comes and knocks thereat. And how joyful will those servants be when the Lord comes and finds them watching. I tell you most assuredly, the Lord will dress himself and have the watchmen all sit down to eat--and he will come and wait on them. And if he should come in the second or the third watch and find it so, those servants will fare extremely well. But you can all be sure of this: had the homeowner known when the thief would come, he would have kept watch, and not allowed his house to get broken into. You, therefore, must ready yourselves; for the Son of Man is coming at a time that you don't know."

"Sir," Peter asked him, "are you referring to us only in this parable, or also to these others?" "Tell me then," the Lord replied, "who is the wise and faithful steward whom the lord will set over his house to measure out the wheat when the time has come? It will truly go well for that servant, whom his lord should find so doing when he returns. Indeed I say to you that he will set him over all he owns. But if that servant should say in his heart, 'My lord is slow in coming home,' and therefore starts beating the male and female servants, and being gluttonous and drinking to excess; that servant's master will come on a day he has not foreseen, and in an hour that he does not know, and hack him to bits, appointing for him the inheritance of unbelievers. I will judge you in line with the way that I find you. That servant who knew the will of his lord, yet failed to get things ready for him, or did not do according to his will, will be beaten with many lashes. He will be beaten with few who, though having done things that are worthy of lashes, did not know. Much will be required from all to whom much has been entrusted; and much more will be demanded of him to whom much has been committed.

JESUS BRINGS ABOUT A DIVISION
(Luke 12:49-59; GTh 10, 16)
Galilee

"I came to set the world on fire, (and indeed) I have. Now behold, I am guarding it until it blazes. How I wish that it was lit already, but I have a baptism to undergo, and how troubled I am until it is done! Do you think that I came to pacify the world? Perhaps people think that I have come to bring them peace on earth. I am telling you not peace, but division. They are unaware that it is instead discord that I have come to cast upon the world--fire, sword, and war. After all, from this time forth, in a house of five, there will be three against two and two against three; a father opposing his son and a son opposing his father, a mother resisting a daughter, and a daughter resisting a mother, a mother-in-law versus her daughter-in-law, and a daughter-in-law versus her mother-in-law, and all of them will stand alone."

He then explained to the multitudes, "When you see a cloud rising up from the west, immediately you say, 'A storm of rain is on its way,' and even so it comes to pass. Also, when a south wind blows, you say, 'It is going to be a scorcher,' and so it goes. You hypocrites! You know enough to read the face of earth and sky, so why can't you read the signs of the times? And besides all that, why is it that you fail to discern righteousness for yourselves? For even as you are on your way to the ruler with your adversary, you diligently try to free yourself for fear that he might drag you before the judge, and that the judge might turn you over to the jailer, and that the jailer might throw you into prison. I am telling you now that you will not get out until you have paid back the very last cent."

JESUS DEMANDS REPENTANCE
(Luke 13:1-9)
Galilee

And some people who were there at the time were discussing with him the topic of the Galileans whose blood Pilate had mingled with their sacrifices. And Jesus said, "Do you imagine that because these people suffered such things, these men of Galilee were sinful beyond all other Galileans? I am telling you no; but all of you will come to this if you should choose not to reform. How about those eighteen who were killed when the tower fell on them in Siloam? Do you imagine that their debt was beyond that of other men in Jerusalem? I am telling you no; but if you should not repent, you will all end up like that."

And he spoke this parable: "A certain man had a fig tree that was planted in his vineyard, and came looking for fruit thereon but never found any, so he complained to the vinedresser, 'Behold, for three years now I have come looking for fruit on this tree and have never found any. Chop it down! Why make fruitless the ground that it uses?' 'Sir,' responded the vinedresser, 'leave it here for one more year, so that I might dig around it, mix in some manure and then see if it bears you any fruit. If it does not, then go ahead and cut it down.'"

PARABLE OF THE SOWER
(Matt 13:1-9; Mark 4:1-9; Luke 8:4-8)
The Sea of Galilee

And that day Jesus left the house and started to teach as he sat down by the sea. A great many multitudes were gathered around him; and they came to him from this town and that. So much so, as a matter of fact, that he got into the boat and sat down on the sea, even as the crowd that had gathered there stood on the shore. And he began to speak to them again and teach them many things in parables. And as he was teaching them, he spoke this parable to them, saying, "Hear this! A sower went out to sow his seed, took a handful and scattered. And it happened that, as he seeded it, some of it fell onto the road, and the seed got trampled down. And the birds came down from the sky, gathered them (and) ate them up. Others fell onto the rock, (or) stony ground where there was not much dirt. These took neither root in the earth, nor did they form any heads of grain. And right away (they all) came up, for the soil there was lacking in depth. Now as soon as they sprang up, the sun arose, and these for their lack of root and want of moisture, were scorched, (and they) withered. Others fell amid the thorns, and the thorns coming up with them, choked the seeds, and the worms devoured them, and so they did not yield their fruit. Still others fell on fertile ground. These came up, grew large, and all of them indeed bore fruit--some of them a hundredfold, some sixty, and some thirty. (Again,) one of them bore thirty-fold, another one bore sixty-fold, and another one a hundred-fold." And he cried out, "Whoever has ears to hear--let him hear!"

WHY JESUS USES PARABLES
(Matt 13:10-23; Mark 4:10-20; Luke 8:9-15;
GTh 5, 9, 7, 41, 56, 62, 80/5-POxy 654;
Quote by Clement of Alexandria, Miscellanies 5.10.63;
Quote By Macarius Of Egypt, Homily 12.17)
Beside the Sea of Galilee

And when Jesus was alone, those who were around him came up to him, along with the twelve disciples, and asked him about the parable, "Why do you speak to them in parables?" (and) "What is the meaning of this parable?" And he answered them, "Whoever has come to see the world has exhumed a cadaver, and of that one who has uncovered the corpse, the world is not worthy. I clarify my mysteries to those <who are worthy> of <my> mysteries. Do not let your left hand in on the workings of your right. My mystery is for me to share with the sons of my house. I am giving you such an inheritance that nothing in this world can compare with it. To you it has been given to know the secrets of the heavenly governance, (and) the mystery of God's rulership, but to these others it has been given only in parables. For to these this knowledge has not been given. No, for outsiders, all things are hidden away in parables, so that in seeing they may see and yet never perceive, and in hearing they may hear and yet never understand, lest they should turn and be forgiven their sins.' For it will be given to the one who has, and he will have it in abundance, and whoever has nothing, even what he does have will be taken away. This is why I use parables when I speak to these, for though they see, they don't perceive, and though they hear they don't discern, and neither do they comprehend.' And fulfilled in them is the prophecy of Isaiah, which says, 'In hearing you will hear, and will never understand, and in seeing you will see, and never will perceive. For this people's heart has grown numb; they heard only wearily with their ears, and their eyes they have closed, lest with their eyes they should see, and with their ears they should hear, and with their hearts understand, that they might return to me to be restored.' But joyful are your eyes that see, and joyful are your ears that hear, for truly do I say to you, that many prophets and righteous men wished to see what you now see, and did not see it, and to hear what you now hear, and did not hear it."

Then he asked them, "Is the meaning of this parable lost on you? How then will you decipher the rest? I am going to give you what no eye has seen, what no ear has heard, what no hand has handled, and what has never risen in the hearts of men. Hear therefore the parable of the sower. The seed stands for the word of God, so what the sower sows is the word. Now those on the road where the word is sown are those who hear. Whenever anyone hears the word of the kingdom and does not understand it Satan, the Devil, the Evil One, comes along and quickly captures and takes the word that was sown in their hearts, lest through their belief therein they might be saved. This is that which was sown on the road.

"As for those who were sown on rock, these are the ones who are likewise sown on rocky ground. These, therefore, are the ones who hear the word, and upon hearing it, immediately receive the word with joy. They are, nonetheless, not firmly rooted in themselves. They, being the ephemeral sort, believe only for a little while, and they quickly lose their footing whenever, for the sake of the word, trial or persecution comes, and they therefore fall away.

"And what was cast onto thorns: these are the ones who have been sown toward thorny places. And even though they hear the word, the age and its worries, the deceitfulness of riches, and the cravings for other things enter in and choke the word, rendering it unfruitful. And those who have heard, and venture forth through troubles and wealth, and the pleasures of this life, are strangled, and do not come to their fruition.

"And that which is sown on fertile ground: these are the ones who, once they have been sown, hear the word, and upon hearing the word with a true and righteous heart, understand it, accept it and hold on to it, and bear their fruit continuously. Some of them a hundredfold, some sixty, and some thirty; one (indeed) bears thirty fold, one sixty, one a hundred fold, and another one a hundred and twenty fold.

And he asked them, "Does one bring out the lamp only to place it under a jar (or) beneath the couch? Is it not meant to be put on a stand? Nobody lights a lamp and covers it up with a vessel or puts it under a couch. He puts it instead upon a stand, so that those who come in might see by its light. Know what is before your face, and what is concealed from you will be revealed to you. You see, nothing is so secret that it will not surface (and) be exposed, nor hidden so well, that it will not become obvious and recognized, and (nothing is) buried that will not be <exhumed.> For there is nothing that was concealed that is not meant to be revealed, nor was anything kept hidden but that it should come to light. If anyone has ears that hear, let him hear.

"And for this reason," Jesus advised them, "consider carefully the way that you hear. It will be measured back out to you in line with the way that you measure, and it will be added to those of you who are able to hear. More will be given to him who has something in hand, but it will be taken away from him who appears to have and yet does not. Those who are holding nothing will be stripped of even the little that they have."

THE WHEAT AND THE TARES
(Matt 13:24-30; GTh 57)
Beside the Sea of Galilee

And he spoke another parable to them: "The kingdom of the skies is like a man who had good seed, which he sowed into his field. His enemy came by night and planted tares among the wheat and ran away while the men were asleep. And when the wheat sprang up and yielded fruit, the weeds appeared along with it. Now the man did not let them pull up the tares. The servants of that householder approached him and asked, 'Sir, did you not sow good seed in your field? Where did all of these weeds come from?' 'An enemy has done this,' he answered. 'Would you have us go and pull them out?' the servants asked. 'No,' the man replied, 'for if you go gathering up the tares, you might uproot the wheat with them. Let the two grow alongside each other until the harvest, for at the time of the harvest, the weeds will be conspicuous, and I will say to the reapers, "Gather up first the tares and tie them into bundles to burn, then gather the wheat into my barn."'"

THE SEED GROWS BY ITSELF
(Mark 4:26-29)
Beside the Sea of Galilee

And he said, "This is how God's kingdom is: it is as though a man should cast his seed upon the ground, and day and night go to sleep and rise again. He has no idea how the seed springs up or grows; for the earth brings forth the grain by itself--first a blade, then an ear, then the grain grows full within it. Now when at last the grain is ripe, the harvest time has come about, so without delay he sends the sickle."

THE MUSTARD SEED
(Matt 13:31-32; Mark 4:30-32; GTh 20)
Beside the Sea of Galilee

"Tell us what the kingdom of the skies is like," the disciples asked Jesus. And he set another parable before them: "What can we liken God's kingdom to, or what parable can we use to describe it? The kingdom of the skies is even as a mustard grain, which a man took and sowed in his field. And when it is cast upon the earth, it is indeed less than any other seed; but whenever it falls upon (or) is planted in prepared soil, it grows to become greater than all other plants. And after it is fully grown, it becomes the greatest of herbs, becoming a tree, (and) a shelter, producing limbs so enormous that the birds of the sky can rest under the shade (of) its branches."

THE WOMAN AND THE LEAVEN
(Matt 13:33; GTh 96)
Beside the Sea of Galilee

He laid another parable before them: "The Father's heavenly kingdom is like leaven, out of which a woman took a small amount and hid it in three measures of meal until the batch was thoroughly leavened. Then she formed <the dough> into giant loaves. Anyone here with ears should hear!

THE WOMAN AND HER JAR OF MEAL
(GTh 97)
Beside the Sea of Galilee?

"The <Father's> kingdom is like a woman who was carrying a full <jar> of meal. As she walked along <a> distant road, the handle of the jar broke and the meal trickled out behind her <along> the path. She did not notice it at the time; but was unaware of her misfortune. Only when she had reached her house, and put down the jar did she learn that it was empty."

JESUS SPEAKS TO THE PEOPLE ONLY IN PARABLES

(Matt 13:34-35)
Beside the Sea of Galilee?

Jesus spoke all these things to the people in the language of parables, and he did not say anything to them except through parables, to fulfill what was spoken through the prophet, "I will open up my mouth in parables, proclaiming things hidden from the world's foundation."

JESUS EXPLAINS THE WHEAT AND THE TARES TO HIS DISCIPLES
(Matt 13:36-43)
In a House with His Disciples

Then Jesus left the crowds behind and entered the house. And his followers approached him and said, "Explain to us the parable of the weeds in the field." And he answered them, "the one who sows the good seed is the Son of Man, the field is the world, and the good seed are the sons of the kingdom. The tares are the sons of the evil one, and the devil is the enemy that sowed them. The harvest is the end of the age, and the reapers are the angels. So even as the tares are gathered up and burned with fire, so will it be at the close of this age. The Son of Man will send forth his angels, and they will gather out of his kingdom everything that stands against it, along with those who commit lawless acts, and toss them into the blazing furnace where there will be weeping and grinding of teeth. Then the righteous ones will shine like the sun in the kingdom of their Father. Whoever has ears that can hear, let him hear.

TREASURE HIDDEN IN THE FIELD
(Matt 13:44; GTh 109;
Quote By Clement Of Alexandria, Homilies 3.71.3)
In a House with the Disciples

"Again, the heavenly kingdom is like someone who had a treasure hidden in his field but knew nothing about it. <When> he died he left it to his <son.> The son knew <nothing> about it either. He took possession of the field and sold it--a man then found the treasure and hid it, and he joyfully went and sold all that he had, and bought that field. The buyer went plowing, <uncovered> the treasure, and started lending money at interest to whomever he pleased." (The word that was given freely must never be sold.)

THE PEARL OF GREAT PRICE
(Matt 13:45-46; GTh 76)
In a House with the Disciples

"Again, the Father's heavenly kingdom is like a businessman who had a supply of merchandise (and) was in search of quality pearls. That dealer was wise; he found one pearl that was especially precious and went and sold all of his goods and bought that singular pearl for himself. And so it goes for you as well, look for His reliable and enduring treasure where no moth devours and no worm destroys."

THE LARGE FISH
(GTh 8)
In a House with the Disciples?

And he said, "The true human is like a wise fisherman who cast his net into the sea and pulled it out full of little fish. The discerning fisherman spotted a large, choice fish among them. He threw all of the smaller ones back into the water, and had no trouble in choosing the large. Anyone here with two good ears should hear!

THE TWO KINDS OF FISH
(Matt 13:47-50)
In a House with the Disciples

"Again, the heavenly kingdom is like a net that was cast into the sea and which took of every kind. And when it was full, men dragged it ashore. Then they sat down, gathering the good ones into baskets and casting the bad ones aside. That is how things will come about at the end of the age. The angels will come and sever the wicked from among the righteous and hurl them into the flaming furnace, where it will be all weeping and grinding of teeth."

CLOSING PARABLES
(Matt 13:51-53; Mark 4:33-34;
Clement of Alexandria, Homilies 8.7)
In a House With the Disciples

Jesus asked them, "Are all these things now clear to you?" "Yes they are," they answered him. "For this reason," he explained, "every scribe who has been initiated into the kingdom of heaven is like a homeowner who brings out of his storehouse things that are both new and old. Someone is counted rich in God when they recognize that the ancient things of ages past are what is 'new,' and that what is 'new' is really 'old.'"

And as far as they were able to hear, he spoke the word to them using many such parables; and he spoke nothing to them except through parables, but when he was alone with his disciples, he would work them all out for them. And so it happened that, after he had finished speaking these parables, Jesus moved on.

THE WINDS AND THE WAVES OBEY JESUS
(Matt 8:18, 23-27; Mark 4:35-41; Luke 8:22-25; AcA&M 8)
By and Upon the Sea of Galilee

My children, who have given your lives over to the Lord, have no fear, because the Lord will never forsake us. At that time we were alone with our Lord. Now on that day, when evening had come, it happened that Jesus saw great masses gathered around him. He then gave orders to travel on to the other side of the lake, saying to [us], "Let us pass to the further shore." And [we] took him into the boat as he was, leaving the crowds behind [us] there. And after he had climbed aboard, we disciples followed after him, and then [we] shoved off. (And there were also other small boats with him.)

And while he was on board, he quietly lied down in order to test us, and fell into a deep sleep as [we] sailed along, though he was not truly asleep. And behold, a great, tempestuous windstorm rose up in the sea, and bore down upon it. And the sea became so rough that the waves were pounding against the boat (and) towering over the sail of the ship, such that it was being filled. And by that time it was almost full and they were all in mortal danger, but he was sleeping on a pillow down in the stern. And [we], his disciples, came up to him saying, "Master, master, we are all about to die! Lord, save us! We are perishing! Teacher, do you not care if we all die?"

And seeing that we were terrified, he woke right up and questioned [us], "Oh you limited of faith, tell me why you're so afraid?" Then he stood to his feet, and reproved the winds and commanded the raging waters of the sea, "Be silent and still!" The waves subsided and the wind was lulled, and a great calm settled in. (All things are obedient to him, you see, for they are all his handiwork.) "Why are you so full of fear?" he demanded. "How have you come to such unbelief? Where is your faith?" And the men, paralyzed with fear, said to each other in utter astonishment, "Who can this be? From where is this man that he even commands the winds and the waves and they obey him?" And for this reason, my children, do not ever be afraid, for the Lord Jesus will never forsake us.

HEALING THE DEMONIAC
(Matt 8:28-34; Mark 5:1-20; Luke 8:26-39)
Eastern Shore of the Sea of Galilee

And he sailed down (with) [them] to the region of the Gadarenes and came to land on the other side of the sea, to the place that was opposite Galilee. And two demoniacs who were so violent that no one was able to pass that way, came out from among the tombs and confronted him. When Jesus had come out of the boat (and) stepped ashore, he was met by (one of) the demon-possessed, filthy spirited [men] who had come out from that town's cemetery to withstand him. This man had worn no clothes for a long time now, nor had he lived in any house, but only there among the tombs. The demon had taken control of him on numerous occasions, and no one was able to keep him tied down any longer, even with a chain. He had been shackled many times, you see, and in spite of being bound-up hand and foot, and constantly kept under watch, he still managed to shatter his chains and demolish his foot irons and be driven by the demon into desolate places. There was no one strong enough to overpower him, and he would cry out day and night amid the tombs and hills, and mutilate himself with rocks.

As soon as he saw Jesus from afar, he ran up to him, fell to his knees before him, (and) shouted out as loud as he could, "Tell me what you want from me, Jesus, Son of the Most High God! I beg you, please, do not hurt me! Swear to God that you won't torment me!" Jesus, you see, had ordered the filthy spirit to leave the man, saying to him, "You unclean spirit, come out of him!"

"What is your name?" Jesus demanded. "Legion," the man replied, "for we are many." Multitudes of demons, you see, had entered into him. "Son of God," they all cried out, "tell us what you want from us! Have you come to torment us before the time?" Now he (and) the demons pleaded persistently with Jesus not to cast them out (and) make them go down to the abyss.

A short distance away from them, on the slope of a nearby hill, a giant herd of pigs was feeding. The demons begged Jesus to let them go into the swine, (saying,) "If you force us out, then send us to that herd of pigs, and let us enter into them." And Jesus agreed, saying, "Go ahead!" So when the evil spirits left the man, they all went into the pigs, and the entire herd--nearly two thousand in number--raced down the steep embankment into the sea where, drowning in the water, they died.

When the herdsmen saw what had been done, they dashed into the city and through the countryside proclaiming all that they had seen--including what had become of the demoniacs. And the whole town went out to meet him, (and) to see all that had happened. And when they came to him and saw him there, they found the man who had been possessed, (but) from whom the legion of demons had fled, sitting at the feet of Jesus, fully dressed and sound of mind; and all of them were petrified.

Those who had seen the event explained to the people what had happened to the demon-possessed man; how [he] had been healed, and about the swine as well. Then everyone in the region of the Gerasenes started begging Jesus to leave their presence (and) their land, for all of them were terrified.

So Jesus went aboard the boat, and as he was climbing in, the man who was formerly possessed by demons asked if he might travel on with him. Jesus would not let him come, but sent him away, saying, "Go back home to your family and let them know how much the Lord God has done for you, (and) the kindness He has shown to you," then he shoved off. So the man went into town, (and) on to the Decapolis and began to proclaim what a marvelous thing that the Lord had done for him, and they were all astonished.

THE FEAST AT LEVI'S
(Matt 9:11-13; Mark 5:21, 2:15-17;
Luke 8:40/5:29-32; Barnabas 5:9)
Capernaum

Now when Jesus had once again crossed over and come again to the other shore of the lake, a large crowd greeted him, and surrounded him, for they had all been awaiting him. A great throng gathered around him and he started teaching them. Then Levi held a feast for Jesus at his home. As Jesus was eating at Levi's house, large numbers of tax-collectors and "sinners" and others came around (and) dined with him and his disciples. (Many, you see, had followed him there.) But the Pharisees and their scribes, saw that he was eating with "sinners" and tax-collectors. They grumbled to his students, demanding, "Why do you (and) your Master eat and drink with tax-collectors and 'sinners?'" When Jesus heard them (asking) this, he answered them, "It is not the healthy who need a doctor, but those who are ill. You ought to go and learn what it means to say 'I long for mercy, and not sacrifice.' It is not the righteous, you see, but the unrighteous instead that I have come to call to repentance." (And it was in his choice of the apostles that he truly showed he was the Son of God, for the ones that he selected were 'sinful' above all others, which was proof that he came to call 'sinners' to repentance, and not saints.)

JOHN'S FOLLOWERS QUESTION JESUS
(Matt 9:14-17; Mark 2:18-22; Luke 5:33-39; GTh 104)
Capernaum(?)

The followers of John were fasting, as were the Pharisees. At that time, some of John's students approached Jesus and asked, "Why is it that we, the followers of John, fast and pray all the time, as do the disciples of the Pharisees, but your disciples never do. To the contrary, they are always eating and drinking?" "Can you compel the guests of the bridegroom to fast while he is yet with them?" Jesus replied. "How is it even possible for the bridegroom's guests to fast (and) mourn while he is there? They cannot so long as the bridegroom remains. But the time is approaching when the groom will be taken from them--then will begin their day of fasting. Their 'fast,' therefore, will be in those days." "Come now," they urged him, "let us all fast and pray." "For what reason?" asked Jesus. "What offense have I committed, or in what way have I been overcome? After the groom has left the bridal chamber, then the people can fast and pray." Then he spoke this parable to them: "No one rips a piece off of new clothing and sews the new patch onto old. If he should, the newer piece would shrink, tearing the older clothing even further; he will have ripped the new garment even more, and the new portion would no longer fit the old. And no men pour fresh wine into used wineskins, either. If they should, the fresh wine would pop the skins, and the wine would flow right out. The wine and the skins would both be destroyed. No, fresh wine has to be put into new wineskins! They (therefore) put it in the new, that way they are both preserved. Also, after drinking the old wine, no one ever wants the new, for they hold that the older is the better."

THE RAISING OF JAIRUS' DAUGHTER;
THE HEALING OF THE BLEEDING WOMAN
(Matt 9:18-26; Mark 5:22-43; Luke 8:41-56)
Capernaum

At that moment, even as he was saying these things, one of the rulers of the synagogue, a man named Jairus, came in. And as soon as he saw Jesus there, he went up to him and knelt before him. And he fell down at his feet and solemnly begged Jesus to go to his house because his only daughter, a twelve year old girl, was near to death. "My daughter is in the throes of death, (and by now) has passed away. But kindly come and place your hands on her, that she might receive her healing, and she will live." So Jesus and his followers got up and went with him.

And as he was on his way, a great crowd followed after him, squeezing him almost to the point of crushing him. And there was this woman there who, for twelve years had been the victim of bleeding, yet no one had been able to cure her. She had suffered a great deal, while under the care of many physicians, and had spent all that she had on doctors; but rather than getting any better, she had only gotten worse. And when she came to hear of Jesus, she said in her heart, "If I were to but touch his clothes, I would be healed!" So right away she snuck up behind him and touched the hem of his robe, and in that instant the woman was healed. Her bleeding stopped, and she perceived within herself that she'd been delivered from her suffering. Jesus immediately sensed power flowing out of him, so he turned around amid the crowd, asking, "Who was it that touched my clothes?" "You see all of these people thronging you," his students replied, "and yet you ask, 'Who touched me?'" But he kept on looking to see who it was. "Who has touched me?" he demanded. When everyone there denied it, Peter responded, "Teacher, the people are swarming all around you and shoving up against you." But Jesus answered him, "Someone here has touched me, though. I am sure that power has flowed from me!"

Jesus turned around and looked at her. Then the woman, realizing what had changed within her and seeing that she could not hide, came and fell at his feet trembling with fear. And she confessed the truth before them all; her reason for touching him and how she had been so quickly cured. "Take heart, my daughter," he assured her, "what healed you was your faith. Go peacefully along your way and be free of your affliction."

And even as Jesus was speaking, a certain man came (with) some from the house of Jairus, a ruler of the synagogue. "Your daughter's dead!" the man declared. "Do not continue to trouble this teacher, (for) it will do you no good." When Jesus heard this, he ignored their words and counseled Jairus, the ruler of the synagogue: "Have no fear, for if you would just believe, then your daughter would be healed."

He allowed only Peter, James, and his brother John to follow him. When he got to the home of Jairus, the synagogue ruler, Jesus saw the people in an uproar, crying out and lamenting, mourning for her as loud as they could. At that point, he went inside, allowing none but Peter, John and James to go in with him, along with the father and mother of the girl. When Jesus entered the ruler's house, he saw the flutists and the disorderly crowd and questioned them, "Why all this lamentation and commotion? Get out! Enough with all of your weeping. This child is not dead, but only sleeping." Still, sure that she was dead already, they all simply laughed at him. But after ushering these people out, he took the father and mother of the girl, along with the disciples who were with him, and went in to where the young child was. He took the young girl by her hand and said, "Talitha koum!" which translates as, "I say young woman, rise up now!" Then her spirit was restored and she immediately got up and started walking around. This utterly astounded them, and he solemnly bound them not to tell anyone what had happened, (nor) to allow anyone to find out about it. Then he had them give her something to eat.

JESUS HEALS THE TWO BLIND MEN
(Matt 9:27-34)
Capernaum?

And as Jesus moved on from there, two blind men followed after him, crying out, "Son of David, have mercy on us." When he got to the house, the sightless men came up to him. "Do you believe that I can do this?" he asked them. "Yes Lord," they answered. Then he touched their eyes and said, "Let it be to you as you believed," and their eyes were opened. Then Jesus ordered them sternly, "See that no one hears of this." But they went right out and spread his name throughout the land. And behold, even as they were leaving, they brought a speechless, demon-possessed man over to him. After the demon had been cast out, the man who had been mute began to speak, and the people cried out in astonishment, "Never has this been seen in Israel!" "It is only through the Lord of Demons," the Pharisees contended, "that this man is ousting demons."

JESUS "DISHONORED IN HIS OWN HOUSE"
(Matt 13:54-58; Mark 6:1-6)
Nazareth

Jesus left that region for his own, and his students followed him. He arrived in his hometown, and when the Sabbath came around, Jesus started teaching the people in their synagogue. And many of those who heard him there were amazed, asking, "Where did this man learn all this? What kind of wisdom is this that has been given to him that he does such marvels? Is this not the carpenter, the son of the carpenter, (and) of Mary? His mother's name is Mary, right? Are not James, Joseph, Judas and Simon his brothers? Are not his sisters here with us?" And they all took offense at him.

But Jesus informed them, "A prophet only lacks honor in his own hometown, in his own household, and in his own family." He was unable to work any wonders there, except to lay his hands upon and heal a few of the sick. And he was astounded by their lack of faith; and it was owing to their unbelief that he did not perform a great many wonders in that place.

JESUS IN THE GENTILE TEMPLE
(AcA&M 12-15)
Nazareth? Jerusalem? Hebron?

(Andrew said,) as we, the twelve disciples, were entering into a Gentile temple with our Lord, that he might make plain to us the ignorance of the devil, it happened that the chief priests, seeing us following after Jesus, chided us, 'Oh you wretches, why do you walk with the one who says that he's the Son of God? Are you trying to say that God has a son? Which of you has ever seen God in the presence of a woman? Is not this the son of Joseph the carpenter, and is not Mary his mother. Are not James and Simon his brothers?' And when we heard these words, our hearts all sank. And Jesus, knowing that our hearts were giving way, took us aside to a secluded spot, and performed amazing miracles before us there, showing His Godhead to us all. Then we appealed to the chief priests, saying, 'You must also come and see--for he has persuaded us.'

And the chief priests followed us. Now after we had entered into the Gentile temple, Jesus brought the heavens into view, to assure us that these things were true. (Now thirty men from the people went in with us, attended by four of the chief priests.) And Jesus, looking over the right and left hand sides of the temple, caught sight of two sculpted sphinxes, one to the right and the other to the left. And turning to us, Jesus said, 'Behold, this is like the sign of the cross, for these are even as the cherubim and seraphim are in heaven.' Then he looked at the sphinx on the right, and said, 'I say to you, image of what is in heaven--that which the hands of artisans have sculpted--leave your place, and come down to give answer to the high-ranking priests, and convict them, and reveal to them whether I am truly God, or just a man.'

And at that moment the sphinx got up from its spot, and in a human voice proclaimed to them, 'Oh you senseless sons of Israel! Not only have these people not been content with the blinding of their hearts, but they long for others to be blind like them, who ascribe human qualities to God. First of all, God made man and breathed His breath into all that live, giving movement to what had never moved. He is the One Who summoned Abraham, cherished His son Isaac, and brought His beloved Jacob back into his land, and revealed Himself to him in the wilderness, and made many great things for him. It was He Who led them forth and gave them water gushing from a rock. He is the Judge of the living and the dead. He is the one who prepares great blessings for those who obey Him, and devises punishments for those who don't. So do not think of me as some mere idol that can be handled; for indeed I say to you, that the temples are better than your synagogues. Now even though we are but stones, the priests themselves have called us gods. And those priests who serve at the temple purify for fear of the demons. For if they have had relations with women, they purify for seven days. It is because of us that they do not enter into the temple--on account of the fear that they show for the name that they have given us--that is to say the name of god. But as for you, after you have fornicated, you take up the law of God, go right into the synagogue of God, purify and then recite--showing no respect for the glorious words of God. I am telling you that because of this, the temples are going to fare better than your synagogues, such that they, too, will become churches of His only begotten Son.' After the sphinx had spoken this, it fell silent.

And we said to the high-ranking priests, 'It would now be fitting for you to believe, for even the stones have convicted you.' 'These stones,' the Jews replied, 'have only spoken through magic, so don't go thinking that it's a God. See, if you had put the words of this stone to the test, you would have recognized its trickery. For where did he meet Abraham, or how did he lay eyes on him? Abraham died a great many years before this man ever lived, so how could he have possibly known him?'

And Jesus again turned to the image and said, 'Since these men do not believe that I have spoken to Abraham, go out into the land of the Canaanites, to the double cave in the field of Mamre, where the body of Abraham lies; and cry aloud before the tomb, "Abraham, Abraham, whose body rests in this sepulcher, and whose soul rests in paradise, He Who fashioned you and made you his friend from the beginning, says this, 'You--and your son Isaac; and Jacob also, the son of your son--rise up now and go to the temples of the Jebusites, so that we might convict the chief priests, that they might come to understand that I know you, and that you know me.'"' And the sphinx, on hearing these words, immediately passed before us all. And she set off for the land of the Canaanites, to the field of Mamre, and there cried out before the tomb as Jesus had commanded her. And the twelve patriarchs suddenly came out alive, and inquired of the sphinx, 'To which of us have you been sent?' 'I have been sent as a sign to the three patriarchs,' the sphinx replied, 'but go back and rest until the time of the resurrection.' And as soon as they heard this, they went back in and fell asleep. And the three patriarchs set out with the sphinx to meet Jesus, where they then convicted the chief priests. Jesus then ordered them, 'Go back to your places,' and off they went. 'Return to your post,' he commanded the image. And she went back up and stood in her spot. And he also worked many other wonders, but they never came to believe in him. And if I were to describe these things to you, you would no doubt think they were untrue.

BOUNTIFUL HARVEST; FEW LABORERS
(Matt 9:35-38; Mark 6:6b; GTh 73;
Quote By Clement of Alexandria, Homilies 3.64.1)
Throughout Galilee

And Jesus went from village to village throughout all of the cities and townships, teaching in their synagogues, proclaiming the good news of the kingdom, and healing every sickness and disease among them. And he felt compassion for the multitudes when he saw them all faint and cast aside, as sheep that were lacking a shepherd. "How great is the harvest," he said to his students, "yet how few are the reapers. You should therefore beg the Lord of the Crop to send more workers into His field. How blessed is the man whom the Lord will assign to the service of his fellow workers."

Robert C. Ferrell

THE TWELVE SENT OUT AS A WITNESS
(Matt 10:1, 5-11:1, 10:16-in Cursive Ms. 1424;
Mark 6:7-13; Luke 9:1-6; GTh 6, 14, 23, 27, 33/27, 33-POxy 1;
GEb 6, Quote by Epiphanius, Heresies 30.16;
GNaz 11, Quote by Eusebius, Theophany 4.12)
Galilee

And he called his twelve disciples to himself and gave them power and authority to cast out the unclean spirits, and to cure every sickness and disease. The disciples asked Jesus, "Would you like us to fast? How should we pray? Should we give alms? What diet should we observe?" "If you fast," Jesus said, "you will bring sin upon yourselves, and if you pray, you will condemn yourselves, and if you give alms, you will damage your spirits. I came to bring all sacrificing to an end, and if you continue to offer up sacrifices, you will never stop experiencing wrath. If you do not fast from the world, you will never find the kingdom of God; if you do not keep the Sabbath Day as a Sabbath, you will never come to see the Father. Indeed you hear with one of your ears, but the other you have closed. Never say anything that is untrue, nor ever do what's hateful to you, for all things lie open in the sight of heaven. Nothing, therefore, is hidden that will not be exposed, nor is anything concealed that will not be revealed. Now when you enter into any land and travel throughout any region, if they should receive you, eat whatever they might place before you, and heal the sick who are with them. For what goes into your mouth cannot defile you. It is instead the things that come from your mouth that bring about your defilement."

Jesus, after giving them instruction, sent these twelve out in pairs to preach the kingdom of God and heal the sick. And these were the guidelines that he gave: "Do not go among the Gentiles, nor into any Samaritan town; but go instead to the lost sheep of the house of Israel. And as you go, proclaim to them, 'The kingdom of heaven has drawn near to you!' Restore the sick, cleanse the leprous, raise the dead, and oust the demons: freely was it given you, so freely you should give it, too. Carry nothing but a staff for your path. Do not take any silver, or gold, or brass in your belts; nor bread or scrip for along the way. Wear sandals on your feet, but do not carry extra coats, or sandals, or staffs--for the worker is worthy of his hire.

"And into whatever town or village that you enter, seek out someone who is worthy, and whenever you go into a house, no matter whose it may be, remain there in his home until such time as you leave that town. On entering into that place, welcome it; and if the house should indeed be worthy, let your peace come over it; and should that place be undeserving, let your peace return to you. And if anyone, (or) the people of any place should refuse to take you in or hear your words, then shake the dust from off your feet as you are leaving that house or town as a testimony against them. I tell you most assuredly, it will be more tolerable for the land of Sodom and Gomorrah on the Day of Judgment than it will be for that town.

"Behold, I am sending you out as sheep amid wolves, so be as sly as snakes, (indeed) be even slier than snakes; you should be as simple as doves. And you must be wary of men, for they will turn you over to councils, and beat you in their synagogues, and you will be brought for my sake before governors and kings for a testimony both to these and to the Gentiles. And when they deliver you up, do not think about what you should say, or how you should say it, because at that very moment what you should say will come to you. You are not yourselves the speakers, you see, but the Spirit of the Father will be speaking in you. A brother, moreover, will deliver his own brother over to death, and a father, his own child. Children will turn against their parents, and they will have them put to death. You will be hated by all for bearing my name, but whoever bears it to the end will be saved. And when they persecute you in this town, escape from there into another, for I am telling you that you will not have passed through all the cities of Israel before the coming of the Son of Man. A student is not above his teacher, nor a servant greater than his lord; it is enough for a disciple to be as his teacher, and a servant to be like his lord. If they have called the ruler of the house Beelzebub, how much more will they those of his own house!

"Therefore have no fear of them, for nothing has been covered that will not be exposed; or made unclear that will not be seen through. What I say to you in darkness, speak in illumination, and what you hear in your ear, the other ear (I mean,) proclaim from your housetops. No one lights a lamp and places it under a basket, nor does anyone hide it away somewhere. One puts it on a stand instead, so that everyone might see its light, whether coming in or going out. And do not be shaken by those who destroy the body, but have no strength to slay the soul. Rather, fear Him Who has the power to destroy both body and soul in Gehenna. Do not two sparrows sell for an assar? Yet apart from your Father, not so much as one of these ever falls to the ground. As for you--even the very hairs of your head have their number. So do not be afraid of them--you are worth more than scores of sparrows.

"Therefore all who will acknowledge me before mankind, I will likewise acknowledge them before my Father in heaven. But whoever denies me before men--him also I will deny before my Father in heaven. Do not think that I came to pacify the world; I did not come bringing peace, but a sword. You see, I came to set a man against his father, and a daughter against her mother; a daughter-in-law versus her mother-in-law; and a man's enemies will be those of his own household. I choose the worthiest for myself--and my heavenly Father has given me the most worthy. Whoever loves his father or mother above me is not worthy of me; and whoever loves his son or daughter above me is not worthy of me. Furthermore, whoever does not accept his cross and follow me is not worthy of me. The one who finds his life will lose it, and the one who loses his life for my sake will find it. Whoever accepts you is accepting me, and the one who accepts me is accepting also Him Who sent me. Anyone accepting a wise man in the name of a wise man will receive the reward of the wise. And the one who accepts a righteous man in the name of a righteous man, will receive the reward of the righteous. And whoever gives one of these little ones so much as a single cup of cold water to drink in the name of a disciple, I tell you most assuredly, he will not be denied his reward. Out of a thousand, I will choose one, and out of ten thousand, I will choose two--and they will stand in peace as one."

And it happened that, when Jesus had finished giving instruction to his twelve disciples, he left that place to teach and preach in their cities. So they traveled through the villages, warning the people to change their ways. They drove out many demons, anointed many of the sick with oil and healed people everywhere.

MINISTRY 3

THE DEATH OF JOHN THE BAPTIST
(Matt 14:1-12; Mark 6:14-29; Luke 9:7-9)
Machaerus

Now by that time, King Herod the Tetrarch had heard stories about Jesus, (and) the kinds of things that he was doing; for his name had gotten around. But Herod was perplexed, because he (and) some (others) were saying, "John the Baptist has been raised from the dead, and for this reason these powers work in him." But others held that Elijah had come: "He is Elijah," they would say. And still others maintained that one of the ancient prophets had come to life: "It is a wise man, like one of the sages of old." Now when Herod heard that, he said to his attendants, "John, whom I had beheaded, has been raised up. But then again, who is this that I have been hearing so much about? I had John's head chopped off! And he sought for a chance to meet with him."

Herod, you see, had sent for John, had him bound up and arrested and put into prison over the issue of his brother Philip's, wife, Herodias, whom he had married. For John had been admonishing Herod, "It is against the law for you to have your brother's wife." Now Herod really wanted to kill John, but since the people believed that he was a prophet, he feared them. Now Herodias nursed a grudge against him and sought to have him put to death, but was not able to make it happen, for Herod feared John, knowing him to be a righteous and holy man, and therefore kept him safe in prison. He would become extremely perplexed (and) do many things whenever he would hear him speak, and he heard that he worked many wonders, yet he continued to hear him gladly.

Then the day came at last. On his birthday, Herod held a banquet for his noblemen and military brass and the foremost of Galilee. When the daughter of Herodias came in and danced for them, she delighted Herod and his guests to such an extent that he promised her on oath to give her anything that she would ask of him. "Ask me for whatever you wish," the king assured the girl, "and I will give it to you." And he solemnly swore to her, "Whatever you might ask of me, I will grant it to you--even if it should be the half of my kingdom." And she went out, and besought her mother, "Tell me what I should ask him for?" Whereupon her mother replied, "The head of that Baptizer, John!"

She hurried right back in to the king, and, at her mother's behest demanded, "I would that you give me John the Baptist's head on a dish right here (and) now." The king regretted it deeply, but for the sake of his oath, and those who were sitting at table with him, he would not break his word to her. He sent an executioner right away, with orders that her request be carried out--that that man's head be brought in on a serving dish. And he went and beheaded him in the prison, and brought his head in on a platter, and handed it to the girl. The girl then carried it to her mother and gave it to her. When his followers heard about it, they came and picked his body up. Then they buried it, laying it in a tomb. And they went back to Jesus and told him these things.

Robert C. Ferrell

JESUS FEEDS FIVE THOUSAND
(Matt 14:13-21; Mark 6:30-44;
Luke 9:10-17; John 6:1-13)
Northeastern Shore of the Sea of Galilee

After this, when the apostles had returned, they gathered all around him, telling him all about what they had done and taught. And when Jesus heard this, he urged them, "Come now, let us go secretly to a secluded spot and take it easy for a while." You see, they had been coming and going so much that they had absolutely no chance to eat. And Jesus took them, boarded a boat with them, and sailed with them to an isolated setting on the far side of the Sea of Galilee, which is the Sea of Tiberias, to a town called Bethsaida.

Now many who were there recognized them, for they had seen the wonders that he had worked on the sick. And the people watched as they went away, so when the throngs of people heard about it and it became known, they all followed after Jesus, running there on foot from all of the towns, and arriving there ahead of him. After Jesus had left that region behind and gone ashore, he saw a great crowd and felt sorry for them, for they were like sheep who were lacking a shepherd. He welcomed them all and started speaking to them and teaching them many things about God's kingdom. Then he healed those who were sick and needed healing.

Jesus climbed up the mountainside and sat with his disciples there, and the Jewish feast day of Passover, was drawing near. Then he lifted up his eyes and saw many people coming to him. Jesus therefore said to Philip, "Where are we to buy bread for these people?" (This he said as a test to him, for he already knew what he would do.) And Philip answered him, "Two hundred denarii worth of loaves would not be enough for each of them to have even a partial serving." And later on, toward dusk that day, his twelve disciples approached him and urged, "This is such a far-flung place, and the day has grown quite long; please tell them to go away. Have them go out into the countryside and villages round about to buy themselves some food to eat, as well as lodging." "They have no need to go away," Jesus answered. "You give them something to eat." Then the disciples asked, "Are we to go out, and with two hundred denarii worth of loaves, give them something?" "How many loaves have you got?" he asked them. "Go and see." One of his servants, Simon's brother Andrew, said to him, "here is a boy, who has five barley loaves and two fish; but what do these amount to among so many?" And when it dawned on them, they said, "We've got nothing here but five loaves and two fish; that is unless we go and buy food for all these people!" (You see, there were close to five thousand men who were there.) And Jesus said, "Bring them over here to me." Then he had the crowd sit down on the green grass. He then said to his disciples, "Have them sit in parties of fifty," and so they did, and there was a lot of grass in that place. They all sat down, by hundreds and by fifties; about five thousand men in all. Upon receiving the five loaves and the two fish, Jesus took the loaves, looked to the sky, and blessed them. And after he had given thanks, he tore apart the loaves and handed them to the disciples to set before the people; and they distributed them among those who were sitting there, and the fish as well. He divided the two fish among them all--as many as the people wished--and they ate their fill and were satisfied. And when the crowd had had enough, he instructed his disciples, "Gather up the leftover fragments, so that nothing might be lacking of them." And they took the leavings, gathering up and filling twelve baskets with what remained of the five barley loaves and the fish that were left by them who had eaten it. And there were five thousand men who ate in that place--not including the women and children!

JESUS REJECTS AN EARTHLY KINGDOM
(Matt14:22-23; Mark 6:45-46; John 6:14-17a)
Northeastern Shore of the Sea of Galilee

When the people saw the sign that he had shown, they said, "This is surely the prophet who is coming into the world!" Then, when evening had come, he immediately constrained the disciples to get into the boat and travel on ahead of him to Bethsaida on the other side, as he stayed behind and dismissed the crowds. His students then went down to the sea, got into a boat and set out for Capernaum, on the opposite shore of the lake. And after he had left them there, Jesus, knowing that the people were about to come and force the kingship on him, headed up to the mountain to pray alone.

JESUS WALKS ON THE SEA
(Matt 14:23b-33; Mark 6:47-52;
John 6:17b-21; AcJn 12, 13)
The Sea of Galilee

By the time evening had come and darkness had fallen, Jesus was all alone upon the land. But he could see the disciples, wind against them, straining at the oars in the boat, already many stadia away, being hurled about by the waves in the midst of the lake. The wind was blowing strong and the waters were growing violent. Even so, Jesus had not yet joined them. Then, in the fourth watch of the night, by the time they had rowed about twenty five or thirty stadia, Jesus went walking out to them on the water. He was just about to pass them by, but when they saw him drawing near to the boat, walking on the surface of the sea, they imagined him to be a ghost. Since they all saw him and were terrified, they cried out in fear, "It is a spirit!" But Jesus immediately spoke up and said, "Be not fearful, but believing, for indeed it is me!" "Master," Simon answered, "if you are who you claim to be, order me to come out to you upon these waters." Jesus said, "Come to me." So Simon got out of the boat and walked out to him upon the water; but he grew anxious when his thoughts turned to the powerful gale. Then Peter began to sink, so he cried out, "Master, save me!" And immediately Jesus caught hold of him and said, "Oh, you limited of faith, why ever did you doubt?" Then they were willing to take him into the ship. He climbed into it with them, and the wind died down just as soon as they had boarded. And right away the boat reached the shore for which they had set out. They were all completely taken aback, since their hearts had been made hard, and they had not understood about the loaves. And the ones who had been in the boat came to him in adoration, saying, "You're assuredly the Son of God."

IN GENNESARET
(Matt 14:34-36; Mark 6:53-56; AcJn 92, 93)
Gennesaret

And after they had passed across, they came to land at Gennesaret, where they cast anchor. And as soon as they had disembarked, the people there immediately recognized him, and raced throughout the region, passing the word along to the surrounding countryside, and the people started bringing their sick up to him on mats wherever they heard that Jesus was.

And everywhere that he would go, be it in villages, townships, or the countryside, they laid those who were in poor health in the markets, and begged him to allow the ill to touch but the fringe of his robe; and as many as touched it were instantly healed.

Again, one time when we disciples were all sleeping in a house in Gennesaret, after I, (John,) had wrapped myself up, I kept a watchful eye on him. At first I heard him say to me, "John, go to sleep." And when I heard this, I pretended to fall asleep; then I saw another who was like him there, whom I also heard saying to my Master, "Jesus, the ones you have chosen still do not believe in you." And my Lord replied, "Indeed they do not, for they are but mortal men."

I will relate another sublime matter to you, my brothers. There were times when I wanted to touch him, and I felt a solid, physical presence; but then there were times when his body seemed unreal to me, and without substance--as if it were not even there at all. Now, if ever he was invited by Pharisee and indeed went to the place where he had been bidden, we would all go with him there. And our host, placing a loaf of bread before each of us, would give him one also. Then he would bless his own and split it among us; and that tiny bit would fill us all, while our own would remain unbroken. Those who had invited him would always be amazed.

And whenever I would walk with him, from time to time I would try to see if he left his prints upon the ground, but I could never make out any. What I did notice, however, was him raising himself up off of the ground. Dearest brothers, I am saying these things to you now that I might stir your faith in him. At this time, however, we must remain silent when it comes to his masterful and amazing works, inasmuch as they are mysterious, and there can be no doubting that they are neither to be expressed with words nor understood with reason.

THE LIFE-GIVING BREAD

(John 6:22-71; John 6:56-in Codex Bezae Cantabrigiensis)
Capernaum

The next day it became clear to the people still standing across the sea that there had been but one boat, and that Jesus had not gotten in with his disciples, but that his followers had gone away all by themselves. Boats from Tiberias, however, did land near the spot where they had eaten the bread after the Lord had given thanks.

When, therefore, it dawned on the people that neither Jesus nor his disciples were there, they boarded the boats and crossed over to the town of Capernaum in search of him. And when they found him on that side of the sea, they asked him, "Rabbi, when did you come to this shore?" "I am telling you the truth," Jesus replied, "you seek me not on account of the signs that you saw, but because you had eaten your fill of the loaves.

"Do not labor for the food that perishes, but for the food that leads to endless life, which the Son of Man will give to you; because God the Father has placed His seal on him." They asked him, "What should we do to bring to pass the works of God?" Jesus answered, "God's 'work' is that you should place your faith in the one He sent." "What sign will you show us then, that we might see it and thereby place our faith in you?" they asked. "What kind of work will you perform? Our ancestors ate the heavenly food out in the wilderness; even as it is written, 'He provided them with bread to eat from on high.' I am telling you the truth," Jesus explained, "it was not Moses who gave you to eat of the heavenly bread; it is, rather, my Father Who gives you of the true bread of heaven. The 'bread' of God is that which comes down from heaven and causes the world to come alive."

"Teacher," they implored him, "give us to eat of this bread." "I am myself that bread of life," Jesus informed them. "Whoever comes to me will never hunger, and whoever trusts in me will never thirst. Even so, all of you have seen me and yet have not believed in me, even as I have spoken it to you. All that the Father gives to me are drawn to me; and anyone who approaches me, I will by no means cast out. For I did not come down from heaven to do my own will, but the will of the One Who sent me; and this is the will of the Father Who sent me: that I should not lose anything that He has given to me, but that I might restore it on the final day. This, you see, is my Father's will: that everyone who looks upon the Son and accepts him should have endless life; and I will lift them up on the final day."

Then the Jews started complaining about him because he said, "I am that bread that came down from heaven." "Is this not Jesus," they marveled, "the son of Joseph; about whom we are certain of father and mother? How is it that he now can say, 'I have come down from heaven?'" "Quit grumbling to yourselves," Jesus replied. "No one can approach me unless they are led by the Father Who sent me; and I will lift him up on the final day. It is written in the Prophets, 'They will all be led by God.' Everyone who hears the Father and learns from Him comes to me. No man has ever seen the Father except for the one who came down from God; this one has truly seen the Father. I am telling you the truth, whoever trusts has endless life; and I am that bread of life.

"Your forefathers ate the manna in the wilderness, and they all died. This, however, is the bread that comes down from heaven, of the which a man might eat and never die. I am that living bread that comes from heaven; so anyone who eats of this bread will live forever. And my flesh is the bread that I give to bring the world to life."

Then the Jews started arguing among themselves, and asking one another, "How can this man give us to eat of his flesh?" Then Jesus revealed to them, "I am telling you the truth, unless you eat the flesh of the Son of Man and drink his blood, you do not have any life within. Whoever eats my flesh and drinks my blood has endless life, and I will raise him on the final day. My flesh is food in truth, you see, and my blood is drink indeed. Whoever eats my flesh and drinks my blood lives within me, and I live within him; even as the Father is within me and I am within Him. I promise you, if you do not take the body of the Son of Man as the bread of life, then you do not have life in him. Even as the living Father has sent me, so also do I live through Him--therefore whoever will partake of me will live through me. This is the bread which came down from heaven, not like that which the fathers ate before and died; whosoever eats this bread will live forever."

He said these things as he was teaching in the Capernaum synagogue. When they heard this, many of his disciples complained, "This is difficult doctrine--who can accept it?" Jesus, however, knowing inwardly that his followers were murmuring about it, questioned them, "Does this offend you? What if you were to see the Son of Man rising up to his former stature?

"The Spirit is what brings you life, but the flesh profits you nothing. The words that I speak to you are spirit and life. Even so, some of you refuse to believe." (For even from the very start, Jesus knew all who would doubt, as well as who would betray him.) "This," he continued, "was why I said to you that no one can approach me unless my Father has empowered him."

After this, many of his disciples went away, and traveled with him no more. "Do you wish to abandon me too?" Jesus questioned the twelve. "Master," Simon Peter answered, "to whom are we supposed to go? Your words lead to endless life. We are confident and do believe that you are the Holy One, the Son of God." "Did I not choose the twelve of you?" Jesus replied. "Even so, one of you is a devil!" He was referring to Judas Iscariot, the son of Simon, who, though he was among the twelve, was to betray him.

CLEAN HANDS--CORRUPT HEARTS
(Matt 15:1-20; Mark 7:1-23; GTh 40)
Capernaum?

Then some Pharisees came to him from Jerusalem, together with some scribes, and gathered around him. And when they saw that some of his disciples were eating with defiled--that is to say, unwashed hands, they looked down on them. The Pharisees, you see, and all of the Jews, mindful of the dictates of the elders, refuse to eat unless they wash their hands religiously. And neither do they dine when they come from the markets, unless they wash themselves first; and there are many other rules which they observe; the cleansing of cups, pots, bronze vessels, and tables. And the scribes and Pharisees questioned Jesus, "Why do your followers break with tradition, and live not by the rules of the elders? They do not wash before they eat; but eat their food with unclean hands!"

Jesus said, "You hypocrites! How well has Isaiah prophesied of you, seeing how it stands written, 'These people glorify me with their lips, but their hearts are far from me. They worship me to no avail, teaching as doctrines what are human commandments. You abandon God's instructions, and hold instead to the laws of men.'"

Then he said, "And how completely do you set aside the law of God, that you might keep to your own teachings! And why is it that you break God's word for the sake of your tradition? For God (speaking through) Moses has said, 'Honor your father and your mother,' and 'Whosoever should curse his father or mother, must die a terrible death.' But you say, 'If someone should say to his father or mother, "What you would otherwise have gotten from me is 'Korban,' that is to say, 'an offering given to God alone,' he is not to use it to 'honor his father or mother.'" You no longer enable him to do anything for his own parents, undermining the law of God for the sake of your own, which you do yourselves impose; and you also do many other things of a like nature."

And again he called them to himself and said, "All of you, listen here and understand: there is surely nothing outside a man which by entering into him can corrupt him. What goes into a man's mouth does not 'defile' him; it is instead the things that come from within a man that bring about his defilement. Anyone here with ears, should hear."

And when Jesus had moved on from there, his disciples came up to him and asked him about the parable: "Did you know that the Pharisees took offense at this?" He answered them, "Every plant that my heavenly Father has not planted will be pulled out by its roots. A grapevine has indeed been planted outside of the Father, but because it is feeble, it will be rooted up and die. Let them be; they are all blind guides. If one blind man should lead another, both will fall right into the ditch."

Peter bid him, "Work this parable out for us." "Do you still not understand?" Jesus replied. "Do you not recognize that whatever enters into a man from the outside cannot defile him, because whatever enters into his mouth does not enter into his heart but his belly instead, and from there passes into the commode? All foods are so purged." Then he said, "It is, to the contrary, what comes out of a man that corrupts a man. For what comes from the mouth proceeds from the heart, and these are the kinds of things that make men 'unclean.' You see, evil thoughts, fornication, theft, murder, adultery, greed, malice, deceit, false witnessing, lewdness, envy, slander, arrogance and folly come from deep within the heart of man. All of these evils proceed from within, and these are the kinds of things that defile a man; but he is not tainted by eating with unwashed hands."

IN TYRE AND SIDON
(Matt 15:21-28; Mark 7:24-30; John 7:1)
Tyre and Sidon

After this, Jesus traveled all around in Galilee, deliberately steering clear of Judea because the Jews there were lying in wait to take his life. And he withdrew to the regions of Tyre and Sidon and entered into a certain house. He did not want anyone finding out about it, but he could not keep it from being known. And right away this Canaanite woman from that area whose daughter had an unclean spirit, heard about Jesus and went to him, crying out, "Lord, Son of David, show me some compassion! My daughter is possessed by demons." Jesus did not speak a word. His followers therefore approached him and said, "Send her away, for she keeps on calling out to us." "I was sent only to the lost sheep of the house of Israel," Jesus replied. The woman, a Syrophoenician Greek by race, came and knelt before him, fell down at his feet and begged him to cast the demon from her daughter. "Help me, Lord!" she pleaded. "Allow the children first to eat," he said to her, "for it is not right to take the children's bread and fling it to the dogs." "Yes my Lord," she answered him, "that much is true. But surely the pups underneath get to eat of the children's crumbs that fall from the table of their master." And he said to her, "Woman, you have tremendous faith. Because you have phrased it thus, you may go. Your request has been granted; the demon has left your daughter." And her daughter was healed from that hour. When she entered into her house, she found her child lying in bed, and the demon gone.

JESUS HEALS THE BLIND, MUTE, LAME AND CRIPPLED
(Matt 15:29-31; Mark 7:31-37)
The Decapolis

Then he left the region of Tyre, and through Sidon, passed alongside the Sea of Galilee into the Decapolis region. He then climbed up onto a mountain and sat down there. Enormous crowds came up to him, bringing the lame, the blind, the mute, and many others along with them--laying them all right at his feet--and he healed them.

And they took this deaf-mute up to Jesus, and pleaded with him to place his hand on him. He then took him privately from the crowd, stuck his fingers into his ears, spat upon and touched his tongue. Then he gazed into the sky, heaved a sigh, and said to him, "Ephphatha," which means, "Be opened!" when translated. And his ears immediately opened up, and his tongue was freed, and he spoke clearly. The crowds were astounded when they saw the mute talking, the disabled made whole, the lame walking and the blind seeing; and they glorified the God of Israel. And he ordered them not to tell anyone; but the more that he forbad them, the more boldly they declared it. Now they were so amazed that they all proclaimed, "He does all things to perfection; he even causes the deaf to hear and the silent to speak."

JESUS FEEDS THE FOUR THOUSAND
(Matt 15:32; Mark 8:1-9a)
The Decapolis

At that time, when a large crowd had again assembled in that place, they had nothing there for them to eat. He therefore called his followers to himself and said, "I feel sorry for these people, for they've been with me three days now, and they have got nothing to eat. I do not wish to send them away hungry, (for) some have come great distances, and if I were to send them off, they might just faint along the way." And his disciples answered him, "Where can anyone get enough food to feed this crowd in such a remote location?"

Jesus therefore questioned them, "Tell me how many loaves you have?" They answered him, "Seven, and a few meager fish." Then he had the crowd sit down upon the ground. He took the seven loaves, and the fish as well, gave thanks to God, tore the loaves and gave them to his followers to place before the people, and so they did. And after blessing the few small fish that they had with them, he ordered his disciples to set them before the multitudes. Everybody ate their fill; and they took up seven baskets full of leftover broken bits. And those who ate were four thousand in number, not including the women and children.

THE SIGNS OF THE TIMES
(Matt 15:39-16:4a; Mark 8:9b-12; GTh 91)
Bethsaida

Then he sent the crowd away, climbed into the boat with his disciples, and arrived in the region of Dalmanutha, (which is also known as) Magadan.

The Pharisees and Sadducees came up to put Jesus to the test, looking to him to show them some heavenly sign. "Reveal yourself to us," they prodded him, "so that we might believe in you."

He then groaned deeply in his spirit, and questioned them, "Why does this generation need a sign? When evening comes, you say, 'The sky is red, so today it will be sunny,' and in the morning you say, 'Today the sky is red and cloudy, so today it will be stormy.' You know how to examine (and) interpret the face of the earth and sky, but have not recognized the one who is before your eyes. You are unable to read this moment, nor yet read the signs of the times. A wicked and adulterous people seeks after some kind of miraculous sign, but I am telling you the truth, no sign will be given to this generation, unless it be the sign of Jonah."

THE LEAVEN OF THE PHARISEES, SADDUCEES, AND HEROD
(Matt 16:4b-12; Mark 8:13-21)
Bethsaida, The Sea of Galilee

Then Jesus went away, leaving all of them behind. He climbed back into the boat and shoved off for the other side. And they forgot to take bread for their trip across the lake, and only had one loaf with them in the boat. And he cautioned them, saying, "Watch yourselves, and beware the leaven of the Pharisees and Sadducees, as well as that of Herod."

And they discussed it among themselves, imagining, "It must be for our lack of bread. We forgot to bring bread with us!" And Jesus, aware of their thoughts, reproached them: "You stunted of faith, why do you reason to yourselves that it's for your lack of bread? Do you not yet see or understand? Have your hearts been hardened? Do you have eyes that do not see, and ears that do not hear? Do you therefore not recall when I broke the five loaves for the five thousand? How many baskets full did you gather?" They answered him, "Twelve." "And when I broke the seven loaves for the four thousand; how many baskets full of broken bits did you pick up?" And they answered him, "Seven." And he questioned them, "How do you not yet recognize that I was not talking to you about bread? You ought, rather, to guard against the leaven of the Pharisees and the Sadducees." Only then did they realize that he was not telling them to guard against the yeast used in the baking of bread, but against the teaching of the Pharisees and Sadducees instead.

HEALING THE BLIND MAN IN BETHSAIDA
(Mark 8:22-26)
Bethsaida

They came to Bethsaida; and the people brought this blind man up to him, and begged Jesus to touch him. And he took the blind man by the hand, and guided him right out of town. There he spat into his eyes, placed his hands upon him, and asked, "Are you able to see anything?" And the man looked up and said, "I see men; but they appear to me as walking trees." After he placed his hands upon his eyes, this man's vision was restored, and he saw everything clearly. Then he sent him home, saying, "Do not go back into town, or reveal it to anyone there."

THOMAS' INSIGHT AND JESUS' WORDS TO HIM:
PETER'S INSIGHT
(Matt 16:13-20; Mark 8:27-30; Luke 9:18-21;
GTh Prologue, 1, 2, 13/1, 2-POxy 654)
The Villages near Caesarea Philippi

Jesus and his followers moved on to the villages around Caesarea Philippi. And one day, along the way, when Jesus had entered into [that] district, he was praying privately, and his disciples were all with him. "Equate me with something," Jesus bid his students, "and explain to me what I am like." Simon Peter answered him, "You are even as a godly angel." Matthew said, "You are like a wise philosopher." "Master," said Thomas, "my mouth is completely at a loss to put into words what you are like." Jesus said, "I am not your master, for you have grown drunk, having partaken of the living spring that I myself have measured out." And he took him aside and spoke three sayings to him. When Thomas returned to his companions, they asked him, "What did Jesus say to you?" Thomas answered, "If I were to tell you one of the sayings that he spoke to me, you would pick up stones and throw them at me--flames would then shoot out of them and burn you up."

These are the mysterious things that the living Jesus spoke and which Didymus Judas, <who is> also known as Thomas, wrote down. He said, moreover, "Whoever finds what these words mean, will not ever taste of death. The seeker should keep on seeking until they find, and when they find, they will be shaken, and when they are shaken, they will be astonished, and will rule over everything, (and <when they reign>, then they will <rest.>)"

Then he questioned his disciples, "Who do the people say that the Son of Man is, (and) the multitudes, that I am?" And they answered him, "Some say that you are John the Baptist, others say that you're Elijah, others say you're Jeremiah, and still others, that you're one of the prophets--that one of the prophets from ages past has come alive." "Well then," he asked, "who do you say that I am?" Simon Peter answered him, "You are God's Messiah; the Son of the Living God." And Jesus answered, "How blessed are you, Simon, son of John, because it was not flesh and blood that revealed this to you, but it was my Father in heaven. And I am here to say to you that you are a rock, and on this rock I will build my church, and the gates of Hades will not prevail against it. I will hand the keys of heaven's kingdom over to you; and whatever you bind on earth will be, having been bound up in the sky, and whatever you loose on earth will be, having been loosed up in the sky." He then forbad his servants from telling anyone about him, that he was Jesus the Christ.

JESUS STARTS TEACHING ABOUT HIS PASSION AND HIS RESURRECTION
(Matt 16:21-23; Mark 8:31-33; Luke 9:22)
Near Caesarea Philippi

And from that time forward Jesus started teaching (and) explaining to his students that he, the Son of Man, must travel up to Jerusalem and be subjected to many ordeals. He said, "The Son of Man has many sufferings to undergo; and to face rejection by the elders, chief priests, and scribes, and after that be put to death. Then, after three days, (that is to say,) on the third day, he will be raised back up to life." This he spoke quite clearly.

Then Peter took him and started to reproach him. "Not so, my Lord!" he protested. "This will never be to you!" But Jesus, turning and looking at his disciples, rebuked him, saying, "You get behind me, Satan! You are an obstruction to me, for you are not concerned with the things of God, but merely with the things of men."

JESUS TEACHES ABOUT DISCIPLESHIP
(Matt 16:24-28; Mark 8:34-9:1; Luke 9:23-27)
Near Caesarea Philippi

Then he called the people and his disciples to himself and counseled them, "If any man would follow me, let him first deny himself, carry his cross every day and then follow me. For whoever would save his life will end up losing it; but whoever would lose his life for my sake, and that of the gospel, will find it (and) save it. For what profit is there for a man if he should come to possess even the entire world and do harm to himself (or) forfeit his soul? Or what does any man have to offer in exchange for his soul? You see, whoever despises me and my words in this adulterous age of corruption, the Son of Man will likewise despise him when he comes in the fullness of his splendor and the majesty of the Father--in the presence of the holy angels and their grandeur. For the Son of Man will truly come with all his angels in the glory of the Father, and at that time, He will pay all men in line with their works."

And he said to them, "I am telling you the truth; there are some who are standing here who will not die before they have seen the kingdom of God coming in power (and) the Son of Man, in his reign."

THE TRANSFIGURATION
(Matt 17:1-8; Mark 9:2-8;
Luke 9:28-36; AcJn 90; 2Pet 1:18)
Mount of Transfiguration

After six (whole) days had passed, about eight days after Jesus had said all this, he took Peter and James and me, John, the brother of James, and led [us] apart by [our]selves to his usual prayer spot high up the mountain, in order to pray. And even as he was in the midst of prayer, he was changed before [us] there. And we saw such light upon him that it is impossible for a man to describe it in human terms. His face transformed, and beamed like the sun, and his clothing began shining white as snow; whiter, in fact, than any fuller on earth could possibly whiten them; as white as light, and as bright as a lightning bolt.

Just then two men, Moses and Elijah, appeared to them in glorious splendor, and they were discussing his imminent departure, which he was soon to bring about in Jerusalem. Peter and his companions were all quite drowsy, but once they had awakened fully, they beheld his glory and that of the two men who were standing there with him. As the men were departing from Jesus, Peter said to him, "Master, Sir, it is good that we are here; if you would, let us set up three tabernacles, one for you, one for Moses, and another for Elijah." Now he did not know what to say, (or even) what he was saying, for all of them were terrified. And behold, even as he was speaking, a bright cloud appeared and overtook them all, and as the cloud enveloped them there, they were paralyzed with fear. And a voice came from the cloud, saying, "This is my beloved Son, the Elect One; I am truly pleased with him. You must hear him." When the voice had spoken (and) the disciples had heard it, they fell to their faces on the ground in fear. But Jesus came and touched them. "Rise up, and fear not," he said. All of a sudden they looked up (and) around, and no longer saw anyone there with him. Jesus was all alone and in their midst, and they let no one know at the time about what they had seen. (And we did ourselves hear this voice from the heavens, for we were with him on the sacred mountain.)

A SECOND TRANSFIGURATION
(AcJn 90, 91)
Mount of Transfiguration

He led the three of us up the mountain again in a similar way, saying, "Come up with me." Once again we went along, and we saw him praying at a distance. Now because he loved me, (John,) I drew near to him silently, just as if he would not see, and stood and watched him from behind. Now I could tell that he was not wearing clothes, but appeared to us as naked, yet not the least bit like a mortal. His feet were so much whiter than snow that they lit up the very ground beneath him, and his head reached into the sky, and the sight was such that I shrieked in fright. Then he turned around and appeared as small as any man! And he took hold of my beard, and pulling it he said to me, "John, do not be doubtful, but believing; and stop being so nosy." "Lord," I asked, "what did I do?" And let me tell you, my brothers, for thirty days I suffered such agony where he grabbed me by my beard, that I complained to him, "Lord, if your lighthearted tug has caused me such pain, what would it have been like if you had drubbed me but good?" And he answered me, "From this time forth, make it your business never to provoke the One Who is not to be tempted."

But Peter and James were angered by my discussion with the Lord and gestured for me to come to them and leave the Lord alone. So I went over to where they were, and they both prodded me, "Who was the Lord talking to on the mountain top, for we heard two of them speaking?" And when I thought about the extent of his compassion as it relates to his all-encompassing nature and his wisdom, which has never grown weary of watching over us, I replied, "If you were to ask this of him, you would get your answer."

JESUS REVEALS THAT
JOHN THE BAPTIST IS ELIJAH
(Matt 17:9-13; Mark 9:9-13; Luke 9:37a)
Mount of Transfiguration

And the following day, as they were coming down the mountainside, he constrained them, "Do not tell anyone what you have seen until the Son of Man has risen from the dead." So they kept it to themselves, but wondered what he meant by, "rising up from the dead."

And the disciples asked him, "So why is it that the scribes and Pharisees maintain that Elijah must appear beforehand?" And Jesus answered them, "When Elijah does come, he will restore all things--even as it stands written of the Son of Man--that he must undergo many sufferings and be despised. But I am here to tell you, Elijah has already come, yet these people never acknowledged him. They did just what they wanted to do to him, even as it is written about him. The Son of Man is to suffer the same fate at their hands. The disciples then recognized that he was talking to them about John the Baptist."

THE DEMON THE DISCIPLES
COULD NOT CAST OUT
(Matt 17:14-21; Mark 9:14-29; Luke 9:37b-43a)
At the Foot of the Mount of Transfiguration

Now when they had come down from the mountain and to the disciples, they saw a great crowd surrounding them, and some scribes clashing with them. And when everyone caught sight of him, they were startled, and all of them grew fearful. They then ran up to welcome him. Now when they had assembled together, Jesus asked the people there, "What are you talking to the disciples about?" And someone from the crowd went up to Jesus and knelt before him, crying out, "Teacher, Sir, I have brought you my son. I'm begging you, have a look at him (and) show him some compassion. For he is my only child, and he has been taken with this affliction. He has a spirit of muteness, and he suffers intensely. Wherever it takes hold of him, he screams out suddenly; and it hurls him down in such convulsions that he foams and grinds his teeth and becomes all withered. He is forever falling into fire and water. It hardly ever leaves him and even now is killing him. I brought him here to your disciples and asked, (nay) begged them to cast the spirit out, but they were not able to heal him."

And he answered them, "Oh false-hearted and unbelieving generation, how long must I remain with you? How long do I have to put up with you? Bring your son over here to me." So they took the boy over to Jesus; and just then, even as he was on his way, the filthy spirit caught sight of him, and right away he wracked the boy, throwing him tossing and foaming to the ground.

And he asked his father, "How long has he suffered this?" And he answered, "From his earliest childhood. It has tossed him repeatedly into fire and water in its efforts to destroy him. But if you can help us out, then have mercy on us." Then Jesus asked him, "If you can? All things are possible for one who has faith." The child's father immediately cried out, "I do believe; help me overcome my doubts!" And when Jesus saw that a mob was coming, he commanded the unclean demon spirit, saying to it, "I order you, you spirit of muteness and deafness, to leave him now and never go back."

Then, shrieking and tearing him good, the spirit left him, and he laid there as dead. Most of them, in fact, said that he was dead. But Jesus grabbed the boy by his hand, picked him up, and he arose. And he was healed from that very moment; and Jesus restored him to his father. And they were all amazed by the greatness of God.

Then, on entering into the house, his disciples approached him and asked him in private, "Why could we not cast it out?" And he answered them, "Because you are stunted in your faith. I am telling you the truth, if you had faith as small as a mustard seed, you could say to this mountain, 'Move from this place over to that,' and it would do so. Nothing would be impossible for you. But this kind of spirit cannot leave men except by means of fasting and prayer."

JESUS AGAIN TRIES TO EXPLAIN
TO HIS DISCIPLES ABOUT HIS DEATH
(Matt 17:22-23; Mark 9:30-32; Luke 9:43b-45)
Galilee

Even as they were all marveling at everything that Jesus had done, they moved on into Galilee. Now he did not want anyone knowing about it; because when they had gathered there, he was giving instruction to his disciples. He said, "Listen close to what I say: The Son of man is to be betrayed into the hands of men, and they are going to murder him. After that, on the third day after he has been put to death, he will then be stirred (and) raised to life." But the disciples were dejected, and they did not understand his words. They were hidden from them, that they might not understand them; and they were too afraid to ask him to explain them.

JESUS, PETER, AND THE SHEKEL
(Matt 17:24-27; Mark 9:33a)
Capernaum

When they arrived in Capernaum, the half-shekel collectors came up to Peter and asked, "Does your teacher pay the temple tax?" "Of course he does," he answered them. And on entering into the house, Jesus spoke to Peter first, saying, "Simon, tell me what seems right to you. From whom do earthly kings collect toll or tribute, their own children or those unrelated to themselves?" And when Peter answered, "From outsiders," Jesus explained, "Sons are therefore not obliged. However, so as not to offend them, go and cast a hook into the sea, take the fish that you catch first, and when you open up its mouth you will find a shekel there. Take it and pay them on behalf of both of us."

WHOEVER IS LEAST IS GREATEST
(Matt 18:1-14; Mark 9:33b-50; Luke 9:46-50; GPh 31)
Capernaum

A dispute broke out among the disciples as to which of them would become the more preeminent. Jesus, knowing their thoughts, questioned them, "What were you talking about along the way?" They, however, did not answer, for as they were walking along, they had spoken together as to which of them was to become the most illustrious. And he sat down, summoned the twelve and instructed them, "If anyone would strive to be first, he must be the lowest--even a servant to all people."

Then the disciples came to Jesus, asking, "Who, therefore, is the greatest in the kingdom of heaven?" Calling a child to himself, Jesus took hold of him and had him stand right next to him before them. And drawing him into his arms, he informed them, "I am telling you the truth, unless you transform yourselves and become like children, you will never make it into the kingdom of heaven. For this reason, whoever humbles himself and becomes like this child, will be greatest in the kingdom of heaven. Whoever receives any of these children, such as this one, in my name is, in fact, receiving me; and whoever receives me is not receiving me alone, but also the One Who sent me. You see, the most humble among you will be the most preeminent."

Then John said to him, "Teacher, Sir, we saw this man casting out evil spirits in your name, and we tried to stop him because he was not from those of us who follow you." But Jesus answered, "Do not prevent him, because there is not anyone who could work a miracle in my name and turn around and malign me. See, whoever is not opposed to us is for us, (and) whoever is not against you is on your side. For truly do I say to you, he will never forfeit his reward who, because you are of the Anointed, gives you so much as a cup of water to drink in my name.

"Even so, it would be better for whoever saddens even one of these little ones who trusts in me, to have a giant millstone hung around his neck, (and with that) millstone ringing his neck, be tossed into the sea to drown. Curse the world for its deceit! It is inevitable that deceptions should come, but curse the man by whom these schemes are set in place! Now if your hand leads you to your ruin, then chop it off and cast it out. Better that you should go through life with but one hand, than with two hands to enter into Gehenna, where their worm does not die, and the fire is not quenched. And if your foot should lead you into sin, then cut it off. It is better for you to enter into life with a single foot, than with two feet to walk into the everlasting flames, where their worm does not die, and the fire is not put out. And if your eye should draw you into error, pull it out and throw it away. Better that you should go through life with a single eye (and) enter into the kingdom of God, than with two eyes to be sent into the fire of Gehenna, where their worm never dies, and the fire is not put out. Everyone will be salted with fire, and every sacrifice will be salted with salt. Salt is useful, but if the salt should lose its taste, how ever can you salt it again? Have salt within yourselves, and be at peace with one another." (The apostles taught their disciples, "May the fullness of our offering be salted with salt." Now when they said "salt," what they meant was "wisdom" in code, for without that, no offering is acceptable. Wisdom as it stands today is barren and without a child. She is therefore called a "<hint> of salt." Wherever they <should gather> in their special way, the Holy Spirit will <join with them,> and many are her children!)

"Be careful not to scorn any of these little ones who trust in me, for I am here to tell you that in heaven, their angels gaze endlessly upon the face of my heavenly Father. The Son of Man came to restore what had been lost.

"What do you suppose? If a man should have a hundred sheep and one of them should wander off, does he not leave the ninety nine behind on the hills and go searching for the one that walked away? And if he manages to find it, I tell you most assuredly that he takes greater pleasure in that one than in the ninety nine that never strayed. Likewise, it is not the will of my heavenly Father that even one of these little ones should perish.

JESUS INSTRUCTS PETER TO FORGIVE
(Matt 18:15-35; GTh 30, 48/30-POxy 1;
GNaz 5, Quote by Jerome, Against Pelagians 3.2b)
Capernaum

"If your brother should sin against you, go and, just between the two of you, explain to him where he is wrong. And if he should heed your words, then you will have won him over. But if he should not, then take one or two others along with you, so that 'under the testimony of two or three witnesses, every word might be upheld.' If he refuses to listen even to them, then let the congregation know. And if he then does not give heed, then let him be in your sight as a pagan or a tax-collector. I am telling you the truth, whatever you bind on earth will be, having been bound up above; and whatever you loose on earth will be, having been loosed up above. If, in a single house, two should come to terms together, they will bid the mountain, 'Move away!' and it will be moved. Once again I say to you, if two of you should agree on earth about anything for which they ask, it will be done for them by my Father in heaven. You see, wherever two or three are gathered in my name, there I am in the midst of them. (And) where there are three divine beings, they are gods <apart from> God. And where there are two or even one, I say, 'I live within that one.' Pick up a rock, and you'll find me there. Split apart a chunk of wood, and there will I be."

Then Peter went up to Jesus and asked, "Master, how often should I forgive my brother when he sins against me?" Jesus answered him, "If your brother or sister has slandered you and makes it right, accept him or her seven times a day." Simon, his disciple, questioned him, "Seven times in just one day?" Jesus answered, "I am saying to you, more than just those seven times, but seventy-seven, (even) seventy times seven. For even the prophets themselves, after they had been anointed with the Holy Spirit, were capable of sinful speech.

"Therefore, the heavenly dominion is like a king who wanted to settle accounts with his servants. When he began to reckon with them, one of them who owe ten thousand talents was brought to him; and because he could not pay, his master commanded that he be sold, along with his wife, his children, and everything that he owned as payment. So the servant fell to his knees and begged, 'Lord, if you'll only have patience with me, I will pay you back one hundred percent.' And his master felt sorry for him, canceled his debt, and set him free.

"That very servant went right out and tracked down one of his fellows who owed him a hundred denarii. He latched onto him and started to strangle him, insisting, 'Pay me back everything you owe!' And his fellow servant fell down and pleaded with him, 'Have patience with me, and I will pay it all back.' But he refused; going off instead and having him cast into prison until he could fully repay his debt.

"When some other servants saw that, they became very upset and went and related all that had happened to their master. Then his master sent for him, and reproved him: 'You wicked servant! I forgave your entire debt because you begged me to. Would it not have been fitting for you to have shown mercy to your fellow servant, even as I showed mercy to you?' And his master became angry and turned him over to the jailers, until he could pay his debt in full. Even so will my heavenly Father deal with you, if you refuse to pardon your brother from your innermost beings."

THE SOLEMNITY AND PRICE OF DISCIPLESHIP
(Matt 8:19-22; Luke 9:57-62; GTh 86)
Sea of Galilee

And as they traveled along the way, a certain scribe said to him, "Teacher, I will follow you wherever you go." And Jesus answered, "Foxes have their holes, and the birds of the sky, their nests; but the Son of Man has no place where his head might rest."

And to another, a disciple of his, he said, "Follow me." But he answered him, "Sir, let me go first and bury my father." And Jesus said to him, "Follow me, and leave the dead to bury their own. But as for you, go out and make known the kingdom of God."

Still another one of them affirmed, "I will follow you, Sir, but first let me go and bid my family farewell." And Jesus answered, "No one who puts his hand to a plough while looking behind is suited to the kingdom of God."

JESUS' BROTHERS URGE HIM TO REVEAL HIMSELF
(John 7:2-9)
Galilee

Now the Jewish Feast of Tabernacles was approaching, so his brothers pressured him, "Why not leave and go to Judea, so that your followers might also bear witness to your wonders. After all, no one who wishes to live in the public eye ever does anything on the sly. If you can do all of these things, then show yourself to the entire world." You see, even his own brothers did not believe in him.

Jesus therefore said to them, "It is not my time as yet, but your time is always at hand. The world cannot hate you, but it does hate me for testifying against its evil workings. You go on up to this feast. I am not going up just yet, for my time has not yet come." And when he had spoken these things to them, he remained behind in Galilee.

JESUS SECRETLY HEADS FOR JERUSALEM
(Luke 9:51-56; John 7:10)

Samaria

And after his brothers had set out for the feast, the time came for him to be taken up, so he resolved to go up himself--not openly, mind you, but secretly, as it were. And he sent messengers ahead of him. And after leaving that place, they entered into a Samaritan village to make things ready for him. But the people there did not welcome him, for he was on his way through to Jerusalem. And when his disciples James and John saw this, they asked him, "Lord, would you have us call down fire from the sky to consume them as Elijah once did?" But Jesus turned around and rebuked them, saying, "You do not recognize the nature of your spirit, for the Son of Man did not come to destroy human life, but to restore it." And they moved on to another town.

JESUS AT THE FEAST OF TABERNACLES
(John 7:11-8:1; GTh 38, 53, 59, 108/38-POxy 655;
OSol 30;The Heavenly Dialogue,
Quote by Origen, Against Celsus 8.15)
Jerusalem

So the Jews were looking for him at the Feast, saying, "Where is that man?" And the crowds were bustling with talk about him there; some were saying, "He is a righteous man," but others contended, "No, he is leading the people astray." Even so, no one spoke openly about him for fear of the Jews. And it was about midway through the Feast when Jesus went up into the temple and started to teach. And there the Jews all marveled and asked, "How did this man acquire such knowledge without the benefit of an education?" And Jesus answered, "This is not my own doctrine, but that of the One Who sent me. If anyone should do His will, he will come to recognize whether this teaching comes from God, or if I am speaking on my own. Whoever speaks on his own authority, seeks his own glory, but anyone who seeks to glorify the One Who sends him is authentic, and no falsity exists within him. Did not Moses give you the law? All the same, not even one of you keeps to the law, so why are you looking to murder me?" "You're demon-possessed," the people replied. "Just who is it that is seeking your death?" "I did one miracle and you're all amazed?" Jesus replied. "Still, you will circumcise a child on the Sabbath Day because Moses passed circumcision down to you, though it did not actually stem from him, but the patriarchs instead. So if you can circumcise a boy on the Sabbath to keep from breaking the Mosaic Law, then why are you enraged at me for restoring a man to perfect health on the Sabbath Day? Do not judge by appearances, but by righteousness instead." "Is circumcision beneficial or not?" his disciples asked him. He answered, "If it were of any use, their Father would bring forth from their mothers children who are circumcised already. It is, rather, the true circumcision--that of the spirit--that has become beneficial in its every aspect." Then some of the people of Jerusalem started to ask, "Is this not the man they are trying to kill? And there he goes speaking freely among them. They are not saying a word to him. Have the leaders all concluded that he is the Messiah? We know where this man came from, but when the Messiah comes, no one will know where he came from."

And as Jesus was teaching in the temple, he cried out to them, "You have known me, have you? And where I came from too? I did not come of my own accord. The One Who sent me is genuine, and you have certainly never known Him! I know Him because I came from His very presence, and He was the One Who sent me here." So they tried to apprehend him, but none could get their hands on him, since his time had not yet come. And many who were in that crowd placed their trust in him and proclaimed, "When the Messiah does come, will he do more signs than this man has?"

The Pharisees heard the people speaking these things under their breath about him, so along with the high-ranking priests, they sent officers out to arrest him. Jesus therefore said to them, "I will only be with you a little longer, and then be off to Him Who sent me. You have often longed to hear the words that I am now passing on to you, and you've got no one else to hear them from. Even so, the days are coming when you will seek for me and find me not, and it will be impossible for you to come over to where I am." So the Jews then started asking each other, "Where is he off to, then, that we will be unable to find him? Will he go away and live among the Gentiles, and teach among the Greeks? And what is this saying of his, 'You will seek me, but not ever find me,' and, 'You cannot come to where I am'?" (And) Jesus said, "As long as you remain alive, you must look to the One Who lives; otherwise you just might die, and when you seek for the Living One, you will be unable to find Him."

On the final and most important day of the Feast, Jesus stood and cried aloud, "If anyone is thirsty, let him come to me and drink. Anyone who drinks from my mouth will become like me! I will, in fact, become that man, and the hidden things will open up to him. Many are those who circle the well, yet no one ever draws from it. Why fear now when you've come so far? Isn't it clear to you that I lack neither courage, nor a weapon. Whosoever trusts in me, as it says in the Scripture, 'Rivers of living waters will flow forth from him.'" And in so saying, he spoke of the Spirit, which they who believed in him would soon receive.

> (Drink deeply from the fountain of the Living God,
> For it is open to you now.
> You who thirst, drink your fill,
> And rest yourselves by the spring of the Lord,
> For it is lovely and pure, and brings rest to your soul.
> More pleasing than honey is the taste thereof,
> And the honeycomb is as nothing beside it.
> For it flows from the lips of the Lord,
> And takes its name from his very heart.
> For it approached unseen, and arrived without limit,
> And until it came at last, and was set in their midst,
> No one knew anything about it.
> How blessed are those who drink therefrom,

And come to find their rest thereby.)

Now Jesus had not yet been glorified, since the Holy Spirit had not yet been given. Therefore many in the crowd, hearing his words proclaimed, "This man must certainly be that Prophet." Others said, "This is the Messiah!" And others asked, "Why would the Messiah come from Galilee? Does not the Scripture say that the Messiah comes from the seed of David, and hails from his hometown of Bethlehem?" There was thus a division among the people on his account. And some there wanted to arrest him, but no one managed to get their hands on him. So the officers approached the chief priests and the Pharisees, who asked them, "How is it that you did not arrest him?" "No one else has ever spoken the way that this man has," the officers replied. The Pharisees then questioned them, "Have you been taken in as well? Has anyone from the rulers believed in him? How about the Pharisees? It is only that this crowd is cursed, ignorant as they are about the law!" Nicodemus, the one who had come to him by night, being one of them, asked them, "Does our law pass sentence against a man without first giving him a hearing to find out what it is that he has done?" "Are you also from Galilee?" they rejoined. "Look into it and recognize that the Prophet, (indeed) no prophet rises up from Galilee." And at that they all went home. But Jesus went to the Mount of Olives.

THE WOMAN CAUGHT IN ADULTERY
(John: 8:2-8:11)
Jerusalem

At daybreak he returned to the temple, and everyone came up to him, and he sat down and started teaching them. Now the scribes and Pharisees brought this woman up to him who had been caught in unfaithfulness. And they placed her right in the midst of the crowd and said to him, "Teacher, this woman was caught in the very act of adultery. Now the Mosaic Law states that someone like this should be stoned to death. What do you say?" They put this question to him in order to entrap him, so that they might have some cause for bringing him up on charges.

Then Jesus leaned forward and started writing on the ground with his finger. And when they prodded him for an answer, Jesus sat back up and said, "Let the sinless one among you be the first to cast a stone at her." And he bent back down and continued writing on the ground.

And when they heard this, they started leaving one by one, from the oldest to the youngest, each convicted by their conscience. And Jesus was the only one who remained, and the woman was standing there. And straightening himself back up, he saw no one there except this woman. And he asked her, "Woman, where are your accusers? Is there not a soul left to sentence you?" And she answered him, "No one, Sir." Then Jesus said, "I do not condemn you, either. Now move along and sin no more."

DISPUTATIONS

(John 8:12-59; GTh 77, 82, 83, 84)
Jerusalem

So Jesus addressed the people again, saying, "I am the light of this world. I am the light that's in all things. Whoever follows me will never walk in darkness, but will instead experience a living light. I am the fullness. All that there is has come from me, and all has been achieved in me. Split apart a chunk of wood, and there will I be! Pick up a stone and there you will find me. Whoever is near to me is near to the fire, and whoever is far from me is far from the kingdom."

"You testify about yourself," the Pharisees contended, "your witness is therefore untrue!" Jesus answered them, "Even if I do testify about myself, mine is still a worthy attestation, since I know where I came from as well as where I go. You, on the other hand, have no idea where I came from or where I am going. Your judgments rest on fleshly views. I do not myself judge anyone; but even if I were to judge, my judgments would still be true, since I'm not alone in what I do. The Father Who sent me stands with me. In your law, moreover, you will find that it stands written, 'The testimony of two men is faithful.' Even if I speak of myself, the Father Who sent me testifies about me also."

They therefore asked him, "Where is this 'Father' of yours?" And Jesus answered them, "You have never known me, nor have you ever known my Father. Had you ever come to know me, you would have also come to know my Father. People can truly see the forms, but the light within them remains concealed by the very light of my Father's image. He will make Himself known all right, but it is His light that conceals His image. You are pleased at the sight of your own semblance, but when you come to see your images, which came into being before you, and which neither disappear nor show themselves for what they are, how great a burden you will have to bear!" Jesus spoke these words in the treasury while teaching in the temple. Even so, no one there laid hold of him, since his time had not yet come.

Once again he said to them, "I am about to go away. You will try to find me, but you will perish in your sins. You cannot follow me to where I go." So the Jews inquired, "Because he is saying, 'You cannot follow me to where I go,' does he mean that he will kill himself?" "You are from here below," he explained to them, "whereas I am from up above. You are from this world, but I am not of this realm. This is why I said to you that you will perish in your sins, because you will die in wickedness for not believing that I AM." And so they asked him, "Who are you, then?" And Jesus replied, "Even what I have said from the start! I have many things to speak and judge about you. Even so, the One Who sent me here is faithful, and I will make known to the whole world the things that I got straight from Him." They did not understand that Jesus was speaking to them of the Father, so he advised them, "When you glorify the Son of Man, then you will come to see that I AM, and that I've spoken nothing on my own. But these words that I speak to you are even as my Father has given them to me, and He Who sent me is also with me. The Father never left me alone, because I always do what He finds pleasing."

And even as he was speaking, many put their faith in him. So Jesus advised the Jews who believed in him there, "If you stay faithful to my word, then you are my followers in truth. You will see things as they truly are, and the truth will set you free." "We are of the seed of Abraham," they answered him, "and have never been subject to anyone, so how can you say, 'You are going to be set free'?" Jesus answered them, "I am telling you truly that everyone who is a party to sin is a slave to sin, and the servant is not a permanent member of the house; but the Son belongs forevermore. So if the Son should set you free, then you will indeed be free. I know that you're the seed of Abraham, but you are looking to do me in because you have no place in you for my word. I am telling you what I have seen in the very presence of my Father. You likewise do as you have seen from your father." "Our father is Abraham," they all responded. "If you were truly the children of Abraham," Jesus replied, "you would be doing as Abraham did. As it stands now, you are looking to put me to death, a man who has told you the truth that he got straight from God. Abraham never did that! You are truly doing the will of your father." "It was not we who were born of fornication," they retorted. "We have but one Father, and that is God!" "If God were indeed your Father," Jesus answered, "you would love me, because I came here straight from God, and now I am with you. Neither did I come of my own, but I was sent here by Him. So why do you misconstrue my words? It is even because you cannot understand my speech. Your source--your father--is the devil, and it is your father's will that you will do. He's been a murderer from the very first, and has never stood in the truth, since there is no truth to be found in him. Whenever someone speaks a lie, he speaks it through acquaintance with him, because that person is a liar, even as his father before him. And you do not believe me simply because I speak the truth. Which of you can convict me of sin? And if I should speak the truth to you, why then do you not believe? The one who comes from God understands the words of God. The reason that you do not grasp them is simply that you're not from God."

So the Jews replied, "Are we not right in calling you a demon-possessed Samaritan?" "I have no demon!" Jesus told them, "It is that I am honoring my Father, whereas you are dishonoring me. And I am not seeking to glorify myself; but there is another Who seeks it, and He is the judge. How truly do I say to you, if anyone should keep my word, he will not ever see death." The Jews therefore answered him, "Now we know for certain that you've got a demon! Abraham died, as have the prophets; yet you profess, 'If anyone should keep my word, he will never taste of death.' Are you greater than our father Abraham? He has died, even as the prophets have. Who are you making yourself out to be?" Jesus replied, "If I were to exalt myself, then my glory would come to nothing. The One Who magnifies me is my Father, Who you argue is your God--even though you've never known Him. But I have known Him, and if I were ever to say that I did not know Him, I would be a liar like you! But I truly do know Him and I keep His word. Your 'father' Abraham was thrilled at the chance to see my day, and without a doubt he did see it--and he was overjoyed by it!" So the Jews replied, "You are not yet fifty years old, and you have met Abraham?" Jesus answered them, "I am telling you the truth, before Abraham ever was, I AM!" Then they started picking up rocks to stone him with, but Jesus concealed himself and walked out of the temple through the midst of them all, and such was his departure from them.

HEALING OF THE MAN BORN BLIND
(John 9:1-41)
Jerusalem

And in passing, he saw a man who had been born blind. His followers asked him, "Rabbi, was it his own sin or that of his parents that caused him to be born like this?" Jesus said, "He has not committed sin, and neither have his parents. It happened so that God's works might be shown in him. While daylight remains, it is only right that I should do the works of Him Who sent me. The night is coming, wherein no man can work at all. I am the light of the world so long as I am in the world."

And after he had said all this, he spat upon the ground, made some mud and rubbed it onto the blind man's eyes. At that point he told the man, "Go and rinse in the pool of Siloam," (which translates as 'sent.') So he went away and washed himself, and he came back able to see. His neighbors and those who had seen him before as a blind man asked, "Is this not the same one who used to sit and beg?" Some confirmed, "It is him alright," but others alleged, "It is only that he looks like him." But as for the man himself, he confessed, "I am he!" So they asked him, "Then how was it that your eyes were opened?" The man responded, "This man named Jesus made some mud and daubed my eyes. Then he told me, 'Go to the pool of Siloam and wash up there.' And I went away and washed myself, and after that I was able to see." "Where is this man?" they questioned him. And he answered them, "I do not know."

They then took the man who had been blind up to the Pharisees. Now the day upon which Jesus had made the mud and opened his eyes was a Sabbath. So the Pharisees asked him once again how it was that he could see. "He smeared my eyes with mud," he said. "After that, I washed it off, and now I can see!" Several of the Pharisees therefore contended, "This man does not come from God, since he does not keep the Sabbath Day." Some others asked, "How is a sinful man able to show such signs?" They were therefore split in their opinions.

And once again they questioned the blind man, "Tell us what you think of him, seeing how it was your eyes that he opened?" "He is a prophet," he responded. The Jews, however, did not believe that the man had been born blind and had received his sight until they had summoned the parents of the one who had come to see. "Is this your son, who you claim was born blind?" the Jews asked the parents. "How is it now that he can see?" "We know that this man is our son," his parents replied, "and that he's been blind since he was born, but we have no idea how he now can see, or who it was that opened his eyes. He is old enough, so ask it of him. He is free to speak this for himself."

His parents put it like this since they were both afraid of the Jews. The Jews, you see, had already conspired to throw anyone who acknowledged that he was the Christ right out of the synagogue, and this was why his parents said, "Ask it of him, for he is of age." And they sent again for the man who had been blind, and ordered him, "Praise God for this miracle. This man we know to be a sinner." So he replied, "I don't know if he's a sinner, but I do know one thing; that I used to be blind, but now I can see!" And once again they asked the man, "Tell me what he did to you. How did he open up your eyes?" "I have explained it to you already," he retorted, "and you would not listen. Why do you want to hear it again? Do you wish to become another of his students?" "You are one of this man's followers," they replied, "but we are all disciples of Moses. We recognize that God spoke to Moses, but we don't know where he came from." "What an unbelievable thing it is," the man replied, "that you cannot tell where he is from, when here he has opened up my eyes! All of us understand that God does not acknowledge sinners, but He does listen to anyone who worships Him and does His will. To open the eyes of one born blind is something completely unheard of. This man would be able to do nothing at all if he did not come from God." And to this they said, "You were born in utter sin--and do you dare to preach to us?" And they threw the man right out of there.

Now when Jesus heard that he had been cast out, he found the man and asked him, "Do you believe in the Son of God, (who is also) the Son of Man?" "Sir," he asked, "who is he, that I might believe in him?" "Not only have you seen him already," said Jesus, "but he is speaking right to you." And the man replied, "Lord, I do believe!" and he fell to his face before him. "I came into this world," Jesus explained, "in order to create this distinction: that the blind might come to see, and that those who see might be made blind." And some Pharisees who were there with him heard all of this and said, "Tell us, then, are we blind too?" And Jesus said, "If indeed you had been blind, you would not be guilty of sin. But since you say that you can see, your sin lingers on.

THE GOOD SHEPHERD
(John 10:1-21; Gospel of the Ebionites
in Clementine Homilies III.52)
Jerusalem

"I am the door that leads to life. Whoever passes through me enters into life. Assuredly I say to you, whoever does not enter the sheepfold through the door, but climbs over from some other side is a thief and a robber. The shepherd of the sheep enters in through the door. The porter opens up for him and the sheep all hear his voice. And he calls his own sheep by name and guides them out. And after drawing out those that belong to him, he goes out ahead of them. And the sheep follow after him because they recognize the sound of his voice. But they will not follow a stranger. They all run away from him, for they recognize not a stranger's voice." Jesus spoke this to them in a parable, but they did not understand what he was telling them.

So Jesus again affirmed to them, "Most assuredly I say to you, I am the sheep gate. All who have gone before me were thieves and robbers. The sheep, however, never listened to them. I am that door. If any should go in through me, he will be kept safe, and will come in and go out, and find pasture. The only reason that the thief comes is in order to steal, to kill, and to destroy; but I have come to give them life--that they might have it to a greater extent!

"I am the good shepherd. The good shepherd lays his life down for the sheep. But the hired hand, who is not the shepherd to whom the sheep belong, runs away when he sees the wolf approaching. The wolf then catches them, and the sheep are all dispersed. The hired servant runs away, for he is but a wage earner, and is not worried about the sheep.

"I am the good shepherd. I know my own and they know me, even as the Father knows me, and I know Him. And I lay down my life for the sake of the sheep. What is more, I have other sheep which are not of this fold which I must likewise bring along. These will also hear my voice, and there will be a single flock, with a single shepherd. This is why my Father loves me: because I lay my life down that I might take it up again. No one deprives me of it. It is of my own will that I lay it down; and I have the power to take it up. This instruction was given to me by my Father."

And there arose yet another rift among the Jews over these words. Many among them contended, "He has a demon!" and "He is demented!" and "Why do you even listen to him?" But others insisted, "These are not the words of a demoniac. Can a demon open the eyes of the blind?"

THE SEVENTY TWO SENT OUT
(Luke 10:1-24; DTry 35:3;
Acts of Paul, Gospel Fragment in Coptic)
Perea

Now after this, the Lord appointed another seventy(two,) and sent them out in pairs before him into every city and region where he was soon to go. Then he informed them, "Truly it is a bountiful crop, but there are scarcely any harvesters. So appeal to the Lord of the harvest to send more gatherers into His field. Now move along.

"Divisions and heresies are sure to come. I am sending you out as sheep among wolves, (for) many will come outwardly draped in sheepskins and bearing my name, but deep within they are ravenous wolves. Do not carry a bag, or a wallet, or any sandals. Do not so much as say 'hello' to anyone along the way. And into whatever house you go, even before you do anything else, say, 'May peace come upon this home.' And if there should be a son of peace in that place, your peace will come to rest on it. And if this is not the case, your peace will then come back to you. Remain there with them in that house, and eat or drink what they provide for you, because the laborer is worthy of his hire. Do not move from house to house.

"And into whatever town you go and they receive you, eat whatever they give to you. Heal the sick among them, and say to them, 'God's kingdom has drawn near to you.' And into whatever town you go and they do not take you in, go out into its open places and proclaim, 'Even the dust of your town that sticks to us, we scrape off against you! Even so, be sure of this: the kingdom of God has drawn near to you.' I can assure you that when the day comes, it will be more tolerable for Sodom than it will be for that place.

"Curse you, Chorazin! Curse you, Bethsaida! For had the mighty works that were done in you been carried out in Tyre and Sidon, they would have sat long ago in sackcloth and ashes and repented. But the judgment will be more tolerable for Tyre and Sidon than it will be for you. As for you, Capernaum, have your praises reached the skies? Well, you will be brought down to Hell! Whoever hears you, also hears me; and whoever dismisses you dismisses me; and anyone who rejects me is also rejecting Him Who sent me."

And the seventy(two) returned in joy, saying, "Lord, even the demons subject themselves to us under your authority!" And he replied, "I have seen the Adversary fall like lightning from the sky. Behold, I have given you power to trample down snakes and scorpions, and the Enemy's every strength. There is nothing that can harm you at all. But do not rejoice over the fact that the spirits submit to you, but delight in the knowledge that your names have been written up in the heavens. There is something above the raising of the dead and the feeding of the multitudes--blessed indeed are those who with their whole heart have believed."

At that moment, Jesus grew joyful in spirit and said, "Father, I fully agree with You, Lord of heaven and earth, that You have concealed these things from the 'learned' and 'wise,' and have disclosed them instead to mere 'infants.' Indeed, Father, because it was just so pleasing to You! My Father has placed all things into my hands, and no one knows who the Son is, except for the Father, and no one knows who the Father is except for the Son, and those to whom the Son wishes to disclose Him." And he turned to the followers and spoke to them privately, "How privileged are the eyes that see what you do, for indeed I am telling you that many prophets and kings have longed to glimpse what you now see, and never did see it, and to hear what you're being told, but never heard it."

THE GOOD SAMARITAN
(Luke 10:25-37; GTh 25;
Clement of Alexandria, Excerpts from Theodotus 2.2;
Clement of Alexandria, Miscellanies 1.19)
Judea?

Now behold, this lawyer stood up to test him, saying, "Teacher, what must I do to inherit limitless life?" And Jesus replied, "What is written in the Law?

Tell me how it reads to you." And he answered Jesus, "You are to love your God with your whole heart and your whole spirit; from the fullness of your strength and with a thorough understanding; and your fellow man as you do yourself." And Jesus said, "You have given me the right answer. If you've seen your brother, then you've seen your God. Love your friends as you do your soul, defend them as the pupil of your eye. Do all this and you will live. Save yourself and your soul as well!'"

But eager to excuse himself, the man put this question to him, "But who qualifies as my neighbor?" And Jesus, taking it all in, answered him, "This man was on his way down to Jericho from Jerusalem, when he fell prey to bandits. They took his clothing off of him, pounded him severely, and ran away, leaving him there half dead. And a certain priest happened to be passing through. When he saw the man, he passed him by on the opposite side. Likewise, when a Levite who happened on that place got there and saw it, he passed him by on the other side. A Samaritan, however, came to him on his travels. But when this man saw him, he was moved with compassion for him. He walked over to him, bound up his wounds, poured olive oil and wine over them, lifted him up onto his own mount, took him to an inn and cared for him. And the next day as he was moving on, he took out two denarii and gave them to the innkeeper and said, 'Watch over him, and if it should cost you anything more, I will pay you back when I return.' Of these three, which one of them do you suppose turned out to be a 'neighbor' to the one who fell among the robbers?" And he answered, "The one who showed him compassion." Then Jesus charged him, "Go and do things just like him."

MARTHA AND MARY
(Luke 10:38-42)
Bethany

And as they continued on, he came to this certain village where this woman named Martha welcomed him into her home. And she had this sister named Mary, who also sat at Jesus' feet and listened to him as he taught. Now Martha was distracted by all of the serving that she was doing, so she stood by Jesus and asked, "Sir, does it not bother you that my sister has left me to serve by myself? Order her to help me out." And Jesus replied, "Martha, Martha, you are anxious and concerned about many things, but only a few things are necessary--or really just one. Mary has chosen the better one; and she will not be deprived of it."

PRAYER AND THE PARABLE OF
THE PERSISTENT NEIGHBOR
(Luke 11:1-13)
Perea

And it happened that, as he was praying in a certain place, one of his disciples approached him as he was closing and requested, "Lord, teach us how we ought to pray, even as John taught his disciples." And he said to them, "Whenever you pray, you should say:

'Our Father, Who is in heaven,
Blessed be Your name.
May Your kingdom come,
And Your will be done on earth
As it is in heaven.
Give us this day our next day's bread.
And forgive us our sins,
As we forgive our debtors.
And lead us not into temptation,
But save us from the Evil One.'"

Then he asked them, "Who among you that has a friend would go to him at midnight and beseech him, 'Friend, please lend me three loaves. See, this friend of mine has come to me on his travels, and I do not have anything to give him.' And the one inside responding, 'Do not bother me. I have already bolted the door, and my children are all in bed with me. It's not like I can get right up and give it to you!' I am telling you, even if he would not get up solely for the sake of his friendship, he will get up and give him as many as he needs simply because he keeps on pestering him. And so I am telling you: Ask, and it will be given to you; seek, and you will find: knock, and it will open up for you. You see, the one who asks is the one who receives; the one who seeks is the one who finds; and to one who knocks, it is opened right up.

"Fathers, if your son were to ask you for a loaf, which of you would give him a stone. How about a fish? If your son should ask you for a fish, would you give him a snake? Would you hand him a scorpion if he asked for an egg? If even you, as degenerate as you are, know how to give good gifts to your children, how much more will your heavenly Father give the Holy Spirit to those who ask it of Him!"

JESUS HEALS THE BENT WOMAN
(Luke 13:10-17)
Perea

And he was teaching in one of the synagogues on the Sabbath Day, and behold, there was this woman who had suffered from a debilitating spirit for eighteen years. She was altogether bent and could not straighten herself at all. And when Jesus saw her, he summoned her and said to her, "Woman, you have been set free from your infirmity!" And he laid his hands upon her, and she straightened right up and glorified God.

And the synagogue leader, furious that Jesus had healed on the Sabbath, said to those who were gathered there, "There are six days set aside for doing work. Come and be healed on one of those days and not on the Sabbath!" "Hypocrites!" he said to them. "Do not all of you untie your ox or your donkey from its stall and lead it out to have a drink? Then why should this woman, a daughter of Abraham who has been bound up by the Enemy for eighteen years now, not be set free from her bondage on the Sabbath Day?" And when he said this, all of his adversaries were put to shame, but the people were delighted by the marvelous things that he was doing.

THE MUSTARD SEED AND THE THREE MEASURES
(Luke 13:18-21)
Perea

"What is the kingdom of God like?" he asked them. "What can I use as an analogy? It is comparable to a mustard seed, which a man took and sowed in his garden. It grew into an enormous tree, and the birds of the sky settled in among its branches."

Once again he said to them, "What might I liken God's kingdom to? It is even as yeast, which a woman took and hid in three satas of flour until it had worked itself through."

THE DEDICATION FEAST
(John 10:22-39)
Jerusalem

Then came the Dedication Feast in Jerusalem. It was wintertime, and Jesus was on the temple grounds, walking in Solomon's Portico. The Jews therefore gathered around him and asked, "How long will you keep us guessing? If you are the Messiah, then come right out and tell us." And Jesus answered, "I have told you already. It is just that you did not believe. The very works that I do in my Father's name testify about me. It is because you are not my sheep that you do not believe me. It is even as I have told you before; my sheep all recognize my voice. I know them, and they follow me, and I give them endless life. No one takes them from my hand. My Father Who has given them to me is greater than all, (as is) that which my Father has given to me. I and the Father are One."

So once again the Jews gathered stones with which to pummel him. "I have shown you many great works which are from my Father," Jesus retorted, "For which of these works do you stone me?" "We are not stoning you for any good work," the Jews rejoined, "but for speaking wickedly, because you--a mere mortal--are making yourself out to be equal to God." "Isn't it written in your law," Jesus said, "'I have called you gods'? If He addressed the ones to whom the word of God came as gods, and that Scripture can't be set aside, then what about the one whom the Father sanctified and sent into the world. Why is it that you accuse me of blasphemy for saying that I'm the Son of God? If I do not do my Father's works, then do not put your faith in me. But if I should do my Father's works, even if you would not take me at my word, at least accept the works I do, so that you might recognize and believe that the Father is within me, and that I am within Him." And they tried once more to seize him, but he slipped right through their fingers.

JESUS WITHDRAWS TO THE JORDAN, ASKS THE PEOPLE A STRANGE QUESTION, AND WORKS A MIRACLE
(John 10:40-42; Egtn 4)
The Jordan River

Then he returned to the place on the other side of the Jordan where John had first baptized and stayed there. <Jesus said, "This withered tree's fruit has been> locked up <and its productivity> has been subjected imperceptibly. <How much of> its weight <remains> unweighed?" They were bewildered at such an unusual question, so Jesus headed to the riverbank. And as he stood there, he stretched out his right hand and <ground up a withered branch(?)> and scattered it over the <coursing river.> Then <he sprinkled some> water <over> the <dried-up tree> and it <filled out> before their eyes and put forth fruit <in such abundance that there was nothing> into <which it could all fit before them.> And many people came up to him and said, "John never performed any signs, but everything that John taught us about this man turned out to be true." And many placed their faith in him there.

ENTER THROUGH THE STRAIGHT GATE
(Luke 13:22-30)
Perea

And he taught them as he passed through towns and villages, and advanced toward Jerusalem. And someone asked him, "Lord, are there but a few who are saved?" And he answered them, "Strive to enter through the narrow gate, because I am telling you that many will try to gain entrance, but will not be able to. When the homeowner gets up and bolts the door, and you are all standing outside knocking at it and shouting, 'Lord, Lord, open up the door for us!' He will ask you, 'Where did you come from.' Then you will answer him, 'We ate and drank in your very midst! You taught us in our very streets!' Then he will reply to them, 'You horde of evildoers! I know neither who you are, nor the place from whence you came. Get away from me!'

"There will be wailing and tooth grinding there when you see Abraham, Isaac and Jacob, together with every prophet of God's kingdom, even as the likes of you are being thrown out. They will come from east and west, and north and south, and take their seat in the kingdom of God. See, there are last who will be first, and first who will be last."

JESUS IS WARNED ABOUT HEROD
(Luke 13:30-35; GTh 67)
Perea

That day, some Pharisees approached him and said, "Leave this place, for Herod is seeking to murder you." And he answered them, "Go and say to that fox, 'See, today I am casting out demons and preparing remedies. Tomorrow I will do the same. But on the third day I will be perfected.' Nevertheless, it is needful for me to press on today, tomorrow, and the following day, because it cannot be that a prophet should ever die outside of Jerusalem. Jerusalem! Jerusalem! Slayer of prophets and stoner of those who are sent to you! How often I have ached to gather your children together, as a hen gathers her hatchlings under her wings, but you would not have it! Look, your house is being left to you in desolation. Those who know all things, yet are lacking within, are truly lacking in all things. I tell you most assuredly, you will never see me again until you have said, 'Blessed is he who comes in the name of the Lord!'"

HOW TO ATTEND, AND HOW TO GIVE A FEAST
(Luke 14:1-14)
Perea

He entered into the house of this certain prominent Pharisee to eat bread one Sabbath Day, and they monitored him closely. Now behold, before him was this dropsical man, so Jesus questioned the Pharisees and lawyers, "Is it lawful to heal on the Sabbath Day?" They did not answer him at all, so he grabbed hold of the man, made him well and let him go. And he prodded them, "Which of you who has a son, (or) a donkey, or an ox, should they fall into a well on the Sabbath Day, would not immediately pull him out?" And they could not say a thing.

He marked how the guests were competing for the seats of distinction, and spoke this parable to them, "Whenever you are called to a wedding feast, do not sit in the seats of honor, for it might just be that he has invited someone who is more noble than you. The one who invited you might then approach you and say, 'Let this person have your seat.' You will then have to bear the shame of taking the place of least importance. Whenever you are bidden, you ought rather to sit in the lowest position, so when the one who invited you comes, he will say to you, 'My friend, move on up!' Then you will be honored before those seated with you. You see, whoever honors himself will be abased, while those who humble themselves will be honored." And, moreover, he said to those who had invited him, "Whenever you have lunch or dinner guests, do not invite your friends, brothers, family members, or wealthy neighbors, for they might then invite you back, and you will thus be recompensed. Instead, whenever you hold a banquet, summon the poor, the maimed, the lame, and the blind. That way you will indeed be blessed, because they do not have the means to repay; you will receive it back at the revival of the just!"

THE REJECTED INVITATION
(Luke 14:15-24)
Perea

When one of the men seated there with him heard this, he said to him, "How lucky is the man who will eat bread in the kingdom of heaven!" And Jesus answered him, "There was this man who readied an enormous feast and invited many guests. When the time came around, he sent his servant out to say to those who had been invited, 'Everything is set in place, so come right now!' But everyone started making excuses. The first one said, 'I have just now bought a field and I must go and have a look. Please let me off.' Another one said, 'Not long ago I purchased five yoke of oxen, and I must now go to inspect them. Please excuse me.' Yet another said to him, 'I cannot come for I have only just now wed.' That servant returned and passed all of this on to his master. Then the owner of the house became enraged and ordered his servant: 'Go out quickly into the streets and alleys of the city, and come back with the poor, the maimed, the blind, and the lame.' And the servant said, 'Lord, what you ordered done has been carried out, and even now there are settings left.' Then the master charged his servant: 'Go out into the highways and byways and force them to attend, that my house might be filled up. I am telling you, not one of those who were invited will partake of my feast!'"

THE COST OF DISCIPLESHIP
(Luke 14:25-35; GTh 15, 55, 101, 105)
Perea

Enormous crowds of people were following after Jesus, and he turned to them and said, "Whoever does not hate <father> and mother the way that I do is not fit to be my disciple, and whoever does <not> love <father and> mother the way that I do is not fit to be my disciple. My mother <gave me death>, you see, but my true <mother> gave me life. Anyone who knows both the Father and the Mother will be called the child of a harlot. When you come to see the One Who was not born of woman, fall upon your faces in worship, for that One is indeed your Father. Anyone who comes to me and does not hate his 'father' and 'mother,' 'wife' and 'children,' 'brothers' and 'sisters' and even his own life, is not fit to be my disciple. Also, anyone who fails to pick up his cross and follow after me is not worthy of me (and) cannot be my disciple.

"If any of you wished to build a tower, would he not sit down first and figure out his expenses before he started, in order to determine whether he has the means to finish? Because if he has laid the foundation already and cannot complete it, everyone who sees it will begin to mock him, saying, 'This man started out to build, but was not able to finish it off!' Or let's say that one king goes out to battle against another. Would he not sit down first and figure out whether his ten thousand will be able to withstand the twenty thousand sent out to oppose him? If he cannot, he sends envoys out while the other one is still far off and sues for peace.

"Similarly, none of you who fails to leave all of his things behind can be my disciple. The salt is good, but if the salt goes bland, what is there to season it?

It is fit for neither the land nor the manure pile; it is simply thrown away. Whoever has ears that can hear, let him hear."

THE LOST SHEEP AND THE LOST COIN
(Luke 15:1-10; GTh 107)
Perea

Now all of the tax-collectors and 'sinners' gathered closely around him in order to hear him. But the Pharisees and scribes were grumbling, "This man not only takes in 'sinners,' but then goes on to eat with them!"

And he spoke this parable to them, "The kingdom is like a shepherd who had a hundred sheep. The largest of them wandered off. He left the ninety nine and went out looking for that one until he found it. After all of his efforts, he said to that sheep, 'I love you more than the ninety nine!'

"Who among you that owns a hundred sheep, upon the loss of even one, would not leave the ninety nine behind in the field and search for the one that went astray until he has found it? And once he has recovered it, does he not joyfully place it over his shoulders? Then, after the man gets home, does he not gather together his friends and his neighbors and say, 'Join me now in celebration, for I have found the sheep that I had lost.' I am here to tell you that the joy in heaven over a single 'sinner' who repents far exceeds that of ninety nine 'righteous' men, who do not feel the need to reform.

"Or what woman upon losing one of her ten drachmas does not light a lamp and diligently sweep her house until she finds it? And as soon as she recovers it, does she not gather together all of her neighbors and lady friends and say, 'Rejoice with me, for I have found the drachma that I lost!' I hereby say to you that the angels of God rejoice over the conversion of even a single 'sinner.'"

THE PRODIGAL SON
(Luke 15:11-32)
Perea

And he went on, "This man had two sons. The youngest one said to his father, 'Father, give me my share of the inheritance.' So the man divided his estate between them. Not long after that, the younger son gathered together all of his belongings and made away for a distant land, where he managed to fritter away all of his wealth in riotous living. After he had squandered it all, a terrible famine swept over the region, and he became destitute. He joined himself to a man of that land, who sent him out into the fields to feed swine. He longed to fill his stomach with even the husks that the pigs were eating, but no one there would give him any. Then he came to himself and asked, 'How many of my father's hired hands have more than enough bread, but as for me--I'm starving to death! I will rise and go back to my father. "Father," I will say to him, "I have sinned against heaven, and in your eyes. I am no longer fit to be called your son--just let me be as a hireling to you."' And he got up and returned to his father, who, seeing him far away in the distance, beamed with compassion, ran right up to him, wrapped his arms around his neck and kissed him. And then his boy confessed to him, 'Father, I have sinned against heaven and in your sight. I am not worthy to be called your son. Treat me like one of your hired hands.' But the father commanded his servants, 'Bring out my finest robe and clothe him with it; give him a ring for his hand, and sandals for his feet. Bring the fatted calf and slaughter it, so that we might celebrate and feast upon it, for this son of mine was dead, but now he is alive again; who once was lost, but now is found.' And they all began to make merry.

"But the elder son had been out in the field. And as he drew near to the house, he heard the music and the dancing, so he called one of the young men to himself and asked, 'What is all of this about?' And the servant explained, 'Your brother has come back to us, and your father has slaughtered the fatted calf for him, because he has gotten him back all safe and sound!' But his brother seethed with rage and refused to go in, so his father came out and started pleading with him. And he complained to his father, 'Behold, I have worked for you all of these years, and have never disobeyed your commands, yet you never gave me so much as a young goat that I might revel with my friends. But when this son of yours shows up after blowing your substance romping with whores, you go and slaughter the fatted calf for him!' And the man responded, 'Son, you are always here with me, and what is mine is yours as well. We simply had to rejoice and be glad, for this brother of yours was once dead, but now he is alive again; he once was lost, but now is found.'"

THE CLEVER MANAGER
(Luke 16:1-18; Clement of Alexandria, Stromateis 1.28.177;
Quote by Clement of Alexandria, 11.51, 3.50, 18.20)
Perea

And he said to his disciples, "There was this rich man whose steward was charged with squandering his assets. So he called for him and demanded, 'What is this I hear of you? Account for your oversight, for you may no longer manage my affairs.' And the steward said within himself, 'What am I going to do now that my boss is firing me? I am too weak to dig and too proud to beg. I know just what I will do when I am relieved of my duties--get them to welcome me into their houses!' And he summoned all of his master's debtors and inquired of the first, 'How much do you owe my Master?' And he replied, 'A hundred baths of olive oil.' 'Now take your bill, sit down and write fifty.' Then he asked the second one, 'Now as for you, how much do you owe?' He responded, 'One hundred cors of wheat.' So he said to him, 'Here is your invoice, write down eighty.' Then the Lord commended the unjust steward on the shrewdness of his tactics. For the sons of this age are more clever in their strain than the sons of light. And I am here to say to you, be competent money-changers. Make plenty of friends for yourselves with this unholy mammon, so that when you fail, they will receive you into their eternal abodes. Whoever is faithful with what is least will be faithful with what is great; and whoever is unfaithful with what is least will be unfaithful with what is great. So if you can't be trusted with filthy lucre, who will entrust you with the true wealth? And if you cannot be trusted with the things of others, who will give you anything for yourself? Become faithful money-changers! Reject the counterfeit coins and accept only the genuine. No servant can serve two masters, because he will despise the one and love the other, or else he will serve the one and ignore the other. You cannot serve both God and Mammon."

When the money-loving Pharisees heard this, they all scoffed at him. Jesus said to them, "You like to parade your righteousness before mankind, but God knows what's in your hearts, because what is thought commendable in the eyes of men is reprehensible in the sight of God. Until John came on the scene, there was the law and the prophets. And ever since that time, the good news of the kingdom of God has been proclaimed, and everyone forces their way in. Indeed, it would be easier for heaven and earth to pass out of existence than it would be for a tittle of the law to disappear. Whoever divorces his wife and marries another, is committing adultery, and anyone who marries that woman put away by her husband is also committing adultery.

THE RICH MAN AND LAZARUS
(Luke 16:19-31; Recognitions of Clement 2.29)
Perea

Now there was this certain rich man who dressed in purple and choicest linen, and feasted sumptuously on a daily basis. Then there was this poor man named Lazarus, who had been placed at his gate, all covered in sores. He longed to eat even the crumbs that fell from the rich man's table. Dogs even came up to him and licked his sores. So the poor man died, and was whisked by the angels into Abraham's bosom. The wealthy man passed on as well, and he received a burial. And amid his tortures in Hades, he looked up and saw Abraham off in the distance, and Lazarus was in his bosom. Then he cried out, 'Father Abraham, show me some compassion! Send Lazarus to dip his finger into the water and cool my tongue with it, because this flame is tormenting me so.' 'My son,' Abraham replied, 'call to mind all of the good things that you received while you were still alive, as well as the evils that Lazarus has known. He is receiving his consolation now, whereas you are receiving your affliction. And besides all that, a great chasm has been placed between ourselves and you, so that those who would leave and cross over to you cannot, nor can any pass over from that side to this.' 'Then I beg you father Abraham,' the wealthy man replied, 'send him to my father's house, that he might describe this place of torment in detail to my five brothers, so that they don't also end up here.' Abraham then answered him, 'They have Moses and the prophets, let your brothers hear their words.' And he responded, 'But no, father Abraham, if someone should rise up from the dead and go to them, they will truly change their ways!' 'If they will not hear Moses and the prophets,' Abraham rejoined, 'then neither will they be persuaded by someone who rises from the dead.' Curse those who live in extravagance and wealth and yet give nothing to the poor! These will have to give account, for they should have loved their neighbors as themselves. For they showed the poor no compassion in their hardship."

FORGIVENESS AND FAITH
(Luke 17:1-10; Oxy 840:1)
Perea

<Jesus said, "A criminal,> before committing a crime, thinks about his every move. But you should guard against a fate like his, since those who carry out crimes against their fellow men not only get what's coming to them in this life, but (in the next one,) he will have to face punishment and eternal anguish. Stumbling blocks are sure to come," he cautioned his disciples, "but woe to the one who sets them up. It would profit him more to have a giant millstone fitted around his neck and to be thrown into the sea than to cause one of these little ones to lose their footing. You must therefore watch yourselves. If your brother should do you wrong, then reprove him, and if he should change his ways, then forgive him. And if he should injure you seven times in just one day, and seven times that day he should turn around and apologize, then pardon him." Then the apostles said to the Lord, "Give us a more excellent faith." The Lord then answered them, "If your faith were even as a mustard seed, you would have said to this mulberry tree, 'Be pulled up by the roots and planted in the sea,' and it would have obeyed you.

"Which of you, should he have a servant out plowing or feeding, would have him come in from the field and say to him, 'Come here. Sit down and eat!'? Would you not rather say to him, 'You must fix me something to eat. Tie your robe and wait on me while I eat and drink. You can eat when I am done.' Does the servant get any thanks for following orders? I think not! And so it goes for all of you, after doing what you were expected to, say, 'We are all just miserable servants and have only done as we were told.'"

Robert C. Ferrell

MINISTRY 4

JESUS RAISES LAZARUS
(John 11:1-44)
Bethany

Now there was this certain man named Lazarus who was ill. He was from Bethany, the same village as Mary and her sister Martha. Now this was the same Mary who had anointed the Lord with ointment and wiped off his feet with her hair, and the ailing Lazarus was her brother. The sisters therefore sent a message to Jesus, "Lord, the one that you love is ill." Now when Jesus heard this, he said, "This illness will not lead to death, but to the glorification of God; that the Son of God might be exalted thereby." Now Jesus loved Martha and her sister, and Lazarus too. So when he heard about his condition, Jesus stayed where he was for two days. "Let us return to Judea," he said to his students. "Rabbi," the disciples questioned him, "the Jews have just now tried to stone you, and are you going back again?" "Are there not twelve hours in a day?" Jesus replied. "If anyone should walk in daylight, he will not stumble, because he can see by the light of this world. If, however, someone should walk at night, then he will indeed slip up, for there is no light in him." After saying this to them, he explained, "Our friend Lazarus has only fallen asleep; but I am going there to wake him up." So his followers said to him, "Sir, if he is sleeping, then he will get well." Now Jesus meant that he had died, but the disciples imagined that he was talking about some kind of restful slumber. So at that point Jesus came out and said, "Lazarus is dead, but for your sakes I am glad that I was not there, so that you might come to believe. Even so, let us all now go to him." At this, Thomas, who is also known as Didymus, said to the other disciples, "Let us all go with him as well, that we might all die alongside him." So Jesus came and found that Lazarus had already been entombed for four days.

Now Bethany was only about fifteen stadia away from Jerusalem, and many Jews had come to Martha and Mary to comfort them on the loss of their brother. When Martha heard that Jesus would soon be there, she went out to meet him, while Mary sat at home. "Lord," said Martha, "my brother would never have passed on had you been here. But I know that even now, God will give you whatever you might ask of Him." "Your brother will be raised again," Jesus said. "I know," Martha answered. "He will rise again in the resurrection on the last day." Jesus said, "I am the resurrection and I am life. Anyone who trusts in me, even though he passes on, he will indeed live. And everyone who is alive and has faith in me will never, ever die. Do you believe this?" "I do, my Lord," she answered him, "I believe that you are the Messiah, the Son of God who is coming into the world." And after she had said all this, she returned and summoned Mary, and said to her privately, "The Teacher is here, and he's asking for you."

When Mary heard this, she got up quickly and went over to where Jesus was. Now Jesus had not yet entered into the village, but was still waiting there where Martha had met him. The Jews who had been with her in her house, consoling her, when they saw how Mary had sprung up and hurried out, said, "She is going to weep at the tomb," so they followed after her. So when Mary got to the place where Jesus was and saw him there, she fell at his feet and said, "Lord, my brother would never have died if you had been here." When Jesus saw her weeping, and the Jews who came with her also weeping, he was deeply stirred within his spirit, and he grew troubled. Then he asked them, "Where have you laid him?" "Lord," they replied, "come and see." Jesus wept. So the Jews there said, "Look at how deep his love for Lazarus was!" But some of them sneered, "Could not this one who opened up the eyes of the blind man also have kept this man from dying?" So Jesus, once again deeply moved, arrived at the tomb. It was a cave with a stone lying across it. "Remove the stone," he said to them. And Martha, the sister of the deceased, protested, "Lord, the stench of death is on him now, for he has been dead for four days!" "Did I not already say to you," Jesus reminded her, "that if you were to believe, you would see the glory of God?" Then they removed the stone where the dead man lie. And Jesus looked to the sky and said, "Father, I thank You for hearing me. I know very well that You always do, but I said it for the sake of those standing here, that they might believe that You have sent me." And after he had spoken this, he shouted in a loud voice, "Lazarus, come forth!" And the one who had died came out, his grave clothes still bound around his hands and feet, and a cloth still wrapped around his face. And Jesus said, "Unbind him now and let him go."

THE PHARISEES CONSPIRE TO EXECUTE JESUS
(John 11:45-54)
Jerusalem; Ephraim

Many of the Jews who came to Mary and saw what Jesus had done came to put their faith in him. Some of them, however, went to the Pharisees and let them know what he was doing. The high-ranking priests and the Pharisees therefore called a meeting of the Sanhedrin and asked, "What are we supposed to do, seeing that he does so many signs? Were we to let him go on like this, everyone would come to believe in him, and the Romans would come and do away with our temple and our nation." And one of them--that year's high priest, whose name was Caiaphas--questioned them, "Do you understand nothing at all? Can you not see that it is better for one man to die for the sake of the people, than for the entire nation to perish?" Now it was not on his own that he said this to them, but as that year's high priest, he was prophesying that Jesus was soon to die for the sake of the nation. And not just for that nation alone, but to bind together all of God's children who are scattered far and wide, and make them all one. So they plotted his death from that day on. Jesus therefore no longer walked freely among the Jews, but left that place for a town called Ephraim, which was near to the desert, and he stayed with his disciples there.

THE GRATEFUL LEPER
(Luke 17:11-19)
Galilee or Samaria

He was traveling between Galilee and Samaria on his way through to Jerusalem. There he entered into a certain village where there met him ten lepers who were standing off in the distance and shouting, "Jesus, Master, show us some compassion!" And when he saw them, he said to them, "Go and show yourselves to the priests." And even as they went their way, all of them received their cleansing. And one of them, when he realized that he'd been cured, returned praising God loudly. And he fell to his face at Jesus' feet and gave him thanks--and this man was a Samaritan. "Were there not ten who were cleansed?" Jesus marveled. "Where then are the other nine? Were there none found besides this foreigner who would come back and praise God?" Then he said to him, "Rise up now and go your way, for your faith has made you whole."

THE COMING OF THE KINGDOM
(Luke 17:20-37; GTh 3, 18, 29, 51, 61, 113)
Galilee?

And he was prodded by the Pharisees (and) the disciples, "Tell us when God's kingdom will come." He answered them, "The kingdom of God does not come through observation, nor will anyone proclaim, 'Look, here it is,' or 'Look, over there!' You see, God's kingdom lies within you! It is instead that the Father's dominion covers the face of the earth and men fail to discern it." "Explain to us how our end will come," the followers requested of Jesus. Jesus answered them, "Have you found the beginning, then, that you seek for the end? For where the beginning is, there will the end be also. Blessed is the one who takes his stand at the beginning, for he will know the end and will not ever taste of death." His disciples asked him, "When will the dead find rest, and the new world come at last?" He answered them, "What you are looking forward to has already happened, but you do not yet realize it. If those who lead you should say to you, 'Behold, the kingdom is up in the sky,' then the birds of the sky will enter in before you. Should they claim, 'It is under the earth (or) beneath the sea,' then the fish will enter in before you. To the contrary, the dominion lies both within you and without. <Those who> come to the knowledge of <themselves> will discover this. As soon as you recognize who you are, you will become recognized. You will come to see yourselves as the children of the Living Father. If, however, you are unaware of your true nature, then you dwell in poverty, and you are yourselves that poverty! It is truly marvelous that flesh should arise from spirit, but if spirit should break forth by means of the flesh, then that is a marvel bound up in a marvel. Even so, I am truly amazed at how such a vast fortune has made its home in such great poverty! The days are coming," he said to his disciples, "when you will long to behold even one of the days of the Son of Man, and will not see it. They will say to you, 'Look, over here!' and 'Look, over there!' Do not follow after them, because in his day, the Son of Man will be even as a bolt of lightning flashing from one end of the sky to the other. But before that ever happens, he must undergo numerous ordeals, and be rejected by this generation. And just as it was in Noah's day, so also will it be in the days of the Son of Man. They ate, they drank, they married off and were given in marriage right up to the day that he entered the ark. Then came the all-destroying flood. It happened the same way in Lot's time; they ate, they drank, they bought, they sold, they planted and they built. Then, on the very day that Lot left Sodom, He rained fire and brimstone down from heaven, bringing all things down to destruction. On the day of the revelation of the Son of Man, it will be even as these things were. On that day, those of you who are up on the housetop, do not go down for what's in your house. And those of you who are out in the field, do not even turn around. Remember Lot's wife? Anyone looking to save his life will end up losing it, but whoever turns his back on this life will end up saving it. I am telling you that on that night, two will be in the same bed; one will be taken, and the other will be left--one will die and one will live. Two women will be grinding in the very same place; one will be taken, and the other will be left. Two men will be out in a field; one will be taken, and the other will be left." "Where to, my Lord?" they asked him. He answered, "Wherever there is a carcass, the vultures will be sure to gather." Salome said, "Who are you, mister? You have climbed onto my couch and eaten from my table as if sent to me by someone." Jesus answered her, "I am the one who receives his nature from the One Who is whole. The things of my Father have been given to me." "I am truly your disciple," (answered Salome.) "It is for this reason," (Jesus explained to her,) "that I say, 'when a man is unified he will beam with light; but if he should be conflicted, he will be choked with darkness.'"

THE UNJUST JUDGE;
THE PHARISEE AND THE TAX-COLLECTOR
(Luke 18:1-14)
Galilee?

And he related this parable to them so that they might always pray and never lose heart. He said, "There was a certain judge in a particular town who neither worshiped God, nor reverenced men. There was also this widow who lived in that town who kept on coming up to him and saying, 'Carry out justice for me against my enemy.' And for a while, he did not bother. But later on he thought to himself, 'Though I respect neither God nor man, because this woman keeps on pestering me, I will indeed stand up for her, lest she beleaguer me with her endless visits.'" And the Lord said, "Mark the words of the unrighteous Judge. Will not God avenge His elect, who cry out to Him both day and night. Will He keep them waiting? I am telling you that He will carry out justice for them with all due speed. Nevertheless, when the Son of Man does come, will he find faith here on this earth?"

Then he spoke this parable to some who looked down on everyone else, believing in their hearts that they were just: "Two men, a Pharisee and a tax-collector, went up to the temple to pray one day. The Pharisee stood and prayed to himself, 'God, I thank You for the fact that I am not greedy, evil, or adulterous, like other people are, such as this publican over here. I fast two times a week, and pay a tithe on all that I receive.' But the tax-collector stood far away and would not even look up to heaven. He merely struck his chest and said, 'God, have mercy on a sinner like me!' I am here to say to you that this one went down to his house justified, while the other one did not! For everyone who exalts himself will be humbled, whereas those who humble themselves will be exalted."

JESUS TEACHES ABOUT DIVORCE
(Matt 19:1-12; Mark 10:2-12)
Perea

And after Jesus had said all this, he left Galilee for the part of Judea that lies beyond the Jordan. Enormous crowds again came to him (and) followed after him, and he started teaching and healing them there as was his custom. And the Pharisees came to put him to the test, asking, "Is it lawful for a man to divorce his wife for whatever reason?" He replied, "What did Moses say to you?" They answered him, "Moses allowed a man to write out a certificate of divorce and send her on her way." And he asked them, "Have you never read that He Who created them at first created them both male and female?" Then he explained: "This is why a man will leave his mother and father behind and join together with his wife. And so they are to remain; the two are to be one in flesh. Thus, they are no longer two, but one. So do not let anyone tear apart what God has joined." Then they asked him, "So how come Moses said to give her a bill of divorce and send her away?" He answered, "Moses wrote this law for you, allowing you to divorce your wives, because your hearts had been made hard. But this was not how it was at first. I am telling you now that whoever puts his wife away and marries another for any reason but whoredom is committing adultery against her. And whoever marries the woman who has been put away is also committing adultery."

When they all got back to the house, his followers prodded Jesus about this. He responded, "Anyone who puts away his wife and marries some other woman is committing adultery against her. And if she should put her husband away and marry some other man, she is committing adultery against him." "If this is the case between a man and a woman," his disciples remarked, "then it is better to remain unwed." And he informed them, "Not everyone can accept this insight; only those to whom it has been given. You see, there are those who have been born as eunuchs from their mother's womb; and there are the kind that are made eunuchs by men; and there are eunuchs who have kept themselves that way for the kingdom of heaven. Let whoever can, receive this."

JESUS AND THE CHILDREN
(Matt 19:13-15:Mark 10:13-16; Luke 18:15-17;
GTh 4, 22/4-POxy 654; Gospel of The Nassenes,
Quote by Hippolytus, Philosophumena 5.7.20)
Perea

At that time, the people were bringing infants (and) young children over to him so that he might lay his hands on them and pray. But when his disciples saw what the people were doing, they reproached them. But when Jesus saw the disciples hindering the crowds, he became angry, called the children to himself and said, "Let the little ones draw near to me! Do not stand in the way of their coming, for the heavenly kingdom of God is comprised of such as these. Most assuredly I say to you, whoever fails to receive the kingdom of God as a little child will never enter into it." Jesus, spotting some suckling newborns, said to his followers, "You see these infants nursing here? Those who enter the kingdom are just like these." His followers asked him, "So are we to enter in as newborns?" Jesus answered, "Out of the two you should form one, making what is inside like what is outside, and what is outside like what is inside, and what is 'higher' should be brought together with what is 'lower,' and in this way you will transform the 'man' and the 'woman' into that singular union. Thus the man will not be 'male,' nor will the woman be 'female.' And when you should replace an 'eye' with an 'eye,' and a 'hand' with a 'hand,' and a 'foot' with a 'foot,' with one image replacing the other, you will enter into the <kingdom.> Anyone who looks for me will find me in children, for it is in these that I will show myself. The aged man who is full of days will not hesitate to ask a little child who is seven days old about the place of life, and he will live. For there are many who are first who will be last, and many who are last (who will be) first, and they will become singular, one." Then he took the children into his arms and blessed them. And after laying his hands on them, he left that place.

THE PITFALL OF WEALTH
(Matt 19:16-28; Mark 10:17-31; Luke 18:18-30;
GNaz 6, Quote by Origen, On Matthew, 15:14,
regarding Matt 19:16-30;
GTh 110, 81)
Perea

Now as Jesus was moving on from there, a certain ruler ran up to him. And when he had drawn near to him, he asked him, "Good teacher, what is the good that I must do to receive [the] inherit[ance] (of) eternal life?" And Jesus asked him, "Why do you refer to me as good, (and) ask it of me? God alone, and no one else, is the only One Who is good. But if you'd like to enter into life, then you must abide by the commandments." And he asked Jesus, "Which ones?"

And Jesus said, "You know them: 'Do not murder, do not commit adultery, do not steal, do not witness falsely, do not commit fraud, honor your father and your mother, and love your neighbor as you do yourself.'" The young man answered him, "Teacher, I have lived by these from my childhood. What do I yet lack?" When Jesus heard this, he looked at him with love (and) said, "You only fall short in one thing. If you wish to move on to perfection, go and sell the things you own and distribute your substance among the poor. Then you will have treasure in the kingdom of heaven. Only then should you come and follow me."

When he heard this, the young man's face fell, (and) his heart sank. Jesus looked at him and said, "How hard it is for the rich to get into God's kingdom! Truly it is easier for a camel to pass through the eye of a needle than it is for a wealthy man to enter into the kingdom of God." And he went away all dejected, seeing that he had many possessions. And those who heard this asked him, "Then who qualifies for salvation?" Jesus answered, "What is beyond the grasp of men is within the reach of God."

A second wealthy man asked him, "Teacher, what must I do to have life?" Jesus answered, "Sir, you must fulfill the law and the prophets." "I have done that already," the man replied. "Go now," he said, "sell your things and give it all to the poor. Then come and follow me." But the rich man didn't like hearing that, so he started scratching his head. Then the Lord reproved him, saying, "How can you claim to be fulfilling the law and the prophets, when the law demands of you, 'Love your neighbor as you do yourself'? Take a look around you then. Many of your brothers and sisters, Abraham's own sons and daughters, live in squalor and starve to death, while nothing of yours ever makes it out to them." And turning toward Simon, who was sitting nearby, he said to him, "Simon, son of Jonah, it is easier for a camel to pass through the eye of a needle than it is for a rich man to pass into the kingdom of heaven." And Jesus turned and looked at his disciples and said, "The one who discovers the world and finds the wealth, and the one who has authority, ought to renounce the world (and) to reign. In all truth I say to you, a 'wealthy' man can hardly enter into the heavenly kingdom of God."

The disciples were all amazed by his words. But once again he said to them, "Children, how difficult it is for those whose confidence is in their wealth to get into God's kingdom! Once again I say to you, it is easier for a camel to squeeze through the eye of a needle than it is for a wealthy man to enter into the kingdom of God." When his students heard this, they were completely taken aback. "Who then can be saved?" they asked one another. Jesus then looked at his disciples and said, "This is impossible for men, but not for God. For God, all things are possible."

Then Peter asked him, "All of us have forsaken everything to follow you. What, therefore, will we possess?" "Truly do I say to you," Jesus then said to them, "when all things have been made new, and the Son of Man is sitting on his glorious throne, all of you who followed me will likewise sit upon twelve thrones and judge the twelve tribes of Israel. And everyone who left houses, or brothers, or sisters, or father, or mother, or wife, or children, or fields for my sake (and) the kingdom of God, will receive (and) not fail to receive many times over, (even) a hundred fold, homes, brothers, sisters, mothers, children and fields. And though they come with persecutions in this age, their end is eternal life in the age to come. And many who are first will then be last, and many of the last will then be first.

THE WORKERS IN THE FIELD
(Matt 20:1-16; Barnabas 6:13)
Perea

"The kingdom of heaven is like a man who owned some land. One morning he went out to hire some workers for his vineyard. He contracted with the workmen for a denarius that day, and sent them out to work in it. And at about the third hour, he went back and saw some others who were standing around in the marketplace not doing anything. 'You also go into the vineyard," he said to them, "and I will pay you what is right,' and away they went. And he went out and did the same thing at the sixth, and the ninth hours. Now at about the eleventh hour, he found yet others who were standing idly by, so he asked them, 'Why have you stood around here doing nothing all day?' 'Because,' they said, 'no one would hire us.' 'You also go out,' he ordered them, 'and you will be paid what is right.' And at dusk, the owner said to his overseer, 'Summon the workers and pay them, starting with the last and ending with the first.' And those who were hired at about the eleventh hour came up, and each of them received a denarius. And when those who were first came up to him, they expected to be paid the more, but they also received a denarius apiece. And upon receiving it, they started railing against the owner of the estate, 'These latecomers have worked scarcely even a single hour, yet you have placed them on par with the likes of us, who have shouldered the better part of the work, not to mention the heat of the day.' 'Friend,' he answered one of them, 'I have not wronged you. Did you not agree with me to work for a denarius? Take what's yours and move along. I wish to give to these who were last even as I have given to you. Do I not have the right to distribute my substance any way that I see fit? Or does my generosity elicit your avarice?' This is how the last will be first, and the first will be last. Behold, I do myself cause the first things to become last and the last things to become first. Many are the called, you see, but the chosen are few."

JOURNEY TO JERUSALEM
(Matt 20:17-28; Mark 10:32-45; Luke 18:31-34;
SMk 1; Matt 20:28ff in certain mss.)
Perea, Bethany

Now Jesus led them out as they moved on to Jerusalem. The disciples were amazed, and those who followed were troubled and afraid. He took the twelve disciples aside privately and informed them once again about what he was soon to undergo, "See, we are headed up to Jerusalem, and all that the prophets have written about the Son of Man are to be fulfilled. The Son of Man will be delivered up to the chief priests and the scribes. They will then condemn him to death, and hand him over to the Gentiles so that they might mock him, insult him, spit on him, beat him, crucify and kill him. And three days later, he will rise up, being raised to life on the third day." The disciples did not get this at all. Its meaning was lost on them, and they did not realize what he was talking to them about.

Then they came to Bethany. There was a woman there whose brother had recently died, so she knelt down before Jesus. "Son of David," she implored him, "show me compassion!" But the disciples reproved her. Then Jesus became angry, and went with her into the garden where his tomb was. At that moment, a voice was heard from within the tomb. Then Jesus went to the entrance and rolled away the stone. He went in to where the young man was, took him by his hand and lifted him up. The man looked on Jesus with love, and begged him to remain with him. They then came out of the tomb and entered into the young man's home. (Who, by the way, was very wealthy.) Six days later, Jesus gave him instruction: the man came to him that evening, clad only in a linen cloth. He stayed there with him overnight, for Jesus taught him the mystery of the kingdom of God. Then he left that place and crossed back over to the far side of the Jordan.

Then the mother of the sons of Zebedee approached him, together with her sons, knelt down before him and asked him to do her a favor. Jesus asked her, "What would you like?" James and John said, "Teacher, we would like you to grant us our request." And he responded, "What would you have me do for you?" They answered, "Allow us to sit in your glory, one to your right, and the other to your left." "Please," the mother asked Jesus, "order that one of these two sons of mine might sit to your right in your kingdom, and the other to your left." But Jesus responded, "You don't know what you're asking of me. Are you able to drink from the cup of which I must soon partake, or of experiencing the same baptism which I am soon to undergo?" "Yes we are," they answered him. "Indeed you are to drink of my cup," he informed them, "and go through the same baptism with which I will be baptized. Nevertheless, it is not for me to grant a seat, either to my right or to my left. It belongs instead to those for whom my Father has prepared it."

When the ten heard about this, they were furious with the two brothers, James and John. So Jesus called them to himself and said, "You know how those who are reckoned as governors over the Gentiles lord it over them, and how their superiors subjugate them as well. This is not how it will be with you. Rather, let anyone among you who aspires to greatness become your servant, and whoever would be first must be servant to you, (and indeed) to all; even as the Son of Man has. For the Son of Man did not come to be served, but in order to render service, and to offer his life as a ransom for many. You ought rather to try and outgrow smallness, foregoing greatness to become small. Upon receiving a dinner invitation, for example, do not go in and sit among the places of distinction, lest someone more illustrious than you should come along, and the host be compelled to approach you and say, 'Move on down,' and thus embarrass you. It would work more to your advantage for you to seat yourself in a lesser spot. That way if someone less distinguished should come, the host will therefore say to you, 'Move on up!'"

ZACCHAEUS THE PUBLICAN
(Luke 18:35-37; 19:1-10; Mark 10:46a; SMk 2; Traditions of Matthias, Quote by Clement of Alexandria, Stromateis 4.6.35)
Jericho

As Jesus was approaching Jericho, this blind man was sitting and begging by the side of the road. When he heard all the people who were headed that way, the blind man asked, "What is all of this about?" The people replied, "Jesus of Nazareth is passing by."

They then arrived in Jericho. Now the sister of the young man whom Jesus loved was there, as were both his mother and Salome. Jesus, however, would not visit them as he was only passing through.

There was this rich man there named Zacchaeus, who was a chief tax-collector. He was determined to get a glimpse of Jesus. He wanted to see which one he was, but owing to the throngs and his diminutive stature, he was not able. So he ran on ahead and climbed up a sycamore tree in order to get a look at him, seeing how he was soon to pass that way. Now when Jesus came to that place, he glanced up and looked at him. "Zacchaeus," Jesus beckoned him, "hurry on down, for I must spend the day at your house!" Zacchaeus then clambered down and received him with delight. And when they saw that, everyone started grumbling, "He has gone to stay with a 'sinful' man!" But Zacchaeus stood and said to the Lord, "Look, Sir! I am giving half of all that I own to the poor, and if I have defrauded anyone out of anything, I will pay it back four times over." And Jesus said to him, "The Son of Man has come this day and restored what had been lost; for it was in order to search out and save what was lost that the Son of Man came. Today deliverance has come to this house, for this man also is a son of Abraham."

THE TEN MINAS
(Luke 19:11-28)
Jericho

Now as they were hearing his words, he went on to speak a parable to them, because he was near to Jerusalem, and they were under the impression that the kingdom of God was about to unfold. For this reason Jesus said to them, "There once was this highborn man who traveled to a faraway land to accept a kingship and return. He therefore summoned ten of his servants and distributed ten minas among them. He said, 'Put this money to good use until I return.' Now his subjects all hated him, so they sent a delegation after him to declare, 'We do not want this man reigning over us.' And after being installed as king, the man came home. Then he gave orders that those to whom he had entrusted the money should be brought to him so that he might determine how each of them had followed through on his task. The first one came to him and said, 'Sir, your mina has made you another ten.' And he replied, 'Great work, you able servant! Now because you have proven yourself faithful over something small, take authority over ten cities!' The second one then approached him and said, 'Lord, your mina has increased fivefold.' Accordingly he said to him, 'As for you, command five cities!' Then another one came up and said, 'Master, behold, here is your mina. I had it tucked away in a handkerchief. You see, I feared your austere disposition. You take what you did not lay down, and harvest where you did not plant.' 'You wicked servant!' he answered him, 'I will judge you by your very words.' So you knew me to be a austere man, taking up what I never laid down and reaping where I never sowed? In that case, would it not have been better to have put my money in the bank, so that I could have at least gotten it back with some interest on my return?'

"And he ordered those who were standing nearby: 'Confiscate his mina and give it to the man who has ten.' At this point they all replied, 'But Sire, he already has ten minas!' Even so, I can assure you that everyone who has will be given the more, but as for someone who lacks, even what he does have will be taken away from him. But as for these, my enemies, who do not wish to bow to my lordship over them, bring them here and slay them before me.'" And after he had said all this, he ventured on, leading the way up to Jerusalem.

BARTIMAEUS AND HIS COMPANION
(Matt 20:29-34; Mark 10:46b-52; Luke 18:38-43)
Leaving Jericho for Jerusalem

A great crowd was following Jesus as he and his followers were leaving the city of Jericho; and two blind men were sitting over by the side of the road. (One of them,) Bartimaeus, which means 'the son of Timaeus,' was sitting there begging. Now when they heard that it was Jesus of Nazareth who was passing that way, they started to shout, "Lord Jesus, Son of David, have mercy on me!" "Show us some compassion!" Many people, the forepart of the crowd, reproved them, saying, "Be quiet!" But they simply shouted louder (and) longer, "Lord, Son of David, show me some compassion!" "Please have pity on us both!" Jesus immediately stopped and commanded that the man be brought before him. "Summon him," Jesus said. So they called to the blind man, "Take courage, mister. He is calling out for you, so get up!" And tossing his cloak to the side, Bartimaeus sprang to his feet and went to Jesus. And when the man had drawn near to him, Jesus asked him, "What would you have me do for you?" "Rabbi, Sir," said the sightless man, "How I wish that I could see." And each of them pleaded, "We would like our eyes to be opened." Jesus felt for them and touched their eyes. And all of a sudden they received their sight, and traveled down the road with him. Then the man gave praises to God, and when the crowd saw that, they also started to glorify God.

ARRIVAL IN BETHANY; MARY ANOINTS JESUS
(John 11:55-12:1, 9-11)
Bethany, near Jerusalem

Now the Jewish Passover was drawing near, and many went up to Jerusalem from the countryside before the Passover to purify themselves. They were keeping an eye out for Jesus. And the people stood there asking one another in the temple, "What do you suppose? Will he absent himself from the feast?" Now the chief priests and the Pharisees had issued a decree to the effect that if anyone should know of his whereabouts, he must disclose it, that they might arrest him. This was why six days prior to the Passover, Jesus came to Bethany, where Lazarus was, who had died, and whom Jesus had raised from the dead.

And many of the Jews heard that he was there, so they came, not only to see Jesus, but also to see Lazarus, whom he had raised. Now the chief priests had made a similar pact to murder Lazarus, because many of the Jews were going off and believing in Jesus on account of him.

THE TRIUMPHAL ENTRY
(Matt 21:1-11, 14-17; Mark 11:1-11; Luke 19:29-44; John 12:12-19; POxy 840-2:1-9, GTh 28/28-POxy 1)
Bethphage, Bethany, Mount of Olives, Jerusalem

By the following day, the great multitude that showed up for the feast had heard that Jesus was coming to Jerusalem. And they drew near, approaching (and) arriving in Bethphage, then Bethany, as far as the hill known as the Mount of Olives. Then Jesus sent out two of his followers, saying to them, "Go on ahead to the village that lies before you, and even as you are going in, you will see a donkey tethered there, and a colt which no one has ever ridden before, tied alongside her. Untie them both and bring them here. And if anyone says anything to you, (or) asks you, 'What are you up to?' (or) 'Why are you untying it?' simply respond, 'The Lord is in need of them.' He will send [them] back here shortly, (and) without hesitation.'" So the disciples went and did as Jesus had said. Those he sent went out and found everything precisely as Jesus had described it to them. They went and found a colt tied to a door in the open street. As they were untying the colt, the owners happened to be standing there. They then asked the disciples, "What are you doing, untying that colt?" They replied as Jesus had instructed them: "The Lord has need of [them]," they answered. So the people let them leave with [them]. They brought back the ass and its colt, draped their garments across them, and seated him thereon. So Jesus found himself a young donkey and mounted it. And all of this came to pass in order to fulfill what had been spoken through the prophet who said,

'Say to the Daughter of Zion,
"Fear not, Oh Daughter of Zion.
Behold, your King is coming to you,
Humbly mounted on a donkey,
Upon a colt--the foal of a beast of burden."'

His students did not get this at first, but after Jesus had been glorified, they recognized that all of these things were written about him and had been fulfilled in him.

And as he moved on from there, the better portion of the crowd continued to spread their clothing out along the road, while others cut palm branches from trees that were out in the fields. They went out to meet him shouting, (and) scattering the branches all over the road. When he came to the crest of the road on the Mount of Olives, the host of disciples--the great crowd that was leading the way, and also those who were trailing behind--started praising God with joyful cries for all the wonders they had seen. They were all clamoring,

"Hosanna to the Son of David!
Blessed is the King who comes in the name of the Lord!
Blessed is the King of Israel!
Blessed is the coming of the kingdom of our father David!
Peace in heaven, and glory in the highest!
Hosanna even in the highest!"

Then some of the Pharisees from among the people reproved Jesus: "Teacher, admonish your disciples!" "I can assure you," he answered them, "if these were to silence themselves, the very stones would cry aloud."

And as he drew near to Jerusalem and caught sight of the city, he mourned for it, saying, "If only you, yes you, had understood what would have brought you peace this very day, which even now is hidden from you. The days are coming when your adversaries will raise up an embankment against you, surrounding you and shutting you in on every side, and will throw you right down to the ground, along with the children within your walls. They will not leave so much as a single stone upon another--all because you did not recognize the time of your visitation!"

Now the people who were with Jesus when he called Lazarus out of the tomb and raised him from the dead were there describing the event to everyone. And because they heard that Jesus had worked this wonder, many people went out to meet him. And as he entered into Jerusalem, the entire city trembled, asking, "Who is this?" And the crowds proclaimed, "This is Jesus, the prophet from Nazareth of Galilee!"

And he went over to the temple, where blind and lame men came up to him, and he healed them there. And when the high-ranking priests and the scribes saw the wonderful things that he was doing, and the children crying out in the temple, "Hosanna to the Son of David," they became extremely angry. "Do you not hear what these children are saying?" they questioned him. "Yes I do," Jesus said, "have you never read, 'You have praises prepared from the mouths of babes and children'?" So the Pharisees concluded among themselves, "Face it, we are getting nowhere with this. Look at how the whole world chases after him!"

And Jesus went up into the temple, taking <his students> along with him. He led them all the way into the innermost sanctuary and started wandering through the temple grounds, looking around at everything.

A high-ranking Pharisee priest named Levi also went in and confronted them, demanding of the Savior, "Who authorized you to walk around in this inner sanctum and look upon these hallowed objects, seeing how you have not performed the ceremonial ablution, nor have your followers so much as cleansed their feet? In a polluted state have you encroached upon this ceremonially clean and holy place. No one walks around in here unless they have washed up first and put on clean clothes, nor do they venture to look upon these holy vessels!"

Now the Savior immediately got up with his disciples and said, "And I suppose that you are clean, seeing that you are with us here?" "I'm clean all right," Levi said. "I went down into the Pool of David, washed myself off, and came back up on the other side. I have, moreover, put on ceremonially clean, white clothing. It was only after doing so that I came here and looked upon these sacred things."

"Accursed be the blind who refuse to see!" the Savior retorted. "You wash in these lifeless waters, where swine and dogs wallow day and night. You cleanse and scrub your skin superficially as any whore or showgirl would. They all rinse and scour--putting on fragrances and painting themselves for the seduction of men--but deep inside they are teeming with scorpions and every manner of filth. You say that my students and I are unwashed, yet we have bathed in the dynamic water of life which comes down from <my Father in heaven.> But curse those <who are hypocritical and blind!> I took my place in the midst of the world, and showed myself to them in the flesh. I found them all to be intoxicated, and not one of them was thirsty. My soul has suffered, (and continues to) suffer, on account of the sons of men, for their hearts are blind and they do not see, for empty did they enter this world, and empty do they seek to leave it--and the whole time that they are here, they continue in their drunkenness. After they have recovered from their wine, they will repent." Now because it was getting to be quite late, he and the twelve left them all behind and withdrew from town to lodge in Bethany.

THE WITHERED FIG TREE
(Matt 21:18-19; Mark 11:12-14)
Outside Jerusalem

Now when Jesus left Bethany early the next morning and headed for the city, he was hungry. He saw this fig tree that was covered with leaves off in the distance, so he went up to it to see if there was any fruit on it. When he got there, he found nothing on it but leaves, for it was not the season of figs. Jesus therefore said to the tree, "From this time forward, may you never again bring forth. May no one ever eat any fruit from you!" His disciples heard him saying this, and at that, the fig tree withered.

THE SECOND CLEANSING OF THE TEMPLE
(Matt 21:12-13, Mark 11:15-19; Luke 19:45-48)
Jerusalem

And when they got to Jerusalem, Jesus entered into God's temple and threw out those who were buying and selling within it. He turned over the tables of the money-changers, together with the benches of those who sold doves, and would not let anyone carry goods through the temple grounds. And as he was instructing them, he said, "Is it not written, 'My house will be called a house of prayer for each and every nation'? That indeed is how it reads," he said. "Yet you have converted it into a hideaway for bandits!" And when they heard this, the chief priests and the scribes, fearing Jesus, started looking for some way to put him to death. The entire multitude, you see, was astounded by his teaching. He taught them at the temple every single day. Even so, the chief priests and the scribes, with the support of the leading citizens, were looking to put him to death. But they could not find a way, since the people hung upon his every word. And when it got to be late in the day, he left the city (with them.)

THE SECOND ENCOUNTER WITH THE FIG TREE
(Matt 21:20-22; Mark 11:20-25; Luke 21:37-38)
Jerusalem

And early the next morning, as they were traveling along, they saw how the fig tree had been withered from its very roots. And Peter, calling it to mind, said to Jesus, "Rabbi, look at that! The fig tree that you cursed has dried up!" And when the disciples saw it, they marveled, "How quickly has this fig tree withered!" And Jesus replied, "You must put your faith in God. I tell you most assuredly, if you have faith in God, and do not doubt, not only will you do what has been done to this fig tree, but if you should say to this mountain, 'Be taken up and cast into the sea,' it will happen. And all that you ask for in prayer, think about how you have received it already, and it will become a reality for you. I am telling you the truth, if anyone harboring no doubts within his heart, should say to this mountain, 'Be picked up and tossed into the sea,' believing most sincerely that it will happen, it will be carried out for him. For this reason do I say to you, whatever your request may be, when you pray believe that you've received it already, and it will indeed be yours. And if you should hold anything against anyone, even as you are standing there in the midst of prayer, forgive him. You see, you have but to forgive the sins of other men, and God will forgive you of your own."

CHRIST'S AUTHORITY CHALLENGED
(Matt 21:23-27; Mark 11:27-33; Luke 20:1-8)
The Temple, Jerusalem

And it happened again on one of those days that they entered into Jerusalem and arrived in the temple. And as he conducted himself there, teaching the crowd (and) preaching, the chief priests and the scribes came up to him, along with the elders of the people, and stood nearby, demanding, "What right have you to do all this?" And, "Who has given you the authority to do these things?" Jesus therefore answered them, "I will also question you about a certain point, and you give me a reply. And if you should answer me, I will reveal to you the power by which I do these things. What was the source of John's baptism? Was it from heaven, or from men? Enlighten me!" Now all of them were afraid of the people, since they all considered John a prophet, so the ones who were confronting him started speaking among themselves, saying, "If we should say that it comes from heaven, he will answer, 'Why didn't you believe in him?' If we should say that it comes from men, we have all these people to fear. They will stone us all to death, since they are persuaded that John is a prophet!" And they answered that they did not know. "We have no idea," they said to him. Jesus answered, "Then neither do I reveal to you the power that enables me to do the things I do."

WHO IS THE TRUE WORKER?
(Matt 21:28-32)
The Temple, Jerusalem

"Now tell me how this seems to you? This man had two children. He approached the first one and said, 'My child, go out and work in the vineyard today.' And the boy replied, 'I do not care to go.' Later on, however, he felt that he should reconsider, so he did go after all. The father then approached the other one and said as before. And the young man answered him, 'I will, sir,' but afterward he did not go. Of the two, which one did his father's will?" "The first one did," they answered him. Jesus said, "How truly do I say to you that publicans and harlots are entering into God's kingdom ahead of you. For John approached you in the way of righteousness, but you did not believe in him. Yet the tax-collectors and prostitutes did. Even so, you were not then moved to give his teaching a second thought."

PARABLE OF THE WICKED HARVESTERS
(Matt 21:33-46; Mark 12:1-12; Luke, 20:9-19; GTh 65, 66)
The Temple, Jerusalem

Then he started speaking to the people in parables: "Hear, therefore, this parable: There was this righteous (and) wealthy landowner, who planted a vineyard, hedged it about, dug a pit for a winepress, and set up a tower. He then leased it to some tenants and went away for a certain time. And he sent some of his servants to the groundskeepers during the season to receive its fruit. And the tenants took his servants and scourged one, killed another, and stoned yet another one. He sent one servant to those tenants at about the time of harvest, that they might render some of the fruits of the vineyard to him. But the tenants took him, beat him almost to death, and sent him away with nothing at all. Then the servant went and told his lord. His master said, 'Maybe it was because he did not know them.' Then he sent another to them. But they drubbed that one as well, beating him over the head, treating him with contempt, and sending him away with nothing. He sent them yet another one, and they injured this third one also, throwing him out and murdering him. He again sent more servants--even more than he had before--and they treated them all the same; some they beat and some they killed. Then the owner of the vineyard said, 'What am I supposed to do?' There remained to him a beloved son. 'I will send my cherished son to them; perhaps they will esteem my son.' So he sent him, last of all, saying, 'Surely they will humble themselves before my son (and) show him some respect!' But as soon as they caught sight of him, those tenants started scheming among themselves, saying, 'This one is the heir. Come now, we would do well to murder him. That way, we will command his estate.' They grabbed him, killed him, and threw him out of the vineyard. So when at last the owner comes, what will he do to those tenants?" "What a bunch of wicked men!" they answered him. "He will come and destroy them all, and lease the vineyard out to others--the kind who will hand the produce up to him when harvest time comes around!" "Anyone with ears to hear, had better hear!"

And when they heard that, the people said, "May this never come to pass!" Then Jesus looked at them and said, "Have you never read, 'The stone that the workers cast aside was placed as the cornerstone. This was all the Lord's own doing, and yet we look upon it in amazement'? So what is this that has been written? 'Show me the stone that the builders rejected; that one is the corner stone'? And because of this I say to you that the kingdom of God will be taken away from you and given to the kind who will produce its fruit. The one who stumbles over this stone will be broken to bits. (Indeed) everyone who falls on that stone will broken, but those on whom the stone should fall, them the stone will grind to chaff." And when the scribes, chief priests, and Pharisees caught these parables, they immediately resumed their attempt to lay hold of him and take him into custody, since they recognized that he had spoken this parable against them. Even so, they feared the crowd, for they held him as a prophet, so they let him be and went away.

THE INVITATION TO THE WEDDING FEAST
(Matt 22:1-14)
The Temple, Jerusalem

And Jesus answered them again in parables, saying, "The empire of the skies is likened to a king who was planning a wedding for his son. He sent his servants out to call on those invited to the marriage feast, but none of them were willing to go. Again he sent out other servants, saying to them, 'Say to those who have been called, "Behold, my banquet is set already--my bullocks and my fatted stock have all been slaughtered. All of it is now prepared, so come at once to the wedding feast!"' But the invited all went casually away, one to his field, another to his trade. As for the others, they seized his servants; then they beat and murdered them. Now this so enraged the king that he sent his soldiers forth. He then wiped those killers out and burned down their entire town. Then he said to his servants, 'Truly the wedding feast is ready, but those invited were undeserving. Therefore go to the ends of the streets and invite any and all that you come across to the wedding feast.' Then those servants went all through the byways rounding up everyone that they could find, whether they were good or bad, and the banquet hall was filled with those seated.

"The king then came in to inspect the arrangement. He saw a man in attendance there who was not dressed in the proper attire. So he confronted him, 'My friend, how did you get in here without wedding clothes?' And the man was lost for words. The king then commanded his servants, 'Bind him by his hands and feet and cast him into the outer darkness; the place where there will be wailing and grinding of teeth.' For without question those bidden are many, yet those chosen are few."

GIVE CAESAR WHAT BELONGS TO CAESAR
(Matt 22:15; Mark 12:13-17;
Luke 20:20-26; GTh 100; Egtn 3)
The Temple, Jerusalem

Now the Pharisees went off and discussed how they might entangle him in a remark. And keeping him under close surveillance, they sent some of the followers of the Pharisees and Herodians, (as) spies posing as righteous folk, in order to catch him by some statement (or) to lay hold of something he might say, so as to deliver him up to the governor's control and jurisdiction. They came and put this question to him: "Master Jesus, we know that you come <from God>, because the things that you do place you above all of the prophets. We know that you are sincere, that you speak and teach what is right, and that you are swayed by none, since you show neither respect of persons, nor do you defer to any man. Quite to the contrary, you teach God's way in line with truth." And they said, "Caesar's people demand that we pay taxes. So tell us what you think. Would it be right or wrong for us to pay Caesar's poll tax? Should we have to pay or not?" Jesus, however, sensing their spite, and marking their cunning, was aware of their hypocrisy. "Why are you putting me to the test?" he asked them. "You hypocrites! Let me see the coin for the tax. Bring me a denarius, and let me have a look at it!" So the men brought one up to Jesus (and) handed it over. Then he asked them, "Whose image is this, and what is inscribed thereon?" The men answered him, "Caesar's." At that Jesus said to them, "So give to Caesar what belongs to Caesar, and to God what belongs to God, and give me what belongs to me." And when they heard that, they were amazed by him (and) his response, (and) they kept silent. So right there in the sight of all, they failed to take him in his words. So they went away and let him be.

THE WIFE OF THE SEVEN BROTHERS
(Matt 22:23-33; Mark 12:18-27; Luke 20:27-38;
GEb Quote in Clementine Homilies 3.50)
The Temple, Jerusalem

And that same day some Sadducees, those who claim that there will be no resurrection, approached him. And they asked him a question: "Teacher, Moses wrote to us, saying that if someone's brother should die having a wife, but no child, (thereby) leaving his wife behind, and leaving no children, his brother should thenceforth take his wife, (and) through her he should marry in, causing seed for his brother to proceed from her. Now there were seven brothers among us, and the first one took a wife and passed away childless. He therefore left his wife to his brother, neither having (nor) leaving any seed. Then the second took her to himself, and he also passed away, leaving no seed behind. And the third, all the way through the seventh, likewise took her. And in like fashion, not even one of the seven left any children (or) seed behind. So each of them passed on, and afterward, last of all, the woman also passed away. Now when the resurrection comes and these rise up, which of the seven will this woman become wife to? Whose wife will she be, since all seven of them had her as his?" And Jesus answered them, "Aren't you being misled by this, having understood neither the Scriptures nor the power of God? You misjudge because you do not know the precision of the Scriptures. It is because of this that you don't see the power of God. How is it that you do not understand that the Scriptures are based on soundness of reason? It is only the children of this age who wed and are given in marriage. But as for the ones deemed worthy to achieve that resurrection age, upon rising in the revival from the dead, they will neither marry nor be given in marriage. You see, it won't even be possible for them to die anymore, because they will be celestial--even as the angels are in heaven--and as the sons of the resurrection, they will therefore be the Sons of God. Now as for the resurrection of the dead, did you never read the word that God spoke to you in the book of Moses? Moses, referring to the Lord, pointed out at the burning bush, that the dead are to be raised again, saying, 'I am the God of Abraham and the God of Isaac and the God of Jacob.' He is, therefore, not the God of the dead, but of the living instead, because to Him all are alive. You are being led astray in a serious way." And the multitudes were moved by his teaching.

WHICH COMMANDMENT IS THE GREATEST?
(Matt 22:34-40; Mark 12:28-34)
The Temple, Jerusalem

And a lawyer from the scribes came to them and listened in on their debate. And seeing how well Jesus had answered them, he put this question to him: "Teacher, which is the most fundamental command--the greatest in the Law?" And Jesus answered him, "The foremost is 'Hearken, oh Israel! Our Lord and God reigns alone; and your love for the Lord your God will be from your whole heart, soul and mind--even from the fullness of your strength.' This is the great and overriding commandment. And the second, which is similar to it, is this: 'You must love your neighbor as you do yourself.' Of all the commandments, not a single one surpasses these. The fullness of the law and the prophets flows from these two teachings." "Well put, teacher," the scribe confessed, "In saying that He is One, and that no other exists but Him, you have spoken truly. For to love Him completely, in the fullness of your strength, and to love a neighbor even as yourself outshines all burnt offerings and sacrifices." And Jesus, seeing how wisely the scribe had answered, said to him, "You are not far from the kingdom of God." And no one there dared to question him further.

"DAVID CALLS HIM 'LORD'"
(Matt 22:41-46; Mark 12:35-37; Luke 20:41-44)
The Temple, Jerusalem

As Jesus was teaching in the temple, he posed to them, "How can it be as the scribes assert--that the Messiah will be a son of David? In the book of Psalms, David proclaims through Divine Inspiration, 'The Lord has said unto my Lord, 'Sit here to my right until I make your enemies a stool for your feet.' Now if none other than David calls him 'Lord,' where do they get that he's his son?" And when the Pharisees had assembled there, Jesus asked them this question: "What do you think about the Messiah? Whose son is he supposed to be?" And they answered, "David's." Jesus therefore questioned them, "How is it that in Spirit David calls him 'Lord,' saying, 'The Lord said to my Lord, "Sit here to my right until I place your enemies beneath your feet."' If David himself calls him 'Lord,' therefore, how then can he be his son?" And the great crowd took enormous pleasure in hearing him. None could respond with even a word, nor did anyone risk questioning him from that day forward.

EXPOSING THE SCRIBES AND THE PHARISEES
(Matt 23:1-39; Mark 12:38-40; Luke 20:45-47;
GTh 39, 89, 102, 103/39-POxy 655;
Justin, Dialogue With Trypho 116:2;
Hippolytus, Philosophumena 5.3)
The Temple, Jerusalem

And even as he lectured them, the entire crowd listened attentively to him. Jesus began cautioning his disciples and the people: "Watch out for (and) beware of the scribes and the Pharisees! They have placed themselves on the seat of Moses, so keep to and carry out whatever they should tell you to; but do not imitate their ways. For they say one thing and do another. They tie up heavy and unmanageable loads, and place them on the backs of men. Even so they will not so much as lift a finger to budge them. They do all things to be seen by men; for they make their phylacteries really wide, (and) love to walk in flowing robes, flaunting their elongated tassels, delighting in the salutations they receive in the marketplaces, and cherishing the foremost seats in the synagogues. They love the places of distinction at feasts, and to be referred to as 'Rabbi' by men. They consume the homes of widows and then go on to pray at length. When these are sentenced, they will be severely punished.

"But you must not be called 'Rabbi,' since you have but one Master, and all of you are brothers. Moreover, do not refer to anyone upon this earth as your 'father,' for only One is your Father--the One Who is in heaven. Neither let yourselves be called 'Teachers,' for Christ will be your only guide. And the greatest among you is to be your servant, since whoever honors himself will be abased, and whoever abases himself will be honored.

"Curse the scribes and Pharisees! For they are even as a dog that lies atop a cattle trough; he eats nothing, nor does he let the cattle eat. The Pharisees and the scribes have taken and hidden the keys of knowledge. These have failed to make it in, and have stood in the way of those who were trying. You, on the other hand, become as slippery as snakes, and as simple as doves. If you keep my word, you will recognize the eternal kingdom in advance. How lucky is the man who knows where the thieves are going to enter, since he will be able to arise and prepare from the very start that which pertains to the kingdom before they manage to break into it.

"Curse you, scribes and Pharisees, you phonies! You shut the empire of the skies in the face of all mankind. You do not go in yourselves, and you block off those who are trying to get in. Curse you, scribes and Pharisees, you phonies! You devour the homes of widows and then pray long and pretentious prayers to conceal it. You will therefore receive a stiffer sentence. Curse you scribes and Pharisees! You travel across sea and land to gain a single proselyte; and when you've turned him into one, you cause him to be twice the child of Gehenna that you are. Curse you, you blind leaders! You say, 'Should anyone declare an oath upon this sanctuary, it means nothing; but should anyone swear by the gold of the temple, his debt remains.' You blind fools! Which is greater: the gold, or the temple that sanctifies it? What is more, you declare, 'If anyone should swear by the altar, it means nothing; but if anyone should swear by the offering upon it, his oath is binding. You blind men! Which is greater: the gift, or the altar that sanctifies it? So then, whoever swears by the altar swears by both it and what's on it. And whoever swears by the temple swears by it and the One Who dwells therein. And anyone swearing by heaven is swearing by the throne of God--(even) the One Who is seated thereon. Curse you, scribes and Pharisees, you phonies! You have tithed of your mint, dill and cumin, but have neglected the weightier matters of the law; justice, mercy and faith. You ought to have kept to the latter, without being negligent of the former. You blind guides! You strain out the gnat, but swallow the camel. Curse you, scribes and Pharisees, you phonies! You clean the outer portion of the dish and cup, but on the inside you are filled with greed and self-indulgence. Why is it that you wash the outside? Is it because you fail to recognize that the One Who created the inside is also the One Who created the outside? You blind Pharisee! Start by scrubbing the inside of the dish and cup. That way their outsides will also be cleansed. Curse you scribes and Pharisees, you phonies! You are like whitewashed tombs, which appear beautiful on the surface, but in your core you are filled with skeletons of dead men and all manner of filth, for the living man is not in you. That is how it goes with you. On the surface, you appear as righteous before the people, but deep inside, you are full of hypocrisy and vice.

"Curse you, scribes and Pharisees, you phonies! You build sepulchers for the prophets and adorn the graves of the upright. Then you profess, 'Had we been around in the days of our fathers, we would never have had a part in the shedding of their blood.' You are in effect commending yourselves for being the seed of those who slew the prophets. So bring to completion the sins of your fathers. You serpents! You brood of vipers! How ever will you escape the judgment of Gehenna? For this reason I am going to send prophets to you; wise men and teachers, too. Some you will kill and crucify, others you will beat in your synagogues, hounding them from town to town. That way every drop of righteous blood that has been shed upon this earth will find its way straight back to you, from the blood of the righteous Abel all the way down to that of Zechariah, son of Berechiah, whom you murdered between the temple and the altar. I say to you most assuredly, every bit of this will fall upon this generation.

"Oh Jerusalem! Jerusalem! Slayer of the prophets and stoner of those who are sent to her! How many times have I longed to gather your children together as a hen gathers her nestlings under her wings--but you would not have it. Look, your house is being left to you in desolation. For I am here to say to you, from this very day until such time as you proclaim, 'Blessed is he who comes in the name of the Lord,' you will never see me again."

Robert C. Ferrell

THE WIDOW'S MITE
(Mark 12:41-44; Luke 21:1-4)
The Temple, Jerusalem

And he sat down opposite the treasury, looked up and started watching the crowds as they dropped coins into the depository. He saw the rich proffering their gifts, and many of the wealthier ones were donating rather large sums. Then he noticed a certain poor (and) needy widow, who came and placed two lepta, which amount to a quadrans, therein. And calling his disciples to himself, he said, "Truly do I say to you that this poor widow has put more into the treasury than all the rest. You see, these others offered up out of what remained to them. This widow, on the other hand, has given completely, all that she had of her livelihood, out of her poverty (and) want--even to the very last."

THE HOUR HAS COME
(John 12:20-50)
The Temple, Jerusalem

Now there were some Greeks who had also gone up to worship at the feast. They went over to Philip, who was from Bethsaida in Galilee, and said to him, "Sir, we would like to meet with Jesus." So Philip went and informed Andrew, then they went over to Jesus and let him know. "The hour has come for the Son of Man to be glorified," said Jesus. "Truly and most assuredly I say to you that unless the grain of wheat that falls to the earth should happen to die, it would simply remain alone. Nevertheless, because it dies, it brings forth an abundance of fruit. Whoever loves his life will lose it, but whoever despises his earthly existence lays it up for endless life. If anyone would do for me, let him follow after me; and wherever I should be, there also will be the one serving me. My Father will honor anyone who attends to me. Now my heart is shaken, and what should I say, 'Father, rescue me from this moment'? On the contrary, it was for this very reason that I came to this moment. Father, magnify Your name!" Then a voice came out of heaven, "I have magnified it already, and will magnify it even more." So when the crowd standing there heard it, they all said that it sounded like thunder. Others claimed that an angel had spoken. "It was not for my sake that you heard this voice," Jesus explained, "but for your own. A judgment has befallen the world, and the Ruler of this Realm will be driven out. And if I should be raised from the earth, I will draw mankind to me." This he said to indicate the nature of his death. Then the multitude responded, "From the Law we have learned that the Messiah will remain forever, so how can you say that 'the Son of Man has to be raised up?' Who then is this 'Son of Man'?" So Jesus said, "The light will only be with you a little longer, so walk as long as you have light, that you might not be overtaken by darkness. The one who walks in darkness has no idea where he is going. As long as the light endures for you, you must continue in the light, so that you might be the sons of light." Jesus spoke these words to them, then he went and hid from them. And even though he had done so many signs before them, they still did not believe in him. This happened to fulfill the word of Isaiah the prophet, who said, "Lord, who has believed our account? To whom has the arm of the Lord been revealed?" This was the reason that they could not believe him, for again Isaiah prophesied, "He has blinded their eyes and hardened their hearts, lest with their eyes they should see, and perceiving in their hearts, they should return that I might heal them!" Isaiah prophesied these things because he had been a witness to his glory and had spoken this about him. Yet in spite of all these things, many leaders did believe in him. But these were all afraid to admit it lest the Pharisees should bar them from the synagogue. You see, they valued the praises of men over the praises of God.

Then Jesus cried out to them, "The one who believes in me is not believing just in me, but also in the One Who sent me, and the one who looks on me isn't seeing only me, but also the One Who sent me. I have come as a light into the world, so that all who place their faith in me might not remain in darkness. And if anyone should hear my words and not conform himself to them, I will not be his judge, because I did not come to judge the world, but to save the world. Whoever rejects me, and fails to accept my words already has a judge. On that final day, the very word that I have spoken will condemn him. For it was not on my own that I spoke these things, but it was the Father Who sent me that gave me orders as to what I should say and how I should say it. And I know that His teaching leads to endless life. So the things that I speak, I speak in line with the command that was given me by my Father."

THE APOCALYPSE OF JESUS
(Matt 24:1-51; Mark 13:1-37; Luke 21:5-36;
Clementine Recognitions, 4.4; Barnabas 12:1b;
2Bar 25:1b-4; SbOr 2:6-38; ApEl 3:1-18;
2Esd 2:13, 5:1-12, 13:29-31, 15:12-19;
Papias, Quote from Irenaeus, Against Heresies 33.3, 4)
The Temple, Mount of Olives

Then Jesus left the temple. And as he was on his way out, his disciples came up to him and called his attention to the buildings thereof. Now some of them talked about how it was adorned with beautiful stones and gifts. "Master," one of his followers said, "behold what manner of stones and structures these are!" But Jesus answered him, "See all of these magnificent buildings (and) objects? As for all that you see here, I am telling you truly that the days are coming when there will not be so much as a single stone left on another that will not be thrown down. And this generation will not pass until the destruction begins. For they will come and sit in this very place and lay siege to it, and in this place they will slay your children."

As he sat upon the Mount of Olives across from the temple, the disciples, Peter, James, John, and Andrew asked him privately, "Master, tell us when all of this will come to pass. What will be the sign that all these things will be fulfilled, and what will be the sign of your coming and the end of the age?" And Jesus replied, "Take care that no man deceives you, because many people will come in my name and claim, 'I am the Messiah!' and 'The time is upon us!' and they will deceive many. So don't go chasing after them. The Son of Lawlessness will show himself and say to you, 'I am the Christ,' although he is not. Don't you believe him! You will start to hear of wars, and reports of wars and agitations, but when you do, see to it that you are neither frightened nor disturbed thereby. These, you see, are but the foreshadowings; so do not be afraid, for the end has not yet come. The consummation will not take place all at once." Then he informed them, "Behold, the days are coming when the Most High will arrive to rescue those who live on earth. Confusion of mind will overtake those who dwell thereon, causing them to plot wars one against the other, city against city, region against region. Nation will move against nation, and kingdom against kingdom, and major earthquakes will break forth in this place and that, as will famines, pestilences, and horrifying spectacles--and momentous omens will appear from out of heaven. When, however upon the earth come violent shakings, thunders and lightnings, mildews upon the land, frenzies of jackals and wolves, the slaughtering and devastation of men, the bellowing of oxen, four-footed cattle, domestic mules and goats and sheep, then great expanses of farmland will become barren and through neglect not render their fruit. The selling of free men into slavery will become commonplace as will the robbing of temples. When all of these things come to pass, the tenth generation of men will appear at last, when He Who shakes the earth and brings forth the lightnings will destroy the glory of the idols, and shake down those of the seven-hilled Rome. Vast amounts of wealth will perish, burning in the great fire of the flame of Hephaestus. Then blood will rain down out of heaven; but the earth with its countless men will slay each other in their madness. During this time of unrest, God will impose famines, diseases, and thunderbolts upon those who do not judge according to justice. There will be such a dearth of men on the face of the earth, that one would marvel to see the footprints of another on the ground. These are but the onset of labor pains. But before these trials take place, they will take you into custody and hand you over to councils to be tortured, so look to yourselves. They will persecute you, turn you over to synagogues and imprisonment, and you will be beaten there. And all the nations will despise you on account of me; and you will be brought as witnesses before governors and kings for the sake of my name. This will be your occasion to testify. (The gospel, however, must first be preached before the nations.) Now when they lead you up and turn you in, do not rehearse what you will speak. Simply resolve in your hearts not to plan your rebuttal in advance, for I will provide you with a mouth and a wisdom which none who oppose you will be able to deny or withstand. Instead, speak whatever is given to you at that time, because the words will not be coming from you, but rather from the Holy Spirit.

"Many will be displeased at this, and will turn each other over and despise one another. At that point many false prophets will rise up and seduce many, and unrighteousness will increase to a level beyond that which you now see, nor have you ever heard of before. And owing to the proliferation of lawlessness, the love of the many will grow cold. You will even be turned over by parents and siblings; friends and relatives. So a brother will hand his own brother over to be killed, and a father, his son. Children will rise against their parents, and they will see to it that some of you are executed. And they will be hateful toward you and put you to death for bearing my name. Even so, not a single hair that is on your head will be lost. The one who perseveres to the very end will be saved. And through your persistence you will save your souls. This gospel of the kingdom will be proclaimed at that time as a sign to the world. That is when the moment will come. Then when you see Jerusalem surrounded by armies, recognize that its destruction is at hand. So when you see the abomination that causes devastation, as spoken of by Daniel the prophet, standing in the holy place where it does not belong, (let whoever reads this understand it,) then let those who are in Judea flee to the mountains, let those who are inside get out, and let not those in the surrounding areas go in. Let not the one who is on top of his house go back down to take anything from it. Let not the one who is in the field go back to retrieve his clothing. You see, these are days of retribution, for the fulfillment of all that has been written.

"Let Egypt mourn from its foundations for the plague of chastisement and punishment being brought upon it by the Lord. Let those weep who till the soil, for indeed their seed will fail, and their trees all wither from blight and hail and terrible tempest. Woe to the world and to those who dwell therein, for misery and sword draw near to them, and nation will rise up, sword in hand, to battle against nation. For unrest will there be among mankind, and stronger and stronger will they grow against one another: showing respect for neither king nor commander. A man will wish to enter a town, but will be turned back. Cities will remain in confusion on account of their pride, houses will then be destroyed, and the people there will live in fear. A man will show no mercy to his neighbor, but for his hunger's sake and the extent of his suffering will he use his sword to plunder his neighbor for his household goods. But curse any who are pregnant and nursing in those days! For there will be a great travail in the land, and a wrath against this people. They will all fall by the sword and be taken captive into every nation. And Jerusalem will be trampled down by Gentiles until the times of the Gentiles are fulfilled.

"Pray that your flight does not come in the winter or on the Sabbath, because there will come a time of trouble unrivaled since the time when God first brought the world into being until now, nor ever could it happen again. And someone will reign over the world, whom none on earth will anticipate; and the birds will fly away, and the Sea of Sodom will cast up fish. Then will the one whom the multitudes know not cause his voice to be heard by night, and his voice will be heard by all. Chaos, also, will reign in many places, fires will break out, wild animals will wander beyond their usual places, and menstruous women will bring forth monsters. Salty water will be found in the sweet, and friend will overpower friend. Then reason will go into hiding, and wisdom withdraw into its abode, and many will seek after it, but no one will find it. Then unrighteousness and lack of restraint will increase upon the earth. A nation will then ask its neighbor, 'Has righteousness or anyone who does what is right passed through you?' And the answer will be, 'Not at all.' And in those days men will hope, but not receive; labor, but their efforts will be for nought. Had the Lord not shortened those days, no flesh would at all be saved. But those days will indeed be cut short by the Lord, who has shortened them for the sake of the elect. Ask and you will receive; pray that your days might be few in number, that your days might be cut short. Then if anyone should say to you, 'Look, the Messiah is here,' or, 'Look, over there!' don't you believe it, because false Christs and false prophets will come along and do signs and wonders to deceive, if it were possible, even the elect. But that Son of Lawlessness will once again take his stand in hallowed places, (even) in the holy place. To the sun he will command, 'Descend,' and it will go down. 'Shine,' he will say, and it will blaze forth; 'Darken,' he will declare, and it will grow dark. To the moon he will demand, 'Become bloody,' and so it will be. Like them he will sweep across the sky. With a word he will decree: 'Walk upon the rivers and seas,' and on river and sea will he tread as if he were on dry land. The lame he will cause to walk, the deaf to hear, the mute to speak, and the blind to see. The lepers he will cleanse, and the ill he will heal. He will cast out demons and multiply his signs and wonders before all men. All the works that the Christ performed he will likewise replicate, except for the raising of the dead alone. This is how you will know that he's the Son of Lawlessness, for he has no power to give life.

"But the kingdom is even now prepared for you, so look to yourselves! See, I have told you all things in advance. So if they should say to you, 'Look, he is out in the desert!' do not go forth, 'Look, in the innermost rooms!' do not believe it. You know how lightning strikes in the east and lights up the west; the coming of the Son of Man will be just like that! And the land that you see ruling now will be laid waste and untrodden, and all of mankind will see its desolation. (Wherever there is a carcass, the vultures will be sure to gather!) But if the Most High grants that you should live, after the third day you will see it thrown into confusion.

"But in the days immediately following the distress of those times, there will be signs in the sun, the moon, and the stars. Now with regard to the signs: the sun will be dimmed, and the moon will not furnish her light. Then the sun will suddenly shine at night, and the moon during the day. A tree will bend down and stand upright, blood will drip from out of wood, and stone will speak, and the people will be distressed, and the stars will fall from the sky. And in this world, nations will be tormented and perplexed by the roaring and billowing of the sea. Behold, the days are coming when fear will seize all of those who live on earth, and the land will be devoid of faith. Men will grow cold with fear and dread because of what is taking place, for the powers of heaven will all be shaken. Then the sign of the Son of Man will appear in the sky, and the nations of the world will beat their breasts. At that time, they will see the Son of Man coming on the clouds of heaven with tremendous power and magnificent glory. On the day that the Messiah comes, it will be even as a flock of doves surrounding him as a crown. He will tread upon the vault the heaven, led forth by the sign of the cross. The whole world will see him even as the sun shining from the eastern to the western horizons. All of his angels will surround him at his coming.

"And he will send them forth at the great trumpet call, and they will gather all his chosen ones from the four winds--from one end of heaven to the other, (and) from the farthest reaches of the earth to the uttermost regions of heaven. And when all of these things begin to take place, it will be time to rise and lift your heads, for your deliverance has finally come!" Then he spoke a parable to them: "Take the fig tree, and every other tree as well. Now work out the mystery of the fig tree: when its tender limbs grow out and sprout leaves, at that moment you can see for yourselves and know that summer is coming. And so it will be that when you see all of these things begin to unfold, understand that God's kingdom is at hand; even at the very doors! I am telling you the truth, this generation will not have passed before all these things are fulfilled at last. Heaven and earth will pass away, but never my words. Therefore at the end of days, this will be the sign that the Most High will show in the sight of all who dwell on earth; when terror overtakes those who are living in the world and they fall into terrible torments and tribulations. It will then come about that because of their many troubles, they will say in their hearts, 'The Mighty One no longer takes thought for the earth.' It will be even as they are losing all hope that the time will awaken. Furthermore, the great God Who dwells in the skies will become in every way a savior to all men of virtue. At that time a profound peace and understanding will begin, and the bountiful land will once again bring forth fruit in profusion, and will no longer remain divided or in servitude. Those who enter into God's kingdom will see the days come when vines will grow with ten thousand runners apiece, and ten thousand branches will grow on each runner, and ten thousand shoots will grow on each branch, and ten thousand sprouts will grow on each shoot, and ten thousand bunches will grow on each sprout. And these bunches will each produce ten thousand grapes; and when they are pressed, each of these grapes will yield twenty-five measures of wine. And if one of the saints should grab one cluster, another one will then proclaim, 'I am better! Take me instead! Glorify the Lord through me!' A grain of wheat will likewise produce ten thousand ears, and these ears will each have ten thousand grains thereon, and each grain will yield five pounds of pure, fine wheat flour twice over. And it will be the same for every other fruit, seed, and plant. And every animal will feed solely on what the earth provides. They will become peaceable and live together in harmony, and will subject themselves obediently to men. Every harbor and port will once again be open to all mankind and shamelessness will exist no more. Then God will again perform a great sign: a star will shine forth like a radiant crown, glorious, and gleaming from the resplendent sky for a great many days. (For at that time, He will show from heaven the crown that is given to men who strive in the war.) But as for the day and the hour, no man knows it, neither do the angels in heaven, nor even does the Son, but only the Father.

"But at the coming of the Son of Man, things will be even as they were in Noah's day. For just as it was in the days before the flood, when they were eating and drinking, getting married and marrying off right up to the day that Noah entered the ark; none gave heed until the flood arrived and did away with all of them. Even so will the coming of the Son of Man be. Two will then be out in the field; one will be taken and the other will be left. Two will be grinding at the mill; one will be taken and the other will be left. So stay alert, for you do not know when your Lord will return.

"Even so, recognize this much, if the homeowner had known before the hour that the thief would come, he would have kept watch, and not allowed his house to get broken into. So also must you be vigilant, for the Son of Man is coming at a time that you do not know. Also, look to yourselves, lest at any time your hearts be overcome by excess, drunkenness, and the concerns of this life, and that day sneak up on you without your being aware. For like a trap it will ensnare all of those who live on earth. Who then is that trusty and sagacious servant whom his lord will set over his household servants, that he might give them their food when the season comes? How lucky will that servant be when his lord arrives and finds him so doing. I tell you most assuredly, he will put him over all that He has. But should that wicked servant say in his heart, 'My master will be gone a long time,' and starts beating his fellow servants, and eating and drinking with the drunkards, that servant's master will come on a day that he's not expecting, and at a time that he's not aware, and hack him to bits, assigning him his part with the hypocrites, where there will be wailing and grinding of teeth.

"So be alert, praying at all times that you might be deemed worthy to escape all that will soon come to pass, and stand in the presence of the Son of Man. Do not let down your guard; watch and pray, since you do not know when that time will be. It is like a man who was going on a distant journey, who, at the time he left his house, charged each of his servants with certain tasks, and commanded the porter to keep watch. So remain vigilant, for you never know when the lord of the house might come; at dusk, midnight, cock's crow, or daybreak. Should he happen to come back on a sudden, do not let him catch you sleeping. And what I say to you, I say to all: Watch!

THE TEN VIRGINS
(Matt 25:1-13; AcAn in P. Utrecht I p.14)
Mount of Olives

"At that time, the kingdom of heaven will be likened unto ten virgins who each took their lanterns and went to meet the bridegroom. Five of them were foolish, and five of them were wise. Now the foolish ones, even though they took their lamps, failed to take any olive oil with them; whereas the prudent ones carried flasks along with their lamps. And as the bridegroom lingered, they nodded off, and lay there sleeping. Then at midnight there came a shout, 'Behold, the bridegroom is coming! Go and meet him.' Then those virgins all got up, and they each trimmed their own lanterns. 'Give us of your olive oil,' said the foolish to the wise, 'for our lamps are burning out!' But the wise ones said to them, 'We fear that there will not be enough for you and us both. You ought rather to go to those who sell and buy some oil for yourselves.' Now after they had gone away to purchase some, the bridegroom came. Those who were ready went in with him to the wedding feast, and the door was secured. After a while, the other virgins came around pleading, 'Lord, Lord, open up the door for us!' But the bridegroom answered, 'I tell you most assuredly that I never even knew you.' So keep watch, because you do not know the day or the hour. Oh virgins, it is not without reason that you have guarded your chastity, nor was it in vain that you persisted in prayer with your lamps burning until the voice came to you at midnight, saying, 'Get up! Go forth and meet the bridegroom.'

THE PARABLE OF THE TALENTS
(Matt 25:14-30)
Mount of Olives

"Again, it will be like a man who was going on a trip, who summoned his servants, and placed them over all that he owned. He gave one five talents; another, two; and still another, one; according to what they each could do. Then the master went away. Not long after that, the servant who had received the five went away and traded with them, earning five more. The servant who had received the two likewise gained another two. But the servant who received the one went off, dug into the ground, and hid away his master's silver.

After some time the master of those servants returned and started to settle accounts with them. And the one who received the five talents approached him and presented him with another five, saying, 'Master, you entrusted me with five talents. Behold, I have made you five more talents!' Then his master said to him, 'Great work, you good and faithful servant. I will put you over many things. Enter into your master's joy.' The servant who received the two talents also approached his master and said, 'Lord, you entrusted me with two talents. See, I have made you two more talents!' His master replied, 'Well done, you good and faithful servant! You have shown that you can be trusted with a few talents, so I will put you over many things. Enter into your master's joy!' And the servant who had received the one came up to him and explained, 'Master, knowing that you are a difficult man, reaping where you never sowed and gathering where you never scattered, I feared you. I went out and hid your talent in the ground. There, now you have what is your own!' His master responded, 'You worthless and indolent servant! Knowing that I reap where I did not sow, and gather where I did not scatter, you ought to have deposited my silver with the money brokers. That way, by the time that I got back, I would have gotten what was mine along with some interest. So confiscate the one he has and give it to the one with ten.' For to everyone who has, it will be given, and he will have it in abundance. But from one who has nothing, even what he does have will be taken away from him. 'Now toss that no account servant into the darkness without, where there will be weeping and grinding of teeth.'"

Robert C. Ferrell

THE COMING OF THE MESSIAH
(Matt 25:31-46; Rev 2:26-27/19:6-8/20:4-6;
1Thess 4:16-17; 2Pet 3:8-10a, 13; Barnabas 15:3-7)
Mount of Olives

"And the Son of Man will sit upon his glorious throne when he comes in all his glory, and all of his angels with him. And every nation will be gathered before him, and he will separate them from each other, even as a shepherd separates his sheep from the goats. He will cause his sheep to stand to his right, and the goats will stand off to his left. Then the king will say to those who are on His right, 'Come now, you whom my Father has exalted, receive the kingdom set aside for you from the foundation of the world. For I was hungry and you gave me to eat, I was thirsty and you gave me to drink. I was a stranger and you welcomed me in, naked and you covered me up. I was ill and you kept a vigil for me, in prison and you visited me.' And the righteous ones will then inquire, 'Lord, when did we ever see you hungry and feed you, or thirsty and give you something to drink? When did we ever see you as a stranger and welcome you in; or naked and cover you up? When did we see you ill or in prison and visit you?' And the King will respond, 'I say to you assuredly, whatever you did for the least of these, my family members, you did it for me.' Then he will say to those who are on his left, 'Away from me, you accursed ones, and enter into the eternal fire which has been set aside for the devil and his angels. For I was hungry and you gave me nothing to eat. I was thirsty and you gave me nothing to drink. I was a stranger and you did not welcome me; sick and in prison, yet you never came to visit me.' Then they will ask, 'Lord, when did we ever see you hungry or thirsty or as a stranger or naked or sick or in prison and not care for you?' Then he will indeed reply, 'I am telling you the truth, inasmuch as you did not do it for the least of these, you did not do it for me.' And these will all depart into everlasting punishment, but the righteous, into everlasting life."

(And I, [John,] heard what sounded like the noise of a great crowd, and the crashing of many waters, along with the violent clapping of thunder, saying, "Hallelujah, for our Lord God Almighty has taken the throne! Let us rejoice and shout in triumph! Give Him the glory, for the marriage of the lamb has come and his betrothed has readied herself. She has been allowed to adorn herself in beautiful linen, glistening and white." (The fine linen, you see, is the righteousness of the saints.) "And to the one who overcomes and keeps my words up to the end, will I give power over all the nations, and he will rule them with an iron scepter." And they were restored to life and assumed their thrones with the Messiah for a thousand years. For the Lord himself will descend from heaven with a shout and the voice of the archangel and the trumpet of God. And the dead in Christ will rise up first. Then we who are alive and have been spared will be caught up with them to the clouds, to meet the Lord up in the air. And in this way we will be with the Lord forever. Those who remained in death did not come back to life again until the end of the millennium. This is the first resurrection. How blessed and holy is the one who has a part in the first resurrection. The second death has no power over these. Instead, they are to be priests of God and of the Messiah, and they will reign alongside him for the thousand years. Even so, my beloved, do not let this one thing escape you; that one day with the Lord is as a thousand years, and a thousand years are as a day. It is not the case that the Lord is slow to carry out his promise. It is only that he is being patient; for it is against his nature that anyone should be lost, but that all should have a change of heart. This is the Sabbath that Moses speaks of at the creation when he says, "For six days, God labored with the works of His hands, and He finished them on the seventh. On that day the Lord rested, and kept it holy." Now children, do not miss what he's saying here: "He completed them in six days," for what he means is this: That the Lord will bring everything to pass after six thousand years. With Him, you see, a "day" means a thousand years. He bears me out Himself on this when he says, "Behold, the Lord's day will be as a thousand years." Thus, my children, we may conclude that in six days--in six thousand years, that is--everything will be completed. And where he says, "He rested on the seventh day," he is saying: At the time that His Son comes, he will bring an end to the days of the Lawless One, call judgment down upon the wicked, then he will change the sun, the moon, and the stars. After that, on the seventh day, His true rest will begin at last. He goes on to explain, "Clean of hand and pure of heart, you will keep it holy." Now if you can say to me that anyone these days is pure enough in heart to be keeping it holy--the day which God Himself has blessed--then I must say that we have been deceived! If, however, when that day does come someone does manage to keep it holy; by entering into that true rest--that which has been opened to us and is received through the fulfillment of that promise, when lawlessness really is no more and all things really have been made new by the Lord--then we truly will be able to keep it holy, for we will have ourselves been made holy. Nevertheless, the Lord's Day will come like a thief in the night. And even as his word declares, we are all awaiting a new heavens and a new earth, where righteousness indeed prevails.)

THE CONSPIRACY AGAINST JESUS
(Matt 26:1-5; Mark 14:1, 2; Luke 22:1, 2)
Mount of Olives

Now the Feast of Unleavened Bread, which is also called the Passover, was drawing near--only two days away at the time that Jesus was saying these things. He said to his followers, "As all of you are well aware, Passover is two days from now, and the Son of Man will be given up to be crucified." Then the chief priests, elders of the people, and the scribes all gathered in the palace of the high priest, whose name was Caiaphas. They plotted together, seeking for some crafty way to arrest Jesus, murder him and be done with him, for they were afraid of the people. They said, "Not during the feast, however, for the crowds might riot."

MARY ANOINTS JESUS
(John 12:2-8; Matt 26:6-13; Mark: 14:3-9)
Bethany, Near Jerusalem

And while Jesus was staying in Bethany, they made him a supper in the house of one known as Simon the Leper. Martha was serving, and Lazarus was among those who were seated with him. So this woman, Mary, took and broke open an alabaster litrai jar that was filled with a very costly spikenard ointment, and poured the perfume over Jesus' head as he reclined at the table. She anointed Jesus' feet, and wiped them off with her hair, and the fragrance of the ointment filled the house. When, however, his disciples saw it, they were incensed. These (and) some others there angrily commented to one another, "Why such a waste of a fine fragrance? It could have been sold for a hefty sum, more than three hundred denarii, and the proceeds could have been given to the poor!" And they reproved her severely. So Judas Iscariot, the son of Simon, who was about to hand him up, demanded, "So why was this ointment not sold, and three hundred denarii given to the poor?" Now he did not ask this out of any concern that he had for the poor, but because he was a thief, and carried the bag, and would pocket some of whatever was put into it. So Jesus answered, "Leave her alone. Why are you troubling this woman? She has done a beautiful thing for me. She has saved it for the day of my embalming. You will always have the poor with you, and any time you feel like helping them, you may do so. But you will not always have me with you. She did what she could. She came beforehand and poured perfume over my body to prepare me for my burial. Assuredly I say to you, wherever this gospel is proclaimed in the world, what she has done for me will also be proclaimed as a memorial to her."

JUDAS STRIKES A BARGAIN
(Matt 26:14-16; Mark 14:10-11; Luke 22:3-6)
Jerusalem

Then Satan entered into Judas who is called Iscariot, who was numbered among the twelve. And intending to hand Jesus over to the chief priests and Captains, he discussed with them how he might betray him, asking, "What would you give me if I were to hand him over to you?" And they rejoiced, agreeing to give him silver. He accepted it gladly, so they counted out thirty silver coins for him. So from that moment on Judas watched for his chance to betray him when there was no crowd around.

KING ABGAR OFFERS JESUS ASYLUM
(AcThad; EpAb)
Edessa, Jerusalem

{This is a copy of a letter which Abgar the Toparch wrote to Jesus, and sent to him in Jerusalem by the hand of the courier, Hananiah, (and also) the copy of the things that Jesus wrote to Abgar the Toparch by the hand of Hananiah the courier:}

In those days there was this governor of a city called Edessa, whose name was Abgar, who had heard of the wonders that the Christ had worked, and of what he taught as well, for his fame had spread both far and wide. He was amazed by him and wished to meet him, but was unable to leave the supervision of his city. Now Abgar was overtaken by a chronic illness right about the time of the Passion of Jesus and the plotting of the Jews, so he sent a letter to Christ by way of Hananiah the courier. It went something like this: "Abgar Ouchama, the Toparch, governor of the land of the Edessenes, to Jesus, who is called Christ, the good Savior who has appeared in the region of Jerusalem, greetings to you. I have heard many things about you; of the many wonders that you have worked, and the healings that you have brought about with neither medicine nor herb. It is reported that you cause the blind to see and the lame to walk; that you cleanse the leprous, heal the paralyzed, exorcise filthy spirits and demons, restore those who suffer from chronic illnesses, and raise the dead back up to life. When I learned these things about you, I figured that you must be one or the other of these two: either you are a god who came down from heaven to bring these things to pass, or you are a son of God. And this is why I have written you; by everything that's good in you, I implore you now to come to us; both to cure me of my illness and to escape the scheming of the Jews. I have heard that the Jews are spreading malicious rumors about you, and that they wish to do you harm. Come and escape the stratagems of the wicked--all that they have set in place against you on account of their own jealousy. And though my city is rather small, it is holy, and large enough for the both of us."

Now Abgar had ordered Hananiah to obtain an accurate description of Christ; what he looked like, how tall he was, about his hair, and, in short, all that there was to know of him. Then Hananiah went and handed him the letter and looked him over carefully, but could not fix his appearance in his mind. And Jesus, as one who understood the heart, requested something with which to wash, and a towel was given him. And after he had washed himself, he patted his face with it, and it left its form in the linen cloth. Then he handed it to Hananiah and said, "Take this back to the one who sent you, with this message: Peace to you and to your town! This is the reason that I came; to suffer on behalf of this world, and to rise again and raise the fathers. How blessed you are for believing in me, for concerning me it has been written, 'Those who have seen me will not believe in me,' and, 'Those who never saw me will believe and live.' Now concerning that part of your letter requesting that I come to you. I need to make it clear that I must complete my mission in this land, and afterward be taken up to Him Who sent me. But after I have passed into the heavens, I will send Thaddeus, a disciple of mine, to be with you. He will heal your illness, open up your eyes, guide you into all truth, and bring you life--along with the people of your town." And after receiving Hananiah, Abgar fell down and worshiped the image, and his disease vanished before Thaddeus arrived.

Robert C. Ferrell

THE PASSOVER PREPARATIONS
(Matt 26:17-20; Mark 14:12-17; Luke 22:7-16, 24-30;
GEb 7, Quote by Epiphanius, Heresies 30.22)
Large Upper Room, Jerusalem

Then came the day of Unleavened Bread, upon which, the custom is that the Passover lamb must be sacrificed. The disciples drew near to Jesus, and he said, "Clearly I've not looked forward to eating this Passover meat with you in its every aspect, have I?" And he sent out two of his disciples, Peter and John, saying, "Go and ready the Passover meal for us, that we might eat." And they asked him, "Where would you have us make it for you?" Go to a certain man in town. And behold, even as you are entering the city, a man carrying a pitcher of water will meet you. Follow him into the house he enters. Then you will say to the one in charge of the house that he goes into, 'The Master says to you, "My time is at hand. My disciples and I will keep the Passover at your house. Where is the room where my followers and I will eat the Passover meal?"' Then he will show you a large upper room which has been spread out and prepared. Arrange it for us in that place." So the disciples went into the city and found things even as he had described it to them, so they readied the Passover there.

That evening, Jesus arrived with the Twelve. And when the time had come, he sat at table with the twelve apostles. Then he explained, "I have longed to eat this Passover with you before my suffering, inasmuch as I say to you that I will in no way eat of it until the time comes when it is fulfilled in God's kingdom."

And a dispute broke out among them as to which of them would be the greatest. At that point he said to them, "The kings of the Gentiles lord it over them, and the ones who are over these are called 'benefactors.' Yet that is not how it will be with you. Let the one who is greater among you be even as the lesser, and the one who rules as the one who serves. For which is the greater, the one seated or the one serving? Is it not the one who sits? Even so, I am here with you as one who serves. You are the ones who have stayed with me through my ordeals, and I am passing a kingdom on to you, even as the Father has passed a kingdom on to me, that you might eat and drink at my table in the kingdom. Then you will sit on thrones, judging the twelve tribes of Israel."

JESUS WASHES THE FEET OF THE DISCIPLES
(John 13:1-20)
The Upper Room, Jerusalem

Now Jesus knew prior to the Passover feast that the time had come for him to leave this world and return to the Father. And out of love for his own who were in the world, he proved to them the extent thereof. At the time that the supper was being served, the devil had already placed in Judas Iscariot, the son of Simon, the resolve to betray him. Jesus was aware that the Father had placed all things into his hands, and that he had come from God and was on his way back to Him. So he rose up from the dinner table, laid down his outer garment, took a towel and wrapped it around himself. Then he poured water into a basin and started washing off and wiping dry the feet of the apostles using the towel with which he had girt himself.

When he got to Simon Peter, he asked him, "Lord, are you going to wash my feet?" Jesus replied, "You do not yet recognize what I'm doing to you, but it will come to you at a later time." "You will never wash my feet!" Peter insisted. "Were I not to wash your feet," said Jesus, "you would have no portion with me." "Lord," Simon Peter answered him, "not my feet only, but my hands and my head as well!" Jesus replied, "Once a man has been cleansed, he needs only to have his feet washed off, otherwise he is clean all over. And you are all clean. Well, not all of you." (You see, he knew who was about to betray him, and that is why he said to them, "Not all of you are clean.")

So after he had washed their feet and put his clothes back on, he went and sat back down again. At that point he said to them, "Have you any idea what I've done for you? You refer to me as 'the Master' and 'the Teacher,' and what you say is indeed the truth, for truly that is what I am. So if I, the 'Master' and the 'Teacher' have washed off your feet, then you should wash each other's feet. I have left you an example, that you may do even as I have done for you. Truly, truly, do I say to you that a servant is not above his master, nor is the one who is sent greater than the One who sent him. If you have understood these truths, you would do well to put them to use. I am not referring to all of you: I know the ones whom I have chosen. But it is to satisfy the Scripture that reads, 'The one eating my bread has raised his heel against me.' I am speaking to you from this age so that when it comes about, you will believe that I AM. Most assuredly I say to you, anyone who receives the one that I send to them is receiving me, and the one who receives me is also receiving the One Who sent me."

JESUS IDENTIFIES JUDAS AS HIS BETRAYER
(Matt 26:21-25; Mark 14:18-21; Luke 22:21-23; John 13:21-30)
The Upper Room, Jerusalem

And his spirit wrenched as he spoke these things. "But look," he said as they were lying there and eating, "the hand of my betrayer is on the table with mine! I am telling you the truth, one of you eating here with me is going to betray me." His followers were saddened and started looking to one another, uncertain as to which of the disciples he had meant. Then they began to deliberate among themselves as to which of them it might be who intended to do this. And one after another they started asking him, "Lord, is it me?" Now one of his disciples, the one whom Jesus loved, was leaning against his breast. Simon Peter motioned to this disciple, seeking an answer as to which of them he was referring to. He therefore leaned against the breast of Jesus and asked, "Who is it, Lord?" And Jesus replied, "It is truly one of the twelve: the one who dips his hand in the bowl with mine; the one to whom I will give this piece of bread after I have drenched it. For truly the Son of Man is to go precisely as it has been written about him; in accordance with what has been prescribed for him. Even so, woe betide that man by whom the Son of Man will be betrayed. It would have been better for him had he never been born." So he dipped the bread and gave it to Judas Iscariot, the son of Simon. Then Judas, his betrayer, said to him, "Surely it is not me is it, Rabbi?" Jesus replied, "You have said it yourself." Then, after the sop, Satan (again) entered into Judas, so Jesus said to him, "Do as you've resolved without delay." But none of the ones lying there had any idea as to why he had spoken this to him. Some imagined that because Judas was in charge of the money bag, that Jesus had said to him, "Buy the things we will need for the feast," or that he should give something to the poor. So he went out after receiving the bread, and it was night.

LOVE ONE ANOTHER
(John 13:31-35; GHb 7-Quote by Jerome,
Commentary on Ephesians 3, regarding Ephesians 5:4;
Quote by Jerome, On Isaiah 11.2)
The Upper Room, Jerusalem

So after Judas had left that place, Jesus said, "Now the Son of Man is prepared for glorification, and through him will God be glorified. And if God is set to be glorified through the Son of Man, then God Himself will glorify him; and how suddenly will He do so! Dearest children, I will only be with you a little while longer. And even as I have said to the Jews, so now do I say to you; you will go looking for me, but not be able to follow me to where I go. I am passing a new commandment on to you: that you should love one another, even as I have loved you. Never think of yourself as truly fulfilled until you can look upon your brother with love. It is among the greatest of sins to sadden the spirit of a brother. If you should show love for one another, then everyone will recognize you as my disciples."

JESUS PREDICTS PETER'S DENIALS
(Matt 26:31-35; Mark 14:27-31;
Luke 22:31-38; John 13:36-38; Barnabas7:11b)
Upper Room, Jerusalem

Simon Peter asked him, "Lord, where are you going?" Jesus answered, "You cannot follow me there just yet, but eventually you will." Then Jesus revealed to them, "All of you will stumble tonight on my account, for it is written, 'I will strike down the shepherd and the sheepfold will scatter.' But after I have been raised up, I will travel on ahead of you into Galilee." "Lord," asked Peter, "why can't I just follow you now?" "Simon, Simon, Satan has requested that all of you be delivered up so that he might sift you as wheat. Those who wish to see me and take hold of my kingdom must receive me in sufferings and trials. But I have interceded on your behalf, that your faith might fail you not. And after your conversion, strengthen your brethren." And Peter replied, saying, "Lord, I am ready to go to prison with you--and even to my death! Even if everyone else should fall away on your account, I never will. I will lay down my life for you." Then Jesus said, "Will you really lay down your life for me? For I am telling you truly, Peter, this very day, before the cock crows twice, you will disown me three times, denying even this very night that you know me." But Peter spoke the more vehemently, "Even if it means that I must die, I will by no means deny you." And all of the other disciples spoke likewise to him. And he asked them, "When I sent you out without bag or wallet or sandals, were you ever in want for anything?" "Not a thing," they said. "But now," he continued, "let whoever has a bag or a wallet take it with them, and let one who has no sword sell his robe and purchase one. I am telling you that what has been written, 'And he was counted among the lawless ones,' must be completed in me. You see, everything that pertains to me is about to be fulfilled." Then they said, "Look, there are two swords right here!" And he said to them, "These will suffice."

THE BREAD AND THE CUP
(Matt 26:26-29; Mark 14:22-25; Luke 22:17-20)
The Upper Room, Jerusalem

And after he had taken the cup, he blessed it and said, "Take this and divide it among yourselves. For I am telling you that I will not drink of the fruit of the vine until the coming of the kingdom of God." And as they were eating, Jesus took a loaf, blessed it and broke it. Then he gave some to each of his disciples, saying, "Take this now and eat of it, for this is my body, which is offered up on your behalf. Do this to bring about my remembrance." After the supper, he took the cup as he had before, blessed it and offered it to them, saying, "All of you, drink of it." And the disciples drank therefrom. "This cup is the new covenant which is in my blood, which is poured out for your sakes (and) many others; that the sins of the many might be forgiven. I am telling you the truth, I will not again drink of the fruit of the vine until such time as I drink it again with you in my Father's kingdom, the kingdom of God.

THE FAREWELL DISCOURSE:
THE WAY, THE TRUTH, AND THE LIFE
(John 14:1-31)
The Upper Room, Jerusalem

"Do not let your hearts be moved. Believe in God and believe in me. My Father's home has many dwellings. I would have told you if it were not true. I am going to ready a place for you, and if I go to make a place for you, then I will come and take you to myself, that you may also be where I am. And you know the way to where I go." Thomas said, "Lord, we do not know where you are going, so how are we to know the way?" Jesus replied, "I am the way, the truth, and the life! No one gets to the Father except through me! If only you had known me, then you would have known the Father. From this time forward, you have both known Him and seen Him." Philip said, "Lord, reveal the Father to us and that will be enough for us." "Have I been with you so long now, Philip," Jesus asked him, "and do you still not see me for who I am? The one who sees me is seeing the Father. Do you not believe that I am within the Father, and that the Father is within me? The very words that I speak to you do not come from me, but from my Father Who lives in me. All the works are done by Him! Believe me when I say that I am within the Father and the Father is within me. If indeed by nothing else, then believe it through the works themselves. Assuredly I say to you, the one who puts his trust in me will do the same things that I do. Indeed, he will do even greater things than these because I go to the Father. Moreover, I will bring to pass all that you might ask in my name, that the Father might be glorified through His Son. If you should ask anything in my name, I will do it for you.

"If you love me, you will keep my commandments. And I will beseech the Father, and another will He send to you; a Comforter who will spend forever with you. The Spirit of Truth, which the world cannot receive, since it neither perceives it, nor even knows of it. But you do know it because it remains among you and will be within you. I will not leave you orphaned here, I am coming back to you. Only a little while longer and the world will see me no more. Even so, you will see me; for because I am alive, so also will you come alive. When that day comes, you will recognize that I am within my Father and that you are within me and that I am within you. The one who loves me is the one who receives my words and keeps them. And whoever loves me will be loved by my Father. I will also love that man and reveal myself to him."

Judas, not Iscariot, asked him, "Lord, in what way will you reveal yourself to us without revealing yourself to the rest of the world?" Jesus answered him, saying, "If anyone loves me, he will keep my word; and my Father will love him too, and we will come to him and make ourselves a home with him, but the one who does not love me does not keep my words; and the word that you hear is not my own, but comes from the Father Who sent me here. I spoke these things to you in the time that I was with you. But that Advocate, the Holy Spirit, which the Father will send you in my name, will bring all things to light for you, and cause you to remember all that I have spoken to you. I leave you now in peace, and peace is what I give to you. I do not give to you as the world gives. Have no fear, neither let your hearts be moved. You have heard me say, 'I am going home and I will come again to you.' Had you loved me, you would have been glad to hear me say, 'I am going to the Father.' The Father, you see, is greater than I am. I have spoken this to you now, before it happens, so that when it does happen, you might believe it. I will not speak much from this time forth because the Ruler of this World is on his way, and he has no inheritance with me. Nevertheless, the love that I have for the Father must be shown by my doing as He has bidden me. Rise up now, and let's move on!

I AM THE TRUE VINE
(John 15:1-17)
Jerusalem

"I am the true vine and my Father is the vinedresser. He removes every unfruitful branch that is within me, and prunes each one that does bring forth, that it may produce even more fruit. You have been pruned already, on account of the word I have spoken to you. Remain in me, with me in you. Just as the branch, apart from the vine, cannot bear any fruit on its own, neither can you unless you should remain in me. I am the vine and you are the branches. Whoever, therefore, remains in me with me inside of him, will bring forth an abundance of fruit; because apart from me you can do nothing at all. Unless a man remains in me, he is thrown away like a withered branch. They gather and toss them into the flames, and in that place they all will burn. If you remain within me and my words remain within you, then you can ask for whatever you wish--you will receive it! My Father is glorified in this: that you should bring forth fruit in abundance, and thereby show your discipleship. As the Father has loved me, so also have I loved you. Therefore you must remain in my love. And if you should keep my commandments, you will truly remain in my love, even as I have kept the commandments of the Father and remained in His love. I have said these things to you so that you might live in my love an brim with all joy. This is my command to you: You must show love for one another even as I have shown love for you. No one has a greater love than this: that one would give his own life for the sake of his friends. You are my friends if you do as I've instructed you. No longer do I call you servants, because the servant is not privy to the affairs of his master. But I have called you my friends, because I have passed all that I have heard from my Father on to you. You have not chosen me, but I have chosen you, that you might go and bring forth fruit, and that your fruit might endure, so that whatever you should ask of the Father in my name, He might give it to you. This is my command to you: Show love for one another.

OPPOSITION
(John 15:18-27)
Jerusalem

"If you are hated by the world, understand that it hated me before it hated you. Had you been of the world, the world would have loved you as its own. You, however, are not of this world. Rather, I have chosen you from out of this world, and this is why the world can't accept you. Recall the words that I spoke to you: 'A servant is not greater than his master.' If they persecuted me, they will persecute you too. If they had kept my word, they would keep yours too. But they will do all these things to you in my name, since they do not know the One Who sent me. Had I not come and spoken to them, they would not be guilty of sin. But now they have no excuse for their sin. Whoever hates me hates my Father. Had I not done works among them that no one else had ever done, they would not be guilty of sin. But these have not just seen these works, but have also despised both my Father and myself. This, however, has come to pass in order to fulfill what was written in their law: 'They have hated me for no good cause.' And when the Helper comes, that Spirit of Truth that I will send you from the Father, it will bear me out on this. It will bear you out on this as well, since you've been with me from the start.

"I AM GOING TO THE ONE WHO SENT ME"
(John 16:1-33)
Jerusalem

"I have spoken all of this to you to keep you from being ensnared. They will force you out of the synagogue. Indeed, the time will come when everyone who murders you will imagine that they are doing God some kind of sacred service. And the reason that they do these things is because they have never known me, nor ever have they known my Father. Nevertheless, I have spoken these things to you so that when the time does come, you might call to mind that I said them. I never told you these things before because I was still with you.

"But now I am off to Him Who sent me, yet not one of you is asking me, 'Where are you going?' Your hearts have instead grown sorrowful over the words I've spoken. Even so, I am telling you the truth, it will work to your advantage if I do go away, because if I were not to go, the Comforter would not come to your aid. But if I do go, I will send it to you. And when it does come, it will prove the world wrong about sin and righteousness and judgment as well. Concerning sin, because they have no faith in me; concerning righteousness, because I am going to the Father, and you will see me no longer; and concerning judgment, because the Ruler of this World has been condemned. I have many things to teach you still, but you cannot bear them at this time. But when it does come, the Spirit of Truth, I mean, it will lead you into all truth. You see, it will not be speaking on its own, but only what it hears, and will fill you in on things to come. It will glorify me by drawing on what is mine and giving it to you. All that belongs to the Father also belongs to me, and this is why I said to you that it takes all that belongs to me and passes it on to you."

THE FAREWELL PRAYER
(John 17:1-26; vss. following John 17:26-in codex evangelii
Johannei Parisii in sacro Templariorum tabulario asservatus;
Pseudo-Cyprian, Against Dice-Throwers 3;
Fragment From The Strasbourg Coptic Papyrus)
Jerusalem

And when Jesus had spoken these things, he lifted his eyes toward heaven and said, "Father, the time has come to glorify Your Son, that he might also bring You glory. For You have given him power over all flesh, to grant limitless life to all that You have given him. And never-ending life is this: that they might come to know You, the only true God, and Jesus Christ, the one You have sent. I have brought You glory here on earth by finishing all that You gave me to do. And now, Father, glorify me with the majesty that I shared with You before the world was made. I have revealed Your name to those that You gave to me from out of the world. All of them belonged to You, and You have given them to me, and they have truly kept Your word. Now they have received assurances that what You have given me is indeed from You. For I have passed the words that You gave me on to them, and they have accepted them, knowing for sure that I came from Your side, and believing that You have sent me. I am praying for the sake of these. I am not praying on behalf of this world, but for the sake of the ones that You have given me, for all of them belong to You. And all that I have belongs to You, and what is Yours is mine as well. And I have been glorified through them. I am no longer in this realm, but these are to remain behind as I come to You. Holy Father, watch over those You have given to me in Your name, that they might become One, even as we are One. While I was with them in this world, I kept them in Your name. I watched over those that You gave to me, and not one of them was lost except for that son of devastation, that the Scripture might be fulfilled. And now I'm coming back to You, having spoken these things in the world, that my joy might be fulfilled in them. I have passed Your word on to them, and the world has despised them, since they are not of this world, even as I am not of this world. I am not asking You to release them from this realm, but that You might guard them against all evil. They are no more of this world than I am. Sanctify them in Your truth. Your Word is truth. I have sent them out into the world even as You have sent me into the world. And I sanctify myself for them, that they might be sanctified through the truth. Not that I pray for these alone, but also for those who will come to believe in me through their testimony, that they might all become One, even as You, Father are within me, and I am within You. This is so that they might be within us, that the world may come to know that You have sent me. And I have given them the same glory that You gave to me, that they may be One, even as We are One--'I AM' in them, and 'YOU ARE' in me, that they might all be made perfect in the 'One'--and that they might recognize while in this world that You have sent me, and that You have loved them in the same way that You have loved me. Father, I truly wish for those that You have given me to come over to where I AM, that they might experience my glory, which You gave to me, because You loved me before the world ever was. Holy Father, truly the world never did know You, but I do know You, and these all know that You have sent me. I have made Your name known to them, and I will again make it known, so that in these might dwell the same love with which You have loved me, and that I might remain in them. Strengthen me now with Your power, so that with me they might endure the world. Amen. I have been given the scepter of the kingdom. All of these have been despised--and since they were lowly, they were never recognized. Through You, oh Father, have I taken my place as king. You will place all things into my hands. And now I will reveal myself to you in the fullness of my glory, and make known to you the scope of your authority, together with the secret of your apostleship."

Then, with uplifted hands, Jesus said to his followers, "Behold, the time for me to drink the cup from which my Father has given me to drink has come. I am off to my Father Who sent me here, so I will remind you one last time: I am sending you out, so do as I've instructed you. Pass what I have taught you on to others, so that the whole world might come to receive it, and so receive the Holy Spirit. The sins of those that you forgive will be forgiven, and the sins of those you do not forgive will remain unforgiven. Hear what I have said to you: I do not come from this world. The Comforter is with you now, so teach through the authority of the Advocate. I am sending you out as the Father has sent me. Do not sadden the Holy Spirit that is living within you. Do not quench the light that is shining within you. This in truth I swear to you, that I am not of this world. John will act as your father until he comes to me in paradise." Then he sanctified them with the Holy Spirit.

THE PARTING HYMN AND DANCE
(AcJn 94-97a)
Jerusalem

Now prior to being arrested by the ungovernable Jews who received their law through the lawless serpent, he gathered us all together and said, "Before I am handed up to them, let us sing a hymn to the Father, and venture forth to what lies ahead." So he had us form a circle together and hold hands with one another. And he stood at the center and said, "Answer me, 'Amen.'" And he sang a hymn, which went like this:

"Glory to You, Father!"

And those of us encircling him answered, "Amen!"

"Glory to you Word! Glory to you, Grace!" "Amen!"
"Glory to you, Grace! Glory to you, Holy One!"
"Glory even unto Glory!" "Amen!"
"Oh Father, how we give You praise!"
"We thank You, Light,
Wherein no darkness dwells." "Amen!"
"Now I will explain to you why we are giving thanks:
 I will be delivered, and I will deliver." "Amen!"
"I will be freed, and I will set free." "Amen!"
"I will be wounded, and I will wound." "Amen!"
"I will be born, and I will bring forth." "Amen!"
"I will consume, and I will be consumed." "Amen!"
"I will hear, and I will be heard." "Amen!"

"I will be understood,
  Being understanding itself." "Amen!"
"I will be cleansed, and I will cleanse." "Amen!"

The Dance of Grace:

"I will pipe. All of you dance!" "Amen!"
"I will grieve. All of you mourn!" "Amen!"
"The Eightfold Power has joined us in song!" "Amen!"
"The Twelfth in number is dancing on high!" "Amen!"
"It is for the All to dance up in the heights!" "Amen!"
"All of those who do not dance,
  Do not know what is taking place!"
"Amen!"
"I will flee, and I will stay!" "Amen!"
"I will beautify, and I will be beautified!" "Amen!"
"I will be united, and I will unify!" "Amen!"
"I have no house, yet I have many houses!" "Amen!"
"I have no place, yet I have many places!" "Amen!"
"I have no temple, yet I have many temples!" "Amen!"
"I am a lamp to all who look on me!" "Amen!"
"I am a mirror to all who know me!" "Amen!"
"I am a door for all who knock on me!" "Amen!"
"I am a path for all who travel." "Amen!"

"Now if you respond to my dance, see yourself as within me who speaks. And when you see the things I do, keep my mysteries to yourselves. Those of you who dance with me, consider my actions carefully, for it is for you to suffer the passion of mankind, which corresponds to my own suffering. You see, you could never have understood your own affliction without realizing that the Father has sent me to you as the Word. Those of you who have seen my actions as suffering have not stood firm, but you have instead been moved. You have me to rest upon as you move toward wisdom; rest upon me! After I depart from you, you will come to see me as I am! I am not as I now seem to you. At the time that you come forth, you will see me as I truly am. Had you known what your passion would entail, you could have avoided it altogether. Learn therefore the way to suffer, and you will gain power over your suffering. I will teach you what you do not know. I am your God, and not that of the betrayer. It is my will that holy souls should join with mine. Listen to the Word of Wisdom! Say again with me.

'Glory to You, Father!
Glory to You, Word!
Glory to You, Holy Spirit!'

As for myself, if you would like to see me as I truly was, I made all things a laughingstock by means of the Word. By no means was I put to shame, but instead I jumped for joy! But you must come to see the greater vision, and once you have grasped it, then you must go on to proclaim, 'Glory to You, Father!'" "Amen!"

AGONY IN THE GARDEN
(Matt 26:30, 36-46; Mark 14:26, 32-42;
Luke 22:39-46; John 18:3a)
Gethsemane

And after the Lord Jesus had danced with us, sung [the] hymn and given us these words, he crossed over the Brook of Kidron, even as he often would, to the Mount of Olives, where there was a garden known as Gethsemane. Then he entered into it, and the disciples followed him. "Sit here," he said, "while I go over there and pray." And he took Peter with him, along with James and John, the two sons of Zebedee. And feelings of sorrow and dread overwhelmed him. Jesus then confessed to them, "My soul is near to death from sorrow. Remain with me and stay awake!" And he went on a little farther, fell to his face on the ground and prayed that if it could be done, the hour might pass him by. "Abba, Father, take this cup from me if You can. All things are possible with You, so may You take this cup away. Nevertheless, not what I will (or) as I will. Rather, let what You would have happen, come about as You would have it." An angel then appeared from heaven and strengthened him. And in anguish of spirit, he prayed the more fervently. And his sweat was as drops of blood falling to the ground.

He then arose from the prayer and returned to the disciples. He found them lying there asleep, overcome by sorrow. "Simon," he asked Peter, "why are you sleeping? Could you not stay awake with me a single hour? Arise! Shake off your slumber and pray that you do not give way to temptation. For the spirit is truly willing, but the flesh is weak."

He went over and prayed the same prayer a second time, saying, "My Father, if it is not possible to remove this cup without my drinking it, let Your will be done." When he returned, he again found them lying there asleep, their eyes having grown quite heavy. They did not know how to answer him. So he left them there and went back and prayed the same words a third time.

Now Judas, his betrayer, knew about this location, since Jesus and his disciples had gathered there on many occasions. So Judas took charge of the band of soldiers, the officers of the chief priests and the Pharisees, and headed to that place as well. Then Jesus returned the third time to his disciples and said, "Sleep on then, and take your rest. Enough of this! The hour is near, (and indeed) has come. The Son of Man is about to be given over to reprobates. Let us all get up and go, for my betrayer is approaching!"

THE ARREST
(Matt 26:47-56; Mark 14:43-52;
Luke 22:47-53:John 18:2-12a)
Gethsemane

And even as he was speaking, Judas, one of the twelve showed up, and with him was a great multitude sent from the chief priests, the scribes, and the elders of the people, all of whom he was leading there. They were carrying torches and lanterns, and were fitted out with swords and clubs as weapons. Now the traitor had worked out a signal with them: "The one to whom I will show affection is he. Arrest him, therefore, and take him away under guard." And going over to Jesus, he said, "Rabbi, rejoice!" He went up to him to give him a kiss, but Jesus simply questioned him: "Judas, is it with a kiss that you betray the Son of Man? My friend, do what you have come to do." And Judas kissed him.

Now Jesus, aware of all that was about to happen to him, came right out and asked them, "Whom do you seek?" And they responded, "Jesus the Nazarene." And he replied, "I AM." Now Judas, the one who had betrayed him, was also there and standing beside them. So when he answered them, "I AM," they all flew back and hit the ground. So he asked them once again, "Whom do you seek?" And they replied, "Jesus the Nazarene." Jesus said to them, "I have answered you already: I AM. So if you are after me, then let these others go." This took place to fulfill the prophecy that says, "I did not lose even one of those You gave to me."

When Jesus' followers saw what was about to happen, they asked, "Lord, are we supposed to strike them down with these swords?" At that moment the soldiers grabbed hold of Jesus and placed him under arrest. Just then, one of Jesus' companions, Simon Peter, who was standing nearby carrying a sword, reached for it, drew it out and struck the servant of the high priest--whose name was Malchus--cutting off his right ear. But Jesus said to Peter, "Enough of this! Put your sword back in its sheath! Behold, everyone who lives by the sword also dies by the sword. Do you not understand that I could call upon my Father? He would immediately place twelve legions of angels at my disposal! How then would the Scriptures that said that it must be this way ever be satisfied? Should I refuse to drink the cup that was given to me by my Father?" And he healed his ear with just a touch. At that point, Jesus said to the crowd--the chief priests, the officers of the temple guard, and the elders, who had come for him--"Have you come to arrest me as against a bandit; brandishing these swords and clubs? I was with you every day, sitting and teaching in the temple, and you never laid hands on me to take me then. But the Scriptures must be satisfied. All of this has come to pass to fulfill the writings of the prophets. But this is your time; when darkness reigns." Then everyone, (including) the disciples, abandoned him and ran away. Then the band, its commander, and the religious leaders grabbed Jesus and bound him up. Now a certain young man, who was wearing nothing but a linen sheet draped around his naked body, was following after Jesus. As soon as they laid hold of him, he left his linen sheet behind and ran away wearing nothing at all.

PASSION 1

PROLOGUE TO THE ACTS OF PONTIUS PILATE
(ALSO KNOWN AS THE GOSPEL OF NICODEMUS)
Jerusalem?

{I am Ananias, an officer of the Praetorian Guard. And as one who is well versed in the Law, I learned of Jesus Christ through the holy writings, which I read with an unwavering trust, and was deemed worthy to receive holy baptism. And I looked high and low for reports that had been made by the Jews, who during and after the time of our Lord Jesus Christ, had written them under orders from Pontius Pilate himself. I found these accounts written in the original Hebrew during the seventeenth year of our Emperor Flavius Theodosius, the sixth year of the ninth indiction of the Nobility of Flavius Valentinianus, and have translated them into Greek both to please God and to enlighten all who call upon the name of our Lord Jesus Christ.

For this very reason, all of you who read this account and copy it into other books, think of me and pray on my behalf, that God might be kindly disposed toward me and forgive all of the sins that I have committed against Him. Peace to all who read this book and come to hear what it has to say, and to those who serve them as well. Amen.

Now these are the things that Nicodemus recorded with regard to the deeds of the chief priests and the rest of the Jews after the Lord had suffered on the cross. He handed them over on the twenty-fifth of March, four years into the two hundred and second Olympiad, eight days prior to the month of April. This same Nicodemus, during the nineteenth year of the reign of Emperor Tiberius of Rome, translated these accounts into the Hebrew tongue. This coincides with the nineteenth year of the reign of Herod, king of Galilee, which was during the consulate of Rufus and Rubellio, when the Jewish high priest was Joseph Caiaphas.}

JESUS BEFORE THE SANHEDRIN
(John 18:12-14, 19-24; Matt 26:57-68;
Mark 14:53-65; Luke 22:63-71; POxy 1224:4)
Jerusalem

Together, the soldiers, the Captain of the Thousand, and the officers seized Jesus, tied him up, and led him away to Annas first, since he was father-in-law to Caiaphas, that year's high priest. Caiaphas, you see, was the one who had counseled the Jews, "Better that one man should die than the entire nation." The high priest then examined Jesus with regard to his students and his teaching. "I spoke plainly and openly before the world," Jesus answered. "I was forever in the synagogue and the temple, speaking where the Jews perpetually convene. I never spoke anything in secret, so why are you interrogating me? Why not ask the ones who heard me teach what I said?" And when he heard this, one of the officers standing nearby struck Jesus and shouted, "Is this the way you answer the high priest?" "If I spoke amiss," Jesus replied, "kindly tell me where I misspoke, but if I spoke the truth, how can you justify hitting me?"

So Annas forwarded him to Caiaphas, the high priest. Those arresting Jesus seized him and led him away still bound into the house of the high priest Caiaphas, where all of the chief priests, teachers of the law, and elders had gathered together. The high-ranking priests and the entire Sanhedrin were looking for false testimony to use against Jesus in order to bring about his execution. But even though many pretenders stepped up and put forth false statements about him, they were unable to produce any. Their stories, you see, did not agree with one another. Then at last two rose to their feet, came forward and hurled this false accusation against him: "Both of us heard him say, 'I can (and) will destroy this temple that was built through manual labor, and in three days raise up in its place one not made with the hands of men.'" But even the testimonies of these two were not in perfect accord.

Then the high priest stood up in the sight of all and examined Jesus: "Are you not going to respond? What can all of the things that these men have testified against you possibly mean? <What are you trying to prove by> not answering? What are you repudiating, anyway? What is this new doctrine they claim that you teach? What is this brand new message that you are preaching? Explain <it to us> and <we will listen.>" But Jesus held his peace and gave no response. Once again the high priest examined him: "I order you to swear by the Living God: Tell us plainly, are you the Messiah, the Son of the Holy God?" "Indeed I am," answered Jesus. "This is what you say yourselves! And to all of you I say that one day you are going to see the Son of Man coming from the sky on clouds, seated to the right hand of Power." Then the high priest ripped his clothing. "His words are blasphemous!" he said. Then he asked, "What need have we of further witnesses? Listen up, now that you have heard his blasphemy, are you ready to render your verdict?" "He ought to be put to death!" they all replied. So each of them passed sentence against him as one deserving the death penalty. Then some of the men guarding Jesus started taunting him: they blindfolded him, spit into his face, beat him, and punched him with their fists. Still others slapped him and demanded: "Hey, Christ, why not prophesy to us! Which of us punched you?" Then the officers took him and drubbed him.

PETER'S DENIALS
(Matt 26:58, 69-75; Mark 14:54, 66-72;
Luke 22:54b-62; John 18:15-18, 25-27; AcPt 7)
Jerusalem

Simon Peter and another disciple were following Jesus. Now because the high priest knew about this follower, he went ahead and accompanied Jesus into the courtyard of the high priest, but Peter had to wait outside at the door. The other disciple, the one that the high priest knew about, returned and spoke to the girl who was posted there and brought Peter in with him. And Peter followed at a distance all the way to the court of the high priest. But after some people had gotten a fire going in the midst thereof, and all of them had seated themselves around it, Peter went right in and sat down alongside them to see how things would turn out, and he basked in the warmth of the fire.

Now Peter was sitting there openly, and a servant girl spotted him sitting in the firelight below. And after looking at him closely she said, "This man was with him." Then one of the servants of the high priest, the girl who was assigned to the door, came up to him and looked him over carefully. "You were right at the side of that Nazarene, Jesus of Galilee," she accused him. "You are another of that man's followers, aren't you?" But he denied Jesus before them all, saying, "I am not! Not only do I not know him, Lady, but I do not so much as know or understand what you are saying!" And he slipped away to another spot over by the entrance, and the cock crowed.

Now the servants and officials were keeping warm together around a fire they had kindled on account of the chill, and Peter stood right there warming himself alongside them. And again another servant girl saw him there and informed those who were standing nearby, "This man was with Jesus of Nazareth. He is one of them!" And a little while later, as Simon Peter stood basking in the warmth, someone else accused him, "You are assuredly another of his students." "Mister," Peter answered, "I am not!" "You most certainly are!" And he denied it again with an oath: "I do not even know that man!"

And about an hour or so after that, another one of them affirmed, "There can be no question, this man had to have been with him, for he is a Galilean." And a short time later, those who were standing nearby went up to Peter and said, "You have got to be one of them! Behold, your Galilean accent gives you away." And Peter answered him, "Mister, I do not know what you are saying!" One of the servants of the high priest, someone related to the man whose ear Peter had cut off, demanded, "Did I not see you in the garden with him?" And once again Peter denied it, calling all manner of curses down upon himself. And he offered this testimony before them all: "I don't even know this man that you're talking about!" And right then, even as he was saying all of this, the cock crowed a second time. Then the Lord turned and looked at Peter. Then Peter called to mind the word that the Lord had spoken to him, "Today, before the cock crows twice, you will deny me three times." And after thinking it through, he went out and started sobbing bitterly.

Precious brothers, I denied our Lord Jesus Christ not once, but three times. Still, the ones who cornered me were vicious dogs, as the Lord's prophet had foretold. Even so, the Lord did not hold it against me. Not at all, but out of his compassion for the weakness of my flesh, he turned and looked at me, prompting me to pour forth bitter tears. And I deeply regretted my lack of faith; how could I have been so taken in by the devil as to turn my back on my Lord's word? You men and brothers who are gathered together in the name of Jesus Christ, I am telling you now that Satan, that deceiver, also shoots his arrows at you, that he might lead you all astray. Never be wanting for faith, my brothers, nor ever waver in your mind. You ought instead to strengthen yourselves. Show some resolve and do not doubt. For if Satan was able to undermine and bring down someone like myself, whom the Lord regarded so highly, even to the point where I denied the light of my hope, convincing me to back down as though the one I believed in were some mere mortal, what do you suppose that he will do to you who are new to this? Do you think that he will not tear you down and turn you into enemies of God's kingdom, dragging you all down to destruction? Everyone he manages to rob of his assurance in our Lord Jesus Christ, you see, becomes forevermore a child of destruction. Therefore, my brothers--those who have been chosen by the Lord--turn yourselves around and be securely founded on the Lord Almighty, the Father of our Lord Jesus Christ, whom no one has ever seen, nor indeed can any behold whose faith is not in him. Recognize where this seduction that has lured you came from. You see, I did not come to convince you with mere words that the one I preach to you is the Messiah, but through faith in Jesus to urge you on instead by supernatural powers and deeds. Let none of you hold out for any other 'savior' besides him who was despised, whom the Jews assailed; this Nazarene who was crucified, and died, and rose again on the third day.

JESUS CONDEMNED BY THE SANHEDRIN
(Matt 27:1, 2a; Mark 15:1a; Luke 22:66-23:1b)
Jerusalem

At daybreak on the following morning, the chief priests, the elders of the people, and the teachers of the law convened for the sole purpose of seeing to the execution of Jesus. So they led him off to their Sanhedrin, where they examined him, "If you really are the Messiah, then why not come right out and tell us." "If I were to tell you that," Jesus responded, "you would not believe me, and if I were to ask it of you, you would not give me any answer, neither would you let me go. From this time forward the Son of Man will be seated to the right hand of God's strength." "Do you claim to be the Son of God?" they all demanded. "It is because I am that you are accusing me of it," he retorted. Then they said, "What need have we of further witnesses? We have heard it ourselves from his very lips." Then they tied him up and led him off, and the council stood to their feet.

JUDAS COMMITS SUICIDE
(Matt 27:3-10; Acts 1:18, 19)
Jerusalem

Now when Judas saw that Jesus had been condemned, he became very sorry for having betrayed him, so he returned the thirty silver coins to the chief priests and the elders, saying, "I have committed a serious offense: I have betrayed innocent blood!" "What is that to us?" they asked, "That was all your own doing!" So Judas threw the coins into the sanctuary and went right out and hanged himself. And he dove head first; his belly split open, and out gushed his guts!

Now this man bought a field with his evil reward; the chief priests picked the coins up off of the floor and said, "Since this is blood money it cannot lawfully be put into the treasury." So they decided to spend the money on a potter's field and use it as a cemetery for foreigners. And everyone who lived in Jerusalem heard about it. As a matter of fact, the name of that field found a place in their tongue. "Akeldema," means "The Field of Blood," and that is why it is called "Blood Field" to this very day. Then were fulfilled the words spoken by Jeremiah the prophet, "They accepted the thirty silver coins, the price that the people of Israel had set on him, and used them to purchase the potter's field, even as the Lord had ordained for me."

THE JEWS ACCUSE JESUS BEFORE PILATE
(Matt 27:2b; Mark 15:1b; Luke 1b, 2;
John 18:28-32; GNc 1:1-3:1)
Palace of Pontius Pilate, Jerusalem

Then, while it was still early in the morning, the Jews led Jesus away from Caiaphas and over to the Praetorium, and delivered him up to Pilate the governor. Now they all wanted to eat the Passover meal, so to avoid ceremonial defilement, they did not go in. And Annas, Caiaphas, Semes, Dathaes, Gamaliel, Judas, Levi, Naphthali, Alexander, Jairus, and all of the other Jews started charging Jesus with a whole range of offenses, so Pilate went out to them and requested, "What is the precise charge that you are bringing against him?" "We would not have brought him here to you," they responded, "if he were not a criminal." Then they started accusing him, saying, "We found this man to be undermining our nation; forbidding that taxes be paid to Caesar. We know for a fact," they insisted, "that this man is the son of Joseph the Carpenter and that he was born of Mary; but he claims to be the Messiah, the Son of God, and a King as well! And as if that were not enough, he desecrates the Sabbath Day and seeks to do away with the law of our fathers." Then Pilate questioned them, "And what things does he do that show he wants it done away with?" "In our law," the Jews replied, "it says that no healing should be done on the Sabbath. But this man, by his evil ways, has healed the lame, the crippled, the withered, the blind, the paralyzed, the deaf, and the demon-possessed--all upon the Sabbath Day!" "And in what way are these actions evil?" Pilate asked. "He is a sorcerer!" they retorted. "It is through none other than Beelzebub that he casts the evil spirits out. They are all at his command." "What you say cannot be true!" Pilate answered. "No filthy spirit can cast out another; only the gods can do that."

"Your excellency," the Jews bid Pilate, "we implore you; please take him and try him yourself before your court." And Pilate called them near and asked, "Since I am but a governor, kindly explain to me how I am supposed to interrogate a king?" "Now hold on right there!" they said. "We never said that he was a king. Only that he claims to be one!" Then Pilate called his messenger over and directed him, "Give Jesus a proper escort into this place." So the messenger went right out. And as soon as he saw that he was the Christ, the messenger worshiped him. Then he took his cloak in hand and spread it out on the ground below. Then the man addressed him thus, "Lord, the governor is summoning you, so please pass across this as you enter." But when the Jews saw how the messenger had acted, they denounced Pilate, demanding, "Why did you send this herald out to call him in, and not a bailiff instead? For as soon as this messenger laid eyes on him, he worshiped him, spreading his cloak upon the ground and asking him to walk across it as though he were some kind of king!" Then Pilate called for the messenger and questioned him, "Why did you spread your cape on the ground and have Jesus pass over?" "Lord Governor," replied the messenger, "when you sent me over to Alexander in Jerusalem, I saw this man seated on a donkey, and the children of the Hebrews were carrying branches in their hands and making a commotion. And other people were spreading their own clothes out before him and proclaiming, 'You, who rest in the highest, rescue us now! Praises to the one who comes bearing the Lord's name!'"

"The children of the Hebrews were crying out in Hebrew," the Jews called out to the messenger, "so how could you, who speak Greek, possibly have understood what they said?" "I simply asked one of the Jews," the messenger replied, "'What is this that they are shouting in Hebrew?' and he interpreted it for me." Then Pilate demanded, "And just what were they crying out in Hebrew?" "Hosanna membrome baruchamma Adonai," the Jews answered. "And just how do 'Hosanna' and all of those other words translate?" Pilate asked. "You who rest in the highest, rescue us now," conceded the Jews. "Praises to the one who comes in the name of the Lord." Then Pilate asked them, "If you admit that these are the words that the children spoke, then why are you faulting this messenger?" And none of them could say a thing. Then the governor bid the messenger, "Go out and bring him back in any way that you see fit!" At this, the messenger went right out and did as he had done before, saying to Jesus, "Lord, the governor is summoning you, please come inside."

And as he was going in, Jesus passed by the ensigns who were holding the standards up. Then the images at the tops of the standards started of themselves to bow down and worship him. And when the Jews saw what those images had done, bowing themselves in worship to Jesus, they clamored against the standard bearers. But Pilate asked them, "Are you not amazed that the images bowed down and worshiped Jesus?" "We saw the standard bearers lowering them in reverence to him!" the Jews answered Pilate. Then the governor called the ensigns over and demanded, "Why have you done this?" "We are all Greek," they said, "and servants of the temples. Why would we worship him? We were trying to hold the images up, but they bowed down and worshiped him on their own."

Then Pilate ordered the synagogue rulers and the elders: "Pick out some strong men to support the standards, and let us all see if the images lower themselves then." So the Jewish elders chose the twelve strongest men and had them hold the standards up, and they stood in groups of six before the bar of the governor. And Pilate instructed the messenger, "Walk him out of the

The Super Gospel

Praetorium, and come back in with him any way that you like." Jesus and the messenger then left the hall. Pilate then summoned the ensigns who had held the standards with the images up the first time, and informed them, "I have sworn by Caesar's life that if the standards do not bow down when Jesus comes in, I will have your heads chopped off!" And the governor ordered Jesus to enter in a second time. So the messenger did as he had before, inviting Jesus to walk across his cape. He stepped across and went inside, and as he was going in, the standards fell down in reverence to him, even as they had before.

And when Pilate saw this, he was stunned, and nearly got up out of his seat. And even as he was coming to terms with this, his wife, who was some distance away, sent him this message: "Do not get mixed up with this honorable man, because last night I agonized much over a dream I had about him!" And Pilate, calling the Jews before him said, "You know that my wife is devout, and that she is every bit the practicing Jew that you are." Then they replied, "We are all aware of that." "Look," said Pilate, "my wife just now sent this message to me: 'Do not get mixed up with this honorable man, because last night I agonized much over a dream I had about him.'" "Did we not say that he was a sorcerer?" the Jews replied. "You see, he was the one who sent your wife that dream!" Then Pilate called for Jesus and asked, "What are these men testifying against you? Will you not have your say?" "They would not be saying anything at all had they not been given the power to do so," Jesus replied. "Everyone has the ability to bring about either good or evil with the power of the tongue. They will therefore see to it."

Then the Jewish elders challenged Jesus, "And just what ought we to see, anyway? All of us know, first of all, that you were born through fornication; second, that your birth brought about the slaughter of the children of Bethlehem; and third, the reason that your father and mother, Joseph and Mary, had to run away into Egypt was because the people all hated them." But some of the more fair-minded among the Jews who were standing nearby spoke up, "We do not agree that his was an illegitimate birth because we know for sure that Joseph was betrothed to Mary, and it therefore did not constitute fornication." Then Pilate said to the Jews who had alleged that Jesus was born out of wedlock, "Your charge is baseless, because there had been a betrothal by then. Even your fellow countrymen say that!" Annas and Caiaphas then answered Pilate, "All of us here maintain that his birth was through fornication, and you still do not believe us? These are disciples and proselytes of his." Then Pilate called Annas and Caiaphas to himself and said, "Tell me, what are proselytes?" "Proselytes," they explained, "are people who are born to Gentile parents and convert to Judaism." Then Lazarus, Asterius, Antonius, James, Amnes, Caras, Samuel, Isaac, Phinees, Crispus, Agrippa, and Judas, the ones who had vouched for his legitimacy, contended, "None of us are proselytes. We are all of Jewish heritage, and are telling you the truth, for we were there at the betrothal of Joseph and Mary."

Pilate then called these twelve who denied that he was born of fornication over to himself and said, "I order you to swear by Caesar's life that your claim-- that his birth was not of fornication--is true." But they all answered Pilate, "We are forbidden by our law ever to swear, because for us to do so would be a sin. You ought to have them swear on Caesar's life that it is not as we have said, and we will accept the penalty of death." Pilate then questioned Annas and Caiaphas, "Will you not respond to these things?" Annas and Caiaphas answered Pilate, "You are crediting these twelve men who hold that he is legitimate, even though we and the crowd assembled here are clamoring that he was born through fornication, that he practices sorcery, and that he not only claims a kingship for himself, but then goes on to say that he is God's Son, and we are given no credence?" Pilate then ordered the entire crowd to leave except for the twelve men who denied that he had come through fornication. And after ordering that Jesus be taken out of earshot, he asked them, "Why are they so anxious to have him executed?" "They cannot accept the way he performs his healings on the Sabbath Day," they replied. Pilate then asked, "Do you mean that these men want to kill him for doing a kindness?" "That is indeed the case," they answered him.

And Pilate, growing indignant, left the Praetorium and announced to all who were assembled there, "As the sun is my witness, I do not find any guilt in this man." "We would never have handed him over to you if he were not a criminal," the Jews replied to the governor. At that point Pilate declared, "Take him to yourselves, therefore, and judge him as your law directs!" Now in order to bring to pass the word that was spoken by Jesus prefiguring the kind of death that he would suffer, the Jews responded, "It is unlawful for us to put a man to death." And Pilate asked them, "Did your God intend for that command to apply to you alone and not to me?"

JESUS BEFORE PILATE
(Matt 27:11-14; Mark 15:2-5; Luke 23:1-6;
John 18:33-38; GNc 3:2-9:1a)
Jerusalem

Then Pilate went back into the Praetorium and summoned Jesus. And when Jesus was standing before the governor, Pilate asked him in confidence, "Are you indeed the King of the Jews?" But Jesus asked him, "Are you asking because you were moved to ask, or did other people tell you that?" "Am I a Jew?" asked Pilate. "Your own people, and their chief priests, have placed you into my hands. Now what did you do to deserve this?" "It is that my kingdom is not of this world," Jesus answered. "You see, if mine were an earthly kingdom, my servants would fight to keep me from being handed over to the Jews. The source of my kingship lies not in this realm." "Then indeed you are a king!" Pilate declared. Jesus replied, "It is you, therefore, who are calling me king! This was why I was born and sent--that everyone who is of the truth might hear my voice." Then Pilate asked him, "What is truth?" Jesus said, "Truth comes from heaven." So Pilate asked him, "Is there not any truth on earth?" "You have seen for yourself," Jesus answered Pilate, "that those who speak the truth on earth are condemned by those in authority."

Then Pilate, leaving Jesus in the Praetorium, went out to the Jews and proclaimed, "I do not find any guilt in him." "This man said," the Jews rejoined, "'I am able to destroy this temple and to build it again in just three days.'" "Which temple?" Pilate asked them. "The one that took Solomon forty-six years to construct," the Jews answered. "He says that not only will he destroy it, but that in three days he will restore it!" Pilate then declared, "I am free of this righteous man's blood; you see to it yourselves!" "May the bloodguilt fall on us and our children as well!" answered the Jews.

And Pilate called the elders, the priests and the Levites over to himself and charged them privately, "Do not conduct yourselves this way. Your allegations involve healing and Sabbath breaking. None of the things you have accused him of warrants the death penalty." The elders, chief priests, and Levites replied, "Should a man be put to death for speaking blasphemy against Caesar?" "He does deserve to die for that," Pilate responded. "A man qualifies for the death penalty if he curses Caesar," the Jews answered Pilate, "but this man has blasphemed God Himself."

The chief priests and the elders started denouncing Jesus, but he never responded to any of it. Then Pilate asked him, "Do you not hear how many charges they are bringing against you?" But Jesus did not answer him, which astonished the governor to no end. The chief priests went on charging him with a whole range of offenses, so Pilate asked him once again, "Are you not going to defend yourself? Look at how many crimes they are charging you with!" But Jesus still did not respond, and Pilate was amazed.

Then the governor ordered the Jews to leave the Praetorium. And he called Jesus to himself and asked, "What am I to do with you?" "Even as it was given to you," answered Jesus. Then Pilate requested, "And just how was it given to me?" Jesus replied, "Moses and the prophets forespoke of both my death and my resurrection."

Now the Jews were trying to hear what they were saying, and as soon as they heard that, they asked Pilate, "What do you need to hear over and above that man's blasphemy?" And Pilate answered the Jews, "If this qualifies as blasphemy, then take him into your synagogue, charge him with it, and judge him as your law directs!" Then the Jews informed Pilate, "Our law stipulates that if one man should wrong another, he should receive thirty-nine lashes, but it calls for the stoning of anyone who blasphemes God." "Then take him," Pilate answered them, "and punish him as you see fit!" The Jews then said to Pilate, "We would like to see him crucified." "He does not deserve to be crucified," Pilate responded. Then the governor studied the great number of Jews who were standing there closely. And when he saw that many of them were shedding tears, he observed, "Not all of them wish to see him killed." But the Jewish elders then retorted, "Each of us has come in order to bring about his execution." Then Pilate asked the Jews, "Why ought he to be put to death?" "Because he claims to be the Son of God," the Jews replied, "and a king as well."

Nicodemus, who was there among the Jews, stood before the governor and pleaded, "Your Honor, I implore you, allow me to speak a few words." "You may speak," Pilate said. And Nicodemus explained, "I inquired of the elders, priests, Levites, and all who were in the synagogue, 'What are you planning to do with this man? He performs signs and wonders which are far too numerous to count, and which no one else has ever done or ever will do. Set him free, and do not long for evil to befall him. The signs that he presents will endure if indeed they come from God; but if not, they will never amount to anything. You see, when God sent Moses into Egypt, He ordered him to perform many signs before Pharaoh, King of Egypt. Now Pharaoh had these two magicians, Jannes and Jambres, who also pulled off numerous signs like those that Moses did, and the Egyptians were convinced that they were gods. But because the signs they showed did not really come from God, they perished along with those who believed in them, as you Pharisees and teachers of the law are well aware. Now set this man free, for he has done nothing that is worthy of death.'"

At that point the Jews replied, "You are a convert and a disciple of his." "Has the governor also converted, and become his disciple?" Nicodemus asked. "Did not Caesar himself appoint him to this high office?" And when the Jews heard this, they became enraged and started to grind their teeth against Nicodemus. Then Pilate asked them, "Why are you gnashing your teeth against him when you know that he is telling the truth?" The Jews then said to Nicodemus, "May you receive his inheritance along with his teaching." "Yes indeed," Nicodemus affirmed, "may it be to me as you have said."

Then one from among the Jews got up and asked if he might say something. "If you've got something to say," the governor responded, "then you may speak." And he testified, "I laid in agony on a mat for thirty-eight years, but then Jesus came healing many of the demon-possessed, as well as those crippled by various diseases. Now a few young men felt for me and carried me over to him on my stretcher. And when he saw me, this Jesus pitied me, and said to me, 'Pick up your bed and walk.' So I picked up my bed and started walking!" "Ask him the day on which he received his healing," the Jews bid Pilate. "It was on the Sabbath Day," admitted the man who had been healed. Then another of the Jews rose up and asked the governor if he might say a few things. And the governor replied, "Say what you will." This man therefore testified, "I lay in horrible pain over by the sheep pool in Jerusalem for thirty-eight years waiting to be healed. Now at a certain time, one of God's angels would come along and rouse the water, and that is when the remedy would come. The first one in, you see, would be the one to receive healing for whatever the affliction. And when Jesus saw me suffering there, he asked me, 'Would you like to be made whole?' 'Sir,' I replied, 'I've got no one to help me in at the stirring thereof.' 'Stand up!' he ordered me, 'Now pick up your bed and walk.' And I was immediately healed, so I picked up my bed and started walking." The Jews then asked Pilate, "Please, Governor, ask him the day on which he was healed." The man who had been ill said, "It was on the Sabbath." The Jews then said to Pilate, "Did we not say to you that he does his healing on the Sabbath Day? And it is by the Prince of Demons that he exorcises demons!" And another from the Jews stepped up and affirmed, "I was born blind. I could hear things just fine, but I could not see anything. One day, as Jesus was walking by, I heard this passing multitude, so I asked what it was all about, and

I was told that it was Jesus. So I screamed as loud as I could, 'Son of David, have mercy on me!' All of a sudden he stopped and had me brought before him. Then he asked me, 'What would you have me do for you?' And I answered him, 'I would like to have my sight.' And out of compassion for me he touched my eyes and said to me, 'Receive your sight!' and just like that I was able to see! Then I followed after him, rejoicing and giving thanks." Then another of the Jews stood up and declared, "I was hunched over, and with only a word he caused me to stand up straight!" "I had a skin disease," affirmed another, "and he cleansed me with just a word!" Then a woman named Veronica testified, "I was plagued for twelve years by a continual flow of blood. Then I touched the hem of his robe, and right away my bleeding stopped." At that point the Jews replied, "Our law does not admit the testimony of a woman."

And after many others had put forward their accounts, another one of the Jews added, "I saw when Jesus was invited to a wedding in Cana of Galilee. After the wine had run out, he ordered the servants to fill six jugs brimful with water, and so they did. Then he blessed them, changing the water into wine. Everybody drank of it, and this miracle amazed us all!" Then another from among the Jews stepped forward and declared, "I saw Jesus when he was teaching in the synagogue in Capernaum. Now in that place there was this demon-possessed man. 'Leave me alone!' the demon screamed. 'What have we to do with you, Jesus of Nazareth? I know that you're God's Holy One.' But Jesus reproved him, saying, 'Be silent, you filthy spirit, and leave this man at once!' And right away he left that man, not harming him at all." Then a Pharisee testified: "I saw an enormous crowd from all parts of Galilee gather together around Jesus; from Judea, the seaside, and the many regions around the Jordan. And even though so many sick came up to him, he healed each and every one of them. I heard the filthy spirits screaming, 'You are the Son of God!' but Jesus ordered them most emphatically, 'Don't you tell a soul!'"

And after this, another one, who was known as Centurio, testified, "I saw Jesus in Capernaum. 'Master,' I begged him, 'my servant back home is wracked with paralysis.' And Jesus said, 'Then I will go and heal him.' 'But Lord,' I said, 'I am not even worthy that you should enter my house. Just say the word and my servant will be restored.' 'Go on then,' he said to me, 'may it be to you as you believed.' And it was from that time that my servant was healed." Then a certain prominent man chimed in, "I had a son who was laying at death's door back in Capernaum. And when I heard that Jesus had come into Galilee, I went and begged him to come down to my house and restore my son, for he was at the point of death. He said to me, 'Your son is alive!' and it was from that very moment that my son was made well!"

And a host of others shouted, "Surely he's the Son of God and a prophet too, seeing how with his word alone he cures every manner of illness, and subjugates every demon." Then Pilate asked those who were claiming that the demons were under his authority, "Why, then, are your Teachers not also subject to him?" "We have no idea," they replied. But other people then affirmed, "Only God can give this kind of power." "Why then are your Teachers unable to control them?" Pilate asked the Jews. Some maintained, "The power to command demons comes from God alone," but others contended, "Jesus raised Lazarus from the dead after he had been entombed for four days!" Then the governor shuddered, and questioned the entire assembly of Jews, "Why are you so eager to shed innocent blood?"

Pilate then summoned Nicodemus and the twelve who held that Jesus was not born of fornication, and asked them, "What am I supposed to do? The people are divided." "We do not know," they answered him, "those who incite the crowds will see to it."

Then he went out to the Jews again and proclaimed to the chief priests and the assembled multitude, "I do not find any guilt in this man." But they grew all the more insistent, saying, "He's been teaching all over Judea, getting the people all worked up! He started out in Galilee and has continued to this very place!" But when Pilate heard these words from them, he asked if Jesus were a Galilean. And when he realized that Jesus fell under the jurisdiction of Herod, he forwarded Jesus to him, who at the time was also in Jerusalem.

HEROD TRIES JESUS
(Luke 23:8-12)
Jerusalem

Now Herod was very pleased to meet Jesus. He had heard quite a bit about him and had been longing to meet him for some time. He was eager to see him work some kind of wonder. And even though Herod interrogated him at length, Jesus never gave him any answer, and the chief priests stood there accusing him with all vehemence. Then Herod and his soldiers treated him shamefully. They mocked him, decked him out in beautiful finery and sent him back over to Pilate. And though Herod and Pilate had been enemies up to that time, that day marked the start of their friendship.

JESUS' TRIAL BEFORE THE PEOPLE
(Matt 27:15-26; Mark 15:6-15; Luke 23:13-25;
John 18:39-19:1-16a; GNc 9:1b-9:5; GPt 6-9, 1, 2;
GNaz 9-Quote by Jerome, Commentary on Matthew 4)
Jerusalem

Now it was the governor's practice at this feast to free any prisoner that the crowd desired. At the time there was this rather infamous inmate named Jesus Barabbas, the meaning of which is "the son of their teacher, who during the rebellion had committed murder and been locked away with the other insurgents." Then Pilate again rounded up the Jews: the chief priests, the rulers, and the people. And when the crowd had assembled there, they approached Pilate and asked him to do what he would customarily do for them. "You brought this man before me," Pilate declared, "as someone who corrupts the nation. Now behold, I have tried him here before you all and have found him to be not guilty of the charges you have brought against him, as has Herod. Just look, he has even sent him back to us. Nothing that this man has done qualifies him for the penalty of death. Now it is your custom that I should release to you a prisoner at Passover, the Feast of Unleavened Bread. I have this inmate named Barabbas who has been condemned for murder, and this King of the Jews, Jesus, who is standing here before you all, and in whom I have found no guilt. I will punish him and set him free." (He was now under obligation to release one man among them during the feast.) "So which one would you like to have let loose among you?" Pilate asked, "Would you rather have me free Jesus Barabbas, or Jesus who is known as the Messiah, the King of the Jews?" (He knew full well, you see, that it was out of jealousy that the chief priests had turned Jesus over to him. And as Pilate sat at his bar, his wife sent him this word: "Do not get mixed up with this honorable man because I have agonized much today over a dream I had about him.") But the chief priests and the elders worked the crowd into a frenzy, and convinced them to have Jesus put to death, and to have Barabbas released in his stead. And they all cried out as one, "Not him; take this man away from us! Set Barabbas free instead; give us this man in his place." (It was in that very city, you see, that Barabbas had taken part in an uprising and had been imprisoned for rebellion and murder.)

And out of his desire to free Jesus, Governor Pilate once again pleaded with them, asking, "Which of the two should I release to you?" "Barabbas!" they answered him. "What then," asked Pilate, "would you have me do with Jesus the Christ--the one you call the King of the Jews?" "Crucify him!" the crowd responded with a shout. And they kept on screaming, "Crucify him! Crucify him!"

Pilate appealed to them yet a third time, asking, "Why should I? What is his crime? I have found no basis whatsoever for putting him to death, so I will see to it that he is beaten and then have him released." But they just screamed the louder, "Crucify him!"

Then Pilate took Jesus and ordered him beaten. The soldiers twisted a crown of thorns, then they put it on his head and dressed him in a purple robe. They approached him repeatedly and mocked, "Hail to you, oh King of the Jews!" Then they slapped him in the face.

Pilate then went out to them again and said, "Look, I am bringing him back to let you know that I have found no guilt in him." Then Jesus came out wearing the crown of thorns and the purple robe. "Just look at this man!" Pilate bid them. When the chief priests and the officials saw him, they shouted, "Crucify him! Crucify him!" And Pilate said to them, "You take and crucify him, for I have found no guilt in him!" "We have a law," the Jews replied, "and according to that law he should be put to death for calling himself the Son of God." When Pilate heard them saying this, he grew even more disturbed. And he went back into the Praetorium and questioned Jesus, "Where did you come from?" but Jesus did not answer him. "So you're not going to answer me," Pilate said to him. "Do you not realize that I have both the authority to free you, as well as to have you crucified?" "You would never have had such power," said Jesus, "had it not been given to you from above, so the one who handed me over to you is committing the more serious offense." Now Pilate was all the more anxious to let him go after he heard him say this, but the Jews kept on clamoring, "If you free this man, you cannot be Caesar's friend, because he has made himself out to be the Son of God, and a King as well. Would you have him take Caesar's place as king? Anyone who declares himself king does so in opposition to Caesar!" And when Pilate heard this, he brought Jesus out and sat on the judgment seat at a spot known as "the pavement," but in Aramaic it is called "Gabbatha." This took place at about the sixth hour on the day of Preparation, during the week of Passover. And Pilate said to the Jews, "Behold your king!" But they just roared, "Away with him! Take him away and crucify him!" "Is it my role to crucify your king?" asked Pilate. The chief priests responded, "We recognize no king but Caesar!"

Now the Jews had Pilate really upset. "Yours has always been a seditious people," he retorted, "forever in opposition to those who wish to do you good!" "And who might they be?" the Jews demanded. "The way I heard it," Pilate answered, "your God rescued you from unbearable slavery under the Egyptians, and guided you across the Red Sea as if by dry land. He supplied you with manna and quails in the desert, quenched your thirst with water from a rock, and entrusted you with His own law. Yet in spite of all this, you infuriated your God. A molten calf was all you wanted, and this so enraged your God that He would have wiped you out completely had Moses not intervened on your behalf. And even though you were spared, you have the nerve to implicate me as one who despises the emperor!" He then got up from his judgment seat and started to leave. And the Jews all shouted, "We recognize only Caesar, not Jesus. Magi from the east brought him gifts that were fit for a king, and when Herod heard the Magi say that a king had been born, he tried to have him put to death. But as soon as his father Joseph learned of it, he took him and his mother and fled into Egypt. When Herod found out about this, he had all of the Hebrew infants of Bethlehem killed."

When Pilate heard these words from them, his blood ran cold, and he had the boisterous crowd pipe down. Then he asked them, "Do you mean that this is the one that Herod sought?" "Indeed he is," the Jews replied. "The very same."

And they stubbornly persisted with deafening shouts that Jesus be crucified, and their shouts prevailed. When Pilate sensed that he was getting nowhere with this, but was only stirring up a greater commotion, he took water in the sight of all, washed his hands before the sun and said, "I am free of this man's blood. You will have to bear the blame." And everyone responded, "Let his blood fall on us and our children as well!" But none of the Jews there washed their hands, and neither did Herod or any of his magistrates. Then Pilate got up, since none of them would wash. And King Herod commanded that the Lord be taken away, saying, "Do as I've instructed you!" And Pilate, wishing to pacify the multitudes, ordered that the people's will be carried out. Pilate set Barabbas, the man who had been imprisoned for rebellion and murder, free among them, for he was their chosen one.

Pilate then gave the command, and the curtain across from his judgment seat was pulled back. Then he said, "Jesus, your own people have convicted you for being their king. I have ordered that you be beaten as the law of the righteous emperors directs, and hung upon a cross in the very garden where you were taken. And the two evildoers, Gestas and Dysmas are to be crucified alongside you."

Now Joseph, a mutual friend to both Pilate and Jesus, was standing there. And when he realized that they were about to crucify him, Joseph approached Pilate and requested the Lord's body, so that he might bury it himself. Then Pilate sent a message to Herod, requesting his remains. "Pilate, my good friend," Herod answered, "we would have buried him whether or not anyone had asked, seeing that the Sabbath Day is almost here. You see, it stands written in the Law, 'The sun must not be allowed to set on anyone who has been put to death.'" And Herod handed him over to the crowds on the eve of the Feast of Unleavened Bread.

So they grabbed the Lord, shoving him as they drove him on, saying, "Let us drag God's Son along now that he is subject to us." They placed a purple robe on him and set him on the judgment seat. "Judge fairly, oh King of Israel!" they sneered. Then one of them brought a crown of thorns and placed it on the head of the Lord. Now some of those who were standing there spat into his eyes, while others slapped him in the face, and still others poked him with a stick. Some pounded him and jeered, "Let us pay respect to the Son of God!"

But Pilate (had) ordered that Jesus be beaten, so the governor's soldiers seized the Lord Jesus, led him away and ushered him into the palace, which is called the Praetorium, where the entire company of soldiers marshaled around him. They stripped his clothing off of him, placed a bright red (and) a purple robe on him. Then they twisted thorns into a crown and placed it upon his head. And after putting a staff into his right hand, they dropped to their knees before him and taunted him. Over and again they approached him in pretended worship and gibed, "Oh, King of the Jews, how we glorify you!" Time and again they took that staff and beat him over the head with it, spitting all over him, and dropping to their knees in feigned worship to him. Then at last Pilate turned him over to them to be crucified.

THE CRUCIFIXION OF JESUS
(Matt 27:31-45; Mark 15:20-33; Luke 23:26-44;
John 19:17-24; GNc 10:1-11:1a; GPt 4-5a; AnaPlt 7a)
Golgotha (Gethsemane), Outside Jerusalem

Now after they had finished mocking him, they took the purple robe away from him and put his clothing back on him. Jesus then left the Praetorium, along with the two lawbreakers. Then Jesus was handed over to the soldiers, who conducted him out (and) led him away to be crucified.

He pushed on toward the Skull Place, which in Aramaic is called Golgotha, carrying his own cross. And as they were heading out, (the soldiers) leading him along the way, they ran into Simon of Cyrene, father to Rufus and Alexander, who was on his way in from the countryside. They laid the cross upon his back and forced him to carry it behind Jesus. A great crowd followed after him, and some women were weeping and wailing over him. And Jesus turned and said to them, "Do not weep on my account, oh Daughters of Jerusalem, but for yourselves and for your children! You see, the time is approaching when you will say, 'How blessed are the barren women; the wombs that never bore and the breasts that never nursed!' Then they will beg the mountains, 'Collapse on us!' and the hills, 'Shelter us!' For if men act this way while the tree is still green, what will they do after it has withered?"

And they brought Jesus to a spot known as Golgotha, which means the Place of the Skull. And these two lawbreakers were also being taken out to be put to death with him. Then (and) there they gave him wine blended with myrrh (and) gall to drink, and after he had tasted it, he refused to drink of it. They undressed him, wrapped him in a linen cloth, and placed a crown of thorns upon his head. Then they brought (the) two criminals and crucified the Lord Jesus along with [the] others; one to either side of him. But he held his peace and hid his pain. "Forgive them, Father," said Jesus, "for they do not know what they are doing."

Now it was about the third hour when they crucified him, and they seated themselves there and kept watch over him. Now after Pilate had passed sentence against him and the cross had been raised up, he had a proclamation of the crime he was charged with readied and affixed above his head upon the cross stating, as the Jews themselves had laid to his charge, that he was the King of the Jews. The judgment they wrote against him as his title on the notice read: THIS IS JESUS OF NAZARETH, KING OF THE JEWS, KING OF ISRAEL. And many there from among the Jews read this sign. (The place where Jesus was crucified was near to the city, you see, and the notice was written in Aramaic, Latin and Greek.) "Do not write, 'The King of the Jews,'" the chief priests objected to Pilate. "Instead write, 'This man claimed to be the king of the Jews.'" "I have written what I have written," Pilate replied.

Two robbers were also being crucified along with Jesus--one to his right, and another to his left--fulfilling the Scripture that says, "He was reckoned among the lawbreakers." Passers-by fired put-downs at him, shaking their heads at him and heckling, "Oh! You who are to destroy the temple and build it again in just three days. If you are the Son of God, then deliver yourself--come down from the cross!" As the people stood around and gawked, the leaders--the chief priests, the scribes, and the elders--derided him among themselves in like fashion, ridiculing him relentlessly. "This man has delivered others," they taunted, "but he cannot even save himself. Let this man rescue himself if he is the Elect One, the Anointed of God. He is Israel's King! This Messiah, this King of Israel, ought to prove to us that he can come down from the cross right now, for then we would believe in him. He trusts in God, so if God likes him so well, then let God deliver him now. He did boast, 'I am God's Son,' you know." The soldiers also went up to Jesus and mocked him. They presented him with sour wine and scoffed, "If you really are the Jewish King, then why not just deliver yourself." (Over him a written proclamation read: THIS IS THE KING OF THE JEWS.) Even the robbers being crucified there alongside him showered him with abuse.

Now after the soldiers had put Jesus on the cross, they piled his garments up before him, and then they all laid claim to his clothes. They divided them into four portions among themselves, one for each, and cast lots to see who would get what. Only his undershirt remained, but from top to bottom it was seamless and of a single woven fabric. So instead of ripping it apart, the soldiers agreed, "Let the lot decide who gets to keep it." This took place in order to fulfill the word (of) Scripture as spoken through the prophet, "My clothing they split among themselves and for my garments they cast their lots."

At that point one of the criminals started reproaching them, "It is for our own evil deeds that we are suffering, but what crime has this man, who has become Savior to us all, committed against you?" And he so infuriated them that they ordered that his legs not be broken, so that he might die in agony. These were the things that the soldiers did.

Even so, one of the crucified outlaws who was hanging there kept raining insults down on him, "Are you not supposed to be the Messiah? Deliver yourself and us as well!" But Dysmas, the other thief, reproved him, saying, "Do you have no fear of God, seeing as [we] are both suffering the same penalty? We are suffering justly, for ours is an appropriate sentence, seeing that our punishment is in line with our crimes. But this man has not sinned at all." "Jesus," he pleaded, "When you come in your kingdom and the fullness of your splendor, please remember me!" "Truly and most assuredly I say to you," Jesus answered him, "you will this very day see me in paradise!"

By now it was about the sixth hour, and from the sixth hour to the ninth, darkness fell over the land of Judea, (and indeed) the entire world, for the sun went dark and the stars appeared, but they had no glint in them, and the light of the moon gave out, as though it had been turned to blood. And all of them grew anxious and fearful, lest the sun had gone down already, knowing that he was still alive, for against them it stands written, "The sun had better not set on the one who has been put to death."

JOHN'S VISION OF THE CROSS OF LIGHT
(AcJn 97-102)
Mount of Olives

Now after the dance, dear ones, and the departure of the Lord, we apostles were all like men gone astray, and we fled in all directions. But even I, (John,) as I was watching him suffer, did not stay to witness his passion. Instead I ran to the Mount of Olives, weeping over what had happened. Now that Friday at about the sixth hour, after he had been hung upon the cross, darkness overtook the earth. Just then my Lord stood in the heart of the cave, filling the entire place with light. Then my Lord expressed to me, "John, as far as those who are down in Jerusalem are concerned, I am being crucified. They are lancing me with spears and sticks, and giving me gall and vinegar to drink. Even so, I am right here speaking with you, so listen close to what I say. I was the one who put it into your head to climb up this mountain, so that you might hear some teachings that a student can only receive from his master, and which a man can only learn from his God."

After saying this, he revealed to me a cross of light which had been set up. Now there was an enormous crowd around this cross which was not of a single stamp; but within this cross there was both a unified form and a singular likeness. And I saw the Lord above this cross, shapeless and consisting of nothing but a voice. Now this voice was not like the one we were used to hearing, but heavenly, captivating and kindhearted. "John," the voice conveyed to me, "it is essential that someone hear these things from me, because I am in need of someone who will hear. It is for your benefit that I sometimes call this shining cross the Word. Now at other times I refer to it as Mind, or Jesus, or Christ, or the Door, or the Way, or the Bread, or the Seed, or the Resurrection, or the Son, or the Father, or the Spirit, or Life, or Truth, or Faith--and there are times when I call it Grace. It is, in fact, for the sake of mankind that I couch it in such terms. Now as it is understood in itself and as it is spoken to us, it is truly the demarcation of all things, the raising up of, and the basis for those things which have been set in place, but have hitherto remained unsettled; namely the harmony in the wisdom and the wisdom in the harmony. But to the right and to the left there exist powers, principalities, authorities, demons, implementations, intimidations, fury, devils, Satan and the secondary basis, from which proceed the essence of ephemeral things.

"So you see, this is the cross which through the Word has brought all things together, severing off the transitory and lower things, and consolidating all things into one. But this is not the wooden cross, which you are going to see when you go down there, and neither am I the one thereon, who you do not see now, but whose utterance you now hear. I was taken to be something that I am not, for I never revealed my true self to those many others. They will think of me as something else instead; something that is base and utterly beneath me. As a result, even as the place of rest is neither perceived nor even discussed, I, the Lord over this place will be perceived and discussed all that much less.

"Now the people you see crowded around the cross, which represents the baser essence, are not of a singular form, and the ones that you see within the cross do not maintain a unified aspect. This is because not every member of the one who has descended has been assembled together with them. But after human nature has been lifted up, when the kind who obey my voice approach me, then whoever is able to hear me will unite with it. It is to remain above them, and will no longer appear as it does now. No, it will be elevated above them, even as I am right now. You see, I will never be as I once was as long as you do not speak of yourself as belonging to me. But if you should hear the things I have to say and take these words of mine to heart, then you will become as I am now. But once I have taken you to myself, you will become as I once was, for herein lies your source. Therefore pay no mind to the multitudes, but steer clear of them instead, for they are far removed from the mystery! Recognize that I exist entirely within the Father, and that the Father exists within me.

"Accordingly, I never did suffer the things that these people will claim that I suffered. You know that suffering that I showed you and the others in that dance, well I want it to be spoken of as a mystery. For you see, what I have shown you is in fact yourself as you truly are. Even so, only I know myself as I truly am, and these other ones do not. Do therefore allow me to hold on to what is mine. And it is through me that you must perceive what belongs to you. As I have said to you already, it is impossible to see me as I truly am unless you can see me as one who is akin to me.

"You have heard of my suffering, but that I was not the one who suffered; that I felt no pain, yet my agony was real; that I was pierced, yet I was not injured; hanged, and yet I was not hanged; that my blood poured out, yet it did not flow and, in brief, in no way did I suffer the things that they will claim that I suffered. Not at all. Even so, I have endured things that they never mention. But even now I will reveal to you the true nature of my sufferings, since I know that you will understand. Recognize me as the Word--and that the Word was what was put to death; that the Word was pierced, that the Word dripped blood, that the Word was maimed, the Word was hung, the Word was what endured the passion, the Word was nailed, and that the Word was what died. This is how I have expressed it, making a place for the man. Your reasoning, therefore, ought to begin with the Word. Then you will come to perceive the Lord, and in the third place, the man, and the sufferings that he has endured."

After he finished telling me all of these things, as well as others that I could not express to you as he would have me, he was raised up, and no one in that crowd there noticed it. But later on, after I had gone back down, I laughed them all to scorn, because he had revealed to me beforehand all that they were saying about him. Nevertheless, I held this one thing very firmly in my mind: that the Lord put every single detail into symbolic language, as a gift to be given to mankind, that their hearts might be transformed thereby and thus receive deliverance.

THE OVERTHROW OF HADES
(Dec 2:1, 4:1-5:1; DecLtA 2:1-5:3a; DecLtB 2:1-6:2)
The Underworld

Oh Lord Jesus Christ, life and resurrection of the world, and the Son of the Living God, give us grace to speak of your resurrection, of the miraculous deeds that you have performed in Hades, and of the wonders that you have worked in the underworld. Grant us leave to utter mysteries through your death upon the cross, for you have adjured us all and strictly forbidden your servants to reveal to any man the secrets of your divine majesty which you have wrought in Hades.

Now after being placed alongside our fathers in the abyss, the shadow of death, that deep darkness wherein lie all who have died since the creation of the world, something like the sun shone suddenly upon us and illumined us all. And how great was that light--the golden radiance of the sun and the hue of royal purple. And we could see each other in that midnight hour.

And the father of the whole human race rejoiced together with Abraham, the patriarchs and the prophets. And they all cried out to one another, "This light is shining from a great illumination! This light can be none other than the author of everlasting life, who has promised to give us the light of eternity." Then Isaiah, one of those who was standing there, cried aloud, "Father Adam and all of those who are gathered around, listen to the words I speak. In the days that I walked the earth, I prophesied the coming of this light by the teaching of the Holy Spirit through whom I sang,

> 'Land of Zebulun and Napthali beyond the Jordan,
> Galilee of the Gentiles,
> The people sitting in the midst of darkness
> Have seen a great light;
> And among those who dwell
> Beneath the shadow of death,
> A shining light has broken forth.'

Now it has finally come and illumined us who sit in death." And when they heard his words, they turned his way. "Who are you?" father Adam asked him, "For you have spoken the truth." "I am Isaiah," he replied.

And even as we were celebrating in the light that had dawned in our midst, our father Simeon came to us rejoicing and saying, "Give glory to the Lord Jesus Christ, the Son of God; for when he was an infant in the temple, I took him into my arms. And the Holy Spirit prompted me to declare, 'Now my eyes have seen Your salvation. You have laid it out before us all--a light of revelation to the Gentiles, and for the glorification of your people Israel.'" And after hearing this, the host of saints rejoiced the more, even as Hades and the gates of death all trembled.

Then we heard the rumbling voice of the Son of the Most High Father as he thundered, "Oh Princes, raise the portal; hoist the everlasting gates, and the King of Glory, Christ the Lord will come up and enter therein." And behold, Satan, the luminary of death, rose up even as the saints exulted, fled in terror to his officials and infernal authorities and said, "My officers and nether powers, hurry up and shut the gates! Secure them now with iron bars! Resist them all and bravely fight, lest they should capture us and keep us bound in chains." Then all of his unholy minions were disturbed, and went off with all diligence to shut the gates and to carefully fasten all the locks and iron bars; and they brandished their weapons as they howled in a most frightful and gruesome voice.

Then Satan, the Prince and Heir of Darkness, and Ringleader of Death, approached Hades and gloated, "Most insatiable devourer, hearken to my speech. Brace yourself to receive the one that I am bringing down to you. For there is this one from among the Jewish race named Jesus who calls himself the Son of God." And to this voice Hades replied, "That voice that cried out indeed belonged to none other than the Son of the Most High Father. The entire earth, you see, even down to the regions below, shook so hard at the sound of it that I think that now both myself and my dungeons lie exposed." And Satan, that Leader of Death replied, "What has gotten you so teary-eyed? My most ancient and vile friend, have no fear; I have turned the whole race of Jews against him! They struck him with blows to the face just as I commanded them. I even managed to turn one of his own disciples against him! He's the same as any man; so afraid to die. Just look, it was out of fear that he cried aloud, 'My soul is almost dead from sorrow.' And I was the one who brought him down. For he is nothing but a man, and he has just now been lifted up and hung upon a cross, so get ready to secure him here. He caused me a great deal of trouble when he walked up there among the living. He has wronged me and taken his stand against me at every turn. He has cast out as many of my servants as he has come across. He has cured all whom I had disabled through his word alone-- the blind, the lame, the leprous, and the like. He has even reclaimed the dead that I have delivered over to you."

"Is he really so powerful," Hades challenged Prince Satan, "that he does all this with his word alone? If he fears death so much, then who must he be to have such authority? Will you indeed be able to hold your own against him, if he has this kind of clout? Look, through your might you have brought down and subjected great people to my rule. So if you have this kind of authority, and he manages to frustrate your command, what kind of power must lie behind this man Jesus who is so 'afraid of death'? I am telling you the truth, if he shows this kind of ability as a human being, then he must truly be all-powerful and divine. None can stand against such strength! And if it is, as you allege, that he said he feared death, he only said it to deride and to ridicule you, with an eye toward seizing you with the hand of strength. And woe, woe to you forevermore."

"Oh Hades, most insatiable devourer," answered Satan, Prince of Tartarus, "tell me why you have such doubts? Why are you so afraid to receive Jesus, our mutual nemesis? I am not afraid of him. I have tempted him, stirred up the religious fervor and righteous indignation of my ancient people, the Jews, against him, sharpened a spear to pierce him with, mixed gall and vinegar for him to drink, readied a tree to crucify him on, and gathered thorns to prick him with. Soon he will be dead and I will be able to bring him here to you, subject both to you and me! Therefore when he does get here, be prepared to hold him fast."

"Oh Heir of Darkness," Hades retorted, "Son of Damnation and devil, you have just now told me that through his word alone he has brought many back to life whom you had readied for burial. You have informed me that he has himself drawn the dead from me. I have held a great many here who managed to take the dead from me when they lived upon the earth. It was not through their own power that they did this, but through their prayers to God, and it was their Almighty God Who drew them from me. Who then is this Jesus, who takes the dead from me without such prayers? If, then, he has released other people from the grave, by what means or strength are we to detain him here? A short time ago I swallowed up this dead man named Lazarus, and not long thereafter he was forcibly removed from my entrails by the word of one from among the living, and I think it was the one of whom you speak." Then Satan, the Prince of Death said, "It was Jesus all right." And after hearing this, Hades remarked, "If it is that same one who by order of his word alone caused Lazarus to fly like an eagle from my bosom after four days of death, then he is not a man from the human race, but God in all His majesty. Were we to let this man in here, then I fear that we could lose everyone else as well. Just look, I can sense the unrest of all whom I have devoured since the world was made. Oh, how my belly aches! The taking of Lazarus from me seems to me an ill omen, for he was not taken from me like an ordinary dead man. No, the earth cast him forth as swift as an eagle. Now Satan, Master of all Evils, I implore you, by your strength as well as mine, do not bring him here to me! For I fear that even as we are expecting to capture him, he will take us captive instead. Just look, if all it took was his voice alone to destroy every bit of my power, what do you suppose that he will do when he shows up here in person? For as soon as I heard the word of his command I shook with horror and dread, and all who serve me were likewise mortified. So I am now quite sure that any man who could do all this must indeed be God Himself, powerful in dominion, mighty in humanity, and Savior to all mankind. Behold, I fear that his entire purpose for coming down here is to raise the dead. And I am telling you, by the darkness that surrounds us all, if you should bring him here to me, he will free all those who are locked away in the cruelty of prison, shackled by the unbreakable chains of their sins. He will bring them into the eternal life of his divinity, and not so much as one from the dead will be left for me!" "Do not be such a coward!" Satan retorted. "You had better ready yourself, because he is hanging on the cross already and there is nothing else that I can do." "If there is nothing you can do," Hades replied, "then recognize that your destruction is at hand. Now I will no doubt remain cast down and in disgrace, but you will be placed to suffer torments in my embrace."

And all of a sudden, even as Satan and Hades were arguing it all out, a voice thundered and spirits cried forth, "Raise your gates, you rulers, and be lifted up, you everlasting gates; the King of Glory is on his way!" Now when Hades heard this, he cast Satan out of his kingdom, saying to him: "Go and fight him if you can! Go on then, get out of my house! If you are such a mighty warrior, then go and battle against the King of Glory," Satan therefore left his presence. Then Hades ordered his most wicked and demonic servants, "Shore up the cruel gates of brass, and firmly fasten the iron bars. Tighten and secure them all, and hold fast my bolts. Stand tall and keep your eyes open for anything. Take courage and resist, that we who hold captivity might not ourselves be taken captive, for if he should get in here, calamities will befall us all."

Now the saints could hear the conflict between Satan and Hades, for they did possess knowledge, though they did not yet recognize one another. "Ruler of

Death," our holy father Adam answered Satan, "tell me why you shake with fright? Behold, the Lord is coming to demolish all that you have contrived. He will lay hold of you and bind you up forevermore." And when the saints heard the voice of our father Adam, and the boldness with which he had answered Satan, they were strengthened in their joy, and they all came running up to father Adam and crowded around him. Then our father Adam stared out over the great multitude and wondered in astonishment if all in the world were a descendant of his.

JOHN THE BAPTIST
(Dec 2:2; DecLtA 2:3; DecLtB 5:2)
The Underworld

After this another man, an anchorite from the wilderness, stepped into their midst. "And who might you be who clothe yourself in such raiment?" the patriarchs asked him. "I am John," he replied, "the last of the prophets. I made straight the ways of God's Son, and ventured out ahead of that very Lord to clear the rugged and barren places into tidy paths. Mine was the finger that pointed him out to the people of Jerusalem, revealing that he was the Lamb of the Lord and the Son of God. I am the voice of the Most High, the prophet. I am going out before his face to prepare his ways before he comes, to deliver the knowledge of salvation to his people, that their sins might be forgiven them.

"And when I saw him drawing near, the Holy Spirit prompted me to say, 'Behold, it is the Lamb of God, who takes the sins of the world away!' I baptized him in the Jordan river with my own hand, and I saw the Holy Spirit alighting upon him as a dove. Then I heard a voice from the sky, 'This is truly the Son of My love, the one in whom I take delight.' And he let me know that he would go down into the nether realms. And now I have indeed come down to this place, and gone before him to let you know that the risen Son of God is about to arrive from on high to visit us who sit in darkness, underneath the shadow of death. He has sent me here to say to you that the only begotten Son of God is coming down; to advise you that all who put their faith in him will be saved, and to caution you that all who refuse to believe will be condemned. So now I'm here to let you know: as soon as you see him, worship him, for this will be your only chance for repentance, because in the vain world above, you sinned through all your idol worshipping, and it will not be possible for you to repent at any other time."

ADAM AND SETH
(Dec 3:1; DecLtA 3:1; DecLtB 4:2b-3)
The Underworld

And when Father Adam heard these words, he cried out in a loud voice, "Hallelujah!" which is to say, "Truly the Lord is coming." And hearing that Jesus had been baptized in the River Jordan, Father Adam, the first man formed, embraced those who were standing around him. And through his bitter tears he sobbed to his son Seth, "Let your sons the patriarchs and prophets know all that you heard from Michael the archangel; with regard to what took place when I was ill and sent you to the gates of paradise to beseech God to send His angel to give you oil from the Tree of Mercy with which to anoint my body." Then Seth, going before the righteous patriarchs and prophets proclaimed, "Patriarchs and prophets, hearken to my speech. When my father Adam, the first man formed, grew terminally ill, he sent me out to the gate of paradise to pray to God, hoping that He would send an angel out to lead me to the Tree of Mercy, that I might take some of the oil therefrom and anoint him therewith, so that he might recover thereby. So I prayed to the Lord, and in tears did I call upon the Guardian of Paradise to give me some. Then Michael the archangel came out and questioned me, 'Seth, why are you weeping? Tell me, then, what you are seeking? For the Lord has sent me here to you, seeing that I have been set over the human race. Is it because your father is ill and you want some of that oil that raises up the sick, or else access to the tree that produces it? It is impossible for you to receive it just yet. But Seth, let me tell you, do not toil through tearful prayer and supplication for the oil of that Tree of Mercy with which to anoint the body of your father, which is stricken by such pain. Realize in advance that the body of your father Adam will not at this time be given this oil of mercy, but only after the passing of many ages. You see, you will only be able to receive it in the final days and times, after the fulfillment of the five thousand five hundred years. For the dearly beloved Son of God will come down out of heaven and enter this world, that he might raise up not only the body of Adam, but indeed those of all the departed. And when he comes, he will be baptized by John in the River Jordan. Then, when he rises up and out of the water, he will anoint the bodies of all who believe in him with the oil of his mercy. That oil of mercy will be for those who are to be delivered unto eternal life, those who are born of water and Divine Inspiration. And when he goes down into the heart of the earth, Jesus Christ, the beloved Son of God, will then rise up, carry our father Adam into paradise, and deliver him at last to that Tree of Mercy. And he will purify himself and his children with water and the Holy Spirit. Then he will be free of every disease, and then will begin the eternal reign of those who have trusted in him. But none of this can happen yet, so go back and say to your father, 'Five thousand and five hundred years from the time that the world was brought into being, God's only begotten Son is going to come down to this realm and take on a human form, and he will be the one to anoint him with the oil of His mercy.'"

And when Seth was heard to say these things, the patriarchs, the prophets and all of the assembled saints, filled with joy and exultation, started to mock and reprove Hades, chiding, "Oh, Hades, who devours all things but is never filled, open wide your gates that the King of Glory might come inside."

DAVID
(Dec 5:2; DecLtA 5:2a; DecLtB 6:1a)
The Underworld

Then another came forward who was set apart by a regal appearance. His name was David, and he cried out, "You who are blind, do you not know that when I lived in the world above, I was the one who spoke that word, 'Lift up your gates, you rulers?' I made known the mercy of God even as I walked the earth, foretelling of the future joy, and also of his coming, saying, 'Let them throughout all the ages, confess to the Lord of his tender mercies and wonderful works on behalf of the sons of men, for he has shattered the gates of brass, destroyed the bars of iron, and raised them from their wicked ways.'"

JEREMIAH
(DecLtB 6:1b)
The Underworld

Then each of the righteous forefathers started to recognize one another and to recite their respective prophecies. The holy Jeremiah, going over what he had said, then addressed the other patriarchs and prophets, saying, "When I lived in the world above, I forespoke of the Son of God, of his coming to this earth, and of the way that he would speak to men."

ISAIAH
(DecLtA 5:2b; DecLtB 5:1)
The Underworld

Following him, Isaiah likewise said to them, "When I lived upon the earth, I spoke of this through the Divine Inspiration, for did I not say to you, 'The dead will arise, and all who are entombed will again rise up; and the peoples of the earth, (and) those beneath will rejoice as one, for the dew of the Lord will heal them all'? And again I said, 'Oh Death, where is your sting? Oh Hades, where is your victory?'"

THE SAINTS
(DecLtA 5:3a; DecLtB 6:2)
The Underworld

And when the saints heard what Isaiah had said, they all started prodding Hades, "Open up your gates, for now you are vanquished. From now on, you are to be weak and defenseless." Then all of the saints, basking in the light of the Lord before the eyes of our father Adam, responding to all that the patriarchs and prophets had said, cried out, "Hallelujah! Blessings on the one who comes bearing the Lord's name." Now their shouts started Satan trembling and seeking some means of escape, but because Hades and his minions had him all bound up and kept in the underworld--surrounded and guarded on every side--all his efforts were for naught. "What has got you shaking?" they taunted. "We are not about to let you out. Take what you've got coming to you from the one you attacked each and every day. And of this you can be sure: he will bind you up and deliver you into my hands."

JESUS SURRENDERS HIS SPIRIT
(Matt 27:46-50; Mark 15:34-37; Luke 23:45b-46;
John 19:25-30; John 19:26-30-in Codex
Evangelii Johannei Templariorum;
GPt 5:2-5; GNc 11:1a)
Jerusalem

And right about the ninth hour Jesus shouted with a thundering voice, "Eloi, Eloi, lama sabachthani!"--which means "My God, my God, why have you forsaken me?" Now when some of those who were standing nearby heard this, they said, "Listen up, he is calling Elijah!" And one of them said, "Give him gall and vinegar to drink." And right away one of the men raced to get a sponge. Then, after stirring up the mixture, he saturated the sponge with sour wine, poked a stick through it, and gave it to Jesus to drink. But he (and some) others said, "Leave this man alone for now. Let us see if Elijah comes to take him down (and) rescue him."

Now Jesus' mother was standing by the cross, as was his mother's sister Mary, the wife of Cleophas, and also Mary Magdalene. And when Jesus saw his mother there, and his beloved disciple close at hand, he said to her, "Precious woman, do not weep, for I am on my way back to my Father, where there is eternal life. Your son is right here! He is going to take my place." And to the disciple he said, "Here is your mother!" And this follower took her into his home from that time forward.

After that, knowing that all was now fulfilled so as to satisfy the Scripture, Jesus said, "I am thirsty." A jug of vinegared wine was sitting there, so they steeped a sponge in it, attached it to the stalk of a hyssop plant, and raised it up to Jesus' lips, bringing all things to a close, and piling their sins upon their heads. And many, thinking it nighttime, went around carrying lanterns, and they lay down. And after he had taken a drink, Jesus cried with a deafening shout, "My Power! My Power! You have forsaken me! It is finished now!" And when Jesus had again cried in a loud voice, "Father, baddach ephkid rouel" which translates as, "Father, I place my spirit into your hands!" he breathed his last, lowered his head, surrendered his spirit and was taken up.

SIGNS ACCOMPANYING JESUS' DEATH
(Matt 27:51-56; Mark 15:38-41; Luke 23:45b, 47-49; John 19:31-37;
GNc 11:1b; GPt 5:6; GNaz 10, Quote by Jerome, Epistle to Hedibia 120.8,
GNaz 10, Quote by Jerome, On Matthew 4, Regarding Matthew 27:51,
AnaPlt 7b; Dec 5:3a; DecLtA 5:3b; DecLtB 7:1)
Golgotha (Gethsemane), Jerusalem

The Super Gospel

And just then the curtain of the temple ripped in two from top to bottom. The ground then shook and the temple's enormous lintel fractured and collapsed, shattering into pieces. And the entire earth was swallowed up by the underworld, such that the very sanctuary of the temple, as they refer to it, could not be seen by the Jews as they fell. The rocks cracked open and they saw an abyss in the earth below; and they heard the rumbling of thunders that came upon it.

And once again, the voice of the Son of the Most High Father came thundering (in Hades,) "Oh you Princes, hoist your gates, and you everlasting gates, be lifted up; the King of Glory is coming in." And seeing that the voice had twice cried out, Satan and Hades then inquired, "Who is this King of Glory?" just as if they did not know. And the voice of the Lord answered them, "It is the great and powerful Lord, the Lord who is almighty in battle." "I recognize those words that were shouted," David answered Hades, "for I spoke those same words through his Spirit. And now I will say to you as I said before, 'It is the strong and mighty Lord, the Lord who is great in battle, indeed he is the King of Glory.'"

And during that horrific event, the bodies of many of the righteous who had died already were seen raised back up to life. They came out of their graves and, following the resurrection of Jesus, entered into the Holy City and appeared to many of its citizens, as the Jews have themselves admitted. They reported that they had seen Abraham, Isaac, and Jacob; the Twelve Patriarchs, Moses, and even Job, who they say died some thirty-five hundred years before. I, (Pilate,) saw great numbers appearing bodily, and they were grieving for the Jews, both for the great iniquity that had happened on their account, as well as the subsequent devastation of their nation and their law.

And after the centurion who was standing before Jesus, and those who were keeping guard with him, had witnessed the earthquake and all of the other signs that had taken place, hearing his shout and seeing how he had died, they grew fearful and gave glory to God, shouting out and confessing, "This righteous man must have been the Son of God!" And when all who had gathered to see this event saw what had happened, they beat their breasts and left for home. But those who knew him were watching him from a distance, (and) among them were some women, Mary of Magdala, Mary, mother of the lesser James, and of Joses and Salome. These women had traveled with him all over Galilee, attending to his every need. There were also many other women who were watching these things from afar who had followed him and made the journey from Galilee all the way up to Jerusalem.

Now it was the day of Preparation for the following day's high Sabbath, and the Jews, not wanting any bodies left hanging on the crosses on the Sabbath Day, asked Pilate to order that their legs be broken and their corpses removed. So the soldiers came and broke the legs of the first man crucified alongside Jesus, then those of the second one. But when they came to Jesus and found that he was dead already, they left his legs unbroken. One of the soldiers, however, did pierce Jesus through his side with a spear, and out of him flowed blood and water. Now all of these things came to pass to bring to fulfillment the Scripture that says, "Not even one of his bones will be broken." And, as it says in another place, "They will look on the one whom they have pierced." And the man who has given this account actually saw it happen, and his is a faithful witness. He knows that he is telling the truth, such that you might also believe.

CHRIST'S BURIAL
(Matt 27:57-58; Mark 15:42-45; Luke 23:50-52;
John 19:38-39; GPt 6a; GNc 11:2a)
Jerusalem

Now it was the day before the Sabbath, the Day of Preparation. And there was in that place a wealthy man whose name was Joseph, a blameless, virtuous (and) distinguished member of the council. He had dissented to both their verdict and their deed. Now, he was from a Judean town called Arimathea, and was waiting for the coming of God. (He was a follower of Jesus, though secretly, for fear of the Jews.) So later on, as the dusk was settling in, he went boldly up to Pilate and asked him for the body of Jesus.

But when Pilate heard that Jesus was already dead, he was astonished, so he called the centurion over to himself and asked if he had indeed passed on; and the centurion filled the governor in on what had happened. And when the governor and his wife heard that the report was true, both of them were deeply moved, and neither of them ate or drank anything that day. And Pilate sent for the Jews and asked: "Did you see all that came to pass?" But they simply replied, "It was an ordinary eclipse of the sun." And at that, Pilate entrusted the body to Joseph.

So with the permission of Pilate, he came and took possession of the corpse, and Nicodemus, the man who had earlier visited Jesus under cover of darkness was with him. Joseph then purchased some clean linen cloth, (and) Nicodemus brought with him a mixture of aloes and myrrh, in all about a hundred litrai. Together they took down the cross, pulled the spikes from the Lord's hands and then they placed him on the ground. And at this, the whole world shook-- and they were seized with fear and dread.

THE END OF DARKNESS
(Matt 27:59-61; Mark 15:46-47; Luke 23:53-56;
John 19:40-42; GPt 6b; GNc 11:2b, 3)
Near Jerusalem

At that point the sun appeared, and it turned out to be the ninth hour. But the Jews rejoiced and turned his body over to Joseph, since he had been a witness to all of the wonderful things that Jesus had done. So the two of them took the Lord, washed him off, and wrapped him up in the linen cloth along with the spices, in accordance with Jewish burial customs. Now there was this garden known as the garden of Joseph near to the spot where Jesus had been crucified, and in that garden there was this new tomb which belonged to Joseph, who had carved it out of the rock himself, and no one had as yet been placed therein. Now they laid him there both because it was nearby, and because it was the Jewish Day of Preparation and the Sabbath Day was drawing near. He then rolled a giant stone against the opening and went away. Now his friends, Mary of Magdala, and Mary, mother of Joses--women who had traveled with Jesus from Galilee--were witnesses to all these things, (including) where (and) how he had been placed, for they were standing in the distance. They then went home, readied spices and ointments, and rested on the Sabbath Day, even as the law directs.

THE THIEF
(DecLtA 5:3b; DecLtB 7:2)
The Underworld

Then the Lord himself looked down on earth from out of heaven to hear the groaning of the fettered and to liberate the sons of the slain. Now after the voice had sounded (in Hades,) a man appeared bearing a cross upon his shoulders, and the look of a thief. He stood outside and cried to them, "Open up and let me in!" So Satan cracked the door a bit and pulled him into his abode, shutting the door behind him. Then all of the saints, seeing him clearly, immediately questioned him, "We all can see that you are a thief, so explain to us what you are carrying upon your back." "Indeed I really was a thief," he replied in all humility, "and the Jews hung me on a cross alongside my Lord Jesus Christ, Son of the Most High Father. I have come to herald his arrival; to let you know that he is following after me."

DAVID'S OUTCRY
(DecLtA 5:3c; DecLtB 7:3a)
The Underworld

Then David raged against Hades, crying out as loud as he could, "Oh Hades, you most evil and disgusting fiend, open up your gates right now, that the King of Glory might come in!" And all of God's saints likewise rose up against Satan, trying to get their hands on him and tear him limb from limb.

JOSEPH DETAINED
(GNc 12:1)
A Windowless House, Jerusalem?

Now when the Jews heard that Joseph had asked for the body of Jesus, they went all over looking for him, as well as the twelve who had held that Jesus was not born out of wedlock; Nicodemus, and the many others who had come before Pilate and borne witness to his wonderful works. They, however, were all in hiding, and the Jews only managed to track down Nicodemus, who was himself a ruler of the Jews. "Why are you in the synagogue?" Nicodemus asked them. "Why indeed are you in here?" the Jews replied. "You are in league with him, and will receive his portion in the life to come!" "Amen, amen," Nicodemus replied. Then Joseph came forward and asked them, "Why are you so put out with me for requesting the body of Jesus? Behold, I have wrapped it up in spotless linen and placed it in my very own freshly hewn tomb, and I rolled a stone against the mouth of the cave. You have dealt very poorly with the Righteous One, for you never once repented the whole time that you were crucifying him. And to top it all off, you went so far as to pierce him with a spear."

But the Jews seized Joseph and had him taken into custody until the first day of the week. "Now realize," they said, "that it is only because the Sabbath is dawning, and the hour prevents us from harming you that we are restraining ourselves. But you can be quite sure of this: you will not even receive a burial. No, we are going to toss your carcass out for the birds of the sky to peck." "This is how the boastful Goliath once reproached the Living God and the righteous David," Joseph answered. "For through the prophet God has said, 'Vengeance is mine,' says the Lord, 'I will repay!' Now behold, someone who was circumcised, though not in the flesh, but in the heart, took water, washed his hands before the sun, and proclaimed before you all, 'I am free of this righteous man's blood. You will therefore see to it.' At that point you said to Pilate, 'May his blood fall on us, and our children too.' Now I fear that the Lord's anger may indeed come upon both you and your children, even as you have said." Now when the Jews heard these words, they all grew bitter in their hearts, and they snatched Joseph away and shut him up in a windowless house. They then stationed guards to watch the door and sealed up the entrance to where he was confined.

THE JEWISH RULERS BEGIN TO SENSE THEIR GUILT
(GPt 7-8a; GHb 9:2, Quote by Jerome, On Famous Men 2)
Jerusalem

Then the Jews, the elders, and the priests, recognizing the evil they had brought upon themselves, started beating their breasts and crying out loud, "Oh, for the calamity of our sins, for our judgment is at hand, and Jerusalem is doomed." Now I, (Peter,) was in mourning with my friends, and we hid ourselves in our hearts' distress. You see, they were, hunting us down as evildoers seeking to set the temple ablaze. Now James had vowed to eat nothing from the moment that he drank of the Lord's cup until such time as he saw Jesus raised up from among those who sleep. And we (also) were fasting as we sat mourning and weeping night and day until the Sabbath. And after the scribes, Pharisees, and elders had convened, they learned that all of the people were groaning, beating their breasts and lamenting, "If his death has caused these amazing signs, this man must have been righteous indeed!"

THE SEALING OF THE TOMB
(Matt 27:62-66; GPt 8b; GNc 12:2)
Jerusalem

This so frightened the chief priests and the Pharisees that the following day, after the Preparation, they went up to Pilate and bid him, "Sir, we recall that while that charlatan was still alive, he claimed that he would rise again after three days. So give us soldiers (and) order the tomb secured until the third day, or else his followers might come and take his body away and then go around telling everyone that he has risen up from the dead! This last lie would be even worse than the first because the people might actually believe that he has been raised from death and do us harm."

"You have your guard," Pilate replied. "Go and make it as safe as you can." And he gave them Petronius the centurion and some soldiers to guard the sepulcher, and elders and scribes went with them there. And all who were there helped the centurion and the soldiers to secure the tomb, rolling the enormous stone against the opening. They then placed seven seals thereon, pitched a tent and kept guard there.

THE HARROWING OF HELL
(Dec 5:3b; DecLtA 5:3d; DecLtB 7:3b-8:1a)
The Underworld

And again the voice went forth (in Hades) and the cry was heard, "Hoist your gates, you princes, and be raised up, you everlasting gates, the King of Glory is on his way." And once again, at this clear voice, Hades and Satan started asking, "Who is this King of Glory?" just as if they did not know. "The Lord of Hosts is that King of Glory," the angels of the Lord proclaimed, "the great and powerful Lord, even the Lord who is mighty in battle!"

And behold, even as the answer came, Hades started trembling, as the gates of brass (and) bolts of death all shattered into pieces and the iron bars fell broken to the ground. Everything was left lying there completely exposed. And we were set free from [our] chains, as were the rest of the dead who had been bound up in it. And Satan was left standing there confounded, spiritless and shackled of foot in [our] midst.

CHRIST DESCENDS INTO HADES
(Dec 5:3b-6:1; DecLtA 5:3e 6:1; DecLtB 8:1b)
The Underworld

And even as David was speaking, the Lord of Majesty came down into Hades in the form of a man, bathed in heavenly light from above. As one who was lowly, yet great, and full of compassion did he who rescues with invincible power descend, chain in hand, illuminating the eternal darkness and breaking the unbreakable chains; visiting us who were sitting in this deepest darkness, underneath the shadow of the death of sins.

And seeing Christ so suddenly in their abode, alarmed over the horrible way that they had been brought down, Hades, Death, their evil minions and their vicious helpers were all aghast that such a light would dawn in their kingdom. And the legions of demons all shouted as one, "Woe to us, for now we are vanquished! You have defeated us! Oh Jesus, so mighty and glorious a man, so wonderful and great, so spotless and so free of sin, where ever did you come from? Just look, the earthly realm so long dominated by ourselves, and which until now has paid us tribute, has never sent us such a dead man nor delivered such gifts into this nether land. Who are you who have brought our master to confusion? Who is the one who passes unscathed through corruption; who in wrath condemns our power with proof of his undefiled majesty? Who are you, so great and yet so small; so lowly and so grand; commander and combatant; mighty in battle yet in the form of a servant--the King of Glory--who died and yet lived; who though he was slain has carried the cross? Who are you, who have invaded our kingdom with such pluck? You not only show no fear of our torments, but as if that were not enough, you are looking to free everyone here from our bonds. You who once lay lifeless in the tomb have now come down as the Living One. All of creation shook at your death, and even the stars themselves trembled. You have been set free among the deceased, and now you have come at last and disturbed our legions. Who are you that you are able to liberate the prisoners who had once been bound by original sin, restoring them to the freedom that they once possessed? Who could you possibly be who radiate such a divine and splendid light, illuminating those who are blinded by the darkness of their sins? Might you be that same Jesus whom our high commander Satan warned us would lay claim to the whole world through his death and his cross?"

JESUS SEIZES SATAN
(Dec 6:2a; DecLtA 6:2b; DecLtB 8:1c)
The Underworld

Just then the King of Glory seized their leader, Satan, by his head, handed him to the angels, and said, "Bind him hand and foot, neck and mouth in irons!"

JESUS DRAWS ALL THE SAINTS TO HIMSELF
(Dec 8:1b; DecLtA 6:2c, 8:1b; DecLtB 9:1a)
The Underworld

Then the kind and gentle Lord Jesus, King of Glory and Savior to all, stretched out his right hand and grabbed Adam by his, lifting him up and drawing him into his brilliance, greeting him and saying to him, "Peace to you, Adam, and your children too, through numberless ages of ages! Amen." And with joy upon his face, our father Adam fell at the Lord's knees and prayed loudly through his tears, "I will praise you, oh Lord, for you have raised me up, and given my enemies no cause to gloat. Oh my Lord, my God, I cried out to you, and you, oh Lord, have restored me! To your majesty, oh Lord, I offer up my gratitude, for you have lifted me from deepest Hades. You have freed my soul from hell, saving me from those who sink into the pit."

THE TESTIMONY OF ADAM AND EVE
(DecLtA 8:1c; DecLtB 9:1b)
The Underworld

Then our forefather Adam fell at the feet of the Lord. And as he was rising up, he started kissing his hands and shedding many tears. And he spoke these things before them all: "Look and see the hands that fashioned me." And to the Lord he said, "Oh King of Glory, you have come to free mankind and deliver them into your eternal reign!" Our mother Eve likewise fell at the feet of the Lord. And lifting herself up, she kissed his hands and poured forth many tears. And she testified before them all, "Behold the hands that fashioned me!"

THE TESTIMONY OF THE SAINTS
(Dec 8:1c; DecLtA 8:1a, d; DecLtB 9:2a)
The Underworld

(And Adam said,) "Oh you, his saints, sing to the Lord and offer thanks to the memorial of his holiness. For in his anger there is wrath, but in the mercy of his will, there is life." Then the saints all worshiped him, crying out, "Blessed is he who comes in the name of the Lord! The Lord God has shined his light upon us all throughout the ages. Amen. Hallelujah for ages of ages! Praise, honor, power, and glory to you, for you have come down to visit us from on high!" Jesus turned to the others; and stretching forth his hand to them, he said, "You who are sanctified, who belong to me and share in my image and my likeness, approach me now (and) come with me. All of you who have perished through the tree that was touched by this man, who on account of the tree the devil and death have been condemned, see now just how the devil and death have perished on account of the tree. Just look, I have raised you all back up to life through the tree of the cross!" Together they sang Hallelujah, rejoicing as one in his glory. Then the saints all ran suddenly beneath the hands of the Lord and assembled together, and all of the saints and the prophets of God likewise fell at the feet of the Lord. They all cried out with one accord, "We thank you, oh Christ, Savior of the world, for you have brought our life back up from destruction. Oh you who ransom all the world--you have come to us at last! Most assuredly you have fulfilled all that you have foretold through the law and the prophets. You have redeemed the living ones through your cross, and through your death thereon you have come down to us, that through your greatness you might save us all from death and the nether realm."

EVENTS OF THE SABBATH:

Robert C. Ferrell

MANY VISIT THE TOMB
THE SYNAGOGUE RULERS SCHEDULE AN ASSEMBLY
THE WOMEN BUY SPICES FOR JESUS
(Mark 16:1; GPt 9a; GNc 12:2a)
The Tomb, Outside Jerusalem

The following morning, when the Sabbath Day had dawned, a crowd came from Jerusalem and the countryside to visit the sealed tomb. On the Sabbath Day, the synagogue rulers, priests, and Levites called for everyone to meet in the synagogue on the first day of the week. (And) when the Sabbath Day had come and gone, when the week was nearly at an end, Mary of Magdala, Mary, the mother of James, and Salome bought aromatic spices with which they wished to go and anoint the body of Jesus.

THE SIGN OF VICTORY
(DecLtA 8:1e; DecLtB 10:1a)
The Underworld

Then everyone whom God had sanctified besought the Lord to leave the sign of his holy cross as a symbol of triumph in the underworld, that its evil officials might not keep as an offender anyone whom the Lord had forgiven. "Oh Lord," they said, "even as you have fixed your glorious name in the heavens and raised your cross upon the earth as a gesture of your redemption, so also, oh Lord, set as a sign in Hades the cross of victory, that death may no longer hold sway." And then it was done: the Lord planted his cross in the heart of Hades; and this, the mark of his conquest, will truly stand forevermore.

LEAVING HADES
(Dec 6:2b, 7, 8:1a, 2a; DecLtA 6:2a, 7:1-8:2a;
DecLtB 8:1d, 9:2b, 10:1b)
The Underworld

And after he had spoken this, the Savior reached out his hand and blessed Adam, placing the sign of the cross upon his forehead. And he did the same to all of the patriarchs and prophets, martyrs and forebears. And through his majesty alone, the King of Glory trampled Death. Then he fixed his holy foot upon his throat and said, "You have performed countless evils through endless ages, and never once have you let up. But today I am giving you over to the everlasting flames." And right away he summoned Hades and commanded him, "Take this wicked and most loathsome creature into your keeping until I say; until the time of my second coming."

And when Hades had taken hold of Satan, he said to him, "Oh Beelzebub, Prince of Damnation and Head of Destruction, heir to fire and torment, enemy of the saints, whom the angels deride and the righteous contemn, why did you seek to do such things? Why did you need to arrange for the crucifixion of the King of Glory? Was it so that he might come down here and strip us bare? Was it just that you were wholly bent on crucifying the King of Glory, through whose death you promised us all such vastness of plunder? Were you really too foolish to see what you were doing? Now behold, this Jesus is dispelling this darkness with the glory of his divinity. He has fractured the firm foundations of our prisons, sending all the captives forth and freeing those who had once been bound. All who used to groan under our torments now deride us. Their prayers have caused the storming of our dominion and the conquering of our kingdom. The race of men now fears us not! And as if that were not enough, the dead, who never before could gloat over us, nor as prisoners could they ever be joyful, torment us now without any fear. Oh Prince Satan, father of all impious scoundrels and renegades, tell me why you did this thing? The howls of those who had given up all hope of ever being saved and living again can no longer be heard. Not a single groan or solitary tear is to be found on any of their faces. Oh Prince Satan, keeper of the keys to the underworld, look around and recognize that no man now lies dead in me! The loss of paradise and all the spoils that you had gained through the tree of transgression you have now lost through the tree of the cross. All of your joy has come to an end. When you hung up that Jesus Christ, the King of Glory, you were not acting against yourself alone, but me as well. You had hoped to kill the King of Glory, but have destroyed yourself instead. So now that I've taken you to myself, you will come to know firsthand of the evils that I will inflict on you from this time forth! You will meet with the everlasting torments and endless punishments that await you in my eternal custody. Oh Prince Satan, Founder of all Death and Fount of all Pride, you should have thought the evil case of that Jesus through. Oh Head of all Devils, Beginning of Death and End of all Evil, where did you find any iniquity in this Jesus to win his destruction? Why did you presume to carry out such a sin? Why did you, for no reason at all and contrary to justice, crucify the one you knew to be sinless? You brought an innocent and righteous man down here to our sphere, thereby releasing all of the guilty, wicked and unrighteous of the world! What were you thinking when you brought this man down into this darkness? Through him you have been stripped of all who have died since the world began. Now all of your joy has been turned into sorrow." And when Hades had thus finished speaking to Prince Satan, the King of Glory said, "Prince Satan is to remain under your authority for ages without end in the place of Adam and his children, my holy ones."

Now Jesus placed Satan into his hands even as he was saying all of this to him. And seizing Hades, the Savior smote him, demanding an account for all things. And right away he took hold of Satan, its prince, shoving him backwards, throwing him and some others down with Hades into Tartarus, dispensing with them--one and all. (And) they fell with him beneath the feet of the Lord into the yawning chasm below, but others he led into the world above. And grasping the hand of Adam, he rose up out of the underworld with all whom he had sanctified streaming behind. And he ordered us, and many others, to rise up bodily and offer to the world our testimony of the resurrection of our Lord Jesus Christ, and of all the things that had been done in the regions below.

THE RESURRECTION
(Matt 28:1a; GPt 9-10; 1Pet 3:18, 19)
The Tomb, The Palace of Pilate

Now later on that night, after the Sabbath had passed and the Lord's Day was drawing near, the soldiers were keeping watch in pairs. And a very great noise came from the sky, and they could see the heavens opening. Then they saw two men coming down in a beam of light. And as they were approaching the tomb, the stone that had been pushed against the door started of itself to roll aside. And when the tomb was opened up, the two young men went into it. And when the soldiers saw all this, they roused the centurion from his slumber, as well as the elders, for they were also keeping watch. And even as they were describing all that they had seen to them, they once again saw: Three men came out of the tomb, two of them were supporting the third, and a cross came following after! Now the heads of the two reached into the skies, but that of the one they were leading by the hand, extended even beyond them. And they all heard a voice from heaven inquire, "Have you preached to those who sleep?" And from the cross the answer came: "Indeed I have!" (Christ, you see, died once for the sins of all mankind--the righteous and unrighteous alike--that he might deliver us to God. His body was put to death, but he was made alive in spirit, in the which he went and preached to the spirits in prison.)

THE ASCENT INTO PARADISE
(Dec 8:2b; DecLtA 8:2b)
Between Paradise And Earth

And as he sailed into the sky, the righteous forefathers trailed behind him singing praises and proclaiming, "Blessed is he who comes in the name of the Lord! Hallelujah! Give him the glory, oh you saints!" Then the righteous David in a loud voice sang, "Sing a new song to the Lord, for he has performed glorious works! His right hand and his holy arm have wrought salvation for us all. The Lord has made known his salvation and has shown forth his righteousness for the nations to behold." Then the host of saints chimed in, "This indeed is the glory of the saints. Amen and hallelujah!"

HABAKKUK
(DecLtA 8:3a)
Between Paradise And Earth

Then Habakkuk the prophet cried, "You went forth to rescue your people and to free your chosen ones." And the saints all shouted, "Blessed is he who comes in the name of the Lord! The Lord himself indeed is God, and he has caused his light to shine on us. Amen and hallelujah!"

MICAH
(DecLtA 8:3b)
Between Paradise And Earth

Then the prophet Micah likewise cried, "What other 'god' is like you, oh Lord? Who else can blot out transgressions and forgive sins? But now you have bridled your anger and confirmed that your desire is for mercy. And even as you have sworn to our fathers in days of old, you have looked away and shown us your forbearance, forgiving us of our misdeeds and causing all of our sins to sink down in the mass of death." "This is our God forever and ever," echoed the saints, "and he will rule us all forevermore. Amen and hallelujah!" So they followed after the Lord, the prophets reciting their holy words and praises, and the saints all responding, "Amen and hallelujah!"

INTO PARADISE
(Dec 9; DecLtA 9)
Paradise

The Lord then took Adam by the hand and delivered him over to the archangel Michael. And the saints all followed after him, who carried them into the wondrous grace of paradise. And two most ancient ones, men who were full of days, approached them as they were passing through the gates. The holy fathers questioned them, "Who are you, for you have neither seen death nor gone down into hell, but have dwelled, body and soul, right here in paradise." And one of them replied, "I am Enoch, who was pleasing to God, and by the word of the Lord was translated here. And the one that you see with me is Elijah the Tishbite, who was taken up in a chariot of fire. Never to this day have we tasted of death, (for) we are to remain alive until the end of the age. But we have been awaiting the arrival of the Antichrist, when God will send us forth to withstand him, that we might do battle against him with heavenly signs and wonders. He will then have us put to death. But three and a half days after killing us in Jerusalem, we will then be raised again. And after the three days, we will again be taken up alive in clouds to meet the Lord."

THE PENITENT THIEF
(Dec 10; DecLtA 10)
Paradise

And even as Enoch and Elijah were addressing the saints, behold, this other most wretched man approached, bearing his cross upon his shoulder. And when the saints caught sight of him, they asked him, "Who might you be, who have the look of a thief? And what is that sign that you are carrying?" And he answered them, "What you say is indeed the truth. You are right to call me a thief, for I did all kinds of terrible things in that world. The Jews crucified me alongside Jesus, and I was a witness to all of the miraculous events that came about as a result of the cross of Jesus the crucified. And I came to accept that he was the Creator of the natural order, the all-powerful King! So I called to him in prayer and said, 'Oh Lord, remember me when you come into your kingdom!' And receiving my plea, he immediately answered me, 'In all truth do I say to you, this very day you will be with me in paradise.' And he gave me this sign of the cross, and said to me, 'Walk right into paradise carrying this sign. And should the angel who is guarding it not let you in, simply show him the sign of the cross and say to him, "Jesus Christ, the Son of God, who has just now been crucified has sent me to you."'

"And I came carrying my cross into paradise, and was met by the archangel Michael, so I said to him, 'Jesus Christ our Lord, who has been crucified, has sent me here, so please lead me to Eden's gate.' And after hearing me say this, he let me pass through. (The flaming sword, when it saw the sign of the cross, opened right up for me.) But he placed me off to the right and said, 'Behold, wait a while and Adam, the father of the human race, will enter in with all of his children, the holy and the righteous. And after the glorious and most victorious ascension of the crucified Lord Christ, they will also be allowed inside.' And now that I have seen you, I have come to welcome you!" And when the saints heard these words, they all proclaimed, "How great is the Lord, and powerful his might! We bless you, oh Almighty Lord, Father of eternal blessings and of all mercies. You have shown yourself merciful to your own, who have sinned, and have brought them all into the delight of paradise and into your fertile pastures, for surely this is the life of the spirit. Amen and amen!"

THE EARTHQUAKE AND THE REPORT TO PILATE
(Matt 28:2-4; GPt 11)
The Tomb

Now those who were at the tomb were advising one another as to how to approach Pilate and break these things to him. And even as they were working it out, a man came down from the sky and entered into the tomb. And when the centurions saw all this, they abandoned the tomb that they had been guarding and hurried over to Pilate under cover of darkness.

Those who saw it were deeply unsettled as they related all that they had seen to him. "This man really was the Son of God!" they confessed. Pilate answered them, "My hands are clean of the blood of God's Son--this was all your own doing!" Then they all closed in on him and pleaded with him to tell the centurion and his soldiers to speak nothing of what they had seen to anyone. "For it is better for us to bear the guilt of the greatest sin before God, than to be stoned to death at the hands of the Jews." So Pilate ordered the soldiers to keep silent about it.

And behold, there was this terrible shaking of the earth, and an angel of the Lord came down from the sky. He went over to the tomb, rolled away the stone and sat down on it. His appearance was like lightning and his clothing was as white as snow. Those who were keeping watch were so afraid that they all shook and lay as dead.

JOSEPH NOT FOUND
(GNc 12:2b)
Jerusalem

And the entire multitude--the synagogue rulers, the priests, and the Levites--got up early and took council in the synagogue as to how they should put Joseph to death. And even as the council sat, they ordered that he be brought before them in disgrace. But after they had opened the door, they found that he was not inside. They all were taken with surprise and dread, since none of the seals had been broken, and Caiaphas still held the key. So they no longer dared to lay their hands on the ones who had stood up for Jesus in the presence of Pilate.

THE WOMEN FIND THE TOMB OPEN;
JESUS APPEARS TO MARY MAGDALENE
AND THE OTHER WOMEN
(Matt 28:1b, 5-10; Mark 16:2-9; Luke 24:2-8;
John 20:1-17; GPt 12, 13; EpAp 9b-10a)
The Tomb

And when Jesus rose up early on the first day, (which is) the Lord's, his first appearance was to Mary Magdalene, out of whom he had cast forth seven demons. In the early morning darkness of the first day of the week, even as the Lord's Day was dawning, Mary of Magdala, one of the Lord's female disciples went with the other Mary to have a look at the tomb. And Mary Magdalene, for fear of the Jews--all of whom were burning with rage--had not done what women customarily do for their loved ones who have died. So she, with the spices they had prepared, took some of her lady friends, (among whom was) the other Mary, and went to visit the sepulcher where the Lord had been placed. Now these three women visited that spot: Mary, Mary Magdalene, and her daughter Sarah. Now they were all afraid that the Jews would see them, so they agreed, "Even though we were not able to weep and mourn for him on the day of his crucifixion, let's all go and do so now." They wept and wailed over what had happened, and they took ointment with them to pour over his body. And as they neared the burial site, they asked each other, "Now who will roll the stone from the mouth of the tomb, so that we might go in, sit at his side and perform what is due?" (The stone, you see, was very large.) "And if someone should see us, as we all fear they might, and we find ourselves unable to do so, let us at least place what we have brought before the door as a memorial to him, and we will weep and beat our breasts all the way home."

But as they were approaching the tomb they looked up, and on their arrival they saw where the giant stone had been rolled away from the opening, and they found the burial spot uncovered. So Mary Magdalene ran over to Simon Peter, and to the other disciple, whom Jesus loved, and said, "They have taken the Lord away from the tomb, and we do not know where they have placed him!"

Peter and the other disciple therefore hurried out and raced to the tomb. The two of them ran there together, but the other disciple outran Peter, arriving first at the burial place. He bent down and saw the linen cloth lying there, but did not enter into it. Then Simon Peter came following him and did go in. And Simon, bending over, saw the burial linens there, and the cloth from his head rolled up and in another spot. And he went away marveling over all that had happened. So the other disciple who got to the tomb first went in and saw, and he believed. (You see, at the time they had not understood from the Scriptures that it was needful for Jesus to rise up from death.)

The women, (however,) went up to the tomb, bent over, opened the door and had a look inside. And right there in the midst of the tomb, they saw a handsome young man sitting, all dressed in dazzlingly bright attire. The angel then asked the women, "Why have you come here? Who are you looking for? Him that was crucified? He has risen up and gone away. But if you should doubt my words, just bend down and look inside." And when they went into the tomb, they did not find the body of the Lord Jesus there. Instead they saw a young man dressed in a white robe sitting off to the right hand side, and they were frightened. "Have no fear," he said to them. "I know that you are seeking Jesus of Nazareth, who was crucified. He is not here, but has risen like he said he would. Come and see where he was put; see that he is not there! Realize that he has risen up and gone back to the place from which he was sent."

And all of a sudden, even as they were marveling at this, two men stood beside them in garments that gleamed like lightning, and the women were so frightened that they fell to their faces on the ground before them. But then those men questioned them, "Why are you looking for the living among the dead? He is not here. He is risen! Call to mind what he said to you while he was yet in Galilee: 'The Son of Man must be handed up to wicked men, undergo crucifixion and on the third day, be raised again.'"

They then recalled the things he said. "Now go quickly to Peter and the disciples and let them know that he has risen from the dead. And behold, he is going on ahead of you into Galilee. Listen, I am telling you as he has told you; you are all to meet him there." Then, frightened and bewildered, they quickly left the tomb and fled in fear and tremendous joy. And without saying anything, they ran to inform his disciples--for they were too afraid to tell anyone about what had happened.

Now Mary stood weeping just outside the tomb. And even as she wept, she stooped down into it and saw two angels sitting there all dressed in white, one at the head and one at the feet where the body of Jesus had been placed. And the angels said to Mary, "Woman, why are you weeping?" "Because they have taken my Lord away," she said, "and I do not know where they have put him." Now after Mary had spoken these words, she turned around and saw Jesus standing there, though she did not yet recognize him. Jesus asked her,

"Woman, why are you crying? Who are you looking for?" And supposing him to be the groundskeeper, she said to him, "Sir, if you have taken him away somewhere, then please tell me where you have placed him and I will go and get him." Then Jesus said, "Mary!" And she turned around and cried, "Rabboni!" which means 'Teacher.' Jesus said, "Do not touch me, for I have not yet ascended to the Father. But go to my brothers and let them know that I am going up to my Father, Who is also your Father, and to my God, Who is also your God."

Now behold, even as the women were mourning and weeping there along the way, the Lord Jesus met them, and appeared to them saying, "Hello there! For whom are you weeping? Stop your crying this instant; I am the one that you are seeking." And they went up to him, took hold of his feet, and worshiped him. "Have no fear," he said to them, "but let one of you go to your brothers, the disciples, and tell them that they should travel on to Galilee and meet me there. Say to them, 'Let's go. The Master has risen from the dead!'"

THE REPORT OF THE SOLDIERS TO THE JEWS
(Matt 28:11-15; GNc 13)
In the Synagogue

Now as they were on their way, even as those who were in the synagogue continued to sit and marvel over what had happened to Joseph, some members of the guard went into the city. The Jews, out of fear that the disciples would come and steal his body and take the Lord away somewhere, had requested them of Pilate to keep the tomb of Jesus safe. These passed along all that had happened to the synagogue rulers, the chief priests, and the Levites. "There was this powerful earthquake," they explained, "and we saw an angel come down out of heaven, who rolled the stone from the mouth of the cave and sat on it. He was as white as snow and like lightning in appearance, and we were all terrified and fell as dead men to the ground. We also heard the voice of the angel speaking with the women who were waiting at the tomb, saying, 'Have no fear. See, I know that you are looking for Jesus, who has been crucified. He is not here, but has risen as he said he would. Come and see the spot where the Lord once lay. Go right now to his disciples and let them know that he has risen from the dead, and is even now in Galilee.'"

"Who were these women that he spoke with?" the Jews inquired. And the members of the guard said, "We have no idea who they were." So the Jews then asked, "And just when did all these things take place?" "In the middle of the night," responded the guard. "Why, then, did you fail to arrest them?" the Jews demanded. "We were so terrified that we became as dead men," the guard explained. "We didn't even hope to see the light of day, so how could we have possibly detained them?" "As the Lord lives," the Jews rejoined, "we do not believe you." "You saw that man perform so many signs," the guard reproved the Jews, "and you still did not believe in him, so why should you take our word for it? You are right when you say that the Lord lives; for he is indeed alive. We have come to learn," added the guard, "that you locked up that man who asked for the body of Jesus. For even though you sealed the door, when you opened it back up, you did not find him there. So why not hand Joseph over to us, and we will hand Jesus over to you." "Joseph is back in his own home town," the Jews affirmed. "And Jesus has risen up, and is in Galilee, as we heard the angel say," replied the members of the guard.

Now these words struck fear in their hearts, so they cautioned them, "Be careful that people don't hear this telling; or else everyone will come to believe in Jesus." And the elders of the Jews took counsel together. They laid out a sufficient quantity of silver, and gave it to the soldiers with these words: "Say, 'His followers all came late at night, even as we slept, and made away with his remains.' Now do not worry, if the Governor should hear of this; we will convince him and keep you out of harm's way." So they took the money and did as they were told. And the Jews put forth this story of theirs, which is spread abroad among all men to this day.

REPORT TO THE DISCIPLES;
THE VISIT OF THE THREE WOMEN
(Mark 16:10, 11; Luke 24:9-12; John 20:18; GPt 12; EpAp 10b)
Outside the Tomb, Jerusalem

When Mary Magdalene, Joanna, Mary mother of James, and the others got back from the tomb, they reported all of these things to the eleven, and to all the other disciples. Then Mary Magdalene brought the news that she had seen the Lord, and related all that he had said to her to those followers who had been with him.

Now the disciples were mourning and weeping, for they had not believed the women. After hearing that Jesus was alive, and that Mary had seen him, they did not accept it, for their words seemed ridiculous to them. Now Mary came and reported it to us (apostles,) but we just asked her, "Woman, what have we to do with you? Can the one who is dead and in the grave possibly be alive again?" (For when she told us that our Savior had risen from the dead, we did not believe her.) She then went back to our Lord and said, "None of them believed me when I told them of your resurrection." "Let another one of you go and tell them again" he said. And Martha came and let us know, but we replied, "Tell us what you want with us? Is it possible for the one who has died and is entombed to be alive again?" (For when she said, "The Savior has risen up from the dead," we did not take her at her word.) She then went back to the Lord and said, "No one believed me when I told them that you were alive." And he said to her, "Let another of you go and tell this to them again." So Sarah came to us and gave us the same report, and we called her a liar. So she went back to our Lord and gave him the same word as Mary had. Then Mary came back and told us again, but we still did not believe her, so she went back to the Lord and reported it to him.

Now it was the final day of Unleavened Bread, and since the feast by then was at an end, many people left the city and returned to their homes. And we, the twelve disciples of the Lord, wept and grieved, and each of us went back home mourning over what had happened. But I, Simon Peter, and my brother Andrew took our nets and headed out for the sea, and Levi, whom the Lord <had called at the tax booth> was with us.

APPEARANCE TO JAMES
(GHeb 9, Quote by Jerome, On Famous Men 2)
Jerusalem

Jesus then appeared to James. (According to the Gospel of the Hebrews, after the resurrection of the Savior, the Lord handed his robe to the servant of the priest. Then he went and showed himself to James. A little while later, the Lord said, "Bring me a table and some bread." And right away he took the bread and blessed it. And after he had broken it, he gave the bread to James the Just and said to him, "Brother, eat this your bread, for the Son of Man has risen up from those who sleep!")

THE WALK TO EMMAUS
(Mark 16:12; Luke 24:13-32)
On the Road to Emmaus

Now behold, later on that day Jesus showed himself to two of them in a different form as they were walking in the countryside, on their way out to Emmaus, a village about sixty stadia from Jerusalem. And together they were going over all the things that had come to pass. And even as they were discussing these issues, Jesus drew near and traveled alongside them. Now their eyes were being held so as not to recognize him; and he asked them, "What are these things that you are saying to one another as you walk all dejectedly along?" And one of them, whose name was Cleophas, answered him, "Are you but a stranger in Jerusalem, unaware of the things that have happened there over the past few days." "What things?" asked Jesus. "With regard to Jesus of Nazareth," they answered him, "this man, this prophet who was mighty in deed and word before God and all the people; how our chief priests and rulers handed him up to the judgment of death, and crucified him. But we were counting on him for the redemption of Israel, and it has been three days now since these things have happened. Now there were these women who went early to his tomb, but were unable to locate his remains. They came and surprised us with news of an angelic vision that they had experienced, and they all claimed that he was alive. Now some of those who were with us went over to the tomb and found things even as the women had described it to them, but they did not see him." "You fools!" he chided them, "and slow of heart to believe all that the prophets had foretold. Ought not the Messiah to have suffered and entered into his glory?" And from all of the prophets, beginning with Moses, he expounded the Scriptures with reference to himself.

And as they drew near to the village for which they had set out, Jesus acted as if he were traveling further. "Stay with us," they said to him, "for evening is approaching and the day has nearly passed." And he turned aside to stay with them. And as they were reclining together, he took the loaf, blessed it, broke it, and divided it among them. Then their eyes were opened up, and they recognized him, and he vanished from their sight. "Did our hearts not burn within us as he spoke with us along the road and clarified the Scriptures to us?" they marveled to each other.

THE REPORT FROM EMMAUS
(Mark 16:13; Luke 24:33-35)

Those men rose up that very hour, went back to Jerusalem and reported it to the others. They found the eleven gathered together in the company of some others. "The Lord has assuredly been raised to life," they affirmed, "and he has appeared to Simon!" They then explained to them all that had happened as they walked along the road, and about the way that he had made himself known in the breaking of the bread, but the disciples did not believe them either.

PASSION 2

JESUS REVEALS HIMSELF TO THE ELEVEN
(Mark 16:14, Freer Logion Codex Washingtonianus;
Luke 24:36-43; John 20:19-20; EpAp 11a)
Jerusalem

Late in the evening, on the first day of the week, Jesus appeared to the eleven. At that time the Lord said to Mary and her sisters, "Let's all go and visit them now." He came to us veiled and found us inside eating. Now for fear of the Jews the doors had been locked in the place where [we] disciples had gathered, and we were full of doubt and lacking faith. But Jesus came and stood in [our] midst even as [we] were discussing these things. "Peace to you!" he said to us. But all [of us] were terrified, and thought that [we] had seen a ghost. So he questioned [us], "Why are you so full of fear, and why do doubts arise in your hearts? Just look at my hands and my feet, it is me all right. A ghost does not have flesh and bones, as you can see that I have." And he showed them his hands, his feet, and his side.

Now as soon as they recognized that it was the Lord, his disciples rejoiced. And in spite of all their joy and amazement, they still could not believe it was him. Then he asked them, "Have you got anything to eat around here?" So they gave him a piece of broiled fish, which he took and ate before them all. Then he rebuked them for repeatedly refusing to believe the ones who had seen him after his resurrection. Now they all apologized and said, "Satan holds sway over this lawless and faithless age. He uses unclean spirits to keep the true power of God from being understood. Let your justice become apparent, therefore," they all besought the Christ. "Satan's time in power is through," the Christ replied. "Even so, other terrible things are about to take place. I was put to death for the sake of those who sinned, that they might have the truth restored to them. And this is how they are to inherit the imperishable glory of the spirit that exists in heaven."

THE DIALOGUE OF THE SAVIOR
(DSav; John 20:21-23; GEgp, Quotes by Clement of Alexandria,
Stromateis 3.6.45, 3.9.63, 3.9.64, 3.9.66,
3.9.67, 3.13.91, 3.13.92, 3.15.97;
Epiphanius, Excerpts of Theodotus 67;
Epiphanius, Heresies 62.2.7.8f; 2Clem 12:2-5;
Quote by Jerome, Commentary on Ezekiel 16.52)
Jerusalem?

"Now the time has come, my followers," said the Savior to his disciples, "for us to abandon our labors and to rest, for the one who rests will rest forever. Now I say to you, be always above <matter and> time. <Yet I> caution you, <do

not be> fearful <of anger, for> to you <it has been given to escape it.> Anger, you see, is fearsome, <and to> stir up anger is <indeed unwise.> However, because you have <understood that anger> comes from <fear, you have become wise.> They spoke these words against anger with fear and trembling, and that placed them under the power of the archons, for nothing had the strength to resist it. But when I came, I made a way for them and disclosed it to the chosen and the solitary, for they, knowing the Father, have had faith in what is true.

> "Now when you offer praise, do it like this:
> Hear us, Oh Father,
> Even as You heard Your only begotten Son,
> Receiving him and giving him rest from his many labors.
> You are He Whose power <is
> Unlimited.> Your armor
> Is <impenetrable and Your word is> light.
> <You are indeed the God of the> living;
> <The One> whom they touch not.
> <You are> the Word of <life,
> Opening the door to> repentance <and to> life.
> <Everything proceeds> from You. You are
> The entire thought and serenity
> Of the solitary. Again, hear
> Us as You heard
> Your elect. By means of Your sacrifice
> Will these enter in; and by means of their
> Good works have they reclaimed
> Their souls from these
> Blind limbs, that they might live
> Forevermore. Amen.

"I will instruct you. When the time of dissolution comes, the first power of darkness will approach you. Have no fear, and do not say, 'Behold! The hour has come!' Rather, when you come to see a single staff, which <indicates that> this <time indeed has come,> you <who have been chosen to receive this instruction,> understand that <which is to come> from the work <you are to bring forth.> And <in anger will> the archons approach you <that they might frighten you.> How truly is fear the power of darkness, so if you are going to be fearful of what will soon come upon you, it will consume you. For there is not so much as one among them who will spare you or show you any mercy. But look at the <great power that lies> within it, for you see, you have prevailed against every statement on this earth. This <will> raise you to the place beyond the authorities, <where there is no> tyrant. When you <get there> you will see all of those who <came before> and <all who will come after you. And so> I tell you that which <you must do with regard to> the design. <For to understand the> design <which exists in the> place of truth <is to find life.>

They, however, <are the sons of falsehood,> whereas you <are children> of the truth. This, <the path to the> living mind, <will be opened up, so> that you might brim with joy. So then <fear not,> that <you might find rest for> your souls, <and doubt not,> lest the word <should become obscured. For > what they have lifted up <is the word, but> they were not able to <overpower it. Make> your inside <the same as your outside, for your inside and> your outside <are one and the same.> Formidable, you see, is that place of crossing that lies before you. Even so, pass it by in singleness of mind! For great is its depth and lofty is its height. <But> in singleness of mind, <you must pass it by!> And the fire that <burns> is <apart from> the waters <in that place, and> all the powers <will subject themselves to> you. They will <all submit,> and the powers <over which> they <rule will likewise succumb.> I am telling you <the truth,> this <soul will> become a <light, which will shine> within everyone <who is of the truth.> You are the <ones who know this truth,> and that <which you bring forth will provide the remedy for the> forgetfulness <that now dominates the> children of <light.> And what you <produce when> you <bring it forth will make them free.>"

Matthew asked, "How <are we to bring out what is inside of us?>"

The Savior replied, <"You do not yet understand> what is within you. <But if you> will abide <in me,> you <will come to know of it.">

"Lord," asked Judas, "<what will be> the works <done by> these souls, these <elect,> these little ones? When <will they come, and> where will they be? <In what way will> the spirit <show itself?>"

The Lord answered, <"The Spirit will assign them their places and their labors, and the truth will itself receive them.> These do not perish <in that day,> nor do they come to destruction, for they have known their consorts, and He Who would accept them. The truth, you see, goes searching for the wise and the righteous.

"The mind is the lamp of the body," the Savior affirmed. "As long as all things are ordered properly within you, that is to say, <in line with the truth,> your bodies will all be luminous. But as long as your hearts remain darkened, the radiance which you await <will not come.> I have called <you here to let you know> that I will travel <on ahead of you. Those who are to reveal> my word with <truth will> I send to <those who seek after it.>"

His followers then inquired of him, "Lord, who is the seeker, and <who is the> revealer?"

"The one who seeks <the truth> reveals <the mysteries of God.>" the Lord replied.

"Lord," asked Matthew, "when I hear <something,> and when I speak it, who is it that <is speaking, and who is it that is> hearing?"

"The one who speaks," the Lord explained, "is also the one who hears, and the one who sees is also the one who reveals."

Mary asked him, "Lord, behold! From where do I carry the body when I am weeping, and from where do I carry it when I am laughing?" The Lord answered, "The body weeps on account of its works, as also for that which remains, and the mind laughs because <it recognizes the> spirit. There is a confusion that leads you to death and a confusion that leads you to life. Should one not stand in the darkness he will not be able to see the light. And so I am telling you <that ignorance> of the light is itself the darkness. And if you do not stand in the darkness, you will never come to see the light. <Flee from that which comes from> the lie, <for> they brought them out <from the place of darkness.> You will give <off a brilliant> light, and <you will> exist for all time in the <blessedness> of one <who will live in peace> forever. Then the powers that are above, as well as those that are below, will <flee from> you. In that place there will be weeping and grinding of teeth with regard to the end of all these things."

Judas said, "Tell us, Lord, what was there before the heavens and the earth came into being?"

The Lord answered him, "There was darkness, and there was water, and there was spirit on the water. And I am here to tell you that what you are searching for and asking about, behold, it lies within you, and <within you lies both> the power and the mystery <of> the spirit, for out of <darkness, light beams forth.> Evil comes <in order to conceal> the real mind and <to alienate you from your true self.> Behold, <it will be unveiled, and you will come to possess it.>"

<One of them> said, "Lord, tell us where the soul is established and where the real mind exists."

The Lord answered, "The fire of the spirit came to be within them both. And for this reason, the <spirit> came to be, and the true mind came into being inside them <both.> If one should place his soul on high, he will be lifted up thereby."

And Matthew said, "<Tell us,> who took it, that is to say <the mind of truth? Surely> it was those who are powerful."

The Lord said, "<You are> more powerful than he <who rules at present. And> you are <more powerful than> he who follows; you and all of the works <that are brought forth from> your hearts. For even as your hearts <have overcome,> so is this the means to overwhelm the powers that are above and also those that are below, <who reign at this time.> I am telling you, let whoever has power renounce it and repent. And let him who knows seek and find and take delight."

"Behold!" said Judas, "I see that everything exists <according to providence,> like the signs that are above the earth. This was why things happened this way."

The Lord said, "When the Father set up the world, He collected water from it and His Word issued forth from it and it came to live in many <places.> It was higher than the path of the stars, which surround the whole earth. They <were all in want of it,> for the water that was collected existed beyond them. <All of them were deprived> of it, a massive fire surrounding them all, even as it were a wall. And <there came a> time when many things became separated from what was within. When the Word was established, He looked upon <the earth> and said, 'Go and cast forth from yourself, that <nothing might> be lacking from generation to generation, and from age to age.' Afterward it spewed forth from itself gushers of milk and wellsprings of honey and oil and wine and fine fruits, along with sweetness of flavor and edible roots, that it might lack nothing from generation to generation, and from age to age.

"And the Word exists above <all things, and there it has been> set, namely <above the firmament.> Its beauty <was great,> and beyond it was a powerful light, luminous and even more dazzling than the one that resembles it, for this is the one that rules over the host of eternal ones, those that are above along with those that are below. The light was taken out of the fire and dispersed over the fullness that exists above and below all of the works that depend on them. They are <set> over the heavens above and the earth below. And all the works depend on them."

And Judas, when he heard these things, bowed down in worship to the Lord and offered him praise.

"These things which you seek of the Son of Man," Mary asked the brothers, "where ever will you keep them?"

"Sister," the Lord answered her, "no one will be able to look into these things except for someone who has a place for them in his heart and is capable of coming forth from this realm and entering into the place of life, that he might not be detained here in this world of poverty."

Matthew said, "Lord, I would like to see that place of life, that place where there is no evil, but only pure light exists!" The Lord answered him, "Brother Matthew, you will never be able to see it as long as you are wearing this flesh." Matthew said, "Lord, even if I will not be able to see it, allow me to discern it!" The Lord said, "All who have come to know themselves have recognized within themselves all that has been given to themselves alone to do, and they have come to resemble it in their virtue."

"Lord," said Judas, "tell me, what causes the shaking that moves the earth?" And picking up a stone, the Lord held it in his hand and asked, "What am I holding in my hand?"

"It is a rock," answered Judas. "What supports the earth," Jesus informed them, "is also what supports the heavens. When a word issues forth from the Greatness, it moves along that which supports the heaven and the earth. You see, it is not in fact the earth that moves, for if it were the thing that moved, it would fall. This, however, does not happen, lest the First Word should fail, for that was what established the universe. Now the universe came into being within it and received its fragrance from it. For whatever things remain unmoved, I <will move> them on behalf of you, the sons of man. That, you see, is your place of origin. You exist within the hearts of those who speak from joy and truth. And even though it goes forth among mankind from the very body of the Father, they are not receptive to it. Even so, it goes back upward to its place.

"He who recognizes not the work of perfection knows nothing at all, and one who does not stand in the darkness will never come to see the light. Whoever understands not how fire was brought into being will burn therein, for they do not know the root thereof. Whoever does not first understand water understands nothing, so what good does it do to baptize him? Whoever does not understand how the wind that blows came into being will blow away with it. Whoever fails to understand how the body that they carry around came into being will perish along with it. And how will he who knows not the Son ever come to know the Father? As for anyone who will not know the root of evil, he is not a stranger to it. Whoever will not know how he came into being, will never know how he is to depart. He is no stranger to this world, which will <perish, and> be humiliated."

Then he took Judas, Matthew, and Mary <out to> the end of heaven and earth. And after placing his hand upon them, they hoped that they might come to see. Judas lifted up his eyes, and there he saw a lofty place, and down below, a great abyss. Judas said to Matthew, "Brother, who can hope to scale this height, or to go down into this depth? For there is a great fire in that place, as well as a great terror." That very moment a Word came from it. And even as it stood there he observed the way in which the Word came down. Then he asked it, "Why have you come down to this place?" And greeting them, the Son of Man said, "A seed from a power was lacking, and it sank down into the abyss of the earth. Then the Greatness remembered it and sent the Word down to it. That Word brought it up into His presence, that the First Word might not fail." His disciples were amazed by all that he had said and they received it all on faith. And they all came to see that it was not necessary to look upon evil. Then he explained to his disciples, "Did I not say to you that like a visible thunder, or the flashing of lightning would the good be taken up to the light?"

Then all of his followers praised him and said, "Lord, who was there to offer you praise before you came here to this place--for all praises exist on your account? Or who is it that will offer you blessings--for all good things proceed from you?" And even as they were standing there, he saw two spirits carrying a single soul with them in a dazzling bolt of lightning. And a word came from the Son of Man, saying, "Present them with their garment!" The small became just like the great; these and the ones receiving them were just alike. <Then he returned with the> disciples whom he had <taken up.>

"<Did you> see evil <among> them from the first <time they saw> one another?" asked Mary. <"Yes I did,"> the Lord replied, <"and> when you see them <unite and> become enormous, they will <all feign their own importance.> But when you come to see the One Who lives forever, that is indeed the great vision."

"Explain it to us!" they all implored. "How would you rather see it," he asked, "in a fleeting vision, or an eternal one?" He said, moreover, "Try to save what can follow after you. Look for it and speak from within it, so all that you seek for may be in harmony with you. Because I am here to tell you, the Living God lives within you, <and you live> within Him."

"How truly I wish <to dwell in that place,"> said Judas. "The Living God lives <within the one who is> whole," the Lord answered, <"whereas> the deficiency <resides within the empty.">

Judas asked, "Who <will come to dwell therein?"> The Lord answered him, <"Those who complete> the works that <remain to be done. As for> that which remains, it is they who you <are to prepare for victory over the angelic rulers.">

"Behold," said Judas, "the archons are above us, so they will be the ones to rule over us!"

"You will be the ones to govern them," Jesus countered, "but only after you have rid yourselves of covetousness. Then you will don the garments of light and enter into the bridal chamber."

"How will our garments be brought to us?" asked Judas. "There are some who will bring them to you," the Lord answered, "and there are others who will receive you. You see, they are the ones who will provide you with your clothes. For who will be able to pass through that place of retribution? Even so, the clothing of life has been given to men since they see the path by which they must go. It is even a challenge for me to pass through." "Hence," said Mary, "'The Trouble Of Each Day,' and 'The Worker Deserves His Wage,' and 'The Disciple Is Like His Teacher.'" (She put forth these expressions as a woman who understood them fully.)

The disciples then asked him, "What is this 'fullness' and what is this 'deficiency'?" "The 'fullness,'" he said, "is where you came from, whereas the 'deficiency' is the place where you currently dwell. But look and see, how His light has poured down on me!"

"Lord," said Matthew, "tell me how the dead pass on, and the living come alive!" The Lord answered him, "You have asked me about the saying; <'You have shown me> what no eye has seen, nor have I heard it from anyone but you.' Nonetheless I say to you, a man is referred to as 'dead' when what animates him is taken away. Now when what is alive escapes from what is dead, it will then be called 'alive' again."

Judas asked: "Why do these die and live again for the sake of truth?" "What the truth brings forth is not what dies," the Lord replied. "That which is born of woman is the thing that dies."

"Lord," Mary said to him, "tell me, was I brought to this place to gain a profit or to suffer a loss?" "You are here," the Lord explained, "to show forth the abundance of the Revealer!" "Is there any place, then, that is unproductive, or in want of truth?" Mary inquired. "In the place that I am not!" the Lord replied. "Lord," said Mary, "you are wonderful and fearsome; an all-consuming fire to those who do not know you."

Matthew asked, "Why can't we all just rest right now?" The Lord answered him, "Once you've laid these burdens down, your rest will come." Matthew asked, "How does the small become one with the great?" The Lord replied, "You will indeed find rest once you have abandoned the works that cannot follow after you."

Mary said, "I would like to see all things as they truly are." "Life is the fortune for him that seeks it," the Lord declared. "The pleasure that this world provides is counterfeit; its gold and its silver are but a delusion."

His followers asked him, "What ought we to do to ensure that our work comes to perfection?" "Be prepared in the face of all things," the Lord replied. "How blessed is the man who has recognized the war, and has seen the battle with his own two eyes, for he has emerged triumphantly, having neither killed nor suffered death."

"Lord," said Judas, "tell me where the path begins." "With love and with righteousness," he answered us. "Had even one of these been among the archons, evil never would have come into existence."

"Lord," said Matthew, "you have spoken openly about the end of all things." The Lord answered, "You have understood and accepted on faith all that I have said to you. They are yours as far as you can understand. If, however, you cannot comprehend them, they are not for you to have."

"What is this place that we are headed for?" they prodded him. The Lord said, "Whatever place lies within your grasp, there you must stand."

Mary asked, "Is it possible to see everything that is established in this manner?" The Lord replied, "The one who sees is the one who reveals, even as I have told you before."

His twelve disciples questioned him, "Teacher, <where is the path to the> peaceful <heart?> Teach us <how we are to attain it.>"

The Lord said, "If you have understood all that I have explained to you, you will achieve immortality. You <are,> after all, <the path that leads to> everything."

Mary said, "There is but one word that I will speak to the Lord with regard to the mystery of the truth in which we have come to stand: We have been revealed to the cosmic beings."

Judas said to Matthew, "We would like to understand the type of garment with which we are to be clothed when we depart from this corrupted flesh." The Lord answered, "The archons and administrators possess garments which have been given to them only for a certain time, and which do not endure. You, however, as children of truth, are not to array yourselves in these temporal vestments. You will instead receive your blessing when you come to undress yourselves! You see, it is no great thing <to strip yourselves and to step> outside."

<One of them> said, <"Lord,> speak <to us about 'The Mustard Seed.'"> The Lord replied, <"It has been sown by> your Father <and it is He that brings it forth."> "What is the nature of that mustard seed?" Mary asked him. "Does it come from heaven, or from the earth?" The Lord answered, "When the Father established the world for Himself, He retained some things from the Mother of all, and this inspires both His speaking and His actions."

"This you have spoken from the mind of truth," Judas remarked. "When we pray, how should we do it?" "Pray in the place where there is no woman," the Lord replied. ("Now by telling us to pray in a place where there is no woman," said Matthew, "he means that we should destroy the works of the female. This does not mean that there is some other way of bringing forth, only that someday women will no longer give birth.") "They will never cease to exist!" Mary protested. "Who is so sure that they won't all dissolve," the Lord replied, "their works being undone in this place too?" (Now when Salome asked, "How long will death continue to reign?" the Lord answered her, "As long as you women continue to bear." You see, the Savior has himself affirmed, "I have come to undo the works of the female." He does not mean that procreation is bad, for such is necessary for the redemption of those who believe. Furthermore, the Lord has said, "Whoever has taken a wife should never forsake her, but whoever has not done so would be better off not getting married." For in the Gospel of the Egyptians many mysterious matters of this nature are passed down as esoteric wisdom given secretly by the Savior, teaching his disciples that the Father, the Son, and the Holy Spirit are a single One. The Naassenes maintain that the soul is difficult to find and to become familiar with. This is because it remains neither in a singular form, nor does it conform to a particular aspect, and as such does not possess a definite appearance such that any pattern or perception of it could possibly describe it. Now since the Word had spoken of the end, Salome was right to ask, "How long are men to suffer death?" Scripture utilizes the word 'man' here in two ways; both as that of the outward, visible form along with the soul, and also with reference to the redeemed and the unredeemed alike. The impulse of the 'male' is used to represent aggression, and the term 'female' is used to indicate lusting. 'Works' signifies both birth and decay. This does not mean that life is a bad thing or that the creation is evil, only that such is the course of nature. You see, when Salome asked, "Then have I done well by not having children?" The Lord replied, "You may eat of every herb, but of the bitter one do not partake." Let us all wait in constant expectation of the arrival of the kingdom of God in love and righteousness, for we do not know the day of God's coming. For you see, when Salome inquired of him, "Tell us when your kingdom will come." the Lord replied, "When you tread underfoot this covering of shame, and when the two should unite, the inner becoming one with the outer, and when the male becomes neither male nor female with regard to the female." Whenever we speak the truth to one another, you see, the two become one, for a single soul, free of all that is false, occupies the two persons. As for the 'outside' being even as the 'inside,' here is the interpretation: With reference to what is within, he means the soul, and with reference to what is without, he means the physical body. So even as your body can be clearly seen, so also ought you to make the character of your soul apparent through your good works. Now when he says, 'the male with regard to the female, neither male nor female,' he is saying, 'when a brother looks upon a sister, he ought not to think of her as female, and she likewise ought not to think of him as male.' Thus he assures us: "If you do these things, my kingdom will appear.")

Judas said to Matthew, "The works of the female will all dissolve. <And when they see it,> the archons will call upon <their every strength.> Is this how we are to become prepared for them?"

The Lord asked, "Can they honestly see you? Can they see the ones receiving you? Behold! A Word is issuing from the Father silently into the abyss, bringing forth like a lightning flash. Are they able to see or overpower it? Not at all, for even now it remains to you! You have known the way which no angel or power has ever seen. But it belongs to the Father and the Son, for they are both a single <One.> You will travel along the path that all of you have come to know, and no matter how great the archons become, they will never be able to attain to it. Even so, listen here--it is a burden even for me to do it."

"When the works dissolve <into nothingness,"> Mary asked the Lord, <"will it be your works> that dissolve a work?" The Lord answered her, "Without question, for <the way> is known to each of you. <Now> if I should dissolve <the works, they> will <each> go back to their place."

"How does the spirit appear?" asked Judas. "How does the sword appear?" answered Jesus. "How does the light appear?" Judas probed. The Lord said, <"You already exist> eternally within it."

Judas asked, "Who forgives the works of whom? Those works which <will condemn> the world. <When the time of judgment comes about,> who is it that forgives the works." The Lord answered him, "Who is it <that condemns?> It is fitting for one who has understood the works to carry out the Father's will. As for all of you, strive to rid yourselves of anger and of envy. Also, strip yourselves of your <worldliness,> and do not <seek after that which is not your own.(?)> <...> <And do not waver when the time comes for you to> reproach <the world.> For I say to you, <the archons will fall on you to strike fear into your hearts.(?)> <...> <When> you take the <word of God to yourselves(?)> you <will rest upon it, and the person> who has sought, and has <come to understand> this, will rest <upon it also.> He will live forevermore. And I say this to you <now, so that> your spirits and your souls might not be led astray." Then Jesus again said to them, "Peace to you! I am sending you forth even as the Father has sent me." And after saying this, he breathed on them and said, "Receive the Holy Spirit! The sins of those you have forgiven will indeed be forgiven, and the sins of those you have not forgiven will remain unforgiven."

JESUS' SECOND APPEARANCE TO THE TWELVE
(EpAp 11b, 12; John 20:24-29)
Jerusalem

But Thomas, one of the twelve apostles--who is also known as Didymus--was not there at the time that Jesus came. And when the other disciples said to him, "We have all seen the Lord!" he answered them, "Unless I see the nail marks in his hand, and place my finger into them, and my hand into his side, I will not believe."

Now after eight days had passed, all of the disciples were again gathered together inside, and the doors were locked, and Thomas was with them. Then Jesus came and stood in their midst, saying, "Peace to you!" Now he presented himself to us in an ethereal form; and we, imagining him to be a ghost, were startled and frightened, still not believing that it could be him. But indeed it was the Lord, so he questioned us, "Why are you so unsettled, and why do doubts arise in your hearts? Come now, and have no fear. I am your master, your teacher; the one you, Peter, denied three times before the crowing of the cock. Are you denying me yet again?"

And we approached him, doubting in our hearts whether it could possibly be him. Then he asked us, "Why this stubborn refusal to believe? Why are you so skeptical? Believe that I am the one who spoke to you about my flesh, my death, and my resurrection. Now just so that you might know it's me, touch me, Peter, and you will see. Place your hand on the nail prints in my hands, and your finger within them." And to Thomas he said, "As for you, Thomas, bring your finger over and inspect my hands. Now bring your hand over and touch the spear wound that was made in my side. Place your finger (and) your hand therein, and be not doubtful, but believing!" And at this Thomas confessed, "You are my Lord and my God!" "Thomas," Jesus questioned him, "does your faith rely on your having seen me? Blessed are those who have not seen and have yet believed. As for you, Andrew, look at my feet and see whether or not they touch the ground, or leave a footprint. You see, in the prophet it stands written, 'The foot of a ghost or a demon neither touches the ground, (nor) leaves any kind of print behind.'"

But now we touched him to know for sure whether he had truly risen in the flesh, and when we had felt him and found that he had indeed risen up bodily, we fell to our faces before him. And confessing our sin, we asked that he forgive us for our faithlessness, for we had not believed him. Then our Redeemer, the Lord and Savior said to us, "Rise up now, and I will reveal to you all that is on the earth, and what is in heaven, and even that which is above the heavens, including your resurrection, the rest that exists in the kingdom of God, and just why it is that my Father has sent me. My Father, you see, has given me power to take you up, along with all who trust in me."

THE MISSION OF THE APOSTLES
(EpAp 13-30)
Jerusalem?

Now this is what he revealed to us: "It so happened that when I had nearly reached this place, even as I was passing through the heavens, on my way down from the Father of all, I put on the wisdom of the Father and clothed myself in His power and might; and when I was in the heavens, I was like the heavens. I passed by the angels and archangels, and being like them in appearance, I passed by the Orders and Dominions, Princes and Powers, possessing in full measure the wisdom of the Father Who sent me. But Michael, who ranks highest among the angels, followed after me. And archangels Gabriel, Uriel, and Raphael, followed me secretly as well, until we arrived at the fifth heavenly plane, in their hearts believing me to be among their ranks, my appearance being like theirs. The Father Himself had given me this power. Then I graced the archangels with the voice of wonder, distracting them all and summoning them to ascend before the altar of the Father to complete the service of their work until such time as I should return to Him. And it was as the image of His wisdom that I did this. I became the all within the all among them, you see, that I might return to the glory of the Father of Majesty, having brought about the merciful will of the One Who sent me. Now have you heard that the angel Gabriel came down bringing the Word to Mary?" "Yes, Lord," we answered him. So he continued, "Now do you recall me saying to you that I became like an angel among the angels?" And we answered him, "Yes, Lord." "Back then," he revealed to us, "it was I who appeared to the Virgin Mary, and it was I who spoke with her, transforming myself into the image of the archangel Gabriel. With faith and laughter did she accept me into her heart. And I, the Word, transformed myself and entered her womb and became flesh. And with regard to Mary, I became a servant to myself, appearing in the semblance of an angel. Even so will I do after I rise again to my Father.

"Now you must observe my passing. If, at the time of Passover, you should commemorate the memorial of my death, then one of you standing here with me will be thrown into prison for the sake of my name. And he will be in great distress and sorrow, lamenting in distant isolation from you even as you are observing it. For the one who is confined will regret that he cannot keep it with you. Now I will send my own power in the form of the angel Gabriel, and the prison doors will be opened up. He will slip away and come to keep the all-night vigil with you, and remain with you until the crowing of the cock. But at the cock's crow, the completion of my Agape and of my remembrance, he will once again be taken away and thrown into prison for a testimony until the time comes for him to leave that place and begin to preach what I have given you in the way that I have instructed you." And we asked him, "Lord, have you not yet finished the drinking of the Passover? Do we, perchance, have to take the cup and drink once more?" And he answered us, "As a matter of fact, it is essential to do so until such time as I return with those who have suffered martyrdom for my sake." And we said, "Oh Lord, what you are now saying to us is great, as is what you have said before. So in what form or power are you about to come?" "How truly do I say to you," he answered us, "that on the wings of clouds will I come, bearing me in glory and bursting forth with a sevenfold brightness--even as the sun--and my cross going before me. I will come down upon the earth to pass judgment on the living and the dead."

And we asked him, "Lord, how many years remain until this happens?" He answered us, "The coming of the Father will take place at the completion of the one hundred and fiftieth year, between Pentecost and Passover, after the hundredth and the twentieth part have passed." (The fulfillment of [these] number[s], you see, corresponds to his crucifixion and his resurrection.) "Now Lord," we said, "up to now you have only told us that you were coming, but just now you said that He Who sent you would come. So how can you say, 'It will be the One Who sent me who will come'?" "I am entirely within my Father," he explained to us, "and my Father is entirely within me."

Then we asked him, "Are you really going to leave us until the time of your return? Where ever will we find a teacher?" "Do you not understand," he answered us, "that even up to now I exist both here and there with the One Who sent me?" "Lord," we asked him, "is it really possible for you to exist both here and there at the same time?" And he said, "I am entirely within the Father, and the Father is within me. I exist after His image and His likeness, after His power, His perfection, and His light." (Now when he said, "I am His perfect Word in its fullest sense," this indicates the work that he did by means of the flesh, even as he said after his crucifixion, when he had died and risen up.) "To

Him," (he continued,) "I have become something like this: I am the perfect thought in the form of a type. Now I came into being on the eighth day, (which is) the Lord's. But through my own redemption you will come to perceive the wonders, and His image, and everything in its perfection--the completion of all things and their conclusion as well. Then you will see me rise again to my heavenly Father, Who is in the sky. Now behold, I am giving you a new command; love one another and defer to one another so that peace might always be with you. Show love to your adversaries, and do to no one else what you would not have done to you. Preach this and teach it among those whose faith is in me. Proclaim the celestial kingdom of my Father; and even as my Father has empowered me, so also do I empower you, that you might bring near the children of the heavenly Father.

"If you preach this, they will believe you! It is your duty to lead His children into heaven!" But we asked him, "Lord, certainly you can do all that you have bidden us to; but just how are we supposed to do it?" "I am telling you the truth," he said, "preach it and teach it, for I will be there at your side. You see, I am more than pleased to remain with you, helping you to become my fellow heirs in the kingdom of heaven, which belongs to Him Who sent me. I am telling you the truth, you will be my friends and brothers, for my Father has delighted in both you and those who will come to believe in me through you. I say to you most emphatically, such a great and wondrous joy has my Father prepared for you that the angels and authorities have long desired, (and still) desire to look upon it and perceive! But they will not be given the vision of my Father's glory." "Oh Lord," we asked him, "what is the meaning of all you are saying?" "You are going to see a light that is brighter than any other light that shines," he replied, "and even more perfect than perfection itself; and the Father of light will perfect the Son. You see, the Father is Perfection itself; and it is through death and resurrection that the Son is made perfect. So the one feat, in fact, outshines the other, and I am in all regards the right hand of the Father, for I exist within the One Who accomplishes; the fullness of the Father <who sent> me." "But Lord," the twelve of us responded, "you have become our life and our salvation, even as you speak such hopeful words to us!" "Believe in it, and take courage in it," he advised us, "and may peace dwell within your hearts, for truly do I say to you that there exists such a rest in store for you in heaven, that place where there is no eating or drinking, no mourning or merrymaking, no worldly concerns, no garment of flesh and no perishing of those who dwell therein. You will not exist as part of the creation below, but you imperishable ones are to receive a share in, and to dwell within the incorruptibility of my Father. And even as I remain continually within the Father, so also does your place of rest lie within me." "Will we appear in the form of an angel," we asked him, "or that of the flesh?" "Behold," he said, "I have put on that flesh of yours. I was born with it, crucified with it, buried with it, and through my heavenly Father, rose again with it. This happened to fulfill the oracle that the prophet David spoke of me, foretelling of both my death and my resurrection:

'Oh Lord, how those who strive
With me have multiplied,
And how many are those
Who rise against me.
Many are those who say to my soul,
"God will never come to your aid."
But You, Oh Lord, are my protection and my glory;
Even the One Who lifts up my head.
Then my voice cried out to God,
And from the mount of His sanctuary
He heard me.
I lay down and slept, and I arose,
For God Himself had raised me up.
You, Oh Lord, are my refuge.
I had no fear of the multitudes
Who rose up against me and hedged me about.
Rise up and deliver me now,
Oh, my Lord and my God!
For You have smitten and cast to the ground
All who have hated me for no good cause.
You have trampled them beneath Your feet,
And You have shattered the teeth of the wicked.
Salvation comes from God alone.
May You sanctify Your own.'

"All that the prophets have spoken has thus been completed, taking place and having its fulfillment in me. I was within them, you see, (and) I myself spoke through them, so with how much more certainty will what I have disclosed to you truly happen, so that you and all who believe in me might bring glory to the One Who sent me!"

But after saying all of this to us, we said, "Lord, you have shown us mercy and it is on your account that we are saved. You have shown us all these things; but if it should seem good to you, we would like to ask you a question." And Jesus answered us, "I realize that you are listening closely and that you long to hear, for truly you will all endure, and even as you listen to me your hearts all fill with joy. Look, ask me anything you'd like to know. As long as you listen close to what I say, it will be my pleasure to speak well with you. How truly do I say to you, even as the Father has awakened me from out of death, so also will you rise up in the flesh. He will transport you to that place that is above the heavens about which I have spoken to you from the first, prepared for you by the One Who sent me here. And this is how I will bring to pass all that has been arranged for your salvation--and it is with this in mind that I have brought mercy to its perfection. For being unbegotten, I was born of mankind, and as one who was without flesh have I worn the flesh and grown up in it. You see, I came to regenerate you who were begotten in the flesh, that through your regeneration you might gain in your fleshly resurrection an imperishable garment. For my Father has delighted in you, and in all of those who hope and place their faith in Him. And I will awaken the hope of the kingdom in whomever I please." At that point we all remarked, "How great is the hope that you inspire, and the way in which you speak!" And he responded, "Do you believe that everything I am telling you will truly happen?" And we answered him, "Yes Lord, we do." "I am telling you the truth," he said, "my Father has given me complete authority to draw all of those who are in darkness into the light and all of those who are in corruptibility into incorruptibility, and those who are in falsehood into righteousness, and those who are in death into life, and those who are in captivity into freedom. You see, it is possible for God to do what mankind cannot. I am hope for the hopeless, a helper for the needy, a treasure for the impoverished, a physician for the ill, and the resurrection for the dead."

And after saying this to us, we asked him, "Lord, will the flesh indeed be judged with the soul and the spirit? Will the one indeed rest in heaven while the other suffers a life of everlasting punishment?" Then he asked us, "How long will you continue to prompt me for answers?" "But Lord," we again prodded him, "it is important that we ask these things of you, since you have commanded us to preach, prophesy and teach, that we might therefore become competent preachers, able to teach them in such a way that they come to believe in you, having learned the certainty of all things through you. This is why we are asking you so many questions." And he answered us, "Truly do I say to you, the flesh of every man will rise up with his soul and spirit still within." And we asked him, "Lord, is it possible for what has passed away and disappeared to live again (and) be made whole? Now we are not asking this because we doubt, for such is not impossible with you, for we believe all that you are saying either has already happened or will someday happen." "Oh you limited of faith," he responded in wrath, "how long will you yet ask of me? Even so, do not be afraid to ask me about what you would like to know; ungrudgingly will I disclose it to you. Simply keep my commandments and do as I say to you without hesitation. Hold nothing back, and do not show respect of persons nor avert your eyes from anyone, that I might not turn my face from you. Rather, serve in a straight, direct, and narrow way. If you should do this, my Father will take great pleasure in you all." Again we said, "Lord, behold, we are taken with distress. We know that we are annoying you with so many questions." At that point he answered us, "I know that in faith, with (and) from your entire being do you inquire of me, and so I am delighted by you. For truly do I say to you, that both myself and my Father within me are pleased that you prod and question me. I rejoice that you have the boldness to do it, for it truly leads you into life." But we were happy to hear him answer this way, for he had spoken meekly to us. We therefore urged him: "Lord, you have shown yourself gracious to us in all things; giving us life by answering all that we have put to you. Will you again reveal to us whatever we might ask of you?" Then he asked us, "Is it the spirit or the flesh that passes away?" "What perishes is the flesh," we answered him. Then he said, "What has fallen will rise again, what is lost will be found, and what languishes will bounce back, that in so doing my Father's glory might be revealed. And even as He has done for me, so also will I do for you who believe in me. For indeed I say to you, the soul will not rise up without the flesh so that on that day an accounting might take place. This is so that they might own up to their works, be they either good or bad, and face their judgment accordingly, that a selection and presentation of those who have been faithful and kept the command of the Father Who sent me might thus be made. Then the judgment of bitterness will take place in accordance with my Father's will, Who said to me, 'My Son, on Judgment Day, you are not to fear the rich, nor out of pity are you to spare the poor. No, you are to deliver each of them over to eternal punishment according to their actions.' But to my beloved, those who have loved me back and have done as the Father Who sent me has commanded, will I grant rest and life in my Father's heavenly kingdom. Look and see what authority He has given me. These will also see the kind of power that the Father has given to me, that I might achieve what I wish in the way that I desire, that I might give it to those in whom I have awakened this hope, those to whom it is my will to give and to provide it. And it was for this reason that I went down to the place of Lazarus and spoke to Abraham, Isaac, and Jacob, preaching the good news to the righteous and the prophets, that they might rise up out of the kind of repose that exists below to that which lies above in heaven, as with you, extending to them the right hand of the baptism of life, together with the remission of sins and the deliverance from all that is wrong. And thus will I offer from this time on to all who place their faith in me. Nevertheless, should someone believe in me and not heed my commands, it will profit them nothing, whatever their view of me might be. Such have run the course in vain, and their lot will be error and destruction and a great and painful punishment, since through their willful disregard they have sinned against my command. But to you, and to all of those who place their trust in me have I granted to become the children of the light, (and) of life in God, free from all evil, and the burden of the judgment, (and) the power of the archons. And everything I have promised you, I will give to all these others too, that they might escape from the prison, the fetters (and) the spears of the archons--and also from their blazing fire!" And at that we said to him, "Lord, you have caused us to rejoice and have given us rest, (and) life, (and) <have bolstered> our faith with amazing works. For in all truth have you preached to our fathers and the prophets, and even so do you preach to us and to all of mankind. Will you now teach us as you taught them?" Then he informed us, "Indeed I say to you and to all who have trusted in me, and to all who will come to believe in the One Who sent me, that I will lead you up and into heaven, to the place which my Father has prepared for the chosen and the most chosen, and the kingdom of the elect in the promised rest, and I will give you endless life. As for those who have sinned against my commandments, teaching something else instead, adding to and taking from them, to inflate their own greatness, who if as a result should estrange and destroy those who believe in me in truth, will I give over to eternal destruction."

But we asked him, "Lord, will others <put forth a> grievance and bring about another teaching besides that which you have given us?" "Just as there are those who do what is appropriate and beautiful," he answered us, "so also must the wicked come, that both good and evil might be made known. Then a just trial will take place in which these will be given over to destruction (and) death, in accordance with their works and deeds." And again we said to him, "Lord, how joyful we are to look on you and hear you speak such words to us, for our eyes have seen all the wonders that you have worked." And he answered us, "How much more joyful are they who have not seen and have yet believed, for they will be called the Children of the Kingdom. They are to be made perfect within the Perfect One, and in my Father's kingdom I will be their life forevermore." Once again we questioned him, "Lord, <seeing> that you are going to leave us, how will anyone ever come to believe us, in light of the fact that you have informed us, 'A day and an hour is coming when I will rise up to my Father'?" He answered us, "Go and preach to the twelve tribes of Israel, and to the Israelites among the Gentiles, from north to south (and) from south to north; from the sunrise in the east to the sunset in the west. Many will believe in me, the Son of God." But we asked him, "Lord, who will believe the things we say? Who will even give us a hearing? How are we to perform or teach or recount the signs, wonders, and powerful works that you have done?" He answered, "Simply go and preach to them, and teach everyone about my return, in the light of my Father's mercy. I will work through you even as the Father has worked through me, since I will be there at your side. I will send my peace to you; my spirit and my power, too. From my very power and spirit will I enable you to prophesy to them unto eternal life. That is how it will be with you--and they will believe you! Indeed, to these also will this power be given and passed along, that they might teach it to the Gentiles in turn."

MARY ASKS JESUS
ABOUT THE NATURE OF HIS FOLLOWERS
(GTh 21)

Mary asked Jesus, "Whom do your followers resemble?" "They are like little children who are living on someone else's land," he answered her. "When the landlords come around, they will say, 'Give us back our estate.' And these will all strip naked in their presence, that they might give them back their field. So this is how I speak of it: should the homeowner realize that the thief is coming, he will keep watch before he comes to steal his things, and not allow him to tunnel into his house, which is his kingdom. You, however, must stand guard from the foundation of the world. Ready yourselves in greatness of strength, that the thieves might not find their way to you; for they will fall upon the power that you look to for help. Let there be in your midst a man who understands. When the fruit burst forth, he came quickly, sickle in hand, and reaped it. Whoever has ears that hear, let him hear."

PETER'S OBJECTION TO MARY

(GTh 114)
Jerusalem?

Simon Peter said to them, "Have Mary depart from us, for women do not qualify for this life." "Behold," Jesus answered him, "I will guide her myself, making her a 'male' like you, so that she might also come alive in spirit. Indeed, any woman who makes herself male will enter into the kingdom of heaven."

THE GOSPEL OF MARY
(GMary, GPh 28, 48b)
Jerusalem?

{Six pages are missing from the manuscript.}

<One of the disciples asked the Savior,> "Will matter be destroyed or not?"
"Every nature," replied the Savior, "every formation, and every creature exists within and among one another. Each will, in turn, be resolved again into its own root, for into its original root does the essence of all matter return. Whoever has ears to hear, had better hear!"
Peter said, "Since you have been revealing all things to us, describe to us also the sin of the world."
"The 'sin' does not lie in this world," the Savior replied. "It is you who bring sin about through your pursuit of the adulterous nature, and this creates the perception of sin. It was to restore every essence of every nature to its proper root that the Good came down to be with you." "This is why sickness and death remain with you," he continued, "for you give yourselves over to the thing that misleads you. Whoever has a mind that can grasp this, let him understand. Matter brought passion into existence, and this passion had no counterpart since it came into being against nature. Then a disturbance arose in the entire body, which was why I told you to be of good cheer, and not to conform yourselves to this flesh, but to that other image of nature instead. Whoever has ears that hear, let him hear."
After saying all these things, the Blessed One said to them all, "Peace to you! Make a place within you for my peace. Be on the lookout for anyone who leads you astray by saying, 'Look, over here!' or, 'Look, over there!' For the Son of Man lies within yourselves, so you must seek after him. Those who search for him will discover him. Now go out and preach the gospel of the kingdom! And do not be like the lawgiver, laying down rules beyond those that I have given you, or else they will come to dominate you." And after speaking these words, he left their presence.
But all of them were deeply saddened, and through their tears they asked, "How are we supposed to go out to the Gentiles and preach the kingdom of the Son of Man? How ever will we escape when they did not even spare him?" Then Mary, standing up and addressing them all, said to her brothers, "Weep not! Do not be sad or lose resolve, for his grace will always be with you, protecting you at all times. Let us instead give praise to his greatness, for he

has readied us all and put us in touch with our true humanity." And after she had spoken this, she turned their thoughts toward the good, and they started discussing the words of the Savior.

(Now there were three Marys who walked with Jesus: his mother, his sister, and Mary Magdalene, who was called his companion. His sister, his mother, and his companion were all called "Mary." But Mary Magdalene <was his> companion, and <he loved> her more than any of the disciples, and he would often kiss her <on the mouth.> <This would offend> the other disciples, <and they used to openly disapprove.> "Why," they would ask, "do you love her more than the rest of us?" The Savior answered them, "Why is my love for you not like my love for her?" If a blind man should stand in darkness alongside someone who can see, what difference is there between the two. But when at last the light breaks forth, the one with sight will see the light, but the blind one will remain in darkness.")

"Sister," Peter questioned Mary, "we know how the Savior favored you above all other women. Tell us what you know and recall of the words that the Savior spoke to you; things that we have not yet known, nor have we so much as heard before." "I will reveal to you all that is hidden from you," answered Mary. And she thus began to speak to them: "I was given a vision of the Lord. And I said to him, 'Lord, this very day have I seen you in a vision!' 'How blessed you are for not wavering at the sight of me,' he answered her, 'for the treasure is in the same place as is the mind.' 'Lord,' I asked, 'is it through the soul or the spirit that the one who sees a vision experiences it?' 'It is through neither the soul nor the spirit that he comes to see,' the Lord replied. 'It is through the mind instead, which exists between these two that the vision is experienced. And it is <through the mind that the soul and the spirit come together.'" (And Mary continued to relate the hidden things of the Lord to them.)>

{Four pages are missing from the manuscript.}

<(Then she related a vision of the soul's passage to them.) "After meeting up with and overcoming the first power, which is called Darkness, the soul approached the second power, which is called Desire, and spoke with> it. And Desire said, 'I never saw you going down, yet now I see you going up. Why are you lying to me? You therefore belong to me!' But the soul responded, 'You neither saw, nor recognized me, but I saw you! You have confused my true self with the clothing that I wore. You never saw me for who I was.' The soul, after saying these things, went away rejoicing.

"Then it came to the third power, which is called Ignorance. After closely examining the soul, it demanded, 'Where do you think that you are going? You are caught up in fornication! You dare not pass judgment, therefore, because you are bound up in it!' And the soul responded, 'How can you judge me when I have not myself passed judgment? I have indeed been bound up, but I have not bound up others. No one ever recognized me. Even so, I have recognized the dissolution of all things, both of heaven and of earth.'

"After overcoming the third power, it went on up to and beheld the fourth, which was sevenfold in its appearance. The first form being Darkness, the second, Desire, the third, Ignorance, the fourth, the Impulse toward Death, the fifth, the Empire of the Flesh, the sixth, Foolish Fleshly Logic, and the seventh is the Wisdom of Wrath. These are the seven Wrathful Powers. They posed these questions to the soul: 'Where have you come from, you slayer of men?' and 'Where are you headed, you conqueror of space?' 'What had me bound up has been vanquished,' the soul replied, 'and what had me hedged about has been undone. Desire has lost its grip on me, and my ignorance has died. I was released from this world as an eternal one, and as a type from the type have I been freed from the fleeting fetters of oblivion. From this time and forevermore, throughout the season and the fullness of the age, I will rest in silence.'"

And after saying all this, Mary fell silent, for it was up to this point that the Savior had spoken to her. But Andrew complained to the brothers, saying, "You can say what you like about the things she just said, but I for one do not believe that the Savior said all that. Come on, what do you suppose? For these things seem vastly different from his thinking, (and) these teachings certainly contain some strange ideas!" And Peter seconded, speaking out against these things. He asked them all with regard to the Savior, "Has he really disclosed all of these things secretly to a woman without speaking them openly to us? Are we supposed to turn around and start listening to the likes of her? Does he honestly prefer her to us?"

And through her tears, Mary questioned Peter, "What are you thinking, brother Peter? Do you imagine that I have conjured all of this up out of my own heart, or that I am telling lies about the Savior?" Levi cut in, saying to Peter, "Peter, you have always been hot-tempered; ever inclining toward anger and constantly giving way to it. And even now that is exactly what you are doing, questioning her as though you were her enemy. Are you now going to attack this woman as if she were one of the adversaries? If the Savior thought her to be worthy, then who are you to dismiss her? For he knew her fully and loved her devotedly, and it is because the Savior knows her so well that he loves her more than he does us. Let us therefore be ashamed and clothe ourselves in our ideal humanity. Let us all be on our way and preach the gospel as the Savior has commanded, not laying down any rules or laws beyond those which he laid down for us." And after hearing this, they went and started to publish and to preach.

APPEARANCE AT THE LAKE OF TIBERIAS
(John 20:30-21:25)
Lake of Tiberias (Sea of Galilee)

Now after these things, Jesus again revealed himself to his disciples at the Lake of Tiberias. Simon Peter, Thomas, who is also known as Didymus, Nathanael of Cana in Galilee, the two sons of Zebedee, and two other disciples were with them as well. Simon Peter said to them, "I am going out to fish." And they answered him, "Then we will go along with you." And right away they went to the boat and climbed aboard, and they caught nothing all that night. Now as morning was approaching, Jesus stood upon the shore, but none of the followers recognized him as such. Then he asked them, "Children, have you got anything to eat?" "No we don't" they answered him. Jesus therefore said to [them], "Cast your net over the right hand side and you will find something." Now their catch of fish was so great, that they lacked the strength to haul it in. Then the beloved disciple of Jesus said to Peter, "It is the Lord!" Now Simon Peter was not wearing anything, so when he heard that it was the Lord, he put on his shirt and jumped right in. And since they were not far from the shore, only about two hundred cubits away, the other disciples came ashore inside the tiny vessel, dragging the net that was full of fish. And as they disembarked upon the land, they saw a coal fire there, and a single fish thereon, and a loaf of bread as well. And Jesus said to them, "Now bring the fish that you have caught." Simon Peter went over and dragged ashore the net that was laden with fish. Now there were one hundred and fifty three of them, and these fish were very large. And despite the greatness of the haul, the net never tore. Then Jesus said to them, "Come now, and let's eat breakfast!" And knowing him to be the Lord, none of his followers dared to ask him who he was. Then Jesus took and gave them bread, and he did the same with the fish as well. Now this was already the third time after his resurrection that he had shown himself to his disciples.

And when they had finished their morning meal, Jesus questioned Simon Peter, "Simon, son of John, do you love me more than these?" "Lord," he answered, "of course I do. You know how I love you!" And he responded, "Feed my lambs." And he asked him a second time, "Simon, son of John, do you love me?" He replied, "Yes Lord, you know that I love you." And he bid him, "Tend my sheep." Yet a third time he asked him, "Simon, son of John, do you love me?" Now Peter was saddened that he asked him a third time, "Do you love me?" And he responded, "Lord, you know all things. You know that I love you." And Jesus said, "Feed my sheep. I am telling you the truth, when you were young, you clothed yourself and walked where you pleased. But after you have grown old, you will stretch your hands out toward another, who will dress you up and carry you where you did not wish to go." (This he said to indicate the manner of death by which he would glorify God.)

After saying this to him, Jesus said, "Follow me!" Peter turned around and saw the beloved disciple of Jesus following them; the one who leaned against his breast during the supper and asked, 'Who is your betrayer, Lord?' And when Peter saw him there, he asked Jesus, "Lord, what about this man?" And Jesus replied, "If it is my will that he should stay until I come, why should that be your concern? You must follow after me!" The brothers took this to mean that this disciple would never die. But Jesus never said that he would not die, only "If it is my will that he should stay until I come, what is that to you?" And that disciple is the one who wrote this down. We are certain that his is a reliable witness. There are also many other things that Jesus did. If these were to be written one by one, I suppose that even the world itself would not be large enough to house the scrolls needed to contain them all. Even though Jesus performed many signs and wonders before his followers which have not been written on this scroll, these things have nonetheless been written down so that you might come to believe, (and) continue to believe that Jesus is the Messiah, the Son of God, and that through your faith, you might come to have life in his name. Amen.

THE GREAT COMMISSION
(Matt 28:16-20; Mark 16:15-18)
The Mountain in Galilee Where Jesus Designated the Apostles

The eleven disciples then went away to the Mountain in Galilee where Jesus had appointed them. And when his followers saw him there, they worshiped him, but even so, some of them continued to doubt. And Jesus came to them saying, "All authority in heaven and earth has been given to me. Go out into every corner of the earth and preach the gospel to all creation, and baptize those of every nation, teaching them all about the Father, the Son, and the Holy Spirit. Teach them to abide by all that I have given you. Whoever believes and is baptized will be saved, but whoever does not believe will be condemned. And these are the signs that will follow for the believers: They will cast out demons in my name, and speak hitherto unspoken tongues. They will handle venomous reptiles; and if they should drink any poison, it will in no way harm them. They will lay their hands upon the ill, and they will recover. And behold, I will be with you until the end of the age. Amen."

THE FORTY-DAY INTERIM
(Luke 24:44-49; Acts 1:3-5; 1Cor 15:6, 7; GTh 12)
Various Places?

He was afterward seen by about five hundred witnesses. (Now some of these have fallen asleep, but most are alive until this day.) Then he appeared to all of the disciples at once. Many and unfailing were the proofs by which he showed himself alive to the apostles whom he had selected. He was seen by them for forty days after his passion, and he spoke to them about God's kingdom. And when he was assembled with them, he instructed them not to leave Jerusalem, but to "Wait for the promise of the Father, about which you have heard me speak. For truly John baptized with water, but not many days from now, you will be baptized with the Holy Spirit." And he said to them, "These are the words that I spoke while I was yet with you: 'All that has been written in the Law of Moses, and the prophets, and the Psalms, has to be fulfilled in me.'"

Then he opened their hearts to the Scriptures and explained, "It was along these lines that they were written, so it was fitting for the Christ to suffer this way and to rise from the dead on the third day, and that from Jerusalem even unto all the nations, a change of heart and the remission of sins might be proclaimed in his name. You are witnesses to these things. Now listen! I will be sending you what the Father has promised to give to you, but you are to remain in Jerusalem until you are clothed with power from on high." The disciples said to Jesus, "We realize that you are going to leave us and that we cannot hold you back. Who, therefore, will rise up and rule over us?" And Jesus answered them, "When you get to that place, you must go to James the Just, for whom heaven and earth have come into being."

JESUS TEACHES ABOUT PAUL
(EpAp 31-33)
Jerusalem? Mount of Olives?

"Now behold, you will meet up with a man named Saul, which will afterward be changed to 'Paul.' He is a Jew, circumcised as the law directs. With fear and trembling will he hear my voice from out of heaven, and his eyes will be made dark. Now do for him as I did for you; make a cross of spittle upon him with your hands. And as soon as you deliver him over to others, this man's eyes will be opened up. Then he will be for the praise of God, my heavenly Father. He will become mighty among the Gentiles; and many, when they hear the way that he preaches and instructs, will delight and be saved. Then he will be despised and delivered into the hand of his enemy. He will testify before mortal and perishable rulers. And on him will come the completion of my testimony, for because he started out by persecuting and despising me, he will be converted to me and thereby will he preach and teach. He is to be among my elect, a chosen vessel and a wall that does not fail. The last of the last will then go out and preach to the gentiles according to the perfect will of my Father."

And he spoke this to them in no uncertain terms: "Even as you have come to learn from the Scriptures that your ancestors the prophets spoke of me, and which are fulfilled in me, so also will you be their leaders. And even as it befits you, every word that I have spoken to you and all that you have written of me-- how I am the Father's Word and how the Father is within me--that you must also be to that man. Teach him, having him call to mind what the Scriptures have said, and how they are fulfilled in me. Then he will be for the deliverance of the Gentiles."

"Master," we asked him, "do we share the same hope of inheritance with them?" And he responded, "Are the fingers on the hand alike? Are the ears of corn in the field alike? Do the fruit trees all bring forth the same fruit? Do they not all produce according to their natures?" And we asked him, "Lord, are you speaking to us again in parables?" "Do not feel bad," he answered us. "For truly do I say to you that you are my friends and brothers in the heavenly kingdom of my Father, and He is pleased with this arrangement. Most assuredly I say to you that I will also offer this hope to all who will come to believe through your teaching."

And once again we questioned him, "Lord, when will we come to meet that man, and when will we go to your Father, our Lord and God?" And he answered us, "That man will go forth from the land of Cilicia to Damascus in Syria in order to tear apart the Church, which you must yourselves establish. At that time I will speak through you, and he will quickly come around. This man's faith will indeed be strong, that he might fulfill the word of the prophet that says, 'Behold, out of the land of Syria I will begin the call of a New Jerusalem, and I will subdue and capture Zion,' and 'The one who is without children and barren will bear fruit and be called "daughter" by my Father. I, however, will call her my bride.' Then I will turn that man aside, that he might never reach that place and carry out his evil plans, and through him will my Father's glory be completed. Behold, I will speak to him from out of heaven after I have gone to be with my Father, and it will be to him as I have spoken it to you."

INTRODUCTION TO THE APOCALYPSE OF PETER
(ApPt 1a)
Mount of Olives, Bethany, Outside of Jerusalem

{The Second Coming of Christ and the Resurrection of the Dead, which Christ revealed to Peter. (It was for not keeping the commandment of God their creator that they all perished in their sins.) And Peter pondered it carefully, that he might unlock the mystery bound up in the Son of the Merciful God, who delights in mercy.}

HIS DISCIPLES ASK IF THE TIME OF HIS COMING IS AT HAND
(Luke 24:50a; Acts 1:6-8; ApPt 1b; EpAp 34a)
Mount of Olives

Then he took them out as far as Bethany, and as he sat upon the Mount of Olives his disciples all came up to him. So when they were once again together there, they asked him, "Lord, are you going to restore the kingdom of Israel at this time?" And he responded, "To you it has not been granted to know the times or the seasons, which the Father has fixed according to His own authority. But you will be given power after the Holy Spirit has come to you, and you will be my witnesses in Jerusalem and Judea, and from Samaria to the farthest reaches of the earth." And once again we said to him, "Lord, how profound are the things you have disclosed and preached. You have made things known to us that have never yet been spoken, and you have comforted us and shown yourself gracious to us in all regards. For you have shown us all these things after your resurrection so that we might receive salvation. Even so, you only revealed to us that signs and wonders would take place in the heavens and on the earth. Teach us enough about them to recognize them." And each of us begged and pleaded with him, saying, "Reveal to us the signs of your return, along with those of the end of the world, so that we might know when it will come and thereby make a record of it, for we must teach it to those who are coming after us--those to whom we are to preach the word of your gospel, and whom we are to install in your Church. That way, when they come to hear, they will pay special attention to it and thereby mark the time of your coming." And our Lord affirmed to us, "I will teach you not only all that will befall you, but also what will come of those who will accept your instruction. See that no man leads you astray, causing you to become doubters, thereby serving other 'gods.' Many will come bearing my name and claiming, 'I am the Christ!' Don't you believe them. Do not even draw near to them, for the coming of God's Son will not in any way be seen except as the lightning that flashes from the east and lights up the west.

> In all my glory will I come,
> On the clouds of heaven
> And with a great multitude.
> In all my glory will I come,
> With my cross passing before my face.
> In all my glory will I come,
> Shining seven times brighter than the sun,
> With all of my saints, all of my angels.

At that time, my Father will place a crown upon my head, that I might pass judgment on the living and the dead, and reward them all for what they have done."

AN EXHORTATION
(2Esd 2:15-32)

Mother, embrace your children, and bring them up with joy, as a dove. Plant their feet firmly, for I have chosen you says the Lord. At that time I will raise the dead from their abodes, and bring them all from out of their tombs, for in these have I seen my name. Have no fear, Oh mother of the children, for I have set you apart, declares the Lord. Help will I send to you, even my servants Isaiah and Jeremiah. According to their prophecy have I set aside twelve trees that are replete with fruits of various types, and a corresponding number of springs that are flowing with milk and honey, along with seven great mountains upon which grow roses and lilies, with which I will fill your children with all gladness. Protect the rights of the widowed. Secure justice for the fatherless. Provide for those who are in need. Defend the orphaned. Furnish clothing for the naked. Care for the wounded and the frail. Do not ridicule the lame. Safeguard the wounded, and to the blind, give a vision of My glory. Care for the old and young within your walls. Take and bury the dead whenever you come across them, and I will give you the first place in my resurrection. Peace, My people, and be still, for your rest will truly come. Oh, good nurse, nourish your children and establish their feet. Not one of the servants that I have given to you will be lost, for I will require them from among those who are numbered within you. Fret not, when the day of distress and heaviness comes, others will weep in sadness, but you will rejoice in your abundance. The heathen will all envy you, but be able to do nothing against you says the Lord. My hands will cover you, that your children might not see Gehenna. Oh mother, rejoice with your children, for I will save you says the Lord. Call to mind your babes who sleep, for I will bring them up from the bowels of the earth and show them mercy; for I am merciful says the Almighty Lord. Hold tight to your children until I come and show them what My mercy entails, for My springs flow abundantly and My grace never fails.

THOSE WHO ARE SEALED
(2Esd 2:34b-41)

Oh you nations that hear and understand--watch for your Shepherd, and he will give you everlasting rest, for near at hand is he who comes at the close of this age. Ready yourselves for the treasures of the kingdom, for the eternal light will shine on you forevermore. Flee the specter of this age and receive the joy of your glory! I bear witness openly of my Savior. Accept the gift being given to you. Be completely filled with joy. Give thanks to him who has called you to the heavenly realm. Rise up and stand tall! Behold the number of those who are sealed at the feast of the Lord! These have fled from the shadow of this world and accepted the glorious robes from the Lord. Take again Oh Zion the fullness of your numbers and seal up the measure among you of those who have clothed themselves in white, who have satisfied the law of the Lord. Fulfilled is the number of your children--all of those for whom you have longed. Ask for power from the Lord, that your people, those who were called from the very start, might now be made holy.

THE GREAT MULTITUDE
(2Esd 2:42-48)

And I, (Ezra,) beheld a great and numberless multitude upon mount Zion, and all were praising the Lord with songs. Among them was a young man who was great of stature, much taller than the others there, and he was placing a crown on each of their heads. Still, he was more illustrious than these. And I was fascinated, so I asked the angel, "Who, Sir, are these?" And he answered me, "These are the ones who have taken off their earthly clothes and replaced them with the clothing of immortality. These have all confessed God's name, and even now are being crowned, and they are receiving palms." "Who is that young man who is placing crowns upon their heads and palms into their hands?" "This one is the Son of God," the angel replied, "whom they have confessed in the world." Then I started praising those who had bravely stood for the name of the Lord. Then the angel instructed me, "Go, and let my people know how countless and beyond measure are the wonders of the Lord God which you have seen."

THE FIG TREE
(ApPt 2a; SbOr 2:154-186)
Mount of Olives

"Now take the fig tree as a sign: as soon as its branches grow out and its shoots burst forth, the end of the world will be near at hand."

And I, Peter, said to him, "Explain the parable of the fig tree to me. How can we make sense of this, since the fig tree is forever putting forth its shoots, and each year yields its owner fruits. What then is this parable of the fig tree supposed to mean. None of us understands it."

And the Lord answered me, "Do you not see that the fig tree represents the house of Israel? It is just like the man who planted a fig tree in his garden that bore him no fruit. Now for several years he went out to see if it ever brought any fruit forth. Now when he saw that it did not, he said to his gardener: 'Dig this fig tree out by the roots, that it might not make useless our ground.' And to God he replied, 'We, your servants, would like to clear it, dig into the surrounding earth and water it. If at that time it bears you no fruit, we will not hesitate to pull it up out of the orchard, even by its roots, and plant another in its stead.' Now, have you understood how this fig tree represents the house of Israel? For truly do I say to you, in the last days, after its twigs have sprouted, false prophets will come along and raise the hopes of everyone, saying: 'I am the Christ, and now I am in the world!' When, however, this sign appears throughout the earth: children are delivered with gray temples from their birth, calamities befall all men, mass starvation breaks out, epidemics and warfare arise, at the changing of times, with expressions of grief, and an excess of tears, a great many children among the nations will sadly, and with piteous wails, devour their parents. They will lay cloaks over their corpses and bury them beneath the earth, the mother of all nations, which will have been polluted by blood and dust. What miserable and frightful sinners are those of the final generation, who understand not that when women no longer give birth, the harvest of persuasive men has come. When deceivers come to speak on earth--even in the place of prophets--the gathering will be close at hand. And when Israel comes to see the evil they've done, they who sinned greatly by crucifying the true Christ will turn away and follow them instead, repudiating the one whom our ancestors praised. Beliar will likewise come and perform many signs before mankind, but this charlatan is not the Christ. And with his dagger will he murder the many martyrs who are to reject him. Then will burst forth the branches of the fig tree, which is to say, the house of Israel. Many will be slain by him, and they will therefore become martyrs. Truly in those days there will be confusion of holy, chosen and faithful men. These will be plundered, along with the Jews. Upon these will fall a terrible wrath when a people from among the ten tribes, which the offshoot of the Assyrians had destroyed, will come from the east to seek out the Jews. After these things will the Gentiles perish. From this day forward, the faithful and elect among the Hebrews will rule over very powerful men, subjecting them as in times of old, for their strength has not been lost. The Most High, Who dwells in the heavens and rules over all will then send sleep over mankind, causing all of their eyes to close. How blessed are the servants that the master will find awake at the time of his coming, for they have remained awake throughout the age, watching with sleepless eyes in expectation. For though he should come at dawn, or dusk, or at midday, he will most assuredly come, and you will find it all as I have said. It will come about with the passage of time, for the coming generation, when at midday all of the stars will appear from the heaven of stars, in the presence of the two great luminaries.

COMING OF ENOCH AND ELIJAH
(ApPt 2b, SbOr 2:187-195)
Mount of Olives

"Enoch and Elijah will then be sent in order to instruct them that this is the deceiver coming into the world, that he might mislead it through signs and wonders. At that time the Tishbite, advancing a heavenly chariot at full speed from heaven, will arrive upon the earth and show forth three signs for the entire world, even as life is fading away. Woe to as many as are found to be with child on that day, and as many as are nursing babes, and as many as dwell upon the sea. Woe indeed to as many as will see that day, for a cloud of darkness will envelop the earth, from east to west and south to north. And so it will happen that those who are slain by his hand, will be numbered among the good and faithful martyrs who in their lifetimes have pleased God.

SIGNS OF THE END
(EpAp 34b)
Mount of Olives

"Now there will be some who will hear this man, (Paul,) and come to believe in me through him. And all of this will come to pass in those coming years and days." And again we asked him, "Tell us what will happen then?" And he answered, "The faithful and the unbelieving will together see a trumpet in the sky, the showing forth of mighty stars in broad daylight, a dragon, and wondrous things spanning heaven and earth; stars going down in flames, great hailstones burning in a fantastic fire, the heated battle between the sun and moon, the ceaseless and fearful thunder and lightning, the clapping of thunder and the shaking of earth. Cities will be laid to waste and men will perish in their ruin. The rains will fail and a great drought will follow. There will be a terrible plague accompanied by widespread and often sudden death to such a degree that those who die will lack a grave. Children and family members will be carried out on a single bed. And a parent will not turn to face his child, nor will a child look upon his parent, nor will a man turn toward his neighbor. But those who are forsaken and left behind will rise up and see the ones who abandoned them, in that they hauled them out on account of the plague. All things reflect hatred, affliction and jealousy. They will take from one and give to another. Now mourn for those who have ignored this command, for what follows will be even worse!

MORE PLAGUES, THE COMING OF THE ELECT
(EpAp 35-39)
Mount of Olives

"At that time my Father's anger will be kindled over the depravity of mankind. Many are their crimes, you see, and their lives are corrupt--the horror of their impurity stands against them in so many ways." "Oh Lord," we asked, "what lies in store for those who hope in you?" And he responded, "How much longer will your hearts be dull? How truly do I say to you, even as it has been spoken of me and my people through David the prophet, so will it be for those who come to believe in me. But deceivers and opponents will there be in the world, those who slander what is right. And they will live up to the prophecy of David, who said, 'How quick are their feet to shed blood and their tongues to weave deceit; the venom of serpents is under their lips. And I see you as you travel with a thief, and claim your portion with a fornicator. And to top it all off, you sit there slandering your brother and setting a trap for the son of your mother. What? Do you think that I should be like you?' Notice how God's prophet has encompassed all things by his words. And even as I have told you before, this was so that everything might be fulfilled."

And again we questioned him, "Lord, will the Gentiles not then ask, 'Where is this God of theirs?'" And he responded, "This is how the elect are to be revealed: they will come forth after suffering such an ordeal." And we asked him, "Are they to leave this world through the torment of an affliction?" "They will not," he said to us, "but if they should ever face this trial, it will be as a test of their faith; whether or not they keep these words of mine in their hearts and obey my commands. They will rise up and wait but a few days, that He Who sent me might be glorified, and myself along with Him. All of this I say to you, for He has sent me here to you. But you must pass it on to Israel, and also to the Gentiles, that they might likewise hear of it. They will come to believe in me and have a part in your salvation; and they will escape the torment of this plague. Now such as despise the pains of death will be taken away and kept in prison. There they will be tortured like thieves." "Lord," we asked him, "will they be like the unbelievers, and will you punish those who have fled from this plague in a similar way?" And he said to us, "They have carried out the work of sinners. And even though they have believed in my name, they have nonetheless acted like those who do not." And again we asked him, "Lord, have those who have escaped thus in store for them no portion in life?" And he replied, "Whoever has glorified my Father is the very home of my Father."

And we bid him, "Lord, show us what will happen after this." "In those coming years and days," said Jesus, "there will be wars upon wars. The four corners of the world will be shaken, and they will declare war against one another. Then the clouds will all be stirred, and will bring about darkness, drought, and the persecution of those who believe in me, and also the elect.

Then contentions, hostilities, and evil deeds will rise up between them. Some of them will believe in my name, but will follow after evil--and all they teach will be in vain. Now men will follow after them and bow to their riches, their corruption, their drunken debaucheries, and their bribes; and among them the rule will be to show respect of persons.

"But those who would look upon the face of God, showing no such regard for the sinful rich, nor fear for those who lead them astray, but who would reprove them instead, are to be crowned in the very presence of the Father. Those who reproach their neighbors will be saved as well, for such is the child of wisdom and faith. If, however, he should not become the child of wisdom, he will hate and persecute his brother. He will not turn toward his brother (or) his neighbor, but will despise him and turn against him and cast him out.

"But those who walk in the way of truth and the knowledge of faith in me, loving me and possessing the knowledge of wisdom and perseverance for the sake of righteousness ought to exult, for they have borne up under cruelty, and have walked in poverty, putting up with those who hate and abuse them. For men despise those who strive to make themselves poor, and for all that continue to endure. Great indeed will be their reward. They have been afflicted and made destitute, for even as they have walked in hunger and thirst, men have despised them. But they have borne it all for the blessedness of heaven, so they will spend forever at my side. But curse those who loathe and despise them; those who walk in haughtiness and boasting, for these are destined for perdition."

But we asked him, "Lord, will all of these things truly happen? Surely it does not become you that we should come upon them ourselves!" "How then," asked Jesus, "will the judgment of righteousness be pronounced on either the upright or the wicked?" "But Lord," we said, "on that day, will they not then say to you, 'When it came to righteousness and unrighteousness, light and darkness, good and evil, you never saw to it <before, but> now you have led <everyone> into righteousness, having shown them all both light and darkness, good and evil, (and) separated them.'" Then he said, "At that time I will say to them, 'Adam was given the chance to decide which of the two that he preferred. And he placed his hand upon the light, choosing it and forsaking the darkness, casting it away from him (and) rejecting it. And everyone else has this ability to believe in the light and the life, which is my Father Who sent me. And so everyone who has faith and carries out the labors of life will live, existing within both (the light and the life.) But if he refuses to acknowledge the light's existence and performs the works of darkness instead, then he can say nothing in his own defense. He will not even be able to lift his eyes to look on me, the Son of God.' And I will say to him, 'You found just what you were looking for, and have received that for which you have asked. Oh, man, upon what grounds do you seek to convict me? Why do you condemn us? Why do you fail to understand us? Why did you abandon and disown both my kingdom and myself? You were denying me even as you were acknowledging me. Why do you even now continue to proclaim and yet deny me? Now look and see; does not every man have the power to choose either to believe (and) live or else to die? Whoever has kept my commands and held to them will henceforth be a Son of Light, even a Son of the heavenly Father. I came down from heaven for the sake of those who keep and do my commandments; (but) on account of those who twist my words. I am that Word. I put on the flesh and I labored and I died. I taught that certain people would be chosen and saved, but that others, who were lost, would be lost forever. They will have to suffer eternal torment and devastation, being scourged alive by fire, in their spirit, in their flesh, and in their soul."

THE SPIRITS AT THE JUDGMENT
(ApPt 3)
Mount of Olives

And in his right hand he showed me, (Peter,) the souls of men, and in the palm thereof, the figure of what will come to pass on the last day concerning the upright and how they are to be severed from among the wicked; how the righteous of heart are going to fare, and how the workers of evil will be rooted out forevermore. We saw the sinners weeping and mourning in bitter anguish to such an extent that all who looked were moved to tears, the righteous, the angels, as well as the sinners themselves. And I said to him, "Lord, allow me to say something about these sinners: They would have been better off had they not been born." And the Savior responded, "Oh, Peter, why would you suppose that it would have been better for them had they never been born? Truly you are resisting God. You could never have more compassion for His own image than He does. You see, He made them all and brought them forth, when they did not even exist before. And my heart is heavy because you have seen what will befall the sinners in the final days; but I will show you by what works they have sinned against the Most High.

JUDGMENT DAY
(ApPt 4a; SbOr 2:214-220)
Mount of Olives

"Now have a look at what these will suffer in the closing days, when the day of God begins. On the day that God renders His judgment, the sons of men will all be assembled from east to west before my Father Who lives forever. Then He will issue the command, and hell will open up its bars of steel and surrender those who are detained within. Then the undying angels of the immortal God, Michael, Gabriel, Raphael, and Uriel, who know the evil deeds of all mankind, will lead the souls of all out of the gloomy darkness over to their judgment, to the bar of the great and immortal God. And since it is His will that all men should appear, all of the animals and birds will receive orders to give back all of the flesh that they have consumed. Because all things belong to God, nothing ever perishes for Him, nor is anything impossible to Him. (For at the behest of God, all things come to pass on the day of decision, the day of judgment, as took place when He made the world and gave orders to everything that is therein.)

There is but One Who is everlasting, the Universal Ruler Himself, who will judge all of mankind. Even so will it come about in the final days, for all things are possible with God. (Also, in Scripture He says: "Son of Man, prophesy to all these bones, 'Bones, join together with bones, then on with your joints, tendons, nerves, flesh, skin and hair.'") Then, when God issues the command, Uriel will supply them with their soul and spirit. (God, you see, has put him over the resurrection of the dead when the day of decision comes.)

THE GRAINS OF WHEAT
(ApPt 4b; Macarius Magnes, Apocritica 4.6.16)
Mount of Olives

"Now consider the grains of wheat which are cast to the ground and reflect thereon. Men cast them to the earth as something dried-up and without a soul, yet they live again and bear their fruit. The earth gives them back as received by pledge. Now this that dies and is sown in the earth in the form of a seed represents mankind. And it will stir again and have its life restored--(even) those who will be judged. So with how much greater certainty will God raise up on the day of decision all of those who trust in Him, and who are chosen by Him, and are those for whom He has made the world. And the earth will truly give this back to God on the day of decision, for both it and the heaven which encompasses it are to face judgment alongside them.

A FIGURE OF THE RAISING OF MANKIND AND OF JUDGMENT
(SbOr 2:221-251)
Mount of Olives

At that time, the Heavenly One will give the dead both breath and voice, and bones will be fastened together with all manner of connections; flesh and sinews, veins and skin upon the flesh, as well as each and every hair that was formerly thereon. On a single day will human bodies reconnect and resurrect in a heavenly way, and breathing will commence. Then that mighty angel, Uriel, will demolish the massive bolts of rigid steel. He will throw open wide the gates of hell--which are not forged of metal--and lead all the sorrowful beings away to their judgment, most particularly those of the primordial phantoms, the Titans, and the Giants which were destroyed by the deluge. Those also whom the waves overtook in the sea, along with as many animals and reptiles and birds as were ever devoured, even these will He call before His judgment seat. Moreover, He will also gather and set before it all of those who were destroyed in the flames of the flesh-consuming fire, when Sabaoth Adonai, who thunders from on high, puts an end to fate, raises up the dead, and takes His seat on His heavenly throne, and establishes a mighty pillar. Christ, who is himself imperishable, will come in glory upon a cloud to the One Who lives eternally, in the presence of his holy angels. He will take his seat to the right hand of the Great One, to preside over the trial of life, both of the pious and the impious. And Moses, that great friend of the Most High will come as well, himself having donned the flesh. The righteous Abraham will likewise return in the flesh, together with Isaac and Jacob, as will Joshua, Daniel, Elijah, Habakkuk, Jonah, and all who were ever slain by the Jews. All of the Hebrews after Jeremiah will He devastate in judgment before Him there, that they might receive and render whatever retribution is appropriate for whatever anyone ever did during their earthly existence.

THE CALAMITIES, DESTRUCTION BY FIRE
(ApPt 5-6a, cf. Macarius Magnes, Apocritica 4.7; SbOr 2:196-213; 2Pet 3:10b-12)
Mount of Olives

"Now these are the things that will come to pass on Judgment Day to those who have fallen away from their faith in God and have instead carried out wickedness. A great torrent of scorching fire will proceed from heaven. Flaming rivers will be let loose, darkness and obscurity will arise and envelop the earth, the waters will then transform, changing into fiery embers. All that lies within them will blaze and the sea itself will turn to flame. Under the heaven an unquenchable fire will rage, flowing on account of the judgment of wrath, which will consume every place in every land, the fathomless ocean and shimmering sea, all of the lakes, rivers, and springs, and all of merciless Hades as well, together with the vault of heaven. The flames of fire will burn the stars and the heavenly powers. The heavenly lights will likewise collide with one another into a desolate form, and the stars will fall from heaven and into the sea. All of mankind will gnash their teeth in a blazing stream; fire and brimstone will flash across a flaming plain, and ashes will come to blanket all things. The earthly elements will all be left bare, be they either land, or sea, or air, or light, or the heavenly vault; even all of the days and nights. The countless birds that filled the sky will no longer be, and aquatic creatures no longer swim in the deep; ships filled with cargo will voyage no more on the seas, nor will the plough be pulled by the beasts, and the breeze no longer blow through the trees. All things will at once fuse into one, then diffuse into thin air. The heaven will be rolled up like a scroll and the stars will melt and fall like leaves from a vine, or those of the fig tree, and be as though they never were. The strongholds of heaven, for their lack of water, will cease to exist and be as though they never were. The lightning bolts of heaven, who by their charms will panic the world, will exist no more. And the spirits of the corpses will grow to resemble them; being set ablaze at God's command. On that day the skies will pass away with a whoosh, the elements will flame out of existence, and the earth and everything in it will be brought to judgment. Then, when the entire created order has come undone, those in the east will flee to the west, (and those in the west) will flee to the east; those in the south will flee to the north, while those in the north will flee to the south. But the wrath of the fearsome flames will overtake them everywhere. It will drive them on and deliver them up to the judgment of wrath in streams of unquenchable fire. For it flows and flames with fire, and after its seething waves have broken forth, there will be much grinding of teeth among the children of men. Now since creation itself comes apart like this, think about how you ought to act, what godly and focused lives you should be living! Look forward to the coming of the Day of God. Work diligently to hasten its arrival, for in that day the heavens will be set ablaze until they all disintegrate, and the elements will melt away in the flames.

Then everyone will witness my coming as I arrive on an everlasting shining cloud, in the presence of the angels of God who will sit with me on my glorious throne, to the right hand of my Heavenly Father. He will place a crown upon my head. Every nation will weep for itself--even as they watch it unfold. And He will order them to enter into the river of fire even as they are confronted with their wicked deeds. Each one will be paid back in line with his own works. The elect ones, on the other hand, who have done well will draw near to me and not witness the spectacle of death by the all-consuming fire.

THE PUNISHMENT OF THE WICKED
(ApPt 6b-7a; SbOr 2:252-282)
Mount of Olives

"But as for the evil creatures, the sinners and the hypocrites, they will come to stand in the dark abyss that never ends. The fire is their punishment. The angels will then bring forward their sins and prepare a place for them where they will each be punished forever in accordance with their crime. Uriel, the angel of God, will then bring forward the souls of those who sinned prior to the flood, who live in all manner of idols--in molten images, objects of desire, and paintings, together with those who live on the tops of hills, within the stones and beside the road--all the things that men call 'gods.' Then they all will pass through the fiery river of undying flame. These will then be burned in everlasting fire together with their idols. The righteous ones will all be saved, but the wicked will be destroyed for good, including those who have carried out atrocities or murders, as will their accomplices. Liars, too, will likewise perish, as will crafty thieves and destroyers of homes; the parasites, the adulterers, the slanderers, the violent, the lawless, and the idolatrous, who have abandoned the great and abiding God and become blasphemers, plundering the devout, breaking the faith, and slaughtering the righteous. Also, as many elders and respected deacons as craftily, shamelessly, and hypocritically judged with respect and, trusting in deceitful statements, have dealt unjustly with other people. More destructive than any leopard or wolf, these are assuredly the most depraved. Also, as many as are extremely arrogant, or employ usury, gathering interest upon interest for their own households, who by so doing harm orphans or widows. Even those who give to orphans or widows from what derives from such evils, as also those who reproach others when they give to them of their own labors. Also, as many as neglected their parents in their old age, not giving them anything back at all, refusing to care for them in turn. Moreover, as many as disobeyed or spoke back to their parents, and all who went back on their solemn pledges, and such servants as turned against their masters. Also, those who polluted the flesh through lewdness, and all who secretly engaged in intercourse, undoing the girdle of virginity, and as many as smote what they had in the womb, casting forth their children contrary to the law. And after they have been destroyed, together with their homes, they will afterward be punished forever. Men and women will then come to whatever place befits them best."

THE BLASPHEMERS
(ApPt 7b/21, 22-Akhmim)
Mount of Olives

"And I, (Peter,) saw a dismal place, even the place of punishment. Now those who were being punished there were clothed in a manner befitting the place. They all wore dark clothing, as did their angels of punishment. Now there were some there who were hanging by their tongues. These were the ones who blasphemed the way of righteousness. Beneath them lie spread out an unquenchable flaming fire that tormented them.

THOSE WHO FORSOOK RIGHTEOUSNESS
(ApPt 7c/23-Akhmim)
Mount of Olives

"And behold, there was this other place with a giant pit (and) a lake that was filled with burning mire. Certain men who had forsaken righteousness were bound up there, and tormenting angels were stationed over them, visiting them and stoking the fire of their punishment.

WANTON WOMEN AND MEN
(ApPt 7d/24-Akhmim)
Mount of Olives

"Again, there were these two women hanging over the seething mire from their necks and hair who were being thrown into the pit. These were the ones who adorned themselves (and) braided their hair, not for the sake of comeliness, but in order to invite fornication, that they might lead the souls of men down to destruction. The men who had slept with them and defiled themselves through adultery, were hanging by their feet (and) loins in that flaming place. Their heads were all stuck in the mire, and they cried aloud to one another, 'We did not know, (nor did we) believe that we would end up in this place of eternal anguish!'

THE MURDERERS AND THEIR ACCOMPLICES
(ApPt 7e/25a Akhmim)
Mount of Olives

"And I saw the murderers and their accomplices being thrown into a fiery crevasse--a place that was crawling with reptiles (and) venomous creatures--where myriad worms, like inky clouds, oppressed them all. And in that torment they writhed without rest.

THE SLAIN BEHOLD THEIR KILLERS
(ApPt 7f/25b Akhmim)
Mount of Olives

"Then the angel Ezrael [brought] forward the souls of their victims. And after that, these all stood by and witnessed the suffering of those who had murdered them. And the murderers confessed, 'Oh God, how truly righteous is Your judgment. For truly we have heard that we would come to this place of everlasting judgment, but we did not believe it.'

THOSE WHO ABORT THEIR CHILDREN
(ApPt 8a/26-Akhmim)
Mount of Olives

"And near to this flaming place I saw another gorge. Here flowed in judgment all kinds of horrifying filth from all manner of sources--the excrement and bodily discharge of the tormented--and there it pooled into a lake. And there were women sitting there engulfed by it up to their throats, suffering a most painful punishment. These were the ones who conceived children out of wedlock and then went on to have abortions, destroying the work that God had made.

THE ABORTED
(ApPt 8b)
Mount of Olives

"And across from them there was this place where great numbers of the aborted sat weeping. Both sides live and cry to God. Lightnings flash from these children and pierce the eyes of those who fornicated and brought about their destruction.
"Above these other men and women stand naked, and their children stand across from them in a heavenly place. There they groan, and confidently summon their parents before the judgment seat of Christ and cry aloud to God for what these have done, 'These were the ones who disregarded, set at nought, and did not keep to Your word. They murdered us, cursing the angel who fashioned us and hung us up. They kept from us the light that You have appointed for all.'" (So it has been passed down and received in the Scriptures that are inspired by God.)
"Milk flowed from the breasts of the mother, which then congealed and gave a stench. From it issued tiny flesh-eating monsters, which crawled all over

them, turning against them and tormenting them forevermore along with their husbands, since they overthrew the command of God and murdered their children." (This teaches that punishment comes as a result of sinning.) "These children, who have been exposed by their parents, are then assigned to the angel Temelouchos, who rears them there and nurtures them, causing them to be like one who has been faithful for a hundred years." (Peter in his Apocalypse says that these will receive the better lot, for after receiving this knowledge, they hope to attain to a better existence, as if they had already gone through the suffering they would have undergone had they been allowed to live out a physical existence. The others, by contrast, will be offered salvation as those who have been wronged and who have experienced mercy. They will receive as a reward an existence that is without anguish.) "But those who killed them are to endure an everlasting torment, for even thus is the will of God.

THE PERSECUTORS AND BETRAYERS OF THE RIGHTEOUS
(ApPt 9a/27-Akhmim)
Mount of Olives

"And other men and women stood there in flames stretching halfway up their bodies. Then Ezrael, the angel of wrath, brought forward their half-blazing bodies, and tossed them into the hell of mankind, a black place where there exist all manner of punishments. There they were afflicted by evil (and) wrathful spirits, while never-sleeping worms gnawed tirelessly at their guts. These were those who persecuted and betrayed my righteous ones.

THOSE WHO DOUBT AND BLASPHEME
GOD'S WAY OF RIGHTEOUSNESS
(ApPt 9b/28-Akhmim)
Mount of Olives

"Not far from those who lived like this were other men and women who gnawed at their tongues (and) bit through their lips. There they were being tortured and poked in the eyes with red hot irons. These were the ones who questioned and insulted my way of righteousness.

THE LIARS WHO KILLED THE MARTYRS
(ApPt 9c/29-Akhmim)
Mount of Olives

"And across the way from these there were yet other men and women whose actions were carried out through deception. These all had their lips sliced off, and were biting through their tongues. Fire passed into their mouths and entered their guts. These were the false witnesses who through their lies caused the martyrs to be slain.

THOSE WHO TRUSTED IN THEIR RICHES
(ApPt 9d/30-Akhmim)
Mount of Olives

"And near to that spot there was a place where a pillar of fire stood situated over glowing stones that were sharper than any sword or spit. And men and women dressed in rags and filthy clothes are tossed on them, where they writhe in agony, that they might endure the eternal torture of judgment. And in that place there were the rich, who trusted in their wealth. They showed the widows, the orphans and their mothers no mercy, but have instead despised (both) these (and) the commandment of God, in whose sight <they are precious.>

USERERS
(ApPt 10a/31-Akhmim)
Mount of Olives

"And not far from there was this giant lake that was choked with filth; discharge, blood, and simmering mire. And they were standing there up to their knees in the place where they toss down men and women who lent money and demanded a high rate of interest.

CULTISTS
(ApPt 10b/32-Akhmim)
Mount of Olives

"And other men and women flung themselves from the heights down a steep slope. And when they reached the bottom their torturers, the demons, would drive these idol worshippers to their wit's end. They forced them back to the precipice, where they are again pushed off, and once again fall down from there. And they do this endlessly. They are tormented like this without respite forever. These are the ones who, out of devotion to some 'apostle,' have allowed themselves to be cut, and have defiled their bodies by acting as a woman with a man, and the women with them there are they who have behaved toward one another as a man with a woman.

THE IDOL WORSHIPPERS
(ApPt 10c/33-Akhmim)
Mount of Olives

"And beyond these people, over by the precipice, <there were yet others.> And beneath them Ezrael readies a great fire; a place consumed by a blazing inferno, full of all manner of gold and silver idols, things that looked like cats and lions, reptiles and beasts; works that were fashioned by the hands of men. And the men and women who had formed images in the place of God are to remain there in their fiery chains. Now beside these stood men and women who were holding glowing rods, and they were beating each other without rest. And because of this, their error, these will stand scourging themselves in eternal punishment before the deceitful images, and such is their judgment.

THOSE WHO FORSOOK THE WAY OF GOD
(ApPt 10d/34-Akhmim)
Mount of Olives

"And close at hand were still other men and women who were being roasted and turned in the fire, baking away in the flame of judgment and its perpetual torment. These are the ones who have utterly renounced the way of God and taken instead to following devils.

THOSE WHO DISHONOR THEIR
FATHER AND MOTHER
(ApPt 11a)
Mount of Olives

"And there was this other very high position. In that place there is a furnace and a brazier, where a great fire blazes. And from one end comes a fiery flame. The men and women who take a false step go tumbling down to that frightening place. And once again, as the fire that is readied for them flows, they climb back up only to fall back down and resume their tumbling. And they will be punished this way forevermore. These are the ones who have failed to honor their father and mother, but have intentionally withdrawn from them. And in this way they are punished forever.

THOSE WHO DISOBEY THEIR PARENTS
AND THEIR ELDERS
(ApPt 11b)
Mount of Olives

"Ezrael the angel then brings children and young women over to show them the ones being punished there. Their painful punishment will be to be hung up for flesh-eating birds to peck. These are the ones who trust in their sins, disobey their parents' commands, do not follow the teachings of their forebears, nor do they respect their elders.

THOSE WHO DID NOT PRESERVE THEIR VIRGINITY
(ApPt 11c)
Mount of Olives

"Next to these were young women who were clothed only in darkness. Their punishment will be intense and their flesh will be ripped to shreds. These were those who kept not their virginity until they were given in marriage, and they will feel these torments the whole time they are suffering them.

DISOBEDIENT SERVANTS
(ApPt 11d)
Mount of Olives

"Again, there were these other men who constantly gnawed at their tongues and were being tortured in eternal flames. These were the servants who disobeyed their masters. And this will be their judgment forever.

SELF-RIGHTEOUS HYPOCRITES
(ApPt 12a)
Mount of Olives

"Now not far from this place of anguish, there were men and women who were dressed in white who could neither see nor speak. These were tightly packed together and dropped on coals of inextinguishable fire. These are the ones who make charitable donations and boast, 'We are righteous in the eyes of God,' though they have never yet labored for righteousness.

THE FIERY STREAM OF JUDGMENT
(ApPt 12b; SbOr 2:283-312)
Mount of Olives

"Then Ezrael, the angel of God, allows them to come forth from this fire only to pronounce their final judgment against them. This then becomes their final sentence. And a fiery stream is unleashed on the condemned and they are carried to the midst thereof, and Uriel places them down there." (Now this river of fire symbolizes that closed door by which the ungodly are to be kept out of the kingdom, as Daniel has written, as has Peter in his Apocalypse. "That party of foolish ones will rise up and find the door shut," refers to the blazing river that lies before them.) "Also there exist fiery wheels which, through their revolutions hold these men and women in suspension. These people will be brought by God's wrath near to the pillar around which an unquenchable fiery river swirls, as will the sorcerers and the sorceresses who are among them. Now the ones who blaze in the pit are the sorcerers and the sorceresses. And concerning their judgments, these flaming wheels are without number. Now these are to be suddenly and severely beaten with fiery whips from above by the angels of the eternal God, and bound below with chains of fire and unbreakable bonds. Then, in that darkness of night, they will be hurled before dread beasts of the underworld, where the darkness is indeed profound. But when the angels have inflicted numerous punishments on all of those who were wicked of heart, a flaming maelstrom from the mighty river will afterward close in on them, for they were wholly consumed by evil deeds. To and fro will these all howl, off in the distance, suffering a most lamentable fate.

Fathers and newborn children, mothers and infants weeping at their breast, who will never want for tears, nor will their lengthy cries be heard as they wail most wretchedly here and there, but in obscurity will they shout below in dark and dank Tartarus. In ungodly places and blazing fire will they pay thrice over for the evil they have done. All of these will clench their teeth and wither away from thirst and endless cruelty. They will all will cry out for death, but it will elude them, for neither death nor dark of night will afford them any respite. They will forever cry out in vain to God, the Ruler of Heaven, but He will conspicuously turn His face from them, for He gave seven age-days to an ever-straying mankind, that they might repent through the intercession of the Holy Virgin.

THE RIGHTEOUS BEHOLD
THE PUNISHMENT OF THE WICKED
(ApPt 13)
Mount of Olives

"The angels then brought forward in their arms my chosen and my righteous ones, who have been made perfect in all righteousness, wearing eternal life as their garment. They will see vengeance carried out on those who despised them even as they undergo His punishment. All of them will receive an everlasting torment that is in line with their own actions. And those who suffer will cry as one, 'Show us some compassion, for now we know what God's judgment is, even though He warned us all before and we never listened.' And Tartarouchos the angel will come and inflict even greater torments on them, saying, 'Are you repenting now, when there is no time to repent? Nothing more is left of your lives!' But at that time they will all confess, 'Righteous is the judgment of God! All of us have heard it now, and can perceive that His judgment is just, seeing that our punishment is in line with our crimes.'"

THE APOSTLES' CONCERN FOR THE SINNERS
(EpAp 40-42)
Mount of Olives

"Oh Lord," we said, "how tormented we are on their account!" "That is good," the lord replied, "for the righteous also show concern for the sinners-- praying and appealing to God my Father, and pleading with Him." And once again we said to him, "Oh Lord, does no one supplicate you? How is it that no one fears you?" But he answered us, "Indeed I will hearken to the prayers that the righteous make on their behalf." And when he revealed this to us, we answered him, "Oh Lord, through all that you have said to us, you have truly inspired us, and in showing us mercy have delivered us, that we might preach it to whom it is right, to those who are worthy, and indeed we will, but will we have our reward with you?" But he simply said to us, "Go out and start preaching, and you will become good ministers and servants." "But Lord," we said, "you are even as a father to us. You will be the one to preach through us!" At that point he questioned us, "Is everyone a father, then? Is everyone a servant? Is everyone a teacher? Do not all of you become fathers or teachers." And at that we said to him, "Lord, did you not say to us, 'Do not speak of anyone on this earth as your "father" or your "master," for your Heavenly Father is your Father and your Master.' Now why are you telling us, 'Like me, you are to become fathers to many children, and bring forth teachers and servants.'" And he answered us, "What you have said is indeed the truth. For I say to you that everyone who has come to believe in me by listening to you; through you will he receive from me baptism and the light of the seal that is in my hand. It is through me that you will become fathers and teachers as well as servants."

But we asked him, "Lord, how can we be each of these three? How can it be that the three should be one?" "How truly do I say to you," he expounded, "you will be called fathers first of all, because from your heart and out of your compassion, you have revealed to them the teachings of the kingdom of heaven. Secondly, you will be called servants because it is through you that these will receive the baptism of life and by my hand the forgiveness of sins. And you will be referred to as teachers because ungrudgingly have you disclosed my word to them. Without distress have you cautioned them and your rebuke has caused them to repent. You have not feared their riches nor respected their persons, but instead have kept my Father's command and brought it to completion. And great is your reward with my Heavenly Father, for they will have their sins forgiven them and they will live an eternal life, receiving a share in the kingdom of heaven." "Oh Lord," we said, "if all of us (and) each of them had ten thousand tongues with which to speak, we could not adequately thank you for promising such things to us!" And he responded, "Now what I have done for you, I say, go and do for others too."

THE WISE AND THE FOOLISH VIRGINS
(EpAp 43-45)
Mount of Olives

"Then you will be even as the wise virgins who lit the flame and then kept watch; who did not sleep, but went with their lamps to meet their Lord, the bridegroom, and have entered into the bridal chamber with him. But the foolish ones who spoke with them all fell asleep and proved themselves unable to." And we asked him, "Lord, who are the wise and who are the foolish?" And he answered us, "With regard to what the prophet has said, the five wise and the five foolish are children--for they are the daughters of God. Now allow mankind to hear their names." But we were downcast and anxious, weeping for the sake of those who had fallen asleep (and) been shut out. And he revealed to us, "The five who are wise are Faith, Love, Grace, Peace and Hope. Whenever those who believe in me come into possession of these, they will become guides to others who believe in me and in Him Who sent me. I am both the Lord and the bridegroom, whom they have accepted. They have gone with me into the bridegroom's house and have laid down with me in my bridal chamber and rejoiced. But the five foolish ones slept, and when they woke up they came to the bridegroom's house and knocked at the door, for by then it had been shut tight. Then all of them wept and mourned because the doors had been secured and they were not being opened to them." But we questioned him, "Lord, what about their wise sisters who are there in the bridegroom's home? Did they simply sit inside and not open it for them? Did they not feel sorry for them or beg the bridegroom to open up to them?" "Of course they are sad and anxious for them," he said. "Even so, no matter how they plead with the groom, it avails them nothing, for they cannot afford any grace to these others." "Oh Lord," we asked, "When will the day come for them to be let in for their sister's sake?" And he responded, "Whoever is shut out remains shut out." And we said to him, "We have understood this word of yours, oh Lord, (but) is this truly binding? Who then are these foolish ones?" "Listen up," he said to them, "these are their names; Wisdom, Knowledge, Obedience, Perseverance and Mercy. These have lied dormant in those who have believed in me and acknowledged me. But since those who slept failed to keep my commandments, they are to remain outside of the kingdom and fold of the shepherd and his sheep--and whoever remains outside the sheepfold gets eaten by wolves. And even though he hears, he will nonetheless be judged--and for this reason suffer death. He will undergo much suffering, misery, and hardship. Rest will elude him and he will be unable to persevere. And though his suffering is acute and he is cut to shreds, torn (and) tortured by his prolonged and painful punishment, his will truly be a slow (and) agonizing death." And we said to him, "Lord, how well you have revealed all things to us." And he responded, "Do you understand these words of mine?" "Yes, Lord," we all affirmed. "It is through these (first) five that they hope to gain access to your kingdom, and through the five who are shut out that they are to remain outside. Even so, oh Lord and bridegroom, because of those who fell asleep, those who kept watch and got to be with you will never rejoice." And at that he said to us, "They will rejoice in that they have gone in with the Lord and bridegroom, but those who slept are their sisters, so they will indeed be grieved on their account. Now God the Father does have ten daughters." "Oh Lord," we said, "how truly it befits your greatness that you should shower grace on these, their sisters." And he responded, "This was not your own idea, but that of Him Who sent me, and I agree with Him!"

THE SINNERS RELEASED FROM HADES
(ApPt 14a; SbOr 2:313-338; Jude 22, 23)
Mount of Olives

"But as for their counterparts, those who are interested in justice and righteous deeds, holiness and truly upright thinking, angels will raise them from the burning stream and deliver them unto the light--even to the carefree realm, wherein lies the path of immortality of the Almighty God and the three springs: of wine, of honey, and of milk. Then the world will belong the same to all, with no walls or fences to divide them. It will then, of its own, bring forth fruit in a much greater abundance. People will live their lives as one, and wealth will be distributed evenly. In that place there will be no 'rich' or 'poor,' neither despot, nor any slave. There will, moreover, exist at that time neither the common nor the eminent; neither sovereign nor head of state, for all will be on the same level with one another. It will no longer be said that 'night has fallen' or that 'something will happen tomorrow' or that 'something happened yesterday,' nor will there be days at all to think about. Neither will there be any spring or summer, buying or selling, dusk or dawn, for He will make it all as one long day. To all of these, His righteous ones, the eternal God Who governs all, will grant them something further still: When they ask Him to rescue mankind from the unquenchable fire and perpetual grinding of teeth, He will give them what they long for. And I say definitively, that at that time, I will deliver out of torment whomsoever my righteous and elect ones should ask of me." (Be compassionate to those who doubt, but others you must drag from the fire, despising even the garment that is tainted by the flesh.) "(And) if anyone should cry to me in their affliction, I will grant them to God. Behold, He will Himself pluck them from the undying fire and set them in another place, even into another eternal realm where they will live forever with the immortal ones. Then I will give my righteous and elect ones the precious baptism and the salvation for which they have pleaded with me, there in that deep and abiding Acherusian lake, where He has the broad waves, (and) which is referred to by men as the Elysian field; and all of this for the sake of His own. And their portion will be with my righteous ones, who will be adorned with flowers, and I will go <to them> and rejoice with them. Then I will travel on to my eternal realm exulting with the patriarchs and my elect. I will fulfill the promises that my Heavenly Father and I have made to them. The Gentiles also will I cause to enter my eternal realm. My Father and I will reveal all that I have promised to give to them in all of its eternity."

EXHORTATION TO PREACH
(EpAp 46-50; Traditions of Matthias,
Quote by Clement of Alexandria,
Stromateis 3.4.26, 7.13.82)
Mount of Olives

"All of you, venture forth! Teach and preach in a clear and truthful manner. Stand your ground before all men and don't defer to anyone. Show neither any fear of, nor respect for anyone, but most especially the rich, for they will be found not to have followed my commands, but to have reveled in their wealth instead." "Lord," we asked him, "does this apply to the rich alone?" And he replied, "If anyone should have but a little substance, and not be wealthy, should he give to the needy and not deny the poor soul who has nothing, I am telling you that men will call him a humanitarian. But if that one should stumble under the burden of the sins he has committed, and should do his neighbor wrong, then for the sake of the kindness that this person has shown his neighbor, his neighbor ought to admonish him. Now after his neighbor has reproved him and he has repented, he will be saved, and the one who corrected him will have endless life as his reward. But if a needy person should see someone who has done some good for him sinning away, and he does not rebuke him (but) encourages him (instead,) such a one will be severely judged, for one blind man who leads another will cause them both to fall into a ditch. You see, both the respected and the one who respects, encouraged and encourager alike are to be punished with the same punishment." (For they say that in the Traditions of Matthias the Apostle it always says, 'Should the neighbor of one who is chosen sin, the chosen one has sinned as well. You see, had he conformed himself to the teaching of the word, then his neighbor would have been too ashamed of his lifestyle to live out any life of sin.' Matthias also taught that we ought not to give ourselves license to indulge in sensual delights, but that we ought rather to clash with the flesh and allow the soul to mature through a faith that is mingled with knowledge.) "And even as the prophet has spoken, 'Those whose belly is their god, who encourage a person to sin, who hold a sinner in regard, justifying the ungodly for some kind of reward, are accursed--one and all.' Now do you see how the judgment will be. Recognize that a judgment awaits them. You can be sure that on that day, I will neither fear the rich, nor will I go easy on the poor.

"If you are a witness to another's sin, then just between the two of you, make plain to him where he is wrong, because if he should listen to you, then you will have won him over! Nevertheless, if he should not heed your rebuke, then bring along another one, or even two if it should come to that. Correct your brother (and) offer him guidance! But if after that he still won't listen, then mark him as, and treat him like a Gentile or a tax-collector.

"Should you hear something about your brother, do not give it any credit. Do not slander anyone and do not long to hear it from others, because it stands written: 'Let not your ear ever hearken to slander.' If you have seen something, then denounce it; correct and convert him." "Oh Lord," we said, "you have given us instruction and exhortations in all things. Even so, Lord, ought there to be dissensions and disputes, covetousness and turmoil, hatred and anger among the faithful who believe in the preaching of your name? For you have said, 'They will fault a person without taking their character into account.' Are these not sinning by despising the one who has corrected them?" And he answered us, "Tell me again why the judgment is coming? Is it not so that the wheat might make it into the barn and the chaff, into the fire? <That is how it goes with those> who have this kind of hate. As for the one who loves me and reproves those who do not carry out my commandments, he will be despised for it, and will therefore suffer persecution. Men will abhor and revile them.

And as if that were not enough, they will also deliberately say what is untrue. A conspiracy will arise against those who love me. But these will reprove them, with an eye toward gaining their salvation. But anyone who points out any of their misdeeds and seeks to correct them and exhort them will first be hated, then avoided, and ultimately set at nought. Also anyone seeking to render them any assistance will be kept from doing so. But with the Father, those who have suffered this are to rank as martyrs. For you see, they were eager to see righteousness carried out, and were not motivated by some kind of corruptible zeal." And we asked him, "Will such a thing take place even in our midst?" And he answered us, "Do not fear the greater part, but watch for what a few will do." "Tell us what you mean," we asked. And he said, "Another teaching will arise; a controversy. Now seeking only to glorify themselves, they will come to put forth worthless doctrine. Now this will give rise to a fatal error, which will teach even those who believe in me to turn away from my command, and lead them from eternal life. Damn all those who twist my words and forsake my command for their own ends, and damn them all who give them a hearing, and all who reject the life-giving commandment, for they are to share in their eternal punishment.

EXHORTATION TO PETER
(ApPt 14b/1-3-Akhmim)
Mount of Olives

"And Peter, I have spoken all of this to you, and expounded it, causing you to understand it. Go west therefore, out to that city that rules over the west, and to that vineyard to which I will direct you. <'Show them> by the hand of my sinless Son that even now his work <is done, that the children> of destruction might be made holy.' But you are the one who has been chosen in the hope that I have given you. Go in peace and spread my gospel throughout the world. Drink the cup which I have foretold you must drink at the hand of the son of him who is in Hades, that his destruction might come, and that you might be made worthy of the promise. When people come to see the source of my word, which is in fact the hope of life, the whole world will suddenly be carried off.

"But there will be many false prophets among these people. They will put forth diverse teachings and doctrines of perdition, and will thus become the children thereof. After that, God will come to my faithful ones who hunger and thirst, suffering affliction and the trial of their souls in this life."

A VISION OF THE RIGHTEOUS
(Luke 24:50b-51a; Acts 1:9;
ApPt 15-17a, 18/4-20-Akhmim)
Mount of Olives

"And my Lord and King Jesus Christ said to me, 'Let us climb this holy mount.' And we, his twelve disciples went up, begging and pleading with him to reveal to us even one of our righteous brethren who had departed from this world, that we might have a look at them and see their likeness for ourselves, that we through our boldness might encourage those who should hear us. And at his transfiguration, the Lord showed (me,) Peter, and also James and John, the sons of Zebedee, the clothing of the final days, the day of the resurrection. Now behold, even as we were praying, these two men appeared to us, standing there before the Lord, but we were not able to look their way and see their faces, for they beamed forth even more light than the sun. Their garments were luminous beyond words, and beyond compare, such as has never been seen by any man in this world. The gentleness thereof no mouth can express, nor can any heart conceive of the glory of their adornment or the beauty of their faces. Astonishing and wonderful was their appearance. The greater one, I would venture to say, shone more in his brilliance than a crystal. And we were all amazed at the sight of them. Their bodies were even whiter than snow, and had a redness surpassing any rose. That redness, moreover, was mingled with the whiteness thereof. It is simply not possible for me to put their beauty into words. They had curly hair that framed their faces and shoulders in a delightful manner. And around their foreheads there was a crown of nard--like a garland woven out of nard blossoms--and beautiful blooms of different hues, like a rainbow on the water, (or) in the air was [their] hair; so finely fashioned was their form, and [they] were decked out in all manner of ornamentation. And when we looked on them in all of their splendor we marveled in their presence, and we were startled by their sudden appearance.

"And I went up to our Lord God Jesus Christ and asked, 'Who are these, my Lord?' And he answered me, 'These are your righteous brethren, Moses and Elijah, the ones whose form you wished to see.' Then I asked him, 'Where then are Abraham, Isaac, Jacob and the other holy patriarchs? And what is the nature of that world in which these who have such glory dwell?' The Lord then revealed to us this expansive, otherworldly kind of setting, where all things emanated light--a paradise in the east chosen for Adam by God. The air in that place was charged with shimmering sunlight and plants of exquisite beauty, and was accompanied by the fragrance of perfume--and I saw there many fruits. This garden, the earth, was bursting with unfading flowers--redolent of spices and plants that blossom gloriously; never fading, and bringing forth blessed fruits. The flowers in that land gave off such a wonderful fragrance that when released from there, it carried over to where we were. Those who were living in that realm wore the shining clothes of angels, and their clothing matched the atmosphere of this, their home. In that region, angels walked among them. All who lived in that place were as glorious as the others there. And in the blessedness of that expanse, they praised the Lord God with a common voice. And my Lord and God Jesus Christ asked me, 'Do you recognize the congregation of the patriarchs? This is where your brothers, the high priests and the righteous ones dwell. Those who are to suffer persecution for the sake of my righteousness are to receive both honor and glory, and come to enjoy this very repose.'

"And I rejoiced and believed and came to recognize what was written in the book of my Lord Jesus Christ. And I asked him, 'Lord, would you have me build three tabernacles here; one for you, one for Moses, and another for Elijah?' And in anger he replied, 'Satan battles against you and has veiled your understanding, for you are overwhelmed by the things of this world. Your eyes must be opened, and your ears unstopped that <you might come to see> a tent that has not been fashioned by the hands of men, but one which my Father has made especially for myself and my chosen ones.

[At my] coming, (Jesus said,) [I] will raise up the dead...and cause my righteous ones to shine even seven times brighter than the sun. Their crowns I will cause to gleam like crystal, like a rainbow in the time of rain. Perfumed with nard and beyond all words will be <their crowns,> fully bejeweled with rubies and the gleaming of shining emeralds, topazes, precious stones and yellow pearls that shine forth like the stars of heaven and the rays of the sun-- all of them completely dazzling, and impossible to look upon.' And we were overjoyed at the sight."

And when he had spoken these things to us and ended his discourse with us, once again he said to us, "Now behold, (recall that I said,) 'After three days and three hours, He Who sent me will come and take me with Him.' The Father has committed the judgment of all things to the Son. Have you understood my words to you, (Peter)? It is for you, to know this mystery, but you must not let the sinners know what you have heard me say, for if you do, they will only sin the more and fall into even greater transgression. My Father will grant life to all mankind, giving all this glory to them, as well as the kingdom that never passes. I come for the sake of those who believe in me. And it is also because of these who believed in me that upon their request, I will show mercy to all of mankind." And even as they looked on, he raised his hands and blessed them. Just then there was thunder and lightning and shaking of the earth, (and) a voice from heaven was heard to declare, "This is My beloved Son, in whom I rejoice, and my commandments: hear him." (And growing fearful, we completely lost sight of the things of this life, and all of the things of the flesh as well. And we had no way of understanding the things about which we had been speaking, both because of the wonders that we had seen on that day, as well as the way in which he had revealed his second coming to us on that mountain, together with the kingdom that endures forever.) And even as he was blessing them, he was taken up from among them and carried into heaven. A bright and enormous white cloud formed overhead and bore away our Lord, with Moses and Elijah. And [we] stood there trembling with fright, but then we all looked up and saw the sky spreading apart. We could see flesh-bearing men approaching and welcoming our Lord, along with Moses and Elijah. And we heard the voices of many angels as they rejoiced and proclaimed, "Oh priest, gather us in your glorious light." And as they were approaching the heavenly firmament, we heard him say, "Go in peace!"

And the faces of the angels there surpass even the shining of the sun, and their crowns are even as the rainbow in the time of rain. (They are all) perfumed with nard, and their eyes gleam like the morning star. There are no words to express a beauty like theirs. Their clothes are not woven, but are white like the fuller's, even as the ones that I, (Peter,) saw on the mountain where Moses and Elijah had been.

THE ASCENSION
(Mark 16:19-20; Luke 24:51b-53; Acts 1:10-11;
Rev 1:7; ApPt 17b; AsIs 11:3b-33)
Mount of Olives, The Seven Heavens

The Lord sent forth his twelve apostles as he rose into the sky, but he was not changed into the form of the angels there. Satan himself, and the angels of that firmament saw him there and worshiped him. And great was the anguish in that place, as they cried out, "How did our Lord come down here to our sphere and we not notice his greatness, seeing in him that he was the King of Glory? Only now do we recognize that this was the majesty that was on him even from the sixth heaven." Then they entered into the second heaven, and he was not transformed there, but all of the angels, those to the right, those to the left, as well as the throne that was in the midst, worshiped him and offered him praise, saying, "How did our Lord conceal himself on his way down and we not see it?" And in like fashion did he rise up into the third heaven, and after this same pattern did they praise him and speak. And through the fourth and the fifth heavens, the angels all spoke in precisely the same manner. There was but one glory, and he was not changed. And I, (Isaiah,) beheld his entry into the sixth heaven, that they worshiped him there and offered him praise. Even so, the praises grew louder in each of the heavens. Then I witnessed his ascent into the seventh heaven, where all of the righteous and all of the angels sang his praises. Then I watched him as he took his seat to the right hand of the Great and Glorious God, Whose glory I told you I could not so much as look upon. And I saw the angel of the Holy Spirit seated there and to the left. This fulfilled the word of Scripture that says, "This generation seeks the face of the God of Jacob." And in heaven there was great alarm and amazement. The angels all flocked together to fulfill the Scripture that says, "Oh you princes, open the gates!" (He then) vanished from their sight.

And even as they were gazing intently upward, two men in white clothes stood by them and questioned them, "Oh men of Galilee, why are you standing here staring up into the heavens? This Jesus, who was taken up from among you and received again into heaven, will return in the same manner as you saw him rise up into the sky." (Behold, he is coming with clouds, and every eye will look on him, even those who pierced him; and all the nations of the earth will mourn on his account. Even so, amen!) Then the heavens, which had been opened, were shut back up. They worshiped him (and) said a prayer and went back down the mountainside praising God, Who has the names of the righteous ones written in the book of life, which is in heaven. And they went joyfully back into Jerusalem, remaining in the temple, and praising God ceaselessly.

And after receiving their instructions, they reported to Peter and his companions. Afterward, Jesus himself put them to work as ambassadors in

Robert C. Ferrell

charge of spreading the holy and imperishable word of eternal salvation from one end of the earth to the other. So they went and preached it everywhere, and the Lord worked with them, confirming the word with the signs that followed.

The Super Gospel

Robert C. Ferrell